PEARSON CUSTOM BUSINESS RESOURCES

Compiled by

BUSINESS LAW
Marie A. Comstock, JD

Pearson Learning Solutions

New York Boston San Francisco
London Toronto Sydney Tokyo Singapore Madrid
Mexico City Munich Paris Cape Town Hong Kong Montreal

Senior Vice President, Editorial and Marketing: Patrick F. Boles
Editor: Ana Díaz-Caneja
Development Editor: Abbey Lee Briggs
Operations Manager: Eric M. Kenney
Production Manager: Jennifer Berry
Art Director: Renée Sartell
Cover Designer: Renée Sartell

Cover Art: Courtesy of EyeWire/Getty Images and PhotoDisc/Getty Images. Photodisc, "Globe surrounded by business people on computer monitors," courtesy of Photodisc/Getty Images. Dave Cutler (Artist), "Man Dropping Coins Into Glass Jar," courtesy of David Cutler/Images.com. Dave Cutler (Artist), "Three Coins in Glass Jar," courtesy of David Cutler/Images.com. Dean Turner, "Stock Vector: Global Finance" Courtesy of Dean Turner/iStockphoto. Hal Bergman, "Refinery Silhouette" Courtesy of Hal Bergman/iStockphoto. Dan Barnes, "Cargo Container Ship Aerial View" Courtesy of Dan Barnes/iStockphoto. Franc Podgorsek, "Stock Numbers" Courtesy of Franc Podgorsek/iStockphoto. "Customer in Line at Grocery Store" Courtesy of Digital Vision Photography/Veer Inc. Owaki-Kulla, "Pumping Gas" Courtesy of Flirt Photography/Veer Inc. Lynn Johnson, "Yunnan Province, People's Republic of China" Courtesy of Lynn Johnson/Getty Images, Inc. Thomas Bendy, "Student Typing" Courtesy of Thomas Bendy/iStockphoto.

This special edition published in cooperation with Pearson Learning Solutions.

Printed in the United States of America.

Please visit our web site at *www.pearsoncustom.com.*

Attention bookstores: For permission to return any unsold stock, contact us at *pe-uscustomreturns@pearson.com.*

Pearson Learning Solutions, 501 Boylston Street, Suite 900, Boston, MA 02116
A Pearson Education Company
www.pearsoned.com

PEARSON

ISBN 10: 1-256-03366-9
ISBN 13: 978-1-256-03366-0

Editorial Advisory Board

Contents

ETHICS AND SOCIAL RESPONSIBILITY OF BUSINESS

▲ **Hue, Vietnam** *American companies "outsource" the production of many of the goods that are sold in America (e.g., clothing, athletic shoes, toys). The reason they do so is because they can get the goods produced at a lower cost in foreign countries and then make higher profits when they sell the goods in the United States. By having their goods made in foreign countries, U.S. companies avoid the expenses of occupational safety laws that require workplaces to be safe to work in, the cost of workers' compensation laws that pay workers if they are injured on the job, fair labor standards laws that prevent child labor and require the payment of minimum wages and overtime wages, the payment of health care and pension benefits for employees, the payment of Social Security taxes, and such. Is it ethical for U.S. companies to "export" the production of their goods to foreign workers who have none of these protections?*

CHAPTER OBJECTIVES

After studying this chapter, you should be able to:

1. Describe how law and ethics intertwine.
2. Describe the moral theories of business ethics.
3. Describe the theories of the social responsibility of business.
4. Examine the provisions of the Sarbanes-Oxley Act.
5. Describe corporate social audits.

CHAPTER CONTENTS

"Ethical considerations can no more be excluded from the administration of justice, which is the end and purpose of all civil laws, than one can exclude the vital air from his room and live."

—John F. Dillon
Laws and Jurisprudence of England and America Lecture I (1894)

▶ INTRODUCTION TO ETHICS AND SOCIAL RESPONSIBILITY OF BUSINESS

Businesses organized in the United States are subject to its laws. They are also subject to the laws of other countries in which they operate. In addition, businesspersons owe a duty to act ethically in the conduct of their affairs, and businesses owe a social responsibility not to harm society.

Although much of the law is based on ethical standards, not all ethical standards have been enacted as law. The law establishes a minimum degree of conduct expected by persons and businesses in society. Ethics demands more. This chapter discusses business ethics and the social responsibility of business.

▶ ETHICS AND THE LAW

ethics
A set of moral principles or values that governs the conduct of an individual or a group.

Sometimes the rule of law and the golden rule of **ethics** demand the same response by a person confronted with a problem. For example, federal and state laws make bribery unlawful. A person violates the law if he or she bribes a judge for a favorable decision in a case. Ethics would also prohibit this conduct. However, the law may permit something that would be ethically wrong.

Ethics precede laws as man precedes society.
Jason Alexander
Philosophy for Investors (1979)

Example Occupational safety laws set standards for emissions of dust from toxic chemicals in the workplace. Suppose a company can reduce the emission below the legal standard by spending additional money. The only benefit from the expenditure would be better employee health. Ethics would require the extra expenditure; the law would not.

Another alternative occurs where the law demands certain conduct but a person's ethical standards are contrary.

Example Federal law prohibits employers from hiring certain illegal alien workers. Suppose an employer advertises the availability of a job and receives no response except from a person who cannot prove he or she is a citizen of this country or does not possess a required visa. The worker and his or her family are destitute. Should the employer hire him or her? The law says no, but ethics says yes (see Exhibit 1).

▶ **Exhibit 1 LAW AND ETHICS**

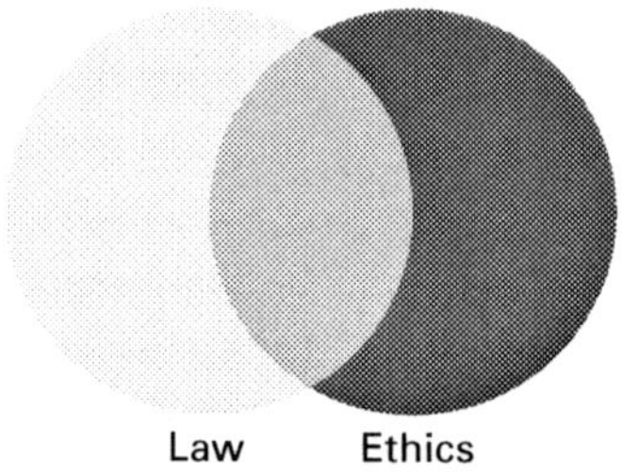

BUSINESS ETHICS

How can ethics be measured? The answer is very personal: What is considered ethical by one person may be considered unethical by another. However, there do seem to be some universal rules about what conduct is ethical and what conduct is not. The following discussion highlights five major theories of ethics.

He who seeks equality must do equity.

Joseph Story
Equity Jurisprudence (1836)

ETHICS SPOTLIGHT

Wal-Mart Pays Big for Meal Break Violations

"At Wal-Mart, not only is there no such thing as a free lunch for employees but, in this sad case, there is no lunch at all."

—Wal-Mart Watch

In recent years, retail giant Wal-Mart has been the target of hundreds of lawsuits by employees in dozens of states, claiming the company violated wage-and-hour laws. In Colorado, Wal-Mart settled with a group of employees for $50 million because of denied meal break violations. In Oregon, workers were rewarded with nearly $2,000 each for similar violations.

A group of California Wal-Mart employees became the first in a series of class action lawsuits involving the denied meal breaks. In *Wal-Mart Stores v. S.C. (Savaglio)*, **Web** 2004 Cal. Lexis 3284 (Supreme Court of California, 2004), both current and former employees argued that Wal-Mart had violated California's meal period law. Wal-Mart fought back, saying that it didn't break any law.

The Oakland, California, jury watched four months of testimony and deliberated for three days before coming back with its verdict: 116,000 current and former Wal-Mart employees were to receive $172 million in general and punitive damages. Wal-Mart employees and community activists felt vindicated and insisted that the company fix the broken system. Wal-Mart Watch, a union-backed group that keeps a very close eye on everything the company does, commented, "At Wal-Mart, not only is there no such thing as a free lunch for employees but, in this sad case, there is no lunch at all."

Less than a year after the meal break case, Wal-Mart was in court in Pennsylvania. This time, the jury hit the company with over $78 million in damages for forcing employees to work "off the clock" and during rest breaks.

Business Ethics Did Wal-Mart act ethically in this case? Why do think Wal-Mart acted as it did in this case?

Ethical Fundamentalism

Under **ethical fundamentalism**, a person looks to an **outside source** for ethical rules or commands. This may be a book (e.g., the Bible, the Koran) or a person (e.g., Karl Marx). Critics argue that ethical fundamentalism does not permit people to determine right and wrong for themselves. Taken to an extreme, the result could be considered unethical under most other moral theories. For example, a literal interpretation of the maxim "an eye for an eye" would permit retaliation.

ethical fundamentalism
A theory of ethics that says a person looks to an outside source for ethical rules or commands.

LANDMARK LAW

The Whistleblower Statute

The Bayer Corporation (Bayer) is a U.S. subsidiary corporation of the giant German-based Bayer A.G. Bayer is a large pharmaceutical company that produces prescription drugs, including its patented antibiotic Cipro. Bayer sold Cipro to private health providers and hospitals, including Kaiser Permanente Medical Care Program, the largest health maintenance organization in the United States. Bayer also sold Cipro to the federal government's Medicaid program, which provides medical insurance to the poor. Federal law contains a "best price" rule that prohibits a company that sells a drug to Medicaid from charging Medicaid a price higher than the lowest price for which it sells the drug to private purchasers.

Kaiser told Bayer that it would not purchase Cipro from Bayer—and would switch to a competitor's antibiotics—unless Bayer reduced the price of Cipro. Bayer's executives came up with a plan whereby Bayer would put a private label on its Cipro and not call it Cipro and sell the antibiotic to Kaiser at a 40 percent discount. Thus, Bayer continued to charge Medicaid the full price for Cipro while giving Kaiser a 40 percent discount through the private labeling program. One of Bayer's executives who negotiated this deal with Kaiser was corporate account manager George Couto.

Everything went well for Bayer until Couto attended a mandatory ethics training class at Bayer at which a video of Heige Wehmeier, then company chief executive, was shown. When the video stated that Bayer employees were to obey not only "the letter of the law but the spirit of the law as well," some of the Bayer executives laughed. Later that day, Couto attended a staff meeting at which it was disclosed that Bayer kept $97 million from Medicaid by using the discounted private labeling program for Kaiser and other health care companies. Two days later, Couto wrote a memorandum to his boss, questioning the legality of the private labeling program in light of Medicaid's "best price" law.

When he received no response to his memo, Couto contacted a lawyer. Couto filed a ***qui tam* lawsuit** under the federal **False Claims Act**—also known as the **Whistleblower Statute**—which permits private parties to sue companies for fraud on behalf of the government. The riches: The whistleblower can be awarded up to 25 percent of the amount recovered on behalf of the federal government, even if the informer has been a co-conspirator in perpetrating the fraud [31 U.S.C. Sections 3729-3733].

After the case was filed, the U.S. Department of Justice took over the case, as allowed by law, and filed criminal as well as civil charges against Bayer. After discovery was taken, Bayer pleaded guilty to one criminal felony and agreed to pay federal and state governments $257 million to settle the civil and criminal cases. Couto, age 39, died of pancreatic cancer three months prior to the settlement. Couto was awarded $34 million, which went to his three children. Did Bayer act ethically in this case? Did Couto act ethically in this case? *United States ex. rel. Estate of George Couto v. Bayer Corporation* (United States District Court for the District of Massachusetts, 2003).

Utilitarianism

utilitarianism
A moral theory that dictates that people must choose the action or follow the rule that provides the greatest good to society.

Utilitarianism is a moral theory with origins in the works of Jeremy Bentham (1748–1832) and John Stuart (1806–1873). This moral theory dictates that people must choose the actions or follow the rule that provides the **greatest good to society**. This does not mean the greatest good for the greatest number of people.

Example If an action would increase the good of 25 people by 1 unit each and an alternative action would increase the good of 1 person by 26 units, then the latter action should be taken.

Utilitarianism has been criticized because it is difficult to estimate the "good" that will result from different actions, it is hard to apply in an imperfect world, and it treats morality as if it were an impersonal mathematical calculation.

Example A company is trying to determine whether it should close an unprofitable plant located in a small community. Utilitarianism would require that the benefits to shareholders from closing the plant be compared to the benefits to employees, their families, and others in the community in keeping it open.

Kantian Ethics

Kantian ethics
A moral theory which says that people owe moral duties that are based on universal rules, such as the categorical imperative "Do unto others as you would have them do unto you." Also known as *duty ethics*.

Immanuel Kant (1724–1804) is the best-known proponent of **duty ethics**, also called **Kantian ethics**. Kant believed that people owe moral duties that are based on **universal rules**. Kant's philosophy is based on the premise that people can use reasoning to reach ethical decisions. His ethical theory would have people behave according to the *categorical imperative* "Do unto others as you would have them do unto you."

Example According to Kantian ethics, keeping a promise to abide by a contract is a moral duty even if that contract turns out to be detrimental to the obligated party.

The universal rules of Kantian ethics are based on two important principles: (1) consistency— that is, all cases are treated alike, with no exceptions—and (2) reversibility—that is, the actor must abide by the rule he or she uses to judge the morality of someone else's conduct. Thus, if you are going to make an exception for yourself, that exception becomes a universal rule that applies to all others. For example, if you rationalize that it is acceptable for you to engage in deceptive practices, it is acceptable for competitors to do so also. A criticism of Kantian ethics is that it is difficult to reach consensus as to what the universal rules should be.

In the following case, a company alleged that a competitor had engaged in false advertising.

CASE 1 Business Ethics

Pizza Hut, Inc. v. Papa John's International, Inc.

227 F.3d 489, Web 2000 U.S. App. Lexis 23444 (2000)
United States Court of Appeals for the Fifth Circuit

"This simple statement, 'Better Pizza.,' epitomizes the exaggerated advertising, blustering and boasting by a manufacturer upon which no consumer would reasonably rely."

—Judge Jolly

Facts

Papa John's International, Inc., is the third-largest pizza chain in the United States, with more than 2,050 locations. Papa John's adopted a new slogan—"Better Ingredients. Better Pizza."—and applied for and received a federal trademark for this slogan. Papa John's spent over $300 million building customer recognition and goodwill for this slogan. This slogan has appeared on millions of signs, shirts, menus, pizza boxes, napkins, and other items, and it has regularly appeared as the tag line at the end of Papa John's radio and television advertisements.

Pizza Hut, Inc., is the largest pizza chain in the United States, with more than 7,000 restaurants. Two years after the Papa John's advertisements began, Pizza Hut launched a new advertising campaign in which it declared "war" on poor-quality pizza. The advertisements touted the "better taste" of Pizza Hut's pizza and "dared" anyone to find a better pizza.

A few weeks later, Papa John's countered with a comparative advertising campaign that touted the superiority of Papa John's pizza over Pizza Hut's pizza. Papa John's claimed it had superior sauce and dough to Pizza Hut. Many of these advertisements were accompanied by the Papa John's slogan "Better Ingredients. Better Pizza."

Pizza Hut filed a civil action in U.S. District Court, charging Papa John's with false advertising in violation of Section 43(a) of the federal Lanham Act. The U.S. District Court found that the Papa John's slogan "Better Ingredients. Better Pizza." standing alone was mere puffery and did not constitute false advertising. The District Court found, however, that Papa John's claims of superior sauce and dough were misleading and that the Papa John's slogan "Better Ingredients. Better Pizza." became tainted because it was associated with these misleading statements. The U.S. District Court enjoined Papa John's from using the slogan "Better Ingredients. Better Pizza." Papa John's appealed.

Issue

Is the Papa John's slogan "Better Ingredients. Better Pizza." false advertising?

Language of the Court

One form of non-actionable statements of general opinion under Section 43(a) of the Lanham Act has been referred to as "puffery." Prosser and Keeton on the Law of Torts (5th edition) define "puffing" as "a seller's privilege to lie his head off, so long as he says nothing specific, on the theory that no reasonable man would believe him, or that no reasonable man would be influenced by such talk."

We turn now to consider the case before us. Reduced to its essence, the question is whether the evidence established that Papa John's slogan "Better Ingredients. Better Pizza." is misleading and violative of Section 43(a) of the Lanham Act. Bisecting the slogan "Better Ingredients. Better Pizza.," it is clear that the assertion by Papa John's that it makes a "Better Pizza." is a general statement of opinion regarding the superiority of its product over all others. Consequently, it appears indisputable that Papa John's assertion "Better Pizza." is non-actionable puffery.

Moving next to consider the phrase "Better Ingredients," the same conclusion holds true. Like "Better Pizza." it is typical puffery. Thus, it is equally clear that Papa John's assertion that it uses "Better Ingredients." is one of opinion not actionable under the Lanham Act. Consequently, the slogan as a whole is a statement of non-actionable opinion. Thus, there is no legally sufficient basis to support the jury's finding that the slogan is a "false or misleading" statement of fact.

Decision

The U.S. Court of Appeals held that the Papa John's trademarked slogan "Better Ingredients. Better Pizza." was mere puffery and a statement of opinion that was not false advertising and did not violate Section 43(a) of the Lanham Act. The U.S. Court of Appeals reversed the judgment of the U.S. District Court and remanded the case to the District Court for entry of judgment for Papa John's.

Case Questions

Critical Legal Thinking What is false advertising? What is puffery? How do they differ from one another?

Business Ethics Do businesses sometimes make exaggerated claims about their products? Are consumers smart enough to see through companies' puffery?

Contemporary Business If the Court of Appeals had found in favor of Pizza Hut, what would have been the effect on advertising in this country? Explain.

Rawls's Social Justice Theory

social contract
A moral theory that says each person is presumed to have entered into a social contract with all others in society to obey moral rules that are necessary for people to live in peace and harmony.

John Locke (1632–1704) and Jean-Jacques Rousseau (1712–1778) proposed a **social contract** theory of morality. Under this theory, each person is presumed to have entered into a social contract with all others in society to obey moral rules that are necessary for people to live in peace and harmony. This implied contract states, "I will keep the rules if everyone else does." These moral rules are then used to solve conflicting interests in society.

The leading proponent of the modern justice theory was John Rawls (1921–2002), a philosopher at Harvard University. Under **Rawls's social justice theory**, fairness is considered the essence of justice. The principles of justice should be chosen by persons who do not yet know their station in society—thus, their "veil of ignorance" would permit the fairest possible principles to be selected.

The notion that a business is clothed with a public interest and has been devoted to the public use is little more than a fiction intended to beautify what is disagreeable to the sufferers.

Justice Holmes
Tyson & Bro-United Theatre Ticket Officers v. Banton (1927)

Example Under Rawls's social justice theory, the principle of equal opportunity in employment would be promulgated by people who would not yet know if they were in a favored class.

As a caveat, Rawls also proposed that the least advantaged in society must receive special assistance in order to realize their potential. Rawls's theory of social justice is criticized for two reasons. First, establishing the blind "original position" for choosing moral principles is impossible in the real world. Second, many persons in society would choose not to maximize the benefit to the least advantaged persons in society.

Ethical Relativism

ethical relativism
A moral theory which holds that individuals must decide what is ethical based on their own feelings about what is right and wrong.

Ethical relativism holds that individuals must decide what is ethical based on their own feelings about what is right and wrong. Under this moral theory, if a person meets his or her own moral standard in making a decision, no one can criticize him or her for it. Thus, there are no universal ethical rules to guide a person's conduct. This theory has been criticized because action that is usually thought to be unethical (e.g., committing fraud) would not be unethical if the perpetrator thought it was in fact ethical. Few philosophers advocate ethical relativism as an acceptable moral theory.

CONCEPT SUMMARY
THEORIES OF ETHICS

Theory	Description
Ethical fundamentalism	Persons look to an outside source (e.g., the Bible, the Koran) or a central figure for ethical guidelines.
Utilitarianism	Persons choose the alternative that would provide the greatest good to society.
Kantian ethics	A set of universal rules establishes ethical duties. The rules are based on reasoning and require (1) consistency in application and (2) reversibility.
Rawls's social justice theory	Moral duties are based on an implied social contract. Fairness is justice. The rules are established from an original position of a "veil of ignorance."
Ethical relativism	Individuals decide what is ethical based on their own feelings as to what is right or wrong.

SOCIAL RESPONSIBILITY OF BUSINESS

Businesses do not operate in a vacuum. Decisions made by businesses have far-reaching effects on society. In the past, many business decisions were based solely on a cost–benefit analysis and how they affected the "bottom line." Such decisions, however, may cause negative externalities for others. For example, the dumping of hazardous wastes from a manufacturing plant into a river affects the homeowners, farmers, and others who use the river's waters. Thus, corporations are considered to owe some degree of **social responsibility** for their actions. Four theories of the social responsibility of business are discussed in the following paragraphs.

Maximizing Profits

The ultimate justification of the law is to be found, and can only be found, in moral considerations.

Lord MacMillan
Law and Other Things (1937)

The traditional view of the social responsibility of business is that business should **maximize profits** for shareholders. This view, which dominated business and the law during the nineteenth century, holds that the interests of other constituencies (e.g., employees, suppliers, residents of the communities in which businesses are located) are not important in and of themselves.

maximizing profits
A theory of social responsibility that says a corporation owes a duty to take actions that maximize profits for shareholders.

Example In the famous case *Dodge v. Ford Motor Company*,[1] a shareholder sued Ford Motor Company when its founder Henry Ford introduced a plan to reduce the prices of cars so that more people would be put to work and more people could own cars. The shareholders alleged that such a plan would not increase dividends. Mr. Ford testified, "My ambition is to employ still more men, to spread the benefits of this industrial system to the greatest number, to help them build up their lives and their homes." The court sided with the shareholders and stated that:

> *[Mr. Ford's] testimony creates the impression that he thinks the Ford Motor company has made too much money, has had too large profits and that, although large profits might still be earned, a sharing of them with the public, by reducing the price of the output of the company, ought to be undertaken.*
>
> *There should be no confusion of the duties which Mr. Ford conceives that he and the stockholders owe to the general public and the duties which in law he and his codirectors owe to protesting, minority stockholders. A business corporation is organized and carried on primarily for the profit of the stockholders. The powers of the directors are to be employed for that end. The discretion of directors is to be exercised in the choice of means to attain that end and does not extend to a change in the end itself, to the reduction of profits, or to the nondistribution of profits among stockholders in order to devote them to other purposes.*

Public policy: That principle of the law which holds that no subject can lawfully do that which has a tendency to be injurious to the public or against the public good.

Lord Truro
Egerton v. Brownlow (1853)

Milton Friedman, who won the Nobel Prize in economics when he taught at the University of Chicago, advocated the theory of maximizing profits for shareholders. Friedman asserted that in a free society, "there is one and only one social responsibility of business—to use its resources and engage in activities designed to increase its profits as long as it stays within the rules of the game, which is to say, engages in open and free competition without deception and fraud."[2]

In the following case, Wal-Mart was accused of unlawfully knocking off another company's product design.

U.S. SUPREME COURT CASE 2 Business Ethics

Wal-Mart Stores, Inc. v. Samara Brothers, Inc.

529 U.S. 205, 120 S.Ct. 1339, 146 L.Ed.2d 182, Web 2000 U.S. Lexis 2197 (2000)
Supreme Court of the United States

"Their suspicions aroused, however, Samara officials launched an investigation, which disclosed that Wal-Mart [was] selling the knockoffs of Samara's outfits."

—Justice Scalia

Facts

Samara Brothers, Inc. (Samara), is a designer and manufacturer of children's clothing. The core of Samara's business is its annual new line of spring and summer children's garments. Samara sold its clothing to retailers, who in turn sold the clothes to consumers. Wal-Mart Stores, Inc. (Wal-Mart), operates a large chain of budget warehouse stores that sell thousands of items at very low prices. Wal-Mart contacted one of its suppliers, Judy-Philippine, Inc. (JPI), about the possibility of making a line of children's clothes just like Samara's successful line. Wal-Mart sent photographs of Samara's children's clothes to JPI (the name "Samara" was readily discernible on the labels of the garments) and directed JPI to produce children's clothes exactly like those in the photographs. JPI produced a line of children's clothes for Wal-Mart that copied the designs, colors, and patterns of Samara's clothing. Wal-Mart then sold this line of children's clothing in its stores, making a gross profit of over $1.15 million on these clothes sales during the 1996 selling season.

(case continues)

Samara discovered that Wal-Mart was selling the knockoff clothes at a price that was lower than Samara's retailers were paying Samara for its clothes. After sending unsuccessful cease-and-desist letters to Wal-Mart, Samara sued Wal-Mart, alleging that Wal-Mart stole Samara's trade dress (i.e., look and feel) in violation of Section 43(a) of the Lanham Act. Although not finding that Samara's clothes had acquired a secondary meaning in the minds of the public, the U.S. District Court held in favor of Samara and awarded damages. The U.S. Court of Appeals affirmed the award to Samara. Wal-Mart appealed to the U.S. Supreme Court.

Issue

Must a product's design have acquired a secondary meaning before it is protected as trade dress?

Language of the U.S. Supreme Court

The Lanham Act, in Section 43(a), gives a producer a cause of action for the use by any person of "any word, term, name, symbol, or device, or any combination thereof which is likely to cause confusion as to the origin, sponsorship, or approval of his or her goods." The text of Section 43(a) provides little guidance as to the circumstances under which unregistered trade dress may be protected. It does require that a producer show that the allegedly infringing feature is likely to cause confusion with the product for which protection is sought. In an action for infringement of unregistered trade dress a product's design is protectable only upon a showing of secondary meaning.

Decision

The U.S. Supreme Court held that a product's design has to have acquired a secondary meaning in the public's eye before it is protected as trade dress under Section 43(a) of the Lanham Act. The Supreme Court reversed the decision of the U.S. Court of Appeals and remanded the case for further proceedings consistent with its opinion.

Case Questions

Critical Legal Thinking What is trade dress? Should it have been protected in this case?

Business Ethics Even if Wal-Mart's conduct was ruled legal, was it ethical?

Contemporary Business What can companies like Samara do to protect themselves from similar conduct by Wal-Mart or other larger companies? Explain.

Moral Minimum

moral minimum
A theory of social responsibility that says a corporation's duty is to make a profit while avoiding causing harm to others.

Some proponents of corporate social responsibility argue that a corporation's duty is to **make a profit while avoiding causing harm to others**. This theory of social responsibility is called the **moral minimum**. Under this theory, as long as business avoids or corrects the social injury it causes, it has met its duty of social responsibility.

Example A corporation that pollutes the waters and then compensates those whom it injures has met its moral minimum duty of social responsibility.

The legislative and judicial branches of government have established laws that enforce the moral minimum of social responsibility on corporations.

Examples Occupational safety laws establish minimum safety standards for protecting employees from injuries in the workplace. Consumer protection laws establish safety requirements for products and make manufacturers and sellers liable for injuries caused by defective products.

LANDMARK LAW

Sarbanes-Oxley Act Prompts Public Companies to Adopt Codes of Ethics

In the late 1990s and early 2000s, many large corporations in the United States were found to have engaged in massive financial frauds. Many of these frauds were perpetrated by the chief executive officers and other senior officers of the companies. Financial officers, such as chief financial officers and controllers, were also found to have been instrumental in committing these frauds. In response, Congress enacted the **Sarbanes-Oxley Act** of 2002, which makes certain conduct illegal and establishes criminal penalties for violations. In addition, the Sarbanes-Oxley Act prompts companies to encourage senior officers of public companies to act ethically in their dealings with shareholders, employees, and other constituents.

Section 406 of the Sarbanes-Oxley Act requires a public company to disclose whether it has adopted a **code of ethics** for senior financial officers, including its principal financial officer and principal accounting officer. In response, public companies have adopted codes of ethics for their senior financial officers. Many public companies have included all officers and employees in the coverage of their codes of ethics.

A typical code of ethics is illustrated in Exhibit 2.

Big Cheese Corporation
Code of Ethics

Big Cheese Corporation's mission includes the promotion of professional conduct in the practice of general management worldwide. Big Cheese's Chief Executive Officer (CEO), Chief Financial Officer (CFO), corporate Controller, and other employees of the finance organization and other employees of the corporation hold an important and elevated role in the corporate governance of the corporation. They are empowered and uniquely capable to ensure that all constituents' interests are appropriately balanced, protected, and preserved.

This Code of Ethics embodies principles to which we are expected to adhere and advocate. The CEO, CFO, finance organization employees, and other employees of the corporation are expected to abide by this Code of Ethics and all business conduct standards of the corporation relating to areas covered by this Code of Ethics. Any violation of the Code of Ethics may result in disciplinary action, up to and including termination of employment. All employees will:

- Act with honesty and integrity, avoiding actual or apparent conflicts of interest in their personal and professional relations.
- Provide stakeholders with information that is accurate, fair, complete, timely, objective, relevant, and understandable, including in our filings with and other submissions to the U.S. Securities and Exchange Commission.
- Comply with rules and regulations of federal, state, provincial, and local governments and other appropriate private and public regulatory agencies.
- Act in good faith, responsibly, with due care, competence, and diligence, without misrepresenting material facts or allowing one's independent judgment to be subordinated.
- Respect the confidentiality of information acquired in the course of one's work, except when authorized or otherwise legally obligated to disclose. Confidential information acquired in the course of one's work will not be used for personal advantage.
- Share knowledge and maintain professional skills important and relevant to stakeholders' needs.
- Proactively promote and be an example of ethical behavior as a responsible partner among peers, in the work environment and the community.
- Achieve responsible use, control, and stewardship over all Big Cheese's assets and resources that are employed or entrusted to us.
- Not unduly or fraudulently influence, coerce, manipulate, or mislead any authorized audit or interfere with any auditor engaged in the performance of an internal or independent audit of Big Cheese's financial statements or accounting books and records.

If you are aware of any suspected or known violations of this Code of Ethics or other Big Cheese policies or guidelines, you have a duty to promptly report such concerns either to your manager, another responsible member of management, a Human Resources representative, or the Director of Compliance or the 24-hour Business Conduct Line.

If you have a concern about a questionable accounting or auditing matter and wish to submit the concern confidentially or anonymously, you may do so by sending an e-mail to (bc.codeofethics@bigcheese.cc) or calling the Business Conduct Line 24-hour number at 1-888-666-BIGC (2442).

Big Cheese will handle all inquiries discreetly and make every effort to maintain, within the limits allowed by law, the confidentiality of anyone requesting guidence or reporting questionable behavior and/or a compliance concern.

It is Big Cheese's intention that this Code of Ethics to be its written code of ethics under Section 406 of the Sarbanes-Oxley Act of 2002 complying with the standards set forth in Securities and Exchange Commission Regulation S-K Item 406.

Exhibit 2 CODE OF ETHICS

Stakeholder Interest

Businesses have relationships with all sorts of people besides their shareholders, including employees, suppliers, customers, creditors, and the local community. Under the **stakeholder interest** theory of social responsibility, a corporation must consider the effects its actions have on these *other stakeholders*. For example, a corporation would violate the stakeholder interest theory if it viewed employees solely as a means of maximizing shareholder wealth.

stakeholder interest
A theory of social responsibility that says a corporation must consider the effects its actions have on persons other than its shareholders.

The stakeholder interest theory is criticized because it is difficult to harmonize the conflicting interests of stakeholders.

Example In deciding to close an unprofitable manufacturing plant, certain stakeholders would benefit (e.g., shareholders and creditors), while other stakeholders would not (e.g., current employees and the local community).

Corporate Citizenship

The **corporate citizenship** theory of social responsibility argues that business has a responsibility to do well. That is, business is responsible for helping to solve social problems that it did little, if anything, to cause.

corporate citizenship
A theory of responsibility that says a business has a responsibility to do good.

In civilized life, law floats in a sea of ethics.

Earl Warren

Example Under corporate citizenship theory of social responsibility, corporations owe a duty to subsidize schools and help educate children.

This theory contends that corporations owe a duty to promote the same social goals as individual members of society. Proponents of this "do good" theory argue that corporations owe a debt to society to make it a better place and that this duty arises because of the social power bestowed on them. That is, this social power is a gift from society and should be used to good ends.

A major criticism of this theory is that the duty of a corporation to do good cannot be expanded beyond certain limits. There is always some social problem that needs to be addressed, and corporate funds are limited. Further, if this theory were taken to its maximum limit, potential shareholders might be reluctant to invest in corporations.

CONCEPT SUMMARY

THEORIES OF SOCIAL RESPONSIBILITY

Theory	Social Responsibility
Maximizing profits	To maximize profits for stockholders.
Moral minimum	To avoid causing harm and to compensate for harm caused.
Stakeholder interest	To consider the interests of all stakeholders, including stockholders, employees, customers, suppliers, creditors, and the local community.
Corporate citizenship	To do well and solve social problems.

CONTEMPORARY ENVIRONMENT

The Corporate Social Audit

It has been suggested that corporate audits should be extended to include not only audits of the financial health of a corporation but also of its moral health. It is expected that corporations that conduct **corporate social audits** would be more apt to prevent unethical and illegal conduct by managers, employees, and agents. The audit would examine how well employees have adhered to the company's code of ethics and how well the corporation has met its duty of social responsibility.

Such audits would focus on the corporation's efforts to promote employment opportunities for members of protected classes, worker safety, environmental protection, consumer protection, and the like. Social audits are not easy. First, it may be difficult to conceptualize just what is being audited. Second, it may be difficult to measure results. Despite these factors, a growing number of companies are expected to undertake social audits.

Companies should institute the following procedures when conducting a social audit:

- An independent outside firm should be hired to conduct the audit. This ensures autonomy and objectivity in conducting the audit.
- The company's personnel should cooperate fully with the auditing firm while the audit is being conducted.
- The auditing firm should report its findings directly to the company's board of directors.
- The board of directors should review the results of the audit.The board of directors should determine how the company can better meet its duty of social responsibility and can use the audit to implement a program to correct any deficiencies it finds.

TEST REVIEW TERMS AND CONCEPTS

Code of ethics
Corporate citizenship
Corporate social audit
Ethical fundamentalism
Ethical relativism
Ethics
False Claims Act (Whistleblower Statute)
Greatest good to society
Kantian ethics (duty ethics)
Maximizing profits
Moral minimum (make a profit while avoiding causing harm to others)
Outside source
Qui tam lawsuit
Rawls's social justice theory
Sarbanes-Oxley Act
Section 406
Social contract
Social responsibility of business
Stakeholder interest
Universal rules
Utilitarianism

CASE PROBLEMS

1 Fraud The Warner-Lambert Company has manufactured and distributed Listerine antiseptic mouthwash since 1879. Its formula has never changed. Ever since Listerine's introduction, the company has represented the product as being beneficial in preventing and curing colds and sore throats. Direct advertising of these claims to consumers began in 1921. Warner-Lambert spent millions of dollars annually advertising these claims in print media and in television commercials.

After 100 years of Warner-Lambert's making such claims, the Federal Trade Commission (FTC) filed a complaint against the company, alleging that it had engaged in false advertising in violation of federal law. Four months of hearings were held before an administrative law judge that produced an evidentiary record of more than 4,000 pages of documents from 46 witnesses. After examining the evidence, the FTC issued an opinion which held that the company's representations that Listerine prevented and cured colds and sore throats were false. The U.S. Court of Appeals affirmed. Is Warner-Lambert guilty of fraud? If so, what remedies should the court impose on the company? Did Warner-Lambert act ethically in making its claims for Listerine? *Warner-Lambert Company v. Federal Trade Commission*, 183 U.S. App. D.C. 230, 562 F.2d 749, **Web** 1977 U.S. App. Lexis 11599 (United States Court of Appeals for the District of Columbia Circuit)

2 Liability The Johns-Manville Corporation was a profitable company that made a variety of building and other products. It was a major producer of asbestos, which was used for insulation in buildings and for a variety of other uses. It has been medically proven that excessive exposure to asbestos causes asbestosis, a fatal lung disease. Thousands of employees of the company and consumers who were exposed to asbestos and contracted this fatal disease sued the company for damages. Eventually, the lawsuits were being filed at a rate of more than 400 per week.

In response to the claims, Johns-Manville Corporation filed for reorganization bankruptcy. It argued that if it did not, an otherwise viable company that provided thousands of jobs and served a useful purpose in this country would be destroyed and that without the declaration of bankruptcy, a few of the plaintiffs who first filed their lawsuits would win awards of hundreds of millions of dollars, leaving nothing for the remainder of the plaintiffs. Under the bankruptcy court's protection, the company was restructured to survive. As part of the release from bankruptcy, the company contributed money to a fund to pay current and future claimants. The fund was not large enough to pay all injured persons the full amounts of their claims.

Is Johns-Manville liable for negligence? Was it ethical for Johns-Manville to declare bankruptcy? Did it meet its duty of social responsibility in this case? *In re Johns-Mansville Corporation*, 36 B.R. 727, **Web** 1984 Bankr. Lexis 6384 (United States Bankruptcy Court for the Southern District of New York)

BUSINESS ETHICS CASES

3 Fraud The Reverend Leon H. Sullivan, a Baptist minister from Philadelphia who was also a member of the board of directors of General Motors Corporation, proposed a set of rules to guide American-owned companies doing business in the Republic of South Africa. The *Sullivan Principles*, as they became known, call for the nonsegregation of races in South Africa. They call for employers to (a) provide equal and fair employment practices for all employees and (b) improve the quality of employees' lives outside the work environment in such areas as housing, education, transportation, recreation, and health facilities. The principles also require signatory companies to report regularly and to be graded on their conduct in South Africa.

Eventually, the Sullivan Principles were subscribed to by several hundred U.S. corporations with affiliates doing business in South Africa. Which of the following theories of social responsibility are the companies that subscribed to the Sullivan Principles following?

1. Maximizing profits
2. Moral minimum
3. Stakeholder interest
4. Corporate citizenship

To put additional pressure on the government of the Republic of South Africa to end apartheid, Reverend Sullivan called for the complete withdrawal of all U.S. companies from doing business in or with South Africa. Very few companies agreed to do so. Do companies owe a social duty to withdraw from South Africa? Should universities divest themselves of investments in companies that do not withdraw from South Africa?

4 Business Ethics Kaiser Aluminum & Chemical Corporation entered into a collective bargaining agreement with the United Steelworkers of America, a union that represented employees at Kaiser's plants. The agreement contained an affirmative-action program to increase the representation of minorities in craft jobs. To enable plants to meet these goals, on-the-job training programs were established to teach unskilled production workers the skills necessary to become craft workers. Assignment to the training program was based on seniority, except that the plan reserved 50 percent of the openings for black employees.

Thirteen craft trainees were selected from Kaiser's Gramercy plant for the training program. Of these, 7 were black and 6 white. The most senior black trainee selected had less seniority than several white production workers who had applied for the positions but were rejected. Brian Weber, one of the white rejected employees, instituted a class action lawsuit, alleging that the affirmative action plan violated Title VII of the Civil Rights Act of 1964, which made it "unlawful to discriminate because of race" in hiring and selecting apprentices for training programs. The U.S. Supreme Court upheld the affirmative-action plan in this case. The decision stated:

> *We therefore hold that Title VII's prohibition against racial discrimination does not condemn all private, voluntary, race-conscious affirmative action plans. At the same time, the plant does not unnecessarily trammel the interests of the white employees. Moreover, the plan is a temporary measure; it is not intended to maintain racial balance, but simply to eliminate a manifest racial imbalance.*

Do companies owe a duty of social responsibility to provide affirmative-action programs? *United Steelworkers of America v. Weber*, 443 U.S. 193, 99 S.Ct. 2721, 61 L.Ed.2d 480, **Web** 1979 U.S. Lexis 40 (Supreme Court of the United States)

5 Business Ethics Iroquois Brands, Ltd., a Delaware corporation, had $78 million in assets, $141 million in sales, and $6 million in profits. As part of its business, Iroquois imported pâté de foie gras (goose pâté) from France and sold it in the United States. Iroquois derived only $79,000 in revenues from sales of such pâté. The French force-fed the geese from which the pâté was made. Peter C. Lovenheim, who owned 200 shares of Iroquois common stock, proposed to include a shareholder proposal in Iroquois's annual proxy materials to be sent to shareholders. His proposal criticized the company because the force-feeding caused "undue stress, pain and suffering" to the geese and requested that shareholders vote to have Iroquois discontinue importing and selling pâté produced by this method.

Iroquois refused to allow the information to be included in its proxy materials. Iroquois asserted that its refusal was based on the fact that Lovenheim's proposal was "not economically significant" and had only "ethical and social" significance. The company reasoned that because a corporation is an economic entity, only an economic test applied to its activities, and Iroquois was therefore not subject to an ethical or a social responsibility test. Is Iroquois correct? That is, should only an economic test be applied in judging the activities of a corporation? Or should a corporation also be subject to an ethical or a social responsibility test? *Lovenheim v. Iroquois Brands, Ltd.*, 618 F.Supp. 554, **Web** 1985 U.S. Dist. Lexis 21259 (United States District Court for the District of Columbia)

ENDNOTES

1. 204 Mich. 459, 170 N.W. 668, Web 1919 Mich. Lexis 720 (Supreme Court of Michigan).
2. Milton Friedman, "The Social Responsibility of Business Is to Increase Its Profits," *New York Times Magazine*, September 13, 1970.

NATURE OF TRADITIONAL AND E-CONTRACTS

NATURE OF TRADITIONAL AND E-CONTRACTS

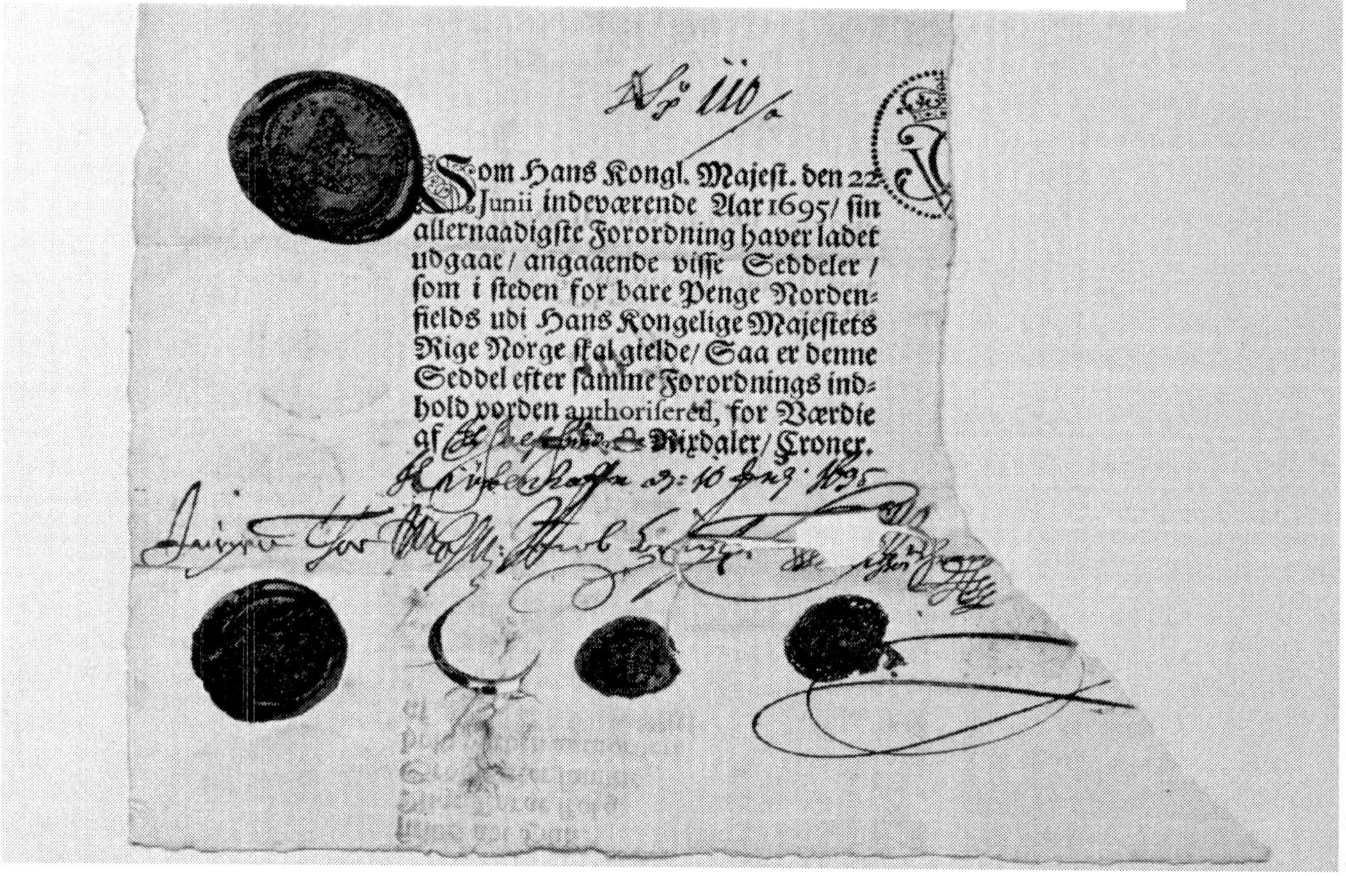

▲ **Norwegian Merchant's Note, with Four Red Seals** *Written contracts have long been used in business to ensure mutual understanding. In many societies, seals such as the ones in this photo were required to establish the document's authenticity.*

CHAPTER OBJECTIVES

After studying this chapter, you should be able to:

1. Define *contract.*
2. List the elements necessary to form a valid contract.
3. Distinguish between bilateral and unilateral contracts.
4. Describe and distinguish between express and implied-in-fact contracts.
5. Describe and distinguish among valid, void, voidable, and unenforceable contracts.

CHAPTER CONTENTS

"The movement of the progressive societies has hitherto been a movement from status to contract."

—Sir Henry Maine
Ancient Law, Chapter 5

INTRODUCTION TO NATURE OF TRADITIONAL AND E-CONTRACTS

Contracts are the basis of many of our daily activities. They provide the means for individuals and businesses to sell and otherwise transfer property, services, and other rights. The purchase of goods, such as books and automobiles, is based on sales contracts; the hiring of employees is based on service contracts; the lease of an apartment is based on a rental contract; and the sale of goods and services over the Internet is based on electronic contracts. The list is almost endless. Without enforceable contracts, commerce would collapse.

Contracts are voluntarily entered into by parties. The terms of a contract become *private law* between the parties. One court has stated that "the contract between parties is the law between them and the courts are obliged to give legal effect to such contracts according to the true interests of the parties."[1]

Nevertheless, most contracts are performed without the aid of the court system. This is usually because the parties feel a moral duty to perform as promised. Although some contracts, such as illegal contracts, are not enforceable, most are **legally enforceable.**[2] This means that if a party fails to perform a contract, the other party may call upon the courts to enforce the contract.

legally enforceable contract
A contract in which if one party fails to perform as promised, the other party can use the court system to enforce the contract and recover damages or other remedy.

This chapter introduces the study of **traditional law** and **e-contract law**. Such topics as the definition of *contract*, requirements for forming a contract, sources of contract law, and the various classifications of contracts are discussed.

DEFINITION OF A CONTRACT

A **contract** is an agreement that is enforceable by a court of law or equity. A simple and widely recognized definition of *contract* is provided by the *Restatement (Second) of Contracts*: "A contract is a promise or a set of promises for the breach of which the law gives a remedy or the performance of which the law in some way recognizes a duty."[3]

Parties to a Contract

Every contract involves at least two parties. The **offeror** is the party who makes an offer to enter into a contract. The **offeree** is the party to whom the offer is made (see Exhibit 1). In making an offer, the offeror promises to do—or to refrain from doing—something. The offeree then has the power to create a contract by accepting the offeror's offer. A contract is created if the offer is accepted. No contract is created if the offer is not accepted.

offeror
The party who makes an offer to enter into a contract.

offeree
The party to whom an offer to enter into a contract is made.

Exhibit 1 PARTIES TO A CONTRACT

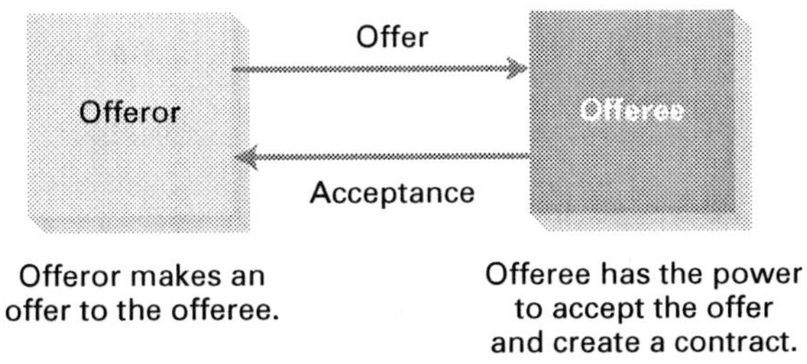

Contracts must not be the sports of an idle hour, mere matters of pleasantry and badinage, never intended by the parties to have any serious effect whatever.

Lord Stowell
Dalrymple v. Dalrymple (1811)

Elements of a Contract

For a contract to be enforceable, the following four basic requirements must be met:

1. **Agreement.** To have an enforceable contract, there must be an **agreement** between the parties. This requires an **offer** by the offeror and an **acceptance** of the offer by the offeree. There must be mutual assent by the parties.
2. **Consideration.** The promise must be supported by a bargained-for **consideration** that is legally sufficient. Money, personal property, real property, provision of services, and such qualify as consideration.
3. **Contractual capacity.** The parties to a contract must have **contractual capacity** for the contract to be enforceable against them. Contracts cannot be enforced against parties who lacked contractual capacity when they entered into a contract.
4. **Lawful object.** The object of the contract must be lawful. Most contracts have a **lawful object.** However, contracts that have an illegal object are void and will not be enforced.

CONCEPT SUMMARY
ELEMENTS OF A CONTRACT

1. Agreement
2. Consideration
3. Contractual capacity
4. Lawful object

Defenses to the Enforcement of a Contract

Two *defenses* may be raised to the enforcement of contracts:

1. **Genuineness of assent.** The consent of the parties to create a contract must be **genuine**. If the consent is obtained by duress, undue influence, or fraud, there is no real consent.
2. **Writing and form.** The law requires that certain contracts be in **writing** or in a certain **form**. Failure of such a contract to be in writing or to be in proper form may be raised against the enforcement of the contract.

The requirements to form an enforceable contract and the defenses to the enforcement of contracts are discussed in this chapter.

CONTEMPORARY ENVIRONMENT
The Evolution of the Modern Law of Contracts

The use of contracts originally developed in ancient times. The common law of contracts developed in England around the fifteenth century. U.S. contract law evolved from the English common law.

At first, the United States adopted a ***laissez-faire*** approach to the law of contracts. The central theme of this theory was *freedom of contract*. The parties (e.g., consumers, shopkeepers, farmers, traders) generally dealt with one another face-to-face, had equal knowledge and bargaining power, and had the opportunity to inspect goods prior to sale. Contract terms were openly negotiated. There was little, if any, government regulation of the right to contract. This "pure law," or **classical law of contracts** produced objective rules, which, in turn, produced certainty and predictability in the enforcement of contracts. It made sense until the Industrial Revolution.

The Industrial Revolution changed many of the underlying assumptions of pure contract law. For example, as large corporations developed and gained control of crucial resources, the traditional balance of parties' bargaining power shifted: Large corporations now had the most power. The chain of distribution for goods also changed because (1) buyers did not have to deal face-to-face with sellers and (2) there was not always an opportunity to inspect the goods prior to sale.

Eventually sellers began using **form contracts** that offered their goods to buyers on a take-it-or-leave-it basis. That is, the consumer has no ability to negotiate the terms of the contract with the seller. The majority of contracts in this country today are form contracts.

Examples Automobile sales contracts, automobile leases, mortgages, and sales contracts for consumer goods, credit card agreements, and software licenses usually use form contracts.

Although the phrase "freedom to contract" is often used, in many situations there is not an absolute ability of freedom of contract. Both federal and state governments have enacted statutes that regulate contracts. Many of these laws are intended to protect consumers, debtors, and others from unfair contracts. Today, under this modern law of contracts, there is substantial **government regulation** of the right to contract.

Examples Federal labor laws protect the rights of workers to unionize and negotiate collective bargaining agreements with their employers. Consumer protection laws protect consumers from certain unscrupulous contracts. Equal opportunity in employment laws protect employees from contracts that attempt to discriminate against them based on race, sex, age, disability, and other protected categories. E-contracts are regulated by federal and state laws that govern transactions over the Internet.

SOURCES OF CONTRACT LAW

There are several sources of contract law in the United States, including the *common law of contracts*, the *Uniform Commercial Code*, and the *Restatement (Second) of Contracts*. The following paragraphs explain these sources in more detail.

common law of contracts
Contract law developed primarily by state courts.

Uniform Commercial Code (UCC)
A comprehensive statutory scheme which includes laws that cover aspects of commercial transactions.

Common Law of Contracts

A major source of contract law is the **common law of contracts,** which developed from early court decisions that became precedent for later decisions. There is a limited federal common law of contracts that applies to contracts made by the federal government. The larger and more prevalent body of common law has been developed from state court decisions. Thus, although the general principles remain the same throughout the country, there is some variation from state to state.

LANDMARK LAW

Uniform Commercial Code (UCC)

A major source of contract law is the **Uniform Commercial Code (UCC).** The UCC, which was first drafted by the National Conference of Commissioners on Uniform State Laws in 1952, has been amended several times. Its goal is to create a uniform system of commercial law among the 50 states. The provisions of the UCC normally take precedence over the common law of contracts.

The UCC is divided into nine main articles. Every state has adopted at least part of the UCC. In the area of contract law, two of the major provisions of the UCC are:

- **Article 2 (Sales). Article 2 (Sales)** prescribes a set of uniform rules for the creation and enforcement of contracts for the sale of goods. These contracts are often referred to as **sales contracts**.

Examples The sale of equipment, automobiles, computers, clothing, and such involve sales contracts subject to Article 2 of the UCC.

- **Article 2A (Leases). Article 2A (Leases)** prescribes a set of uniform rules for the creation and enforcement of contracts for the lease of goods. These contracts are referred to as **lease contracts**.

Examples Leases of automobiles, leases of aircraft, and other leases involving goods are subject to Article 2A of the UCC.

The Restatement of the Law of Contracts

Restatement of the Law of Contracts
A compilation of model contract law principles drafted by legal scholars. The *Restatement* is not law.

In 1932, the American Law Institute, a group comprising law professors, judges, and lawyers, completed the **Restatement of the Law of Contracts**. The *Restatement* is a compilation of contract law principles, as agreed upon by the drafters. The *Restatement*, which is currently in its second edition, is cited in this text as the ***Restatement (Second) of Contracts***. Note that the *Restatement* is not law. However, lawyers and judges often refer to it for guidance in contract disputes because of its stature.

▶ OBJECTIVE THEORY OF CONTRACTS

objective theory of contracts
A theory that says the intent to contract is judged by the reasonable person standard and not by the subjective intent of the parties.

The **objective theory of contracts** holds that the intent to enter into an express or implied-in-fact contract is judged by the **reasonable person standard**. Would a hypothetical reasonable person conclude that the parties intended to create a contract after considering (1) the words and conduct of the parties and (2) the surrounding circumstances? For example, no valid contract results from offers that are made in jest, anger, or undue excitement. Under the objective theory of contracts, the subjective intent of a party to enter into a contract is irrelevant.

▶ E-COMMERCE

As we entered the twenty-first century, a new economic shift brought the United States and the rest of the world into the Information Age. Computer technology and the use of the Internet increased dramatically. A new form of commerce—**electronic commerce**, or **e-commerce**—is flourishing. All sorts of goods and services are now sold over the Internet. You can purchase automobiles and children's toys, participate in auctions, purchase airline tickets, make hotel reservations, and purchase other goods and services over the Internet.

Uniform Computer Information Transactions Act (UCITA)
A model act that establishes uniform legal rules for the formation and enforcement of electronic contracts and licenses.

Much of the new cyberspace economy is based on electronic contracts and the licensing of computer information. E-commerce created problems for forming **e-contracts** over the Internet, enforcing e-contracts, and providing consumer protection. In many situations, traditional contract rules apply to e-contracts. Many states have adopted rules that specifically regulate e-commerce transactions. The federal government has also enacted several laws that regulate e-contracts. Contract rules that apply to e-commerce will be discussed in this chapter.

INTERNET LAW & ONLINE COMMERCE

Uniform Computer Information Transactions Act (UCITA)

The National Conference of Commissioners on Uniform State Laws (a group of lawyers, judges, and legal scholars) drafted the **Uniform Computer Information Transactions Act (UCITA).**

The UCITA establishes uniform legal rules for the formation and enforcement of electronic contracts and licenses. The UCITA addresses most of the legal issues that are encountered while conducting e-commerce over the Internet.

The UCITA is a model act that does not become law until a state legislature adopts it as a statute for the state. Although most states have not adopted the UCITA, the UCITA has served as a model for states that have enacted their own statutes that govern e-commerce. Because of the need for uniformity of e-commerce rules, states are attempting to adopt uniform laws to govern the creation and enforcement of cyberspace contracts and licenses.

▶ CLASSIFICATIONS OF CONTRACTS

There are several types of contracts. Each differs somewhat in formation, enforcement, performance, and discharge. The different types of contracts are discussed in the following paragraphs.

Bilateral and Unilateral Contracts

Contracts are either *bilateral* or *unilateral*, depending on what the offeree must do to accept the offeror's offer. A contract is **bilateral** if the offeror's promise is answered with the offeree's promise of acceptance. In other words, a bilateral contract is a "promise for a promise." This exchange of promises creates an enforceable contract. No act of performance is necessary to create a bilateral contract.

bilateral contract
A contract entered into by way of exchange of promises of the parties; "a promise for a promise."

Example Mary, the owner of the Chic Dress Shop, says to Peter, a painter, "If you promise to paint my store by July 1, I will pay you $3,000." Peter says "I promise to do so." A *bilateral contract* was created at the moment Peter promised to paint the dress shop (a promise for a promise). If Peter fails to paint the shop, Mary can sue Peter and recover whatever damages result from his breach of contract. Similarly, Peter can sue Mary if she refuses to pay him after he has performed as promised.

A contract is **unilateral** if the offeror's offer can be accepted only by the performance of an act by the offeree. There is no contract until the offeree performs the requested act. An offer to create a unilateral contract cannot be accepted by a promise to perform. It is a "promise for an act."

unilateral contract
A contract in which the offeror's offer can be accepted only by the performance of an act by the offeree; a "promise for an act."

Example Mary, the owner of the Chic Dress Shop, says to Peter, a painter, "If you paint my shop by July 1, I will pay you $3,000." This offer creates a *unilateral contract*. The offer can be accepted only by the painter's performance of the requested act. If Peter does not paint the shop by July 1, there has been no acceptance, and Mary cannot sue Peter for damages. If Peter paints the shop by July 1, Mary owes Peter $3,000. If Mary refuses to pay, Peter can sue Mary to collect payment.

Justice is the end of government. It is the end of civil society. It ever has been, and ever will be pursued, until it be obtained, or until liberty be lost in the pursuit.

James Madison
The Federalist No. 51 (1788)

The language of the offeror's promise must be carefully scrutinized to determine whether it is an offer to create a bilateral contract or an offer to create a unilateral contract. If there is any ambiguity as to which it is, it is presumed to be a bilateral contract.

Incomplete or Partial Performance Problems can arise if the offeror in a unilateral contract attempts to revoke an offer after the offeree has begun performance. Generally, an offer to create a unilateral contract can be revoked by the offeror any time prior to the offeree's performance of the requested act. However, the offer cannot be revoked if the offeree has begun or has substantially completed performance.

Example Suppose Alan Matthews tells Sherry Levine that he will pay her $5,000 if she finishes the Boston Marathon. Alan cannot revoke the offer once Sherry starts running the marathon.

A man must come into a court of equity with clean hands.

C.B. Eyre
Dering v. Earl of Winchelsea (1787)

Formal and Informal Contracts

Contracts may be classified as either *formal* or *informal*.

Formal contracts **Formal contracts** are contracts that require a special form or method of creation. The *Restatement (Second) of Contracts* identifies the following types of formal contracts[4]:

formal contract
A contract that requires a special form or method of creation.

- **Negotiable instruments. Negotiable instruments,** which include checks, drafts, notes, and certificates of deposit, are special forms of contracts recognized by the UCC. They require a special form and language for their creation and must meet certain requirements for transfer.
- **Letters of credit.** A **letter of credit** is an agreement by the issuer of the letter to pay a sum of money upon the receipt of an invoice and other documents. Letters of credit are governed by the UCC.
- **Recognizance.** In a recognizance, a party acknowledges in court that he or she will pay a specified sum of money if a certain event occurs.
- **Contracts under seal.** This type of contract is one to which a seal (usually a wax seal) is attached. Although no state currently requires contracts to be under seal, a few states provide that no consideration is necessary if a contract is made under seal.

Informal Contracts All contracts that do not qualify as formal contracts are called **informal contracts** (or **simple contracts**). The term is a misnomer. Valid informal contracts (e.g., leases, sales contracts, service contracts) are fully enforceable and may be sued upon if breached. They are called informal contracts only because no special form or method is required for their creation. Thus, the parties to an informal contract can use any words they choose to express their contract. The majority of the contracts entered into by individuals and businesses are informal contracts.

informal contract
A contract that is not formal. Valid informal contracts are fully enforceable and may be sued upon if breached.

Valid, Void, Voidable, and Unenforceable Contracts

Contract law places contracts in the following categories:

1. **Valid contract.** A **valid contract** meets all the essential elements to establish a contract. In other words, it (1) consists of an agreement between the parties, (2) is supported by legally sufficient consideration, (3) is between parties with contractual capacity, and (4) accomplished a lawful object. A valid contract is enforceable by at least one of the parties.
2. **Void contract.** A **void contract** has no legal effect. It is as if no contract had ever been created. A contract to commit a crime is void. If a contract is void, neither party is obligated to perform the contract, and neither party can enforce the contract.
3. **Voidable contract.** A **voidable contract** is a contract in which at least one party has the *option* to avoid his or her contractual obligations. If the contract is avoided, both parties are released from their obligations under the contract. If the party with the option chooses to ratify the contract, both parties must fully perform their obligations.

   With certain exceptions, contracts may be voided by minors; insane persons; intoxicated persons; persons acting under duress, undue influence, or fraud; and in cases involving mutual mistake.
4. **Unenforceable contract.** With an **unenforceable contract**, there is some legal defense to the enforcement of the contract. If a contract is required to be in writing under the Statute of Frauds but is not, the contract is unenforceable. The parties may voluntarily perform a contract that is unenforceable.

valid contract
A contract that meets all the essential elements to establish a contract; a contract that is enforceable by at least one of the parties.

void contract
A contract that has no legal effect; a nullity.

voidable contract
A contract in which one or both parties have the option to avoid their contractual obligations. If a contract is avoided, both parties are released from their contractual obligations.

unenforceable contract
A contract in which the essential elements to create a valid contract are met but there is some legal defense to the enforcement of the contract.

Executed and Executory Contracts

A completed contract—that is, one that has been fully performed on both sides—is called an **executed contract**. A contract that has not been performed by both sides is called an **executory contract**. Contracts that have been fully performed by one side but not by the other are classified as executory contracts.

Examples Suppose Elizabeth signs a contract to purchase a new BMW automobile from Ace Motors. She has not yet paid for the car and Ace Motors has not yet delivered the car to Elizabeth. This is an executory contract because the contract has not yet been performed. If Elizabeth has paid for the car but Ace Motors has not yet delivered the car to Elizabeth, there is an executory contract because Ace Motors has not performed the contract. If Elizabeth has paid for the car and Ace Motors has delivered the car to Elizabeth, the contract has been fully performed by both parties and is an executed contract.

executed contract
A contract that has been fully performed on both sides; a completed contract.

executory contract
A contract that has not been fully performed by either or both sides.

EXPRESS AND IMPLIED CONTRACTS

An **actual contract** may be either *express* or *implied-in-fact*.

Express Contract

An **express contract** is stated in oral or written words. Most personal and business contracts are express contracts. A contract that is oral or written is an express contract.

express contract
An agreement that is expressed in written or oral words.

Examples A written agreement to buy an automobile from a dealership is an express contract because it is in written words. An oral agreement to purchase a neighbor's bicycle is an express contract because it is in oral words.

Implied-in-Fact Contract

Implied-in-fact contracts are implied from the conduct of the parties. The following elements must be established to create an implied-in-fact contract:

implied-in-fact contract
A contract in which agreement between parties has been inferred from their conduct.

1. The plaintiff provided property or services to the defendant.
2. The plaintiff expected to be paid by the defendant for the property or services and did not provide the property or services gratuitously.
3. The defendant was given an opportunity to reject the property or services provided by the plaintiff but failed to do so.

In the following case, the court had to decide whether the plaintiffs could sue a defendant for breach of an implied-in-fact contract.

CASE 1 Implied-in-Fact Contract

Wrench LLC v. Taco Bell Corporation

256 F.3d 446, Web 2001 U.S. App. Lexis 15097 (2001)
United States Court of Appeals for the Sixth Circuit

"The district court found that appellants produced sufficient evidence to create a genuine issue of material fact regarding whether an implied-in-fact contract existed between the parties."

—Judge Graham

Facts

Thomas Rinks and Joseph Shields created the "Psycho Chihuahua" cartoon character, which they promote, market, and license through their company, Wrench LLC. Psycho Chihuahua is a clever, feisty, cartoon character dog with an attitude, a self-confident, edgy, cool dog who knows what he wants and will not back down. Rinks and Shields attended a licensing trade show in New York City, where they were approached by two Taco Bell employees, Rudy Pollak, a vice president, and Ed Alfaro, a creative services manager. Taco Bell owns and operates a nationwide chain of fast-food Mexican restaurants. Pollak and Alfaro expressed interest in the Psycho Chihuahua character for Taco Bell advertisements because they thought his character would appeal to Taco Bell's core consumers, males aged 18 to 24. Pollak and Alfaro obtained some Psycho Chihuahua materials to take back with them to Taco Bell's headquarters.

Later, Alfaro contacted Rinks and asked him to create art boards combining Psycho Chihuahua with the Taco Bell name and image. Rinks and Shields prepared art boards and sent them to Alfaro, along with Psycho Chihuahua t-shirts, hats, and stickers. Alfaro showed these materials to Taco Bell's vice president of brand management as well as to Taco Bell's outside advertising agency. Alfaro tested the Psycho Chihuahua marketing concept with focus groups. Rinks suggested to Alfaro that instead of using the cartoon version of Psycho Chihuahua in its advertisements, Taco Bell should use a live Chihuahua dog manipulated by computer graphic imaging that had the personality of Psycho Chihuahua and a love for Taco Bell food. Rinks and Shields gave a formal presentation of this concept to Taco Bell's marketing department. One idea presented by Rinks and Shields was a commercial in which a male Chihuahua dog passed by a female Chihuahua dog in order to get to Taco Bell food. Taco Bell did not enter into an express contract with Wrench LLC, Rinks, or Shields.

Just after Rinks' and Shields' presentation, Taco Bell hired a new outside advertising agency, Chiat/Day. Taco Bell gave Chiat/Day materials received from Rinks and Shields regarding Psycho Chihuahua. Three months later, Chiat/Day proposed using a Chihuahua in Taco Bell commercials. One commercial had a male Chihuahua passing up a female Chihuahua to get to a person seated on a bench eating Taco Bell food. Chiat/Day says that it conceived these ideas by itself. In July 1997, Taco Bell aired its first Chihuahua commercial in the United States, and it became an instant success and the basis of its advertising. Taco Bell paid nothing to Wrench LLC or to Rinks and Shields. Plaintiffs Wrench LLC, Rinks, and Shields sued defendant Taco Bell to recover damages for breach of an implied-in-fact contract. On this issue, the District Court agreed with the plaintiffs. The decision was appealed.

Issue

Did the plaintiffs Wrench LLC, Rinks, and Shields state a cause of action for the breach of an implied-in-fact contract?

Language of the Court

The district court found that appellants produced sufficient evidence to create a genuine issue of material fact

(case continues)

regarding whether an implied-in-fact contract existed between the parties. On appeal, Taco Bell argues that this conclusion was erroneous, and asserts that the record contains no evidence of an enforceable contract. We agree with the district court's finding that appellants presented sufficient evidence to survive summary judgment on the question of whether an implied-in-fact contract existed under Michigan law.

Decision

The U.S. Court of Appeals held that the plaintiffs had stated a proper cause of action against defendant Taco Bell for breach of an implied-in-fact contract. The Court of Appeals remanded the case for trial.

Note The U.S. Supreme Court denied review of the decision in this case. In 2003 a federal court jury ordered Taco Bell to pay $30 million to plaintiffs Thomas Rinks and Joseph Shields for stealing their idea for the Psycho Chihuahua commercials. Later, the court awarded an additional $11.8 million in prejudgment interest, bringing the total award to over $42 million.

Case Questions

Critical Legal Thinking What does the doctrine of implied-in-fact contract provide? Explain.

Business Ethics Did Taco Bell act ethically in this case? Did Chiat/Day act ethically in this case?

Contemporary Business What is the purpose of recognizing implied-in-fact contracts? Do you think there was an implied-in-fact contract in this case? If so, what damages should have been awarded to the plaintiffs?

Web Exercise Go to **http://transcripts.cnn.com/TRANSCRIPTS/0306/05/se.03.html** to read about the jury awarding the plaintiffs $30 million. Go to **www.youtube.com/watch?v=B0oEw0IMLXI** for a video clip of Taco Bell's Chihuahua commercial.

Implied-in-Law Contract (Quasi-Contract)

quasi-contract (implied-in-law contract)
An equitable doctrine whereby a court may award monetary damages to a plaintiff for providing work or services to a defendant even though no actual contract existed. The doctrine is intended to prevent unjust enrichment and unjust detriment.

The equitable doctrine of **quasi-contract**, also called **implied-in-law contract**, allows a court to award monetary damages to a plaintiff for providing work or services to a defendant even though no actual contract existed between the parties. Recovery is generally based on the reasonable value of the services received by the defendant.

The doctrine of quasi-contract is intended to prevent **unjust enrichment** and **unjust detriment.** It does not apply where there is an enforceable contract between the parties. A quasi-contract is imposed where (1) one person confers a benefit on another, who retains the benefit, and (2) it would be unjust not to require that person to pay for the benefit received.

Example Heather is driving her automobile when she is involved in a serious automobile accident in which she is knocked unconscious. She is rushed to Metropolitan Hospital, where the doctors and other staff perform the necessary medical procedures to save her life. Heather comes out of her coma, and after recovering is released from the hospital. Subsequently, Metropolitan Hospital sends Heather a bill for its services. The charges are reasonable. Under the doctrine of quasi-contract, Heather is responsible for any charges that are not covered by her insurance coverage.

In the following case, the court found a quasi-contract.

CASE 2 Quasi-Contract

Powell v. Thompson-Powell

Web 2006 Del. C.P. Lexis 10 (2006) Court of Common Pleas of Delaware

"A contract implied in law permits recovery of that amount by which the defendant has benefited at the expense of the plaintiff in order to preclude unjust enrichment."

—Judge Trader

Facts

Samuel E. Powell, Jr., and Susan Thompson-Powell, husband and wife, borrowed $37,700 from Delaware Farm Credit and gave a mortgage to Delaware Farm Credit that pledged two pieces of real property as collateral for the loan. The first piece of property was 2.7 acres of land owned as marital property. Susan had inherited the other piece of property and owned it. Eight years later, Samuel Jr. and Susan defaulted on the mortgage. Samuel Jr. went to his father, Samuel E. Powell, Sr., and orally agreed that if his father would pay the mortgage and the back taxes, he would pay his father back. Samuel Sr. paid off the mortgage and the back taxes owed on the properties. Susan was not a party to this agreement.

Two years later, Samuel Jr. and Susan were divorced. The divorce court ordered that the 2.7 acres of marital real property be sold and the sale proceeds to be divided 50 percent to each party. When the property was sold, Samuel Jr. paid Samuel Sr. one-half of the monies he had previously borrowed from his father. Samuel Sr. sued Susan to recover the other half of the money. Susan defended, alleging that she was not a party to the contract between Samuel Jr. and Samuel Sr. and therefore was not bound by it. Samuel Sr. argued that Susan was liable to him for one-half of the money based on the doctrine of quasi-contract.

Issue

Is Susan liable for one-half the money borrowed by Samuel Jr. from Samuel Sr. under the doctrine of quasi-contract?

Language of the Court

The primary issue in this case is whether the plaintiff can recover from Susan Thompson-Powell on the theory of contract implied in law. A contract implied in law permits recovery of that amount by which the defendant has benefited at the expense of the plaintiff in order to preclude unjust enrichment. To claim restitution, the plaintiff must show that the defendant was unjustly enriched and secured a benefit that it would be unconscionable to allow her to retain.

The essential elements of a quasi-contract are a benefit conferred upon the defendant by the plaintiff, appreciation or realization of the benefit by the defendant, and acceptance and retention by the defendant of such benefit under such circumstances that it would be inequitable to retain without paying the value thereof.

In the case before me the plaintiff paid the mortgage of the son and daughter-in-law at a time when the bank was about to foreclose on the mortgage. If the property had been sold at a foreclosure sale, neither Samuel E. Powell, Jr. nor Susan Thompson-Powell would have received any benefit from the sale of the marital property. Additionally, payment of the mortgage protected Susan Thompson-Powell's inherited property. Thus, because of the plaintiff's acts in preserving the real estate from foreclosure Susan Thompson-Powell received a substantial benefit at the plaintiff's expense. Since the retention of the benefit in this case is unjust, she must repay her share of the money advanced by the plaintiff.

Decision

The court held that Samuel E. Powell, Sr., was entitled to recover from Susan Thompson-Powell one-half of the money advanced for her benefit.

Case Questions

Critical Legal Thinking What does the doctrine of quasi-contract provide? Explain.

Business Ethics Was it unethical for Susan Thompson-Powell to not pay back half of the money borrowed from Samuel E. Powell, Sr.?

Contemporary Business What is the doctrine of quasi-contract designed to prevent? Explain.

Web Exercise Go to **www.oscn.net/applications/oscn/DeliverDocument.asp?CiteID=74212** to read a jury instruction on the issue of quasi-contract.

CONCEPT SUMMARY
CLASSIFICATIONS OF CONTRACTS

Formation

1. **Bilateral contract.** A promise for a promise.
2. **Unilateral contract.** A promise for an act.
3. **Express contract.** A contract expressed in oral or written words.
4. **Implied-in-fact contract.** A contract inferred from the conduct of the parties.
5. **Quasi-contract.** A contract implied by law to prevent unjust enrichment.
6. **Formal contract.** A contract that requires a special form or method of creation.
7. **Informal contract.** A contract that requires no special form or method of creation.

Enforceability	1. **Valid contract.** A contract that meets all the essential elements of establishing a contract.
	2. **Void contract.** No contract exists.
	3. **Voidable contract.** A contract for which at least one party has the option of voiding the contract.
	4. **Unenforceable contract.** A contract that cannot be enforced because of a legal defense.
Performance	1. **Executed contract.** A contract that is fully performed on both sides.
	2. **Executory contract.** A contract that is not fully performed by one or both parties.

▶ EQUITY

equity
A doctrine that permits judges to make decisions based on fairness, equality, moral rights, and natural law.

Recall that two separate courts developed in England: the courts of law and the Chancery Court (or courts of equity). The equity courts developed a set of maxims based on fairness, equality, moral rights, and natural law that were applied in settling disputes. **Equity** was resorted to when (1) an award of money damages "at law" would not be the proper remedy or (2) fairness required the application of equitable principles. Today, in most states of the United States, the courts of law and equity have been merged into one court. In an action "in equity," the judge decides the equitable issue; there is no right to a jury trial in an equitable action. The doctrine of equity is sometimes applied in contract cases.

ETHICS SPOTLIGHT

Equity Saves Contracting Party

"There is only minimal delay in giving notice, the harm to the lessor is slight, and the hardship to the lessee is severe."
—Judge Abbe

The courts usually interpret a valid contract as a solemn promise to perform. This view of the sanctity of a contract can cause an ethical conflict. Consider the following case.

A landlord leased a motel he owned to lessees for a 10-year period. The lessees had an option to extend the lease for an additional 10 years. To do so, they had to give written notice to the landlord three months before the first 10-year lease expired. The lease provided for forfeiture of all furniture, fixtures, and equipment installed by the lessees, free of any liens, upon termination of the lease.

For almost 10 years, the lessees devoted most of their assets and a great deal of their energy building up the business. During this time, they transformed a disheveled, unrated motel into a AAA three-star operation. With the landlord's knowledge, the lessees made extensive long-term improvements that greatly increased the value of both the property and the business. The landlord knew that the lessees had obtained long-term financing for the improvements that would extend well beyond the first 10-year term of the lease. The landlord also knew that the only source of income the lessees had to pay for these improvements was the income generated from the motel business. The lessees told the landlord orally in a conversation that they intended to extend the lease.

The lessees had instructed their accountant to exercise the option on time. Despite reminders from the lessees, the accountant failed to give the written notice within three months of the expiration of the lease. As soon as they discovered the mistake, the lessees personally delivered written notice of renewal of the option to the landlord, 13 days too late. The landlord rejected it as late and instituted a lawsuit for unlawful detainer to evict the lessees.

The trial and appellate courts held in favor of the lessees. They rejected the landlord's argument for strict adherence to the deadline for giving written notice of renewal of the lease. Instead, the courts granted **equitable relief** and permitted the late renewal notice. The court reasoned that "there is only minimal delay in giving notice, the harm to the lessor is slight, and the hardship to the lessee is severe." *Romasanta v. Mitton*, 189 Cal.App.3d 1026, 234 Cal.Rptr. 729, **Web** 1987 Cal.App. Lexis 1428 (Court of Appeal of California)

Business Ethics Did the landlord act ethically in this case? Should the court have applied equity and saved the lessees from their mistake? Why or why not?

INTERNATIONAL LAW

United Nations Convention on Contracts for the International Sale of Goods (CISG)

The **United Nations Convention on Contracts for the International Sale of Goods (CISG)** is a model act for international sales contracts. The CISG is the work of many countries and several international organizations. There are now approximately 70 signatory countries to the CISG. In adopting the CISG, the United Nations stated in its preamble:

PREAMBLE

The State Parties to this Convention,

Considering that the development of international trade on the basis of equality and mutual benefit is an important element in promoting friendly relations among States,

Being of the opinion that the adoption of uniform rules which govern contracts for the international sale of goods and take into account the different social, economic and legal systems would contribute to the removal of legal barriers in international trade and promote the development of international trade,

Have agreed as follows:

The text of the CISG follows the Preamble. The CISG provides legal rules that govern the formation, performance, and enforcement of international sales contracts entered into between international businesses. Many of its provisions are remarkably similar to those of the U.S. Uniform Commercial Code (UCC). The CISG incorporates rules from all the major legal systems. It has, accordingly, received widespread support from developed, developing, and Communist countries.

The CISG applies to contracts for the international sale of goods. The buyer and seller must have their places of business in different countries. In order for the CISG to apply to an international sales contract, either (1) both of the nations must be parties to the convention or (2) the contract may specify that the CISG controls. The contracting parties may agree to exclude (i.e., opt out of) or modify the application of the CISG.

India *The economy of India is growing at over eight percent per year. This once-socialist-inspired country is becoming a major economic power. The second-largest country in the world—with over one billion in population—is transforming itself from an economy based on agriculture and handcrafted goods to an industrial and white-collar economy. Although per capita income remains low, sectors of the Indian economy—such as software engineering, telecommunications, biotechnology, and the provision of back office services—are growing rapidly. International contracts are necessary for India to conduct international trade.*

TEST REVIEW TERMS AND CONCEPTS

Acceptance
Actual contract
Agreement
Article 2 (Sales)
Article 2A (Leases)
Bilateral contract
Classical law of contracts
Common law of contracts
Consideration
Contract
Contractual capacity
E-contract
E-contract law
Electronic commerce (e-commerce)
Equitable relief
Equity
Executed contract
Executory contract
Express contract
Formal contract
Form contract
Genuineness of assent
Government regulation
Implied-in-law contract
Informal contract (simple contract)
Implied-in-fact contract
Laissez-faire
Lawful object
Lease contract
Legally enforceable
Letter of credit
Negotiable instrument
Objective theory of contracts
Offer
Offeree
Offeror
Quasi-contract (implied-in-law contract)
Reasonable person standard
Restatement of the Law of Contracts
Restatement (Second) of Contracts
Sales contract
Traditional law
United Nations Convention on Contracts for the International Sale of Goods (CISG)
Unenforceable contract
Uniform Commercial Code (UCC)
Uniform Computer Information Transactions Act (UCITA)
Unilateral contract
Unjust detriment
Unjust enrichment
Valid contract
Void contract
Voidable contract
Writing and form

CASE PROBLEMS

1 Bilateral or Unilateral Contract G. S. Adams, Jr., vice president of the Washington Bank & Trust Co., met with Bruce Bickham. An agreement was reached whereby Bickham agreed to do his personal and corporate banking business with the bank, and the bank agreed to loan Bickham money at 7½ percent interest per annum. Bickham would have 10 years to repay the loans. For the next two years, the bank made several loans to Bickham at 7½ percent interest. Adams then resigned from the bank. The bank notified Bickham that general economic changes made it necessary to charge a higher rate of interest on both outstanding and new loans. Bickham sued the bank for breach of contract. Was the contract a bilateral or a unilateral contract? Does Bickham win? *Bickham v. Washington Bank & Trust Company*, 515 So.2d 457, **Web** 1987 La.App. Lexis 10442 (Court of Appeal of Louisiana)

2 Implied-in-Fact Contract For six years, Lee Marvin, an actor, lived with Michelle Marvin. They were not married. At the end of six years, Lee Marvin compelled Michelle Marvin to leave his household. He continued to support her for another year but thereafter refused to provide further support. During their time together, Lee Marvin earned substantial income and acquired property, including motion-picture rights worth over $1 million. Michelle Marvin brought an action against Lee Marvin, alleging that an implied-in-fact contract existed between them and that she was entitled to half of the property that they had acquired while living together. She claimed that she had given up a lucrative career as an entertainer and singer to be a full-time companion, homemaker, housekeeper, and cook. Can an implied-in-fact contract result from the conduct of unmarried persons who live together? *Marvin v. Marvin,* 18 Cal.3d 660, 557 P.2d 106, 134 Cal.Rptr. 815, **Web** 1976 Cal. Lexis 377 (Supreme Court of California)

BUSINESS ETHICS CASES

3 Business Ethics The Lewiston Lodge of Elks sponsored a golf tournament at the Fairlawn Country Club in Poland, Maine. For promotional purposes, Marcel Motors, an automobile dealership, agreed to give any golfer who shot a hole-in-one a new Dodge automobile. Fliers advertising the tournament were posted in the Elks Club and sent to potential participants. On the day of the tournament, the new Dodge automobile was parked near the clubhouse, with one of the posters conspicuously displayed on the vehicle. Alphee Chenard, Jr., who had seen the promotional literature regarding the hole-in-one offer, registered for the tournament and paid the requisite entrance fee. While playing the 13th hole of the golf course, in the presence of the other members of his foursome, Chenard shot a hole-in-one. When Marcel Motors refused to tender the automobile, Chenard sued for breach of contract. Was the contract a bilateral or a unilateral contract? Does Chenard win? Was it ethical for Marcel Motors to refuse to give the automobile to Chenard? *Chenard v. Marcel Motors,*

387 A.2d 596, **Web** 1978 Me. Lexis 911 (Supreme Judicial Court of Maine)

4 Business Ethics Loren Vranich, a doctor practicing under the corporate name Family Health Care, P.C., entered into a written employment contract to hire Dennis Winkel. The contract provided for an annual salary, insurance benefits, and other employment benefits. Another doctor, Dr. Quan, also practiced with Dr. Vranich. About nine months later, when Dr. Quan left the practice, Vranich and Winkel entered into an oral modification of their written contract whereby Winkel was to receive a higher salary and a profit-sharing bonus. During the next year, Winkel received the increased salary. However, a disagreement arose, and Winkel sued to recover the profit-sharing bonus. Under Montana law, a written contract can be altered only in writing or by an executed oral agreement. Dr. Vranich argued that the contract could not be enforced because it was not in writing. Does Winkel receive the profit-sharing bonus? Did Dr. Vranich act ethically in raising the defense that the contract was not in writing? *Winkel v. Family Health Care, P.C.*, 205 Mont. 40, 668 P.2d 208, **Web** 1983 Mont. Lexis 785 (Supreme Court of Montana)

ENDNOTES

1. *Rebstock v. Birthright Oil & Gas Co.*, 406 So.2d 636, Web 1981 La. App. Lexis 5242 (Court of Appeal of Louisiana).
2. *Restatement (Second) of Contracts*, Section 1.
3. *Restatement (Second) of Contracts*, Section 1.
4. *Restatement (Second) of Contracts*, Section 6.

AGREEMENT

AGREEMENT

Irene Springer/Pearson Education/PH College

▲ **Lost Dog Sign** *Offers to pay a reward for finding and returning things lead to interesting contract law questions. Someone who found the dog referred to in this photograph would have to have had knowledge of the reward in order to be entitled to collect it.*

CHAPTER OBJECTIVES

After studying this chapter, you should be able to:

1. Define *agreement*, *offer*, and *acceptance*.
2. Describe the required terms of an offer and describe the terms that can be implied in an offer.
3. Describe special forms of offers, including Internet auctions.
4. Define *counteroffer* and describe the effects of a counteroffer.
5. Describe how offers are terminated by acts of the parties and the operation of law.

CHAPTER CONTENTS

"When I use a word," Humpty Dumpty said, in rather a scornful tone, "it means just what I choose it to mean–neither more nor less."

"The question is," said Alice, "whether you can make words mean so many different things."

"The question is," said Humpty Dumpty, "which is to be master–that's all."

--Lewis Carroll
Alice's Adventures in Wonderland (1865)

INTRODUCTION TO AGREEMENT

Contracts are voluntary agreements between the parties; that is, one party makes an offer that is accepted by the other party. Without **mutual assent**, there is no contract. Assent may be expressly evidenced by the oral or written words of the parties or implied from the conduct of the parties. This chapter discusses offer and acceptance.

AGREEMENT

Agreement is the manifestation by two or more persons of the substance of a contract. It requires an *offer* and an *acceptance*. The process of reaching an agreement usually proceeds as follows. Prior to entering into a contract, the parties may engage in preliminary negotiations about price, time of performance, and such.

At some point during these negotiations, one party makes an *offer*. The person who makes the offer is called the **offeror**, and the person to whom the offer is made is called the **offeree**. The offer sets forth the terms under which the offeror is willing to enter into the contract. The offeree has the power to create an agreement by accepting the offer.

In the following case, the court applied the adage "A contract is a contract is a contract."

agreement
The manifestation by two or more persons of the substance of a contract.

offeror
The party who makes an offer.

offeree
The party to whom an offer has been made.

CASE 1 Contract

Marder v. Jennifer Lopez

450 F.3d 445, Web 2006 U.S. App. Lexis 14330 (2006)
United States Court of Appeals for the Ninth Circuit

"Though in hindsight the agreement appears to be unfair to Marder--she only received $2,300 in exchange for a release of all claims relating to a movie that grossed over $150 million. . . ."

--Judge Pregerson

Facts

The movie *Flashdance* tells a story of a woman construction worker who performs at night as an exotic dancer. She performs an innovative form of dancing that includes a chair dance. Her goal is to obtain formal dance training at a university. The movie is based on the life of Maureen Marder, a nightclub dancer. Paramount Pictures Corporation used information from Marder to create the screenplay for the movie. Paramount paid Marder $2,300, and Marder signed a general release contract that provided that Marder "releases and discharges Paramount Picture Corporation of and from each and every claim, demand, debt, liability, cost and expense of any kind or character which have risen or are based in whole or in part on any matters occurring at any time prior to the date of this Release." Marder also released Paramount from claims "arising out of or in any way connected with either directly or indirectly, any and all arrangements in connection with the preparation of screenplay material and the production, filming and exploitation of *Flashdance*."

Paramount released the movie *Flashdance*, which grossed over $150 million in domestic box office receipts and is still shown on television and distributed through

(case continues)

DVD rentals. Subsequently, Sony Music Entertainment paid Paramount for release of copyright and produced a music video for the Jennifer Lopez song "I'm Glad." The video featured Lopez's performance as a dancer and singer. Marder believed that the video contains re-creations of many well-known scenes from *Flashdance*.

Marder brought a lawsuit in U.S. District Court against Paramount, Sony, and Lopez. Marder sought a declaration that she had rights as a co-author of *Flashdance* and a co-owner with Paramount of the copyright to *Flashdance*. She sued Sony and Lopez for allegedly violating her copyright in *Flashdance*. The District Court dismissed Marder's claims against Paramount, Sony, and Lopez. Marder appealed.

Issue

Was the general release Marder signed an enforceable contract?

Language of the Court

The Release's language is exceptionally broad and we hold that it is fatal to each of Marder's claims against Paramount. Such a release of "each and every claim" covers all claims within the scope of the language. Accordingly, the law imputes to Marder an intention corresponding to the reasonable meaning of her words and acts. Here, Marder released a broad array of claims relating to any assistance she provided during the creation of a Hollywood movie. Thus, the only reasonable interpretation of the Release is that it encompasses the various copyright claims she asserts in the instant suit.

Though in hindsight the agreement appears to be unfair to Marder--she only received $2,300 in exchange for a release of all claims relating to a movie that grossed over $150 million--there is simply no evidence that her consent was obtained by fraud, deception, misrepresentation, duress, or undue influence.

We also affirm the district court's dismissal of claims against Sony and Lopez. As we held above, under the terms of the Release, Marder cannot sue Paramount to assert a co-ownership in Flashdance. It is therefore impossible for her to establish a prima facie case of copyright infringement against Sony and Lopez.

Decision

The U.S. Court of Appeals held that the general release Marder signed was an enforceable contract. The Court of Appeals affirmed the judgment of the District Court that dismissed Marder's complaint against Paramount, Sony, and Lopez.

Case Questions

Critical Legal Thinking What is an agreement? Explain.

Business Ethics Did Marder act ethically in bringing this lawsuit? Should Paramount have paid Marder more money after the movie *Flashdance* became a success?

Contemporary Business What does the adage "A contract is a contract is a contract" mean? Was it applied in this case?

▶ OFFER

offer
"The manifestation of willingness to enter into a bargain, so made as to justify another person in understanding that his assent to that bargain is invited and will conclude it." (Section 24 of the *Restatement (Second) of Contracts*)

Section 24 of the *Restatement (Second) of Contracts* defines an **offer** as "the manifestation of willingness to enter into a bargain, so made as to justify another person in understanding that his assent to that bargain is invited and will conclude it." The following three elements are required for an offer to be effective:

1. The offeror must *objectively intend* to be bound by the offer.
2. The terms of the offer must be definite or reasonably *certain*.
3. The offer must be *communicated* to the offeree.

The making of an offer is shown in Exhibit 1.

▶ Exhibit 1 OFFER

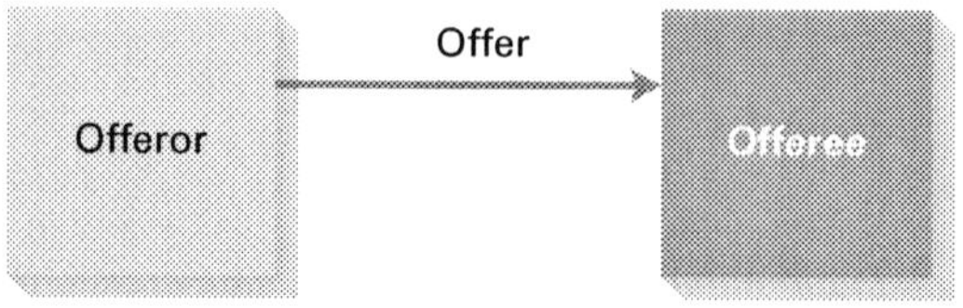

Offeror makes an offer to the offeree.

Objective Intent

The intent to enter into a contract is determined using the **objective theory of contracts**--that is, whether a reasonable person viewing the circumstances would conclude that the parties intended to be legally bound.

objective theory of contracts
A theory that says the intent to contract is judged by the reasonable person standard and not by the subjective intent of the parties.

Example The statement "I will buy your building for $2 million" is a valid offer because it indicates the offeror's present intent to contract.

Example A statement such as "Are you interested in selling your building for $2 million?" is not an offer. It is an invitation to make an offer or an invitation to negotiate.

Offers that are made in jest, anger, or undue excitement do not include the necessary objective intent.

Example The owner of Company A has lunch with the owner of Company B. In the course of their conversation, Company A's owner exclaims in frustration, "For $200, I'd sell the whole computer division!" An offer such as that cannot result in a valid contract.

Express Terms

The terms of an offer must be clear enough for the offeree to be able to decide whether to accept or reject the terms of the offer. To be considered definite, an offer (and contract) generally must contain the following terms: (1) identification of the parties, (2) identification of the subject matter and quantity, (3) consideration to be paid, and (4) time of performance. Complex contracts usually state additional terms.

Most offers and contracts set forth express terms that identify the parties, the subject matter of the contract, the consideration to be paid by the parties, and the time of performance, as well as other terms of the offer and contract.

If the terms are indefinite, the courts usually cannot enforce the contract or determine an appropriate remedy for its breach. However, the law permits some terms to be implied.

A contract is a mutual promise.

William Paley
The Principles of Moral and Political Philosophy (1784)

Implied Terms

The common law of contracts required an exact specification of contract terms. If one essential term was omitted, the courts held that no contract had been made. This rule was inflexible.

The modern law of contracts is more lenient. The *Restatement (Second) of Contracts* merely requires that the terms of the offer be "reasonably certain."[1] Accordingly, the court can supply a missing term if a reasonable term can be implied.[2] The definition of *reasonable* depends on the circumstances. Terms that are supplied in this way are called **implied terms.**

implied term
A term in a contract that can reasonably be supplied by the courts.

Generally, time of performance can be implied. Price can be implied if there is a market or source from which to determine the price of the item or service (e.g., the "blue book" for an automobile price).

The parties or subject matter of the contract usually cannot be implied if an item or a service is unique or personal, such as the construction of a house or the performance of a professional sports contract.

Communication

An offer cannot be accepted if it is not communicated to the offeree by the offeror or a representative or an agent of the offeror.

All things obey fixed laws.

Lucretius (Titus Lucretius Carus)

Example Mr. Jones, the CEO of Ace Corporation, wants to sell a manufacturing division to Baker Corporation. He puts the offer in writing, but he does not send it. Mr. Griswald, the CFO of Baker Corporation, visits Mr. Jones and sees the written offer lying on Jones's desk. Griswald tells his CEO about the offer. Because Mr. Jones never communicated the offer to Baker Corporation, there is no offer to be accepted.

SPECIAL OFFERS

There are several special types of offers. These include advertisements, rewards, and auctions. These special types of offers are discussed in the following paragraphs.

Advertisements

advertisement
An invitation to make an offer, or an actual offer.

As a general rule, **advertisements** for the sale of goods, even at specific prices, generally are treated as **invitations to make an offer.** This rule is intended to protect advertiser-sellers from the unwarranted breach of contract suits for nonperformance that would otherwise arise if the seller ran out of the advertised goods.

There is one exception to this rule: An advertisement is considered an offer if it is so definite or specific that it is apparent that the advertiser has the present intent to bind himself or herself to the terms of the advertisement.

Rewards

reward
An award given for performance of some service or attainment. To collect a reward, the offeree must (1) have knowledge of the reward offer prior to completing the requested act and (2) perform the requested act.

An offer to pay a **reward** (e.g., for the return of lost property or the capture of a criminal) is an offer to form a unilateral contract. To be entitled to collect the reward, the offeree must (1) have knowledge of the reward offer prior to completing the requested act and (2) perform the requested act.

Example John Anderson accidentally leaves a briefcase containing $500,000 in negotiable bonds on a subway train. He places newspaper ads stating "$5,000 reward for return of briefcase left on a train in Manhattan on January 10, 2011, at approximately 10 A.M. Call 212-555-6789." Helen Smith, who is unaware of the offer, finds the briefcase. She reads the luggage tag containing Anderson's name, address, and telephone number, and she returns the briefcase to him. She is not entitled to the reward money because she did not know about it when she performed the requested act.

Auctions

auction with reserve
An auction in which the seller retains the right to refuse the highest bid and withdraw the goods from sale. Unless expressly stated otherwise, an auction is an auction with reserve.

auction without reserve
An auction in which the seller expressly gives up his or her right to withdraw the goods from sale and must accept the highest bid.

At an **auction**, the seller offers goods for sale through an auctioneer. Unless otherwise expressly stated, an auction is considered an **auction with reserve**--that is, it is an invitation to make an offer. The seller retains the right to refuse the highest bid and withdraw the goods from sale. A contract is formed only when the auctioneer strikes the gavel down or indicates acceptance by some other means. The bidder may withdraw his or her bid prior to that time.

If an auction is expressly announced to be an **auction without reserve**, the participants reverse the roles: The seller is the offeror, and the bidders are the offerees. The seller must accept the highest bid and cannot withdraw the goods from sale. However, if the auctioneer has set a minimum bid that it will accept, the auctioneer has to sell the item only if the highest bid is equal to or greater than the minimum bid.

In the following case, the court addressed the issue of an Internet auction.

CASE 2 Internet Auction

Lim v. The.TV Corporation International

99 Cal.App.4th 684, 121 Cal.Rptr.2d 323,
Web 2002 Cal. App. Lexis 4315 (2002)
Court of Appeal of California

"Defendant put the name 'Golf.tv' up for public auction, and plaintiff bid on that name and no other. That was an offer and acceptance, and formed a contract."

--Judge Epstein

Facts

The island nation of Tuvalu was awarded the top-level domain name "tv." Thus, Tuvalu controlled who could use domain names with the suffix "tv" on the Internet. For example, if a person named Jones acquired the suffix tv, her domain name on the Internet could be "jones.tv." Tuvalu hired The.TV Corporation International, a California corporation doing business under the name dotTV, to sell Internet names bearing the top-level domain name "tv." In April 2000, dotTV posted the name "golf.tv" for sale on its website, to be sold to the highest bidder. Je Ho Lim, a resident of South Korea, submitted the highest bid of $1,010 and authorized dotTV to charge his credit card for the amount of the bid. dotTV sent the following e-mail to Lim confirming the sale:

> DotTV--The New Frontier on the Internet
> E-Mail Invoice for Domain Registration
> NAME: Je Ho Lim
> Congratulations!
> You have won the auction for the following domain name:
> DOMAIN NAME: --golf
> SUBSCRIPTION LENGTH: 2 years, starts from activation date
> Amount (US$): $1,010 (first year registration fee)
> Please remember that the annual registration fee increases by 5 annually.
> You have the guaranteed right to renew the registration indefinitely.
> DotTV expects to charge your card and activate the registered domain name by May 15, 2000.
> See ya on the new frontier of the Internet!
> Lou Kerner CEO, dotTV Corporation www.TV

Shortly thereafter, dotTV sent another e-mail to Lim that stated "we have decided to release you from your bid" and that Lim should disregard the prior e-mail because of "an e-mail error that occurred." Later, dotTV publicly offered the domain name "golf.tv" with a beginning bid of $1 million. DotTV claimed that its original e-mail to Lim concerned a different domain name, "--golf," instead of "golf." Lim countered that characters such as two dashes ("--") are not recognized on the Internet and therefore the name "--golf" is an invalid domain name. When dotTV refused to transfer the domain name "golf.tv" to Lim, Lim sued dotTV for breach of contract. The trial court dismissed Lim's case against dotTV. Lim appealed.

Issue

Did Lim properly state a cause of action for breach of contract against dotTV?

Language of the Court

> *Defendant put the name "Golf.tv" up for public auction, and plaintiff bid on that name and no other. That was an offer and acceptance, and formed a contract. The distinction between "Golf.tv" and "--Golf.tv" comes from the acceptance e-mail sent by defendant. Certainly the hyphens preceding the name "golf" could not defeat the existence of an already formed contract. Defendant was accepting plaintiff's bid; it plainly was not making a counteroffer, particularly since, according to the pleading, the name "--Golf" did not "compute"; it did not qualify as a domain name. The e-mail must be read as an acknowledgment of plaintiff's winning bid and acceptance of the contract.*

Decision

The court of appeal held that plaintiff Lim had properly pleaded a cause of action against defendant dotTV for breach of contract and reinstated Lim's case against dotTV.

Case Questions

Critical Legal Thinking What is the difference between an auction with reserve and an auction without reserve. Which type is presumed if there is no other statement to the contrary?

Business Ethics Did dotTV act ethically in this case? Why do you think that dotTV reneged on its e-mail confirmation to Lim?

Contemporary Business Are Internet domain names valuable? How do you register an Internet domain name?

Web Exercise Go to **www.golf.tv**. What types of goods or services are offered on this website? Think up an Internet domain name you would like to have. Go to the Network Solutions website, at **www.networksolutions.com,** and see if that name is available with the top-level domains .com, .org. or .net.

CONCEPT SUMMARY

TYPES OF AUCTIONS

Type	Does the seller offer the goods for sale
Auction with reserve	No. It is an invitation to make an offer. Because the bidder is the offeror, the seller (the offeree) may refuse to sell the goods. An auction is with reserve unless otherwise stated.
Auction without reserve	Yes. The seller is the offeror and must sell the goods to the highest bidder (the offeree). An auction is without reserve only if it is stipulated as such.

TERMINATION OF AN OFFER BY ACT OF THE PARTIES

An offer may be terminated by certain **acts of the parties**. The acts of the parties that terminate an offer are discussed in the following paragraphs.

Revocation of an Offer by the Offeror

revocation
Withdrawal of an offer by the offeror which terminates the offer.

Under the common law, an offeror may revoke (i.e., withdraw) an offer any time prior to its acceptance by the offeree. Generally, an offer can be so revoked even if the offeror promised to keep the offer open for a longer time. The **revocation** may be communicated to the offeree by the offeror or by a third party and made by (1) the offeror's express statement (e.g., "I hereby withdraw my offer") or (2) an act of the offeror that is inconsistent with the offer (e.g., selling the goods to another party). Most states provide that a revocation is not effective until it is actually received by the offeree or the offeree's agent.

Offers made to the public may be revoked by communicating the revocation by the same means used to make the offer.

Example If a reward offer for a lost watch was published in two local newspapers each week for four weeks, notice of revocation must be published in the same newspapers for the same length of time. The revocation is effective against all offerees, even those who saw the reward offer but not the notice of revocation.

CONTEMPORARY ENVIRONMENT

Option Contract

An offeree can prevent the offeror from revoking his or her offer by paying the offeror compensation to keep the offer open for an agreed-upon period of time. This creates what is called an **option contract**. In other words, the offeror agrees not to sell the property to anyone except the offeree during the option period. An option contract is a contract in which the original offeree pays consideration (usually money) in return for the original offeror giving consideration (time of the option period). The death or incompetency of either party does not terminate an option contract unless the contract is for the performance of a personal service.

Example Anne offers to sell a piece of real estate to Hal for $1 million. Hal wants time to investigate the property for possible environmental problems and to arrange financing if he decides to purchase the property, so he pays Anne $20,000 to keep her offer open to him for six months. At any time during the option period, Hal may exercise his option and pay Anne the $1 million purchase price. If Hal lets the option expire, however, Anne may keep the $20,000 and sell the property to someone else. Often option contracts are written so that if the original offeree purchases the property, the option amount is applied to the sale price.

Rejection of an Offer by the Offeree

rejection
Express words or conduct by the offeree that rejects an offer. Rejection terminates the offer.

An offer is terminated if the offeree **rejects** it. Any subsequent attempt by the offeree to accept the offer is ineffective and is construed as a new offer that the original offeror (now the offeree) is free to accept or reject. A rejection may be evidenced by the offeree's express words (oral or written) or conduct. Generally, a rejection is not effective until it is actually received by the offeror.

Example Ji Eun, a sales manager at Apple Computer, Inc., offers to sell 4,000 iMac computers to Ted, the purchasing manager of General Motors Corporation, for $4,000,000. The offer is made on August 1. Ted telephones Ji Eun to say that he is not interested. This rejection terminates the offer. If Ted later decides that he wants to purchase the computers, an entirely new contract must be formed.

Counteroffer by the Offeree

A **counteroffer** by the offeree simultaneously terminates the offeror's offer and creates a new offer. Offerees' making of counteroffers is the norm in many industries. A counteroffer terminates the existing offer and puts a new offer into play. The previous offeree becomes the new offeror, and the previous offeror becomes the new offeree.

counteroffer
A response by an offeree that contains terms and conditions different from or in addition to those of the offer. A counteroffer terminates the previous offer.

Example Fei says to Harold, "I will sell you my house for $700,000." Harold says, "I think $700,000 is too high; I will pay you $600,000." Harold has made a counteroffer. Fei's original offer is terminated, and Harold's counteroffer is a new offer that Fei is free to accept or reject.

CONCEPT SUMMARY

TERMINATION OF AN OFFER BY ACT OF THE PARTIES

Action	Description
Revocation	The offeror *revokes* (withdraws) the offer any time prior to its acceptance by the offeree.
Rejection	The offeree rejects the offer by his or her words or conduct.
Counteroffer	A counteroffer by the offeree creates a new offer and terminates the offeror's offer.

TERMINATION OF AN OFFER BY OPERATION OF LAW

An offer can be terminated by **operation of law**. The ways that an offer can be terminated by operation of law are discussed in the following paragraphs.

Destruction of the Subject Matter

An offer terminates if the subject matter of the offer is destroyed through no fault of either party prior to the offer's acceptance.

Where law ends, there tyranny begins.

William Pitt, first Earl of Chatham
Case of Wilkes (speech)

Death or Incompetency of the Offeror or Offeree

Prior to acceptance of an offer, the death or incompetency of either the offeror or the offeree terminates an offer. Notice of the other party's death or incompetence is not a requirement.

Example Suppose that on June 1, Shari offers to sell her house to Damian for $1,000,000, provided that Damian decides on or before June 15 that he will buy it. Shari dies on June 7, before Damian has made up his mind. The offer automatically terminates on June 7 when Shari dies.

Supervening Illegality

If the object of an offer is made illegal prior to the acceptance of the offer, the offer terminates. This situation, which usually occurs when a statute is enacted or the decision of a court is announced that makes the object of the offer illegal, is called a **supervening illegality**.

supervening illegality
The enactment of a statute, regulation, or court decision that makes the object of an offer illegal. This action terminates the offer.

Example Suppose City Bank offers to loan ABC Corporation $5 million at an 18 percent interest rate. Prior to ABC's acceptance of the offer, the state legislature enacts a statute that sets a usury interest rate of 12 percent. City Bank's offer to ABC Corporation is automatically terminated when the usury statute became effective.

Lapse of Time

lapse of time
A stated time period after which an offer terminates. If no time is stated, an offer terminates after a reasonable time.

An offer expires at the **lapse of time** of an offer. An offer may state that it is effective only until a certain date. Unless otherwise stated, the time period begins to run when the offer is actually received by the offeree and terminates when the stated time period expires.

Example If an offer states "This offer is good for 10 days," the offer expires at midnight of the 10th day after the offer was made. If an offer states "This offer must be accepted by January 1, 2012," the offer expires on midnight of January 1, 2012.

If no time is stated in the offer, the offer terminates after a "reasonable time" dictated by the circumstances. A reasonable time to accept an offer to purchase stock traded on a national stock exchange may be a few moments, but a reasonable time to accept an offer to purchase a house may be a week. Unless otherwise stated, an offer made face-to-face or during a telephone call usually expires when the conversation ends.

CONCEPT SUMMARY

TERMINATION OF AN OFFER BY OPERATION OF LAW

Action	Description
Destruction of the subject matter	The subject matter of an offer is destroyed prior to acceptance through no fault of either party.
Death or incompetency	Prior to acceptance of an offer, either the offeror or the offeree dies or becomes incompetent.
Supervening illegality	Prior to the acceptance of an offer, the object of the offer is made illegal by statute, regulation, court decision, or other law.
Lapse of time	An offer terminates upon the expiration of a stated time in the offer. If no time is stated, the offer terminates after a "reasonable time."

ACCEPTANCE

acceptance
"A manifestation of assent by the offeree to the terms of the offer in a manner invited or required by the offer as measured by the objective theory of contracts." (Section 50 of the *Restatement (Second) of Contracts*)

Acceptance is "a manifestation of assent by the offeree to the terms of the offer in a manner invited or required by the offer as measured by the objective theory of contracts."[3] Recall that generally (1) unilateral contracts can be accepted only by the offeree's performance of the required act and (2) a bilateral contract can be accepted by an offeree who promises to perform (or, where permitted, by performance of) the requested act.

Who Can Accept an Offer?

Only the offeree has the legal power to accept an offer and create a contract. Third persons usually do not have the power to accept an offer. If an offer is made individually to two or more persons, each has the power to accept the offer. Once one of the offerees accepts the offer, it terminates as to the other offerees. An offer that is made to two or more persons jointly must be accepted jointly.

The acceptance of an offer is illustrated in Exhibit 2.

Exhibit 2 ACCEPTANCE OF AN OFFER

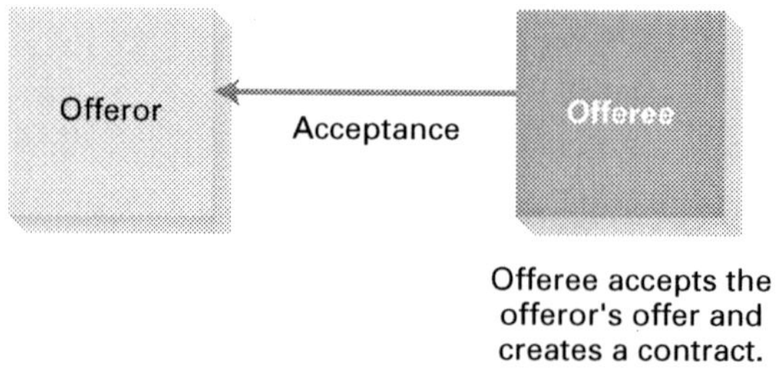

Unequivocal Acceptance

An offeree's acceptance must be **unequivocal**. For an acceptance to exist, the offeree must accept the terms as stated in the offer. This is called the **mirror image rule**.

mirror image rule
A rule which states that for an acceptance to exist, the offeree must accept the terms as stated in the offer.

Example Abraham says to Caitlin, "I will sell you my iPhone for $300." Caitlin says, "Yes, I will buy your iPhone at that price." This is an unequivocal acceptance that creates a contract.

Usually, even a "grumbling acceptance" is a legal acceptance.

Example Jordan offers to sell his computer to Taryn for $450. Taryn says "Okay, I'll take the computer, but I sure wish you would make me a better deal." This grumbling acceptance creates an enforceable contract because it was not a rejection or a counteroffer.

An equivocal response by the offeree does not create a contract.

Example Halim offers to sell his iMac computer to Nicole for $400. Nicole says "I think I would like it, but I'm not sure." This is equivocation and does not amount to an acceptance.

In the following case, the court had to decide whether there had been an acceptance of the offer.

CASE 3 Mirror Image Rule

Montgomery v. English

902 So.2d 836, Web 2005 Fla.App. Lexis 4704 (2005)
Court of Appeal of Florida

"Florida employs the 'mirror image rule' with respect to contracts. Under this rule, in order for a contract to be formed, an acceptance of an offer must be absolute, unconditional, and identical with the terms of the offer."
--Judge Palmer

Facts

Norma English made an offer to purchase a house owned by Michael and Lourie Montgomery (Montgomery) for $272,000. English included in her offer a request to purchase several items of Montgomery's personal property, including paving stones and a fireplace screen. After Montgomery received English's offer, Montgomery made several changes to the offer, including (1) deleting certain items, including the paving stones and fireplace screen, from the personal property section of the offer; (2) deleting a provision regarding latent defects; (3) deleting a provision regarding building inspections; and (4) adding a specific "AS IS" rider. Montgomery signed their counteroffer and delivered it to English. English initialed most of Montgomery's changes except she did not initial the change that deleted the paving stones and fireplace screen --which were worth about $100--from the deal. Montgomery, relying on the "mirror image rule," notified English that she had not completely accepted their offer and that they were therefore withdrawing their offer to sell their house to English. That same day Montgomery signed a contract to sell their house to another buyer for $285,000. English sued Montgomery for specific performance of the contract. The trial court held in favor of English and ordered specific performance. Montgomery appealed.

Issue

Was an enforceable contract made between English and Montgomery?

Language of the Court

Montgomery argue that the trial court erred in denying their motion for summary judgment because the record demonstrated that there had been no meeting of the minds between the parties as to the essential terms of the contract. We agree. Florida employs the "mirror image rule" with respect to contracts. Under this rule, in order for a contract to be formed, an acceptance of an offer must be absolute, unconditional, and identical with the terms of the offer. Applying the mirror image rule to these undisputed facts we hold that, as a matter of law, the parties failed to reach an agreement on the terms of the contract and, therefore, no enforceable contract was created.

Decision

The court of appeal held that because of the mirror image rule, no contract had been created between the parties. The court of appeal reversed the trial court's order of specific performance and remanded the case to the trial court, with instructions to enter summary judgment in favor of Montgomery.

(case continues)

Case Questions

Critical Legal Thinking What does the mirror image rule provide? Explain.

Business Ethics Did Montgomery act ethically when they backed out of selling the house? Did English act ethically by trying to force the sale of the house to her?

Contemporary Business Does the mirror image rule add certainty to contracting? Explain.

Web Exercise English appealed to the supreme court of Florida. Go to English's "Petitioner's Jurisdictional Brief" at **www.floridasupremecourt.org/clerk/briefs/2005/1001-1200/ 05-1186_JurisIni.pdf.** Scroll to the bottom of page 9 and read "II Strict Application of the 'Mirror Image Rule' Produces Harsh and Inequitable Results" on pages 9 and 10, and the "Conclusion" on page 10. The supreme court of Florida denied English's appeal to review the case.

Silence as Acceptance

Silence usually is not considered acceptance, even if the offeror states that it is. This rule is intended to protect offerees from being legally bound to offers because they failed to respond. Nevertheless, silence *does* constitute acceptance in the following situations:

The law has outgrown its primitive stage of formalism when the precise word was the sovereign talisman, and every slip was fatal. It takes a broader view today. A promise may be lacking, and yet the whole writing may be "instinct with an obligation," imperfectly expressed.

Judge Cardozo
Wood v. Duff-Gordon (1917)

1. The offeree has indicated that silence means assent.

   Example "If you do not hear from me by Friday, ship the order."

2. The offeree signed an agreement indicating continuing acceptance of delivery until further notification.

   Example Book-of-the-month and CD-of-the-month club memberships are examples of such acceptances.

3. Prior dealings between the parties indicate that silence means acceptance.

   Example A fish wholesaler who delivers 30 pounds of fish to a restaurant each Friday for several years and is paid for the fish can continue the deliveries with expectation of payment until notified otherwise by the restaurant.

4. The offeree takes the benefit of goods or services provided by the offeror even though the offeree (a) has an opportunity to reject the goods or services but fails to do so and (b) knows the offeror expects to be compensated.

   Example A homeowner who stands idly by and watches a painter whom she has not hired mistakenly paint her house owes the painter for the work.

CONCEPT SUMMARY

OFFER AND ACCEPTANCE

Type of Communication	Effective When
Offer	Received by offeree
Revocation of offer	Received by offeree
Rejection of offer	Received by offeror
Counteroffer	Received by offeror
Acceptance of offer in bilateral contract	Dispatched by offeree

Time of Acceptance

Under the common law of contracts, acceptance of a bilateral contract occurs when the offeree *dispatches* the acceptance by an authorized means of communication. This rule is called the **acceptance-upon-dispatch rule** or, more commonly, the **mailbox rule**. Under this rule, the acceptance is effective when it is dispatched, even if it is lost in transmission. If an offeree first dispatches a rejection and then sends an acceptance, the mailbox rule does not apply to the acceptance.[4]

mailbox rule
A rule that states that an acceptance is effective when it is dispatched, even if it is lost in transmission. Also known as the *acceptance-upon-dispatch rule*.

The problem of lost acceptances can be minimized by expressly altering the mailbox rule. The offeror can do this by stating in the offer that acceptance is effective only upon actual receipt of the acceptance.

Mailbox *The mailbox rule provides that an acceptance is effective when it is dispatched.*

Mode of Acceptance

An acceptance must be **properly dispatched**. The acceptance must be properly addressed, packaged in an appropriate envelope or container, and have prepaid postage or delivery charges. Under common law, if an acceptance is not properly dispatched, it is not effective until it is actually received by the offeror.

proper dispatch
The proper addressing, packaging, and posting of an acceptance.

Generally, an offeree must accept an offer by an *authorized* means of communication. The offer can stipulate that acceptance must be by a specified means of communication (e.g., registered mail, telegram). Such stipulation is called **express authorization**. If the offeree uses an unauthorized means of communication to transmit the acceptance, the acceptance is not effective, even if it is received by the offeror within the allowed time period, because the means of communication was a condition of acceptance.

express authorization
A stipulation in an offer that says the acceptance must be by a specified means of communication.

Most offers do not expressly specify the means of communication required for acceptance. The common law recognizes certain implied means of communication. **Implied authorization** may be inferred from what is customary in similar transactions, usage of trade, or prior dealings between the parties. Section 30 of the *Restatement (Second) of Contracts* permits implied authorization "by any medium reasonable in the circumstances."

implied authorization
A mode of acceptance that is implied from what is customary in similar transactions, usage of trade, or prior dealings between the parties.

TEST REVIEW TERMS AND CONCEPTS

Acceptance
Acceptance-upon-dispatch rule (mailbox rule)
Act of the parties
Advertisements
Agreement
Auction
Auction with reserve
Auction without reserve
Counteroffer
Express authorization
Implied authorization
Implied terms
Invitation to make an offer
Lapse of time
Mirror image rule
Mutual assent
Objective theory of contracts
Offer
Offeree
Offeror
Operation of law
Option contract
Properly dispatched
Rejection of an offer
Revocation of an offer
Reward
Supervening illegality
Unequivocal acceptance

CASE PROBLEMS

1 Objective Theory of Contracts While A.H. and Ida Zehmer, husband and wife, were drinking with W.O. Lucy, Mr. Zehmer made a written offer to sell a 471-acre farm the Zehmers owned to Lucy for $50,000. Zehmer contends that his offer was made in jest and that he only wanted to bluff Lucy into admitting that he did not have $50,000. Instead, Lucy appeared to take the offer seriously, offered $5 to bind the deal, and had Mrs. Zehmer sign it. When the Zehmers refused to perform the contract, Lucy brought this action to compel specific performance of the contract. Is the contract enforceable? *Lucy v. Zehmer* 196 Va. 493, 84 S.E.2d 516, **Web** 1954 Va. Lexis 244 (Supreme Court of Virginia)

2 Terms of a Contract Ben Hunt and others operated a farm under the name S.B.H. Farms. Hunt went to McIlory Bank and Trust and requested a loan to build hog houses, buy livestock, and expand farming operations. The bank agreed to loan S.B.H. Farms $175,000, for which short-term promissory notes were signed by Hunt and the other owners of S.B.H. Farms. At that time, oral discussions were held with the bank officer regarding long-term financing of S.B.H.'s farming operations; no dollar amount, interest rate, or repayment terms were discussed. When the owners of S.B.H. Farms defaulted on the promissory notes, the bank filed for foreclosure on the farm and other collateral. S.B.H. Farms counterclaimed for $750,000 damages, alleging that the bank breached its oral contract to provide long-term financing. Was there an oral contract for long-term financing? *Hunt v. McIlory Bank and Trust*, 2 Ark.App. 87, 616 S.W.2d 759, **Web** 1981 Ark.App. Lexis 716 (Court of Appeals of Arkansas)

3 Implied Terms MacDonald Group, Ltd. (MacDonald), is the managing general partner of Fresno Fashion Square, a regional shopping mall in Fresno, California. The mall has several major anchor tenants and numerous smaller stores and shops, including Edmond's of Fresno, a jeweler. Edmond's signed a lease with MacDonald that provided that "there shall not be more than two jewelry stores" located in the mall. Nine years later, MacDonald sent Edmond's notice that it intended to expand the mall and lease space to other jewelers. The lease was silent as to the coverage of additional mall space. Edmond's sued MacDonald, arguing that the lease applied to mall additions. Who wins? *Edmond's of Fresno v. MacDonald Group, Ltd.*, 171 Cal.App.3d 598, 217 Cal.Rptr. 375, **Web** 1985 Cal.App. Lexis 2436 (Court of Appeal of California)

4 Implied Terms Howard R. Wright hired John W. Cerdes to construct a home for him at a price of $43,150. The contract was silent regarding the time of completion. Construction was not completed after nine months. At that time, Wright obtained an injunction ordering Cerdes to stop work. Wright hired other contractors to complete the building. Cerdes sued Wright for breach of contract, claiming that he was due the contract price. How long should Cerdes have had to complete the house? *Cerdes v. Wright*, 408 So.2d 926, **Web** 1981 La.App. Lexis 5531 (Court of Appeal of Louisiana)

5 Reward Rudy Turilli operated the Jesse James Museum in Stanton, Missouri. He contends that the man who was shot, killed, and buried as the notorious desperado Jesse James in 1882 was an impostor and that Jesse James lived for many years thereafter under the alias J. Frank Dalton and last lived with Turilli at his museum until the 1950s. Turilli appeared before a nationwide television audience and stated that he would pay $10,000 to anyone who could prove that his statements were wrong. After hearing this offer, Stella James, a relative of Jesse James, produced affidavits of persons related to and acquainted with the Jesse James family, constituting evidence that Jesse James was killed as alleged in song and legend on April 3, 1882. When Turilli refused to pay the reward, James sued for breach of contract. Who wins? *James v. Turilli*, 473 S.W.2d 757, **Web** 1971 Mo.App. Lexis 585 (Court of Appeals of Missouri)

6 Counteroffer Glende Motor Company (Glende), an automobile dealership that sold new cars, leased premises from certain landlords. One day, fire destroyed part of the leased premises, and Glende restored the leasehold premises. The landlords received payment of insurance proceeds for the fire. Glende sued the landlords to recover the insurance proceeds. Ten days before the trial was to begin, the defendants jointly served on Glende a document titled "Offer to Compromise Before Trial," which was a settlement offer of $190,000. Glende agreed to the amount of the settlement but made it contingent upon the execution of a new lease. The next day, the defendants notified Glende that they were revoking the settlement offer. Glende thereafter tried to accept the original settlement offer. Has there been a settlement of the lawsuit? *Glende Motor Company v. Superior Court*, 159 Cal.App.3d 389, 205 Cal.Rptr. 682, **Web** 1984 Cal.App. Lexis 2435 (Court of Appeal of California)

7 Acceptance Peter Andrus owned an apartment building that he had insured under a fire insurance policy sold by J. C. Durick Insurance (Durick). Two months prior to the expiration of the policy, Durick notified Andrus that the building should be insured for $48,000 (or 80 percent of the building's value), as required by the insurance company. Andrus replied that (1) he wanted insurance to match the amount of the outstanding mortgage on the building (i.e., $24,000) and (2) if Durick could not sell this insurance, he would go elsewhere. Durick sent a new insurance policy in the face amount of $48,000, with the notation that the policy was automatically accepted unless Andrus notified him to the contrary. Andrus did not reply. However, he did not pay the premiums on the policy. Durick sued Andrus to recover these premiums. Who wins? *J. C. Durick Insurance v. Andrus*, 139 Vt. 150, 424 A.2d 249, **Web** 1980 Vt. Lexis 1490 (Supreme Court of Vermont)

8 Mailbox Rule William Jenkins and Nathalie Monk owned a building in Sacramento, California. They leased the building to Tuneup Masters for five years. The lease provided that Tuneup Masters could extend the lease for an additional five years if it gave written notice of its intention to do so by certified or registered mail at least six months prior to the expiration of the term of the lease.

Six months and three days before the expiration of the lease, Larry Selditz, vice president of Tuneup Masters, prepared a letter exercising the option, prepared and sealed an envelope with the letter in it, prepared U.S. Postal Service Form 3800, and affixed the certified mail sticker on the envelope, and had his secretary deliver the envelope to the Postal Service annex located on the ground floor of the office building. Postal personnel occupied the annex only between the hours of 9 and 10 A.M. At the end of each day, between 5 and 5:15 P.M., a postal employee picked up outgoing mail. The letter to the landlords was lost in the mail. The landlords thereafter refused to renew the lease and brought an unlawful detainer action against Tuneup Masters. Was the notice renewing the option effective? *Jenkins v. Tuneup Masters*, 190 Cal.App.3d 1, 235 Cal.Rptr. 214, **Web** 1987 Cal.App. Lexis 1475 (Court of Appeal of California)

BUSINESS ETHICS CASES

9 Business Ethics Kortney Dempsey took a cruise on a ship operated by Norwegian Cruise Line (Norwegian). In general, suits for personal injuries arising out of maritime torts are subject to a three-year statute of limitations. However, Congress permits this period to be reduced to one year by contract. The Norwegian passenger ticket limited the period to one year. Evidence showed that the cruise line ticket contained the notation "Important Notice" in a bright red box in the bottom-right corner of each of the first four pages of the ticket. The information in the box stated that certain pages of the ticket contain information that "affect[s] important legal rights." In addition, at the top of page 6 of the ticket, where the terms and conditions begin, it is stated in bold letters: "Passengers are advised to read the terms and conditions of the Passenger Ticket Contract set forth below." The clause at issue, which appears on page 8, clearly provides that suits must be brought within one year of injury. More than one year after Dempsey had taken the cruise (but within three years), she filed suit against Norwegian, seeking damages for an alleged injury suffered while on the cruise. Dempsey asserted that the one-year limitations period had not been reasonably communicated to her. Did Dempsey act ethically in suing when she did? Did Norwegian act ethically in reducing the limitations period to one year? Who wins the lawsuit? *Dempsey v. Norwegian Cruise Line*, 972 F.2d 998, **Web** 1992 U.S. App. Lexis 10939 (United States Court of Appeals for the Ninth Circuit)

10 Business Ethics Genaro Munoz owned property that he leased to Goodwest Rubber Corporation (Goodwest) for five years. The lease granted Goodwest the option to buy the property at a fair market value. Goodwest sought to exercise the option to purchase the property and tendered $80,000 to Munoz. When Munoz rejected this offer, Goodwest filed suit, seeking specific performance of the option agreement. The court was presented with a single issue for review: Was a price designation of "fair market value" definite enough to support an action for specific performance? Do you think Munoz acted ethically in refusing to honor the option? Who wins? *Goodwest Rubber Corp. v. Munoz*, 170 Cal.App.3d 919, 216 Cal.Rptr. 604, **Web** 1985 Cal.App. Lexis 2288 (Court of Appeal of California)

ENDNOTES

1. Restatement (Second) of Contracts, Section 204.
2. Section 87(2) of the Restatement (Second) of Contracts states that an offer which the offeror should reasonably expect to induce action or forbearance of a substantial character on the part of the offeree before acceptance and which does induce such action or forbearance is binding as an option contract to the extent necessary to avoid injustice.
3. Restatement (Second) of Contracts, Section 50(1).
4. Restatement (Second) of Contracts, Section 40.

CONSIDERATION AND PROMISSORY ESTOPPEL

CONSIDERATION AND PROMISSORY ESTOPPEL

Philip Entricknap © Dorling Kindersley

▲ **The Inns of Court, London** *The Inns of Court in London are the professional associations to one of which every barrister in England and Wales (and those judges who were formerly barristers) must belong. England follows the common law; that is, cases have been decided throughout centuries, and these cases have become precedent for future cases. The United States modeled its court system on the English system. English courts and U.S. courts hear and decide cases involving international contracts. International contracts support the conduct of trade, business, and e-commerce worldwide. For example, a company in the United States could enter into a contract to purchase goods from a company in England. This would be an international contract. The parties usually agree in their contract which country's courts will hear any cases that arise and which country's laws will be applied in settling the disputes.*

CHAPTER OBJECTIVES

After studying this chapter, you should be able to:

1. Define *consideration* and describe the requirements of consideration.
2. Define a *gift promise* and identify whether gift promises are enforceable.
3. Describe contracts that lack consideration, such as those involving illegal consideration, an illusory promise, a preexisting duty, or past consideration.
4. Define an accord and satisfaction of a disputed claim.
5. Define and apply the equitable doctrine of *promissory estoppel*.

CHAPTER CONTENTS

"The law has outgrown its primitive stage of formalism when the precise word was the sovereign talisman, and every slip was fatal. It takes a broader view today. A promise may be lacking, and yet the whole writing may be "instinct with an obligation," imperfectly expressed."

—Justice Cardozo
Wood v. Duff-Gordon, 222 N.Y.88, 91 (1917)

INTRODUCTION TO CONSIDERATION AND PROMISSORY ESTOPPEL

To be enforceable, a contract must be supported by *consideration*, which is broadly defined as something of legal value. In general, this means that each side to a contract must give something of value for the contract to be enforceable. The consideration can consist of money, property, the provision of services, the forbearance of a right, or anything else of value. Most contracts are supported by consideration.

Contracts that are not supported by consideration are usually not enforceable. This means that a party who has not given consideration cannot enforce the contract. The parties may, however, voluntarily perform a contract that is lacking in consideration. If a contract that was lacking in consideration is performed by the parties, the parties cannot thereafter raise lack of consideration to undo the performed contract. *Promissory estoppel* is an equity doctrine that permits a court to order enforcement of a contract that lacks consideration.

This chapter discusses consideration, promises that lack consideration, and equity doctrines that permit promises that lack consideration to be enforced.

CONSIDERATION

Consideration must be given before a contract can exist. **Consideration** is defined as something of legal value given in exchange for a promise. Consideration can come in many forms. The most common types consist of either a tangible payment (e.g., money, property) or the performance of an act (e.g., providing legal services). Less usual forms of consideration include the forbearance of a legal right (e.g., accepting an out-of-court settlement in exchange for dropping a lawsuit) and non-economic forms of consideration (e.g., refraining from "drinking, using tobacco, swearing, or playing cards or billiards for money"[1] for a specified time period).

consideration
Something of legal value given in exchange for a promise.

Written contracts are presumed to be supported by consideration. This rebuttable presumption, however, may be overcome by sufficient evidence. A few states provide that contracts made under seal cannot be challenged for lack of consideration.

Requirements of Consideration

Consideration consists of two elements: (1) Something of legal value must be given (i.e., either a legal benefit must be received or legal detriment must be suffered) and

(2) there must be a bargained-for exchange. Each of these is discussed in the paragraphs that follow:

legal value
Support for a contract when either (1) the promisee suffers a legal detriment or (2) the promisor receives a legal benefit.

bargained-for exchange
Exchange that parties engage in that leads to an enforceable contract.

1. **Legal value.** Under the modern law of contracts, a contract is considered supported by **legal value** if (1) the promisee suffers a *legal detriment* or (2) the promisor receives a *legal benefit*.
2. **Bargained-for exchange.** To be enforceable, a contract must arise from a **bargained-for exchange.** In most business contracts, the parties engage in such exchanges. The commercial setting in which business contracts are formed leads to this conclusion.

In the following case, the court had to decide whether there was consideration.

CASE 1 Consideration

In the Matter of Wirth

14 A.D.3d 572, 789 N.Y.S.2d 69, Web 2005 N.Y.App. Div. Lexis 424 (2005)
Supreme Court of New York, Appellate Division

"The Pledge Agreement further stated: 'I acknowledge that Drexel's promise to use the amount pledged by me shall constitute full and adequate consideration for this pledge.'"

—Judge Schmidt

Facts

Raymond P. Wirth signed a pledge agreement which stated that in consideration of his interest in education, and "intending to be legally bound," he irrevocably pledged and promised to pay Drexel University the sum of $150,000. The pledge agreement provided that an endowed scholarship would be created in Wirth's name. Wirth died two months after signing the pledge but before any money had been paid to Drexel. When the estate of Wirth refused to honor the pledge, Drexel sued the estate to collect the $150,000. The estate alleged that the pledge was unenforceable because of lack of consideration. The surrogate court denied Drexel's motion for summary judgment and dismissed Drexel's claim against the estate. Drexel appealed.

Issue

Was the pledge agreement supported by consideration and therefore enforceable against the estate of Wirth?

Language of the Court

Pursuant to Pennsylvania's Uniform Written Obligations Act: "A written release or promise, hereafter made and signed by the person releasing or promising, shall not be invalid or unenforceable for lack of consideration, if the writing also contains an additional express statement, in any form or language, that the signer intends to be legally bound." Pursuant to this statute, the Pledge Agreement does not fail for lack of consideration, as the decedent expressly stated his intent to be legally bound by the pledge.

Moreover, even if we were to determine that the decedent, as promisor, anticipated consideration in return for his promise, there was no failure of consideration. The Pledge Agreement, which also was executed by representatives of Drexel, provided that the pledged sum "shall be used by" Drexel to create an endowed scholarship fund in the decedent's name, per the terms of the attached Letter of Understanding. The Pledge Agreement further stated: "I acknowledge that Drexel's promise to use the amount pledged by me shall constitute full and adequate consideration for this pledge."

In our view, pursuant to the terms of the Pledge Agreement, Drexel provided sufficient consideration by expressly accepting the terms of the Pledge Agreement and by promising to establish the scholarship fund in the decedent's name. The fact that the decedent died before the initial gift was transferred into a special account set up by Drexel and therefore the scholarship fund was not yet implemented, did not negate the sufficiency of the promise as consideration to set up the fund.

Decision

The appellate court held that the pledge agreement was supported by consideration and was therefore enforceable against the estate of Wirth. The appellate court reversed the decision of the surrogate court and granted Drexel's motion for summary judgment against the estate of Wirth.

Case Questions

Critical Legal Thinking What is consideration? What happens if there is lack of consideration supporting a promise? Explain.

Business Ethics Was it ethical for the estate of Wirth to try to back out of the pledge agreement Wirth made before he died?

Contemporary Business What special statute did Pennsylvania enact that solves the issue of lack of consideration in many contracts? Does such a statute take precedent over the common law contract rule of consideration? Explain.

▶ GIFT PROMISE

Gift promises, also called **gratuitous promises**, are unenforceable because they lack consideration. To change a gift promise into an enforceable promise, the promisee must offer to do something in exchange—that is, in consideration—for the promise. Gift promises cause considerable trouble for persons who do not understand the importance of consideration.

gift promise
A promise that is unenforceable because it lacks consideration. Also known as a *gratuitous promise*.

Example On May 1, Mrs. Colby promises to give her son $10,000 on June 1. When June 1 arrives Mrs. Colby refuses to pay the $10,000. The son cannot recover the $10,000 because it was a gift promise that lacked consideration. If, however, Mrs. Colby promises to pay her son $10,000 if he earns an "A" in his business law course and the son earns the "A," the contract is enforceable and the son can recover the $10,000.

A completed gift promise cannot be rescinded for lack of consideration.

Example On May 1, Mr. Smith promises to give his granddaughter $10,000 on June 1. If on or before June 1 Mr. Smith actually gives the $10,000 to his granddaughter, it is a completed gift promise. Mr. Smith cannot thereafter recover the money from his granddaughter, even if the original promise lacked consideration.

The case that follows involves the issue of whether a giver can recover gifts that he made.

CASE 2 Gifts

Cooper v. Smith

800 N.E.2d 372, Web 2003 Ohio App. Lexis 5446 (2003)
Court of Appeals of Ohio

"Many gifts are made for reasons that sour with the passage of time. Unfortunately, gift law does not allow a donor to recover/revoke a gift simply because his or her reasons for giving it have soured."

—Judge Harsha

Facts

Lester Cooper suffered serious injuries that caused him to be hospitalized for an extended period of time. While he was hospitalized, Julie Smith, whom Cooper had met the year before, and Janet Smith, Julie's mother, made numerous trips to visit him. Although Julie was married to another man at the time, a romantic relationship developed between Cooper and Julie. While in the hospital, Cooper proposed marriage to Julie, and she accepted. Julie obtained a divorce from her husband. Cooper ultimately received an $180,000 settlement for his injuries.

After being released from the hospital, Cooper moved into Janet's house and lived with Janet and Julie. Over the next couple months, Cooper purchased a number of items for Julie, including a diamond engagement ring, a car, a computer, a tanning bed, and horses. On Julie's request, Cooper paid off Janet's car. Cooper also paid for various improvements to Janet's house, such as having a new furnace installed and having wood flooring laid in the kitchen. Several months later, the settlement money had run out, and Julie had not yet married Cooper. About six months later, Julie and Cooper had a disagreement, and Cooper moved out of the house. Julie returned the engagement ring to Cooper. Cooper sued Julie and Janet to recover the gifts or the value of the gifts he had given them. The magistrate who heard the case dismissed Cooper's case, and the trial court affirmed the dismissal of the case. Cooper appealed.

(case continues)

Issue

Can Cooper recover the gifts or the value of the gifts he gave to Julie and Janet Smith?

Language of the Court

Unless the parties have agreed otherwise, the donor is entitled to recover the engagement ring (or its value) if the marriage does not occur, regardless of who ended the engagement. While we are willing to imply a condition concerning the engagement ring, we are unwilling to do so for other gifts given during the engagement period. Unlike the engagement ring, the other gifts have no symbolic meaning. Rather, they are merely "tokens of love and affection" which the donor bore for the donee. Many gifts are made for reasons that sour with the passage of time. Unfortunately, gift law does not allow a donor to recover/revoke a gift simply because his or her reasons for giving it have soured.

Generally, a completed gift is absolute and irrevocable. We believe the best approach is to treat gifts exchanged during the engagement period (excluding the engagement ring) as absolute and irrevocable gifts unless the donor has expressed intent that the gift be conditioned on the subsequent marriage. Cooper offered no evidence establishing that he gave the gifts on the express condition that they be returned to him if the engagement ended. Thus, the gifts are irrevocable gifts and Cooper is not entitled to their return.

Decision

The court of appeals held that the gifts made by Cooper to Julie (other than the engagement ring) and to Janet were irrevocable gifts that he could not recover simply because his engagement with Julie ended. The court of appeals affirmed the judgment of the trial court, allowing Julie and Janet Smith to keep these gifts.

Case Questions

Critical Legal Thinking Do you agree with the law that requires an engagement ring to be returned to the giver, no matter who breaks off the engagement? Explain.

Business Ethics Did Julie and Janet Smith act ethically in keeping the gifts Cooper had given them? Did Cooper act ethically in trying to get the gifts back?

Contemporary Business Why is there a different rule regarding the returning of engagement rings than for other gifts?

Web Exercise Go to **www.nytimes.com/2006/03/05/business/05goodie.html** to read about gifts to movie stars.

▶ CONTRACTS LACKING CONSIDERATION

Some contracts seem as though they are supported by consideration even though they are not. The contracts described in the following paragraphs fall into this category.

Illegal Consideration

illegal consideration
A promise to refrain from doing an illegal act. Such a promise will not support a contract.

A contract cannot be supported by a promise to refrain from doing an illegal act because that is **illegal consideration**. Contracts based on illegal consideration are void.

Example The statement "I will burn your house down unless you agree to pay me $10,000," to which the homeowner agrees, is not an enforceable contract because the consideration given—not to burn down a house—is illegal consideration. Thus, the extortionist cannot enforce the contract against the homeowner.

Illusory Promise

illusory promise
A contract into which both parties enter but one or both of the parties can choose not to perform their contractual obligations. Thus, the contract lacks consideration. Also known as an illusory contract.

If parties enter into a contract but one or both of the parties can choose not to perform their contractual obligations, the contract lacks consideration. Such promises, which are known as **illusory promises** (or **illusory contracts**), are unenforceable.

Example A contract which provides that one of the parties has to perform only if he or she chooses to do so is an illusory contract.

Moral Obligation

moral obligation
A sense of honor that prompts a person to make a promise. Promises made out of a sense of moral obligation lack consideration.

Promises made out of a sense of **moral obligation**, or honor, are generally unenforceable on the grounds that they lack consideration. In other words, moral consideration is not treated as legal consideration. A minority of states hold that moral obligations are enforceable.

Preexisting Duty

A promise lacks consideration if a person promises to perform an act or do something he is already under an obligation to do. This is called a **preexisting duty**. The promise is unenforceable because no new consideration has been given.

preexisting duty
Something a person is already under an obligation to do. A promise lacks consideration if a person promises to perform a preexisting duty.

Example Many states have adopted statutes that prohibit police officers from demanding money for investigating and apprehending criminals or that prohibit fire fighters from demanding payment for fighting fires. If a person agrees to such a demand, she does not have to pay it because there was no new consideration; public servants are under a preexisting duty to perform their functions.

In the private sector, the preexisting duty rule often arises when one of the parties to an existing contract seeks to change the terms of the contract during the course of its performance. Such midstream changes are unenforceable: The parties have a preexisting duty to perform according to the original terms of the contract.

Sometimes a party to a contract runs into substantial *unforeseen difficulties* while performing his or her contractual duties. If the parties modify their contract to accommodate these unforeseen difficulties, the modification will be enforced even though it is not supported by new consideration.

There is grim irony in speaking of freedom of contract of those who, because of their economic necessities, give their service for less than is needful to keep body and soul together.

Harlan Fiske Stone
Morehead v. N.Y. ex rel. Tipaldo (1936)

Past Consideration

Problems of **past consideration** often arise when a party promises to pay someone some money or other compensation for work done in the past. Past consideration is not consideration for a new promise; therefore, a promise based on past consideration is not enforceable.

past consideration
A prior act or performance. Past consideration (e.g., prior acts) will not support a new contract. New consideration must be given.

Example Felipe, who has worked in management for the Acme Corporation for 30 years, is retiring. The president of Acme says, "Because you were such a loyal employee, Acme will pay you a bonus of $100,000." Subsequently, the corporation refuses to pay the $100,000. Unfortunately for Felipe, he has already done the work for which he has been promised to be paid. The contract is unenforceable against Acme because it is based on past consideration.

In the following case, the court held that there was lack of consideration and there was fraud, and it refused to enforce the contract.

CASE 3 Lack of Consideration

West America Housing Corporation v. Pearson

2007 WY 184, 171 P.3d 539, Web 2007 Wyo. Lexis 196 (2007)
Supreme Court of Wyoming

"The district court stated on the record that he found Joelson's testimony to be wildly unbelievable and likely perjury."
—Justice Hill

Facts

Donald Pearson was 80 years of age and living in an assisted living facility. Jeanne Joelson, whom Pearson knew, convinced Pearson to purchase the Wrangler Road Property, to pay $75,755 as the down payment, and to borrow $279,200 from a lender who retained a mortgage on the property. Joelson told Pearson that she, Bobbie Charles Craver, and West America Housing Corporation (WAHC), which was owned by Joelson, Craver, and Sheena Shoopman, Joelson's daughter, would pay the mortgage payments on the property.

WAHC made the mortgage payments and paid the insurance and property taxes on the property for approximately four years. Joelson then asked Pearson to deed the property to Larry Oltman, Joelson's brother, which Joelson claimed Pearson did. There was a quitclaim deed with Pearson's signature on it that transferred the property to Oltman. The deed transferred ownership of the property to Oltman and indicated that Pearson had received $75,755 "in hand paid" as consideration for the transaction. Oltman subsequently deeded the property to WAHC.

(case continues)

Pearson sued Joelson, Craver, Shoopman, and WAHC, alleging that the transfer of the property from Pearson to Oltman lacked consideration and therefore was a voidable transfer. Pearson also alleged that the transfer of the property from Oltman to WAHC was a fraudulent transfer that was void. Pearson testified that he did not complete or sign the deed transferring the property to Oltman and that he did not receive the consideration indicated on the deed. Joelson testified that she paid Pearson $75,755 in cash that she brought to Pearson in a shoebox at the time of the sale to Oltman. However, Joelson could not produce any withdrawal slip from a bank or any other evidence of the source of the cash. The district court quieted title to the property to Pearson. Joelson, Craver, Shoopman, and WAHC appealed.

Issue

Did the transfer of the Wrangler Road Property from Pearson to Oltman lack consideration and was the transfer of the property from Oltman to WAHC a fraudulent transfer?

Language of the Court

The district court stated on the record that he found Joelson's testimony to be wildly unbelievable and likely perjury. The evidence is at best equivocal that Pearson actually signed the quitclaim deed to Oltman. The only evidence to support the element of consideration was Joelson's "wildly unbelievable" tale of delivering the consideration to Pearson on an unknown date, in the form of cash in a shoe box, for which she obtained no receipt. It was not plain error for the district court to conclude that the deed at issue was void for lack of consideration, despite the language on the face of the deed. It flows virtually without need for discussion that the succeeding deeds were also void. The district court's findings are not clearly erroneous, and its application of the law is not in error.

Decision

The supreme court of Wyoming held that there was no consideration to support the transfer of the deed from Pearson to Oltman. The court also held that the transfer of the property from Oltman to the defendants was fraudulent. The supreme court upheld the district court's decision that quieted title to the property to Pearson.

Case Questions

Critical Legal Thinking What is the result if lack of consideration for a contract is found? Do you think that there was lack of consideration in this case? Explain.

Business Ethics Did Joelson act ethically in this case? Did Oltman act ethically in this case?

Contemporary Business Do you think that there was fraud in this case? Why or why not? Do you think elderly people are often targets of fraud?

Web Exercise Go to **www.fraud.org/elderfraud/hangup.htm.** Read the article "Five Steps to Help Seniors Targeted by Telemarketing Fraud."

CONCEPT SUMMARY

PROMISES LACKING CONSIDERATION

Type of Consideration	Description of Promise
Illegal consideration	Promise to refrain from doing an illegal act.
Illusory promise	Promise in which one or both parties can choose not to perform their obligation.
Moral obligation	Promise made out of a sense of moral obligation, honor, love, or affection. Some states enforce these types of contracts.
Preexisting duty	Promise based on the preexisting duty of the promisor to perform.
Past consideration	Promise based on the past performance of the promisee.

CONTEMPORARY ENVIRONMENT

Special Business Contracts

Generally, the courts tolerate a greater degree of uncertainty as to the issue of consideration in business contracts than in personal contracts, under the premise that sophisticated parties know how to protect themselves when negotiating contracts. The law imposes an obligation of good faith on the performance of the parties to requirements and output contracts.

The following paragraphs describe special types of business contracts that allow a greater-than-usual degree of uncertainty concerning consideration.

Output Contract

In an **output contract**, the seller agrees to sell all of its production to a single buyer. Output contracts serve the legitimate business purposes of (1) assuring the seller of a purchaser for all its output and (2) assuring the buyer of a source of supply for the goods it needs.

Example Organic Foods Inc. is a company that operates farms that produce organically grown grains and vegetables. Urban Food Markets is a grocery store chain that sells organically grown foods. Urban Food Markets contracts with Organic Foods Inc. to purchase all the organic foods grown by Organic Foods Inc. this year. This is an example of an output contract: Organic Foods Inc. must sell all of its output to Urban Foods Market.

Requirements Contract

A **requirements contract** is one in which a buyer contracts to purchase all of its requirements for an item from one seller. Such contracts serve the legitimate business purposes of (1) assuring the buyer of a uniform source of supply and (2) providing the seller with reduced selling costs.

Example The Goodyear Tire & Rubber Company manufactures tires that are used on automobiles. Ford Motor Company manufactures automobiles on which it must place tires before the automobiles can be sold. Assume Ford Motor Company enters into a contract with Goodyear Tire & Rubber Company to purchase all of the tires it will need this year from Goodyear. This is an example of a requirements contract: Ford Motor Company has agreed to purchase all of the tires it will need from Goodyear. Goodyear may sell tires to other purchasers, however.

Best-Efforts Contract

A **best-efforts contract** is a contract that contains a clause that requires one or both of the parties to use their *best efforts* to achieve the objective of the contract. The courts generally have held that the imposition of the best-efforts duty provides sufficient consideration to make a contract enforceable.

Example Real estate listing contracts often require a real estate broker to use his or her best efforts to find a buyer for the listed real estate. Contracts often require underwriters to use their best efforts to sell securities on behalf of their corporate clients. Both of these contracts would be enforceable. Of course, a party can sue another company for failing to use its promised best efforts.

SETTLEMENT OF CLAIMS

The law promotes the voluntary settlement of disputed claims. Settlement saves judicial resources and serves the interests of the parties entering into the settlement.

In some situations, one of the parties to a contract believes that he or she did not receive what he or she was due. This party may attempt to reach a compromise with the other party (e.g., by paying less consideration than was provided for in the contract). If the two parties agree to a compromise, a settlement of the claim has been reached. The settlement agreement is called an **accord**. If the accord is performed, it is called a **satisfaction**. This type of settlement is called an **accord and satisfaction** or a **compromise**. If the accord is not satisfied, the other party can sue to enforce either the accord or the original contract.

accord
An agreement whereby the parties agree to accept something different in satisfaction of the original contract.

Example A contract stipulated that the cost of a computer and software system that keeps track of inventory, accounts receivable, and so on is $300,000. After it is installed, the computer system does not perform as promised. To settle the dispute, the parties agree that $200,000 is to be paid as full and final payment for the computer. This accord is enforceable even though no new consideration is given because reasonable persons would disagree as to the worth of the computer system that was actually installed.

satisfaction
The performance of an accord.

▶ EQUITY: PROMISSORY ESTOPPEL

promissory estoppel
An equitable doctrine that prevents the withdrawal of a promise by a promisor if it will adversely affect a promisee who has adjusted his or her position in justifiable reliance on the promise.

The courts have developed the equitable doctrine of **promissory estoppel** or (**detrimental reliance**) to avoid injustice. This doctrine is a broad policy-based doctrine. It is used to provide a remedy to a person who has relied on another person's promise when that person withdraws his or her promise and is not subject to a breach of contract action because one of the two elements contract requirements (i.e., agreement or consideration) is lacking.

The doctrine of promissory estoppel *estops* (prevents) the promisor from revoking his or her promise. Therefore, the person who has *detrimentally relied* on the promise for performance may sue the promisor for performance or other remedy the court feels is fair to award in the circumstances.

For the doctrine of promissory estoppel to be applied, the following elements must be shown:

- The promisor made a promise.
- The promisor should have reasonably expected to induce the promisee to reply on the promise.
- The promisee actually relied on the promise and engaged in an action or forbearance of a right of a definite and substantial nature.
- Injustice would be caused if the promise were not enforced.

Now equity is no part of the law, but a moral virtue, which qualifies, moderates, and reforms the rigor, hardness, and edge of the law, and is a universal truth.

Lord Cowper
Dudley v. Dudley (1705)

Example XYZ Construction Company, a general contractor, requests bids from subcontractors for work to be done on a hospital building that XYZ plans to submit a bid to build. Bert Plumbing Company, a plumbing subcontractor, submits the lowest bid for the plumbing work, and XYZ incorporates Bert's low bid in its own bid for the general contract. Based on all of the subcontractor's bids, XYZ submits the lowest overall bid to build the hospital and is awarded the contract. Bert Plumbing plans to withdraw its bid. However, the doctrine of promissory estoppel prevents Bert from withdrawing its bid. Since XYZ has been awarded the contract to build the hospital based partially upon Bert's plumbing subcontractor bid, XYZ can enforce Bert's promise to perform under the doctrine of promissory estoppel. Allowing Bert to withdraw its bid would cause injustice.

Courthouse, Santa Barbara, California *This courthouse in Santa Barbara, California, was built in 1929 and is patterned after a Spanish–Moorish palace. The court hears cases, including cases to enforce contracts. To be enforceable, a contract must be supported by consideration. If a contract is lacking consideration, the court will not enforce the contract. However, an exception to this rule is that a court can enforce a contract that is otherwise lacking consideration, using the equitable doctrine of promissory estoppel.*

TEST REVIEW TERMS AND CONCEPTS

Accord
Accord and satisfaction (compromise)
Bargained-for exchange
Best-efforts contract
Consideration
Gift promise (gratuitous promise)
Illegal consideration
Illusory promise (illusory contract)
Legal value
Moral obligation
Output contract
Past consideration
Preexisting duty
Promissory estoppel (detrimental reliance)
Requirements contract
Satisfaction

CASE PROBLEMS

1 Consideration Clyde and Betty Penley were married. Eighteen years later, Clyde operated an automotive tire business, and Betty owned an interest in a Kentucky Fried Chicken (KFC) franchise. That year, when Betty became ill, she requested that Clyde begin spending additional time at the KFC franchise to ensure its continued operation. Subsequently, Betty agreed that if Clyde would devote full time to the KFC franchise, they would operate the business as a joint enterprise, share equally in the ownership of its assets, and divide its returns equally. Pursuant to this agreement, Clyde terminated his tire business and devoted his full time to the KFC franchise. Twelve years later, Betty abandoned Clyde and denied him any rights in the KFC franchise. Clyde sued to enforce the agreement with Betty. Is the agreement enforceable? *Penley v. Penley*, 314 N.C. 1, 332 S.E.2d 51, **Web** 1985 N.C. Lexis 1706 (Supreme Court of North Carolina)

2 Forbearance to Sue When John W. Frasier died, he left a will that devised certain of his community and separate property to his wife, Lena, and their three children. These devises were more valuable to Lena than just her interest in the community property that she would otherwise have received without the will. The devises to her, however, were conditioned upon the filing of a waiver by Lena of her interest in the community property, and if she failed to file the waiver, she would then receive only her interest in the community property and nothing more. Lena hired her brother, D.L. Carter, an attorney, to represent her. Carter failed to file the waiver on Lena's behalf, thus preventing her from taking the devises under the will. Instead, she received her interest in the community property, which was $19,358 less than she would have received under the will. Carter sent Lena the following letter:

> *This is to advise and confirm our agreement—that in the event the J. W. Frasier estate case now on appeal is not terminated so that you will receive settlement equal to your share of the estate as you would have done if your waiver had been filed in the estate in proper time, I will make up any balance to you in payments as suits my convenience and will pay interest on your loss at 6 percent.*

The appeal was decided against Lena. When she tried to enforce the contract against Carter, he alleged that the contract was not enforceable because it was not supported by valid consideration. Who wins? *Frasier v. Carter*, 92 Idaho 79, 437 P.2d 32, **Web** 1968 Ida. Lexis 249 (Supreme Court of Idaho)

3 Past Consideration A. J. Whitmire and R. Lee Whitmire were brothers. R. Lee Whitmire married Lillie Mae Whitmire. For 4 years, A. J. performed various services for his brother and sister-in-law. During this time, R. Lee and Lillie Mae purchased some land. Fifteen years later, in the presence of Lillie Mae, R. Lee told A. J., "When we're gone, this land is yours" At that time, A. J. had not done any work for R. Lee or Lillie Mae for 16 years, and none was expected or provided in the future. Thirty years later, after both R. Lee and Lillie Mae had died, A. J. filed a claim with the estate of Lillie Mae, seeking specific performance of the earlier promise to give him the land. Does A. J. get the property? *Whitmire v. Watkins*, 245 Ga. 713, 267 S.E.2d 6, **Web** 1980 Ga. Lexis 908 (Supreme Court of Georgia)

4 Preexisting Duty Robert Chuckrow Construction Company (Chuckrow) was employed as the general contractor to build a Kinney Shoe Store. Chuckrow employed Ralph Gough to perform the carpentry work on the store. The contract with Gough stipulated that he was to provide all labor, materials, tools, equipment, scaffolding, and other items necessary to complete the carpentry work. Gough's employees erected 38 trusses at the job site. The next day, 32 of the trusses fell off the building. The reason for the trusses having fallen was unexplained, and evidence showed that it was not due to Chuckrow's fault or a deficiency in the building plans. Chuckrow told Gough that he would pay him to reerect the trusses and continue work. When the job was complete, Chuckrow paid Gough the original contract price but refused to pay him for the additional cost of reerecting the trusses. Gough sued Chuckrow for this expense. Can Gough recover? *Robert Chuckrow Construction Company v. Gough*, 117 Ga. App. 140, 159 S.E.2d 469, **Web** 1968 Ga.App. Lexis 1007 (Court of Appeals of Georgia)

5 Illegal Consideration In 1972, Marna Balin was involved in two automobile accidents in which she suffered severe injuries. She hired Norman H. Kallen, an attorney, to represent her. Kallen filed lawsuits on behalf of Balin, seeking damages for her injuries. Kallen repeatedly urged Balin to settle the lawsuits for $25,000. In late 1974, when she became disappointed with Kallen's representation, she retained another attorney, Samuel P. Delug, and instructed him to obtain her legal files from Kallen. The California Rules of Professional Conduct for attorneys provide that an attorney may not retain a client's files [Rule 2-111 (A)(2)]. However, Kallen refused to release the files until Delug agreed to give Kallen 40 percent of the attorneys' fees recovered in the case. The cases were ultimately settled for $810,000, resulting in attorneys' fees of $324,000. When Delug refused to pay Kallen 40 percent of these fees, Kallen sued Delug. Was the fee-splitting agreement between Kallen and Delug supported by legal consideration? *Kallen v. Delug*, 157 Cal.App.3d 940, 203 Cal.Rptr. 879, **Web** 1984 Cal.App. Lexis 2257 (California Court of Appeal)

6 Promissory Estoppel Nalley's, Inc. (Nalley's), was a major food distributor with its home office in the state of Washington. Jacob Aronowicz and Samuel Duncan approached Nalley's about the possibility of its manufacturing a line of sliced meat products to be distributed by Nalley's. When Nalley's showed considerable interest, Aronowicz and Duncan incorporated as Major Food Products, Inc. (Major). Meetings to discuss the proposal continued at length with Charles Gardiner, a vice president and general manager of the Los Angeles division of Nalley's. Gardiner delivered a letter to Major, agreeing to become the exclusive Los Angeles and Orange Country distributor for Major's products, but he stated in the letter "that should we determine your product line is not representative or is not compatible with our operation we are free to terminate our agreement within 30 days." Nalley's was to distribute the full production of products produced by Major.

Based on Gardiner's assurances, Major leased a plant, modified the plant to its specifications, purchased and installed equipment, signed contracts to obtain meat to be processed, and hired personnel. Both Aronowicz and Duncan resigned from their positions at other meat processing companies to devote full time to the project. Financing was completed when Aronowicz and Duncan used their personal fortunes to purchase the stock of Major. Gardiner and other representatives of Nalley's visited Major's plant and expressed satisfaction with the premises. Major obtained the necessary government approvals regarding health standards and immediately achieved full production. Because Nalley's was to pick up the finished products at Major's plant, Nalley's drivers visited Major's plant to acquaint themselves with its operations.

Gardiner sent the final proposal regarding the Nalley's–Major relationship to Nalley's home office for final approval. One week later, Nalley's home office in Washington made a decision not to distribute Major's products. Nalley's refused to give any reason to Major for its decision. No final agreement was ever executed between the parties. Immediate efforts by Major to secure other distribution for its products proved unsuccessful. Further, because Major owned no trucks itself and had no sales organization, it could not distribute the products itself. In less than six months, Major had failed, and Aronowicz's and Duncan's stock in Major was worthless. Major, Aronowicz, and Duncan sued Nalley's for damages under the doctrine of promissory estoppel. Do they win? *Aronowicz v. Nalley's. Inc.*, 30 Cal.App.3d 27, 106 Cal.Rptr. 424, **Web** 1972 Cal.App. Lexis 667 (Court of Appeal of California)

BUSINESS ETHICS CASE

7 Business Ethics Ocean Dunes of Hutchinson Island Development Corporation (Ocean Dunes) was a developer of condominium units. Prior to the construction, Albert and Helen Colangelo entered into a purchase agreement to buy one of the units and paid a deposit to Ocean Dunes. A provision in the purchase agreement provided that:

> *If Developer shall default in the performance of its obligations pursuant to this agreement, Purchaser's only remedy shall be to terminate this agreement, whereupon the Deposit shall be refunded to Purchaser and all rights and obligations thereunder shall thereupon become null and void.*

The purchase agreement provided that if the buyer defaulted, the developer could retain the buyer's deposit or sue the buyer for damages and any other legal or equitable remedy. When Ocean Dunes refused to sell the unit to the Colangelos, they sued, seeking a decree of specific performance to require Ocean Dunes to sell them the unit. Ocean Dunes alleged that the above-quoted provision prevented the plaintiffs from seeking any legal or equitable remedy. Was the defendant's duty under the contract illusory? Was it ethical for Ocean Dunes to place the provision at issue in the contract? *Ocean Dunes of Hutchinson Island Development Corporation v. Colangelo*, 463 So.2d 437, **Web** 1985 Fla.App. Lexis 12298 (Court of Appeal of Florida)

8 Business Ethics Red Owl Stores, Inc., a Minnesota corporation with its home office at Hopkins, Minnesota, owned and operated grocery supermarkets and granted franchises to franchisees to also operate such stores. Joseph Hoffman, who operated a bakery with his wife in Wautoma, Wisconsin, was interested in obtaining a Red Owl franchise to operate a grocery store in Wisconsin. Hoffman contacted a representative of Red Owl and had numerous conversations regarding this proposal. Ten months later, Mr. Lukowitz became Red Owl's representative for the territory comprising upper Michigan and most of Wisconsin. Hoffman mentioned to Lukowitz that he had the capital to invest, and Lukowitz assured him that it would be sufficient to open a Red Owl franchise.

To gain experience in the grocery store business, and upon the advice of Lukowitz and other Red Owl representatives, Hoffman bought a small grocery store in Wautoma. After three months of operating this store, a Red Owl representative came in and took inventory, checked operations, and found that the store was operating at a profit. Lukowitz advised Hoffman to sell the store to his manager and assured Hoffman that Red Owl would find a larger store for him elsewhere. Although Hoffman was reluctant to sell at that time because it meant losing the summer tourist business, he sold on the assurance that he would be operating a Red Owl store at a new location by the fall. Again, Lukowitz assured Hoffman that the capital he had was sufficient to open a Red Owl franchise.

Red Owl had selected a site in Chilton, Wisconsin, for the proposed store. On Red Owl's insistence, Hoffman obtained an option to purchase the site. Hoffman and his wife rented a house in Chilton. Hoffman met with Lukowitz, who assured him, "Everything is ready to go. Get your money together and we are set." Lukowitz told Hoffman that he must sell his bakery business and building in Wautoma and that this was the only "hitch" in the entire plan. Hoffman sold his bakery building but retained the equipment to be used in the proposed Red Owl store. During the next two months, Red Owl prepared various financial projections for the proposed site. Hoffman met with Lukowitz and the credit manager for Red Owl, who demanded that Hoffman have more capital to invest in the store. Hoffman contacted his father-in-law, who agreed to provide the additional money. A week later, Red Owl sent Hoffman a telegram, demanding that he have more capital to invest. When Hoffman could not raise the additional money, the transaction fell through. Hoffman did not purchase the store site in Chilton and forfeited the option payment. The parties had never entered into a final agreement regarding the franchise.

Hoffman sued Red Owl under the doctrine of promissory estoppel, seeking damages for the money lost on the option payment on the Chilton property and the lease payments on the house in Chilton. Did the representatives of Red Owl Stores, Inc., act ethically in this case? Should the equitable doctrine of promissory estoppel apply in this case? *Hoffman v. Red Owl Stores, Inc.*, 26 Wis.2d 683, 133 N.W.2d 267, **Web** 1965 Wisc. Lexis 1026 (Supreme Court of Wisconsin)

ENDNOTE

1. *Hamer v. Sidwa*, 124 N.Y. 538, 27 N.E. 256, **Web** 1891 N.Y. Lexis 1396 (Court of Appeal of New York).

CAPACITY AND LEGALITY

CAPACITY AND LEGALITY

▲ **Las Vegas, Nevada** *Gambling is illegal in many states. However, the state of Nevada permits lawful gambling. A casino must obtain a license from the Nevada Gaming Commission before it can engage in the gambling business.*

CHAPTER OBJECTIVES

After studying this chapter, you should be able to:

1. Define and describe the infancy doctrine.
2. Define *legal insanity* and *intoxication* and explain how they affect contractual capacity.
3. Identify illegal contracts that are contrary to statutes and those that violate public policy.
4. Describe covenants not to compete and exculpatory clauses and identify when they are lawful.
5. Define *unconscionable contract* and determine when such contracts are unlawful.

CHAPTER CONTENTS

An unconscionable contract is one which no man in his senses, not under delusion, would make, on the one hand, and which no fair and honest man would accept on the other.

—Hume v. United States
132 U.S. 406, 10 S.Ct. 134, 1889 U.S. Lexis 1888 (1889)

INTRODUCTION TO CAPACITY AND LEGALITY

Generally, the law presumes that the parties to a contract have the requisite **contractual capacity** to enter into the contract. Certain persons do not have this capacity, however, including minors, insane persons, and intoxicated persons. The common law of contracts and many state statutes protect persons who lack contractual capacity from having contracts enforced against them. The party asserting incapacity or his or her guardian, conservator, or other legal representative bears the burden of proof.

An essential element for the formation of a contract is that the object of the contract be lawful. A contract to perform an illegal act is called an *illegal contract*. Illegal contracts are void. That is, they cannot be enforced by either party to the contract. The term *illegal contract* is a misnomer, however, because no contract exists if the object of the contract is illegal. In addition, courts hold that *unconscionable contracts* are unenforceable. An unconscionable contract is one that is so oppressive or manifestly unfair that it would be unjust to enforce it.

Capacity to contract and the lawfulness of contracts are discussed in this chapter.

MINORS

Minors do not always have the maturity, experience, or sophistication needed to enter into contracts with adults. Common law defines minors as females under the age of 18 and males under the age of 21. In addition, many states have enacted statutes that specify the **age of majority**. The most prevalent age of majority is 18 years of age for both males and females. Any age below the statutory age of majority is called the **period of minority**.

minor
A person who has not reached the age of majority.

Infancy Doctrine

To protect minors, the law recognizes the **infancy doctrine**, which gives minors the right to *disaffirm* (or *cancel*) most contracts they have entered into with adults. This right is based on public policy which reasons that minors should be protected from the unscrupulous behavior of adults. In most states, the infancy doctrine is an objective standard. If a person's age is below the age of majority, the court will not inquire into his or her knowledge, experience, or sophistication. Generally, contracts for the necessaries of life, which we discuss later in this chapter, are exempt from the scope of this doctrine.

infancy doctrine
A doctrine that allows minors to disaffirm (cancel) most contracts they have entered into with adults.

Under the infancy doctrine, a minor has the option of choosing whether to enforce a contract (i.e., the contract is **voidable** by a minor). The adult party is bound to the minor's decision. If both parties to a contract are minors, both parties have the right to disaffirm the contract.

If performance of the contract favors the minor, the minor will probably enforce the contract. Otherwise, he or she will probably disaffirm the contract. A minor may not affirm one part of a contract and disaffirm another part.

Disaffirmance

A minor can expressly **disaffirm** a contract orally, in writing, or through his or her conduct. No special formalities are required. The contract may be disaffirmed at any time prior to the person's reaching the age of majority plus a "reasonable time." The designation of a reasonable time is determined on a case-by-case basis.

disaffirmance
The act of a minor to rescind a contract under the infancy doctrine. Disaffirmance may be done orally, in writing, or by the minor's conduct.

Minor's Duty of Restoration

If a minor's contract is executory and neither party has performed, the minor can simply disaffirm the contract: There is nothing to recover because neither party has given the other party anything of value. If the parties have exchanged consideration and partially or fully performed the contract by the time the minor disaffirms the contract, however, the issue becomes one of what consideration or restitution must be made. The following rules apply:

- **Minor's duty of restoration.** Generally, a minor is obligated only to return the goods or property he or she has received from the adult in the condition it is in at the time of disaffirmance (subject to several exceptions, discussed later in this chapter), even if the item has been consumed, lost, or destroyed or has depreciated in value by the time of disaffirmance. This rule, called the **minor's duty of restoration**, is based on the rationale that if a minor had to place the adult in status quo upon disaffirmance of a contract, there would be no incentive for an adult not to deal with a minor.
- **Competent party's duty of restitution.** If a minor has transferred consideration—money, property, or other valuables—to a competent party before disaffirming the contract, that party must place the minor in status quo. That is, the minor must be restored to the same position he or she was in before the minor entered into the contract. This restoration is usually done by returning the consideration to the minor. If the consideration has been sold or has depreciated in value, the competent party must pay the minor the cash equivalent. This action is called the **competent party's duty of restitution**.

minor's duty of restoration
A rule which states that a minor is obligated only to return the goods or property he or she has received from the adult in the condition it is in at the time of disaffirmance.

competent party's duty of restitution
A rule which states that if a minor has transferred money, property, or other valuables to the competent party before disaffirming the contract, that party must place the minor in status quo.

Most states provide that the minor must put the adult in status quo upon disaffirmance of the contract if the minor's intentional, reckless, or grossly negligent conduct caused the loss of value to the adult's property. This rule is called the **minor's duty of restitution**.

On occasion, minors might misrepresent their age to adults when entering into contracts. Most state laws provide that minors who misrepresent their age must place the adult in status quo if they disaffirm the contract.

The right of a minor to disaffirm his contract is based upon sound public policy to protect the minor from his own improvidence and the overreaching of adults.

Justice Sullivan
Star Chevrolet v. Green (1985)

Ratification

If a minor does not disaffirm a contract either during the period of minority or within a reasonable time after reaching the age of majority, the contract is considered ratified (accepted). Hence, the minor (who is now an adult) is bound by the contract; the right to disaffirm the contract is lost. Note that any attempt by a minor to ratify a contract while still a minor can be disaffirmed just as the original contract can be disaffirmed.

The **ratification**, which relates back to the inception of the contract, can be by express oral or written words or implied from the minor's conduct (e.g., after reaching the age of majority, the minor remains silent regarding the contract).

ratification
The act of a minor after the minor has reached the age of majority by which he or she accepts a contract entered into when he or she was a minor.

Parents' Liability for Their Children's Contracts

Generally, parents owe a legal duty to provide food, clothing, shelter, and other necessaries of life for their minor children. Parents are liable for their children's contracts for necessaries of life if they have not adequately provided such items.

The parental duty of support terminates if a minor becomes *emancipated*. **Emancipation** occurs when a minor voluntarily leaves home and lives apart from his or her parents. The courts consider factors such as getting married, setting up a separate household, or joining the military in determining whether a minor is emancipated. Each situation is examined on its merits.

emancipation
The act or process of a minor voluntarily leaving home and living apart from his or her parents.

Necessaries of Life

Minors are obligated to pay for the **necessaries of life** that they contract for. Otherwise, many adults would refuse to sell these items to them. There is no standard definition of what is a necessary of life. The minor's age, lifestyle, and status in life influence what is considered necessary.

necessaries of life
Food, clothing, shelter, medical care, and other items considered necessary to the maintenance of life. Minors must pay the reasonable value of necessaries of life for which they contract.

Examples Items such as food, clothing, shelter, and medical services are generally understood to be necessities of life.

Examples Goods and services such as automobiles, tools of trade, education, and vocational training have also been found to be necessaries of life in some situations.

The seller's recovery is based on the equitable doctrine of **quasi-contract** rather than on the contract itself. Under this theory, the minor is obligated only to pay the reasonable value of the goods or services received. Reasonable value is determined on a case-by-case basis.

CONTEMPORARY ENVIRONMENT

Special Types of Minors' Contracts

Based on public policy, many states have enacted statutes that make certain specified contracts enforceable against minors—that is, minors cannot assert the infancy doctrine against enforcement for these contracts. These usually include contracts for:

- Medical, surgical, and pregnancy care
- Psychological counseling
- Health insurance
- Life insurance
- The performance of duties related to stock and bond transfers, bank accounts, and the like
- Educational loan agreements
- Contracts to support children
- Contracts to enlist in the military
- Artistic, sports, and entertainment contracts that have been entered into with the approval of the court.

Many statutes mandate that a certain portion of the wages and fees earned by a minor (e.g., 50 percent) based on an artistic, sports, or entertainment contract be put in trust until the minor reaches the age of majority.

MENTALLY INCOMPETENT PERSONS

Mental incapacity may arise because of mental illness, brain damage, mental retardation, senility, and the like. The law protects people suffering from substantial mental incapacity from enforcement of contracts against them because such persons may not understand the consequences of their actions in entering into a contract.

To be relieved of his or her duties under a contract, a person must have been legally insane at the time of entering into the contract. This state is called **legal insanity**. Most states use the *objective cognitive "understanding" test* to determine legal insanity. Under this test, the person's mental incapacity must render that person incapable of understanding or comprehending the nature of the transaction. Mere weakness of intellect, slight psychological or emotional problems, or delusions does not constitute legal insanity.

legal insanity
A state of contractual incapacity, as determined by law.

The law has developed two standards concerning contracts of mentally incompetent persons: (1) adjudged insane and (2) insane but not adjudged insane.

Adjudged Insane

In certain cases, a relative, a loved one, or another interested party may institute a legal action to have someone declared legally (i.e., adjudged) insane. If after hearing the evidence at a formal judicial or administrative hearing the person is **adjudged insane**, the court will make that person a ward of the court and appoint a guardian to act on that person's behalf. Any contract entered into by a person who has been adjudged insane is **void**. That is, no contract exists. The court-appointed guardian is the only one who has the legal authority to enter into contracts on behalf of the person.

adjudged insane
Declared legally insane by a proper court or administrative agency. A contract entered into by a person adjudged insane is *void*.

Insane but Not Adjudged Insane

If no formal ruling has been made about a person's sanity but the person suffers from a mental impairment that makes him or her legally insane—that is, the person is **insane but**

insane but not adjudged insane
Being insane but not having been adjudged insane by a court or an administrative agency. A contract entered into by such person is generally *voidable*. Some states hold that such a contract is void.

Insanity vitiates all acts.

Sir John Nicholl
Countess of Portsmouth v. Earl of Portsmouth (1828)

not adjudged insane—any contract entered into by this person is voidable by the insane person. Unless the other party does not have contractual capacity, he or she does not have the option to void the contract.

Some people have alternating periods of sanity and insanity. Any contracts made by such persons during a lucid interval are enforceable. Contracts made while the person was not legally sane can be disaffirmed.

A person who has dealt with an insane person must place that insane person in status quo if the contract is either void or voided by the insane person. Most states hold that a party who did not know he or she was dealing with an insane person must be placed in status quo upon avoidance of the contract. Insane persons are liable in *quasi-contract* to pay the reasonable value for the necessaries of life they receive.

CONCEPT SUMMARY

DISAFFIRMANCE OF CONTRACTS BASED ON LEGAL INSANITY

Type of Legal Insanity	Disaffirmance Rule
Adjudged insane	Contract is void. Neither party can enforce the contract.
Insane but not adjudged insane	Contract is voidable by the insane person; the competent party cannot void the contract.

INTOXICATED PERSONS

intoxicated person
A person who is under contractual incapacity because of ingestion of alcohol or drugs to the point of incompetence.

Most states provide that contracts entered into by certain **intoxicated persons** are voidable by those persons. The intoxication may occur because of alcohol or drugs. The contract is not voidable by the other party if that party had contractual capacity.

Under the majority rule, the contract is voidable only if the person was so intoxicated when the contract was entered into that he or she was incapable of understanding or comprehending the nature of the transaction. In most states, this rule holds even if the intoxication was self-induced. Some states allow the person to disaffirm the contract only if the person was forced to become intoxicated or did so unknowingly.

Men intoxicated are sometimes stunned into sobriety.

Lord Mansfield
R. v. Wilkes (1770)

The amount of alcohol or drugs that must be consumed for a person to be considered legally intoxicated to disaffirm contracts varies from case to case. The factors that are considered include the user's physical characteristics and his or her ability to "hold" intoxicants.

A person who disaffirms a contract based on intoxication generally must be returned to the status quo. In turn, the intoxicated person generally must return the consideration received under the contract to the other party and make restitution that returns the other party to status quo. After becoming sober, an intoxicated person can ratify the contracts he or she entered into while intoxicated. Intoxicated persons are liable in *quasi-contract* to pay the reasonable value for necessaries they receive.

LEGALITY

One requirement to have an enforceable contract is that the object of the contract must be lawful. Most contracts that individuals and businesses enter into are **lawful contracts** that are enforceable. These include contracts for the sale of goods, services, real property, and intangible rights; the lease of goods; property leases; licenses; and other contracts.

illegal contract
A contract that has an illegal object. Such contracts are *void*.

Some contracts have illegal objects. A contract with an illegal object is *void* and therefore unenforceable. These contracts are called **illegal contracts**. The following paragraphs discuss various illegal contracts.

Contracts Contrary to Statutes

Both federal and state legislatures have enacted statutes that prohibit certain types of conduct. Contracts to perform activities that are prohibited by statute are illegal contracts.

Examples An agreement between two companies to engage in price fixing in violation of federal antitrust statutes is illegal and therefore void. Thus, neither company to this illegal contract can enforce the contract against the other company.

Usury Laws

State **usury laws** set an upper limit on the annual interest rate that can be charged on certain types of loans. The limits vary from state to state. Lenders who charge a higher rate than the state limit are guilty of usury. These laws are intended to protect unsophisticated borrowers from loan sharks and others who charge exorbitant rates of interest.

usury law
A law that sets an upper limit on the interest rate that can be charged on certain types of loans.

Most states provide criminal and civil penalties for making usurious loans. Some states require lenders to remit the difference between the interest rate charged on the loan and the usury rate to the borrower. Other states prohibit lenders from collecting any interest on the loan. Still other states provide that a usurious loan is a void contract, permitting the borrower not to have to pay the interest or the principal of the loan to the lender.

Most usury laws exempt certain types of lenders and loan transactions involving legitimate business transactions from the reach of the law. These exemptions usually include loans made by banks and other financial institutions, loans above a certain dollar amount, and loans made to corporations and other businesses.

Contracts to Commit Crimes

Contracts to commit criminal acts are void. If the object of a contract becomes illegal after the contract is entered into because the government has enacted a statute that makes it unlawful, the parties are discharged from the contract. The contract is not an illegal contract unless the parties agree to go forward and complete it.

In the following case, the court had to determine whether a contract was illegal.

CASE 1 Illegal Contract

Parente v. Pirozzoli

87 Conn.App. 235, 866 A.2d 629, Web 2005 Conn.App. Lexis 25 (2005)
Appellate Court of Connecticut

"Thus, in the case of a contract whose inherent purpose is to violate the law, if both parties thereto are *in pari delicto*, the law will leave them where it finds them."

—Judge Lavery

Facts

Andrew Parente had a criminal record. He and Mario Pirozzoli, Jr., formed a partnership to open and operate the Speak Easy Café in Berlin, Connecticut, which was a bar that would serve alcohol. The owners were required to obtain a liquor license from the state of Connecticut before operating the bar. Because the state of Connecticut usually would not issue a liquor license to anyone with a criminal record, it was agreed that Pirozzoli would form a corporation called Centerfolds, Inc., to own the bar, sign the real estate lease for the bar in his name, and file for the liquor license in his name only. Pirozzoli did all of these things. Parente and Pirozzoli signed a partnership agreement that acknowledged that Parente was an equal partner in the business. The state of Connecticut granted the liquor license, and the bar opened for business. Parente and Pirozzoli shared the profits of the bar.

Six years later, Pirozzoli terminated the partnership and kept the business. Parente sued Pirozzoli for breach of the partnership agreement to recover the value of his alleged share of the business. Pirozzoli defended, arguing that the partnership agreement was an illegal contract that should not be enforced against him. The trial court held that the partnership agreement had been breached and awarded Parente $138,000 in damages. Pirozzoli appealed.

Issue

Was the partnership agreement an illegal contract that was void and unenforceable by the court?

Language of the Court

Here, the partnership agreement was not offensive on its face, but had an illegal, ulterior purpose, namely, to

(case continues)

evade the strictures of the liquor control laws. Because the partnership agreement was made to facilitate, foster, or support patently illegal activity, we conclude that it is illegal as against public policy and, consequently, that the court's enforcement of it was improper.

Although the end result of holding the partnership agreement illegal may be to allow Pirozzoli a windfall at Parente's expense, this result is common and necessary in many cases in which contracts are deemed unenforceable on the grounds of furthering overriding policies. It is in order to effectuate an underlying public policy, rather than sanction a party seeking to enforce an illegal contract, that courts refuse to lend assistance to those who have contributed to the illegality that taints the contract. Thus, in the case of a contract whose inherent purpose is to violate the law, if both parties thereto are in pari delicto, *the law will leave them where it finds them. Knowing that they will receive no help from the courts and must trust completely to each other's good faith, the parties are less likely to enter an illegal arrangement in the first place.*

Decision

The appellate court held that the partnership agreement between Parente and Pirozzoli was an illegal contract that was void and unenforceable. The appellate court reversed the judgment of the trial court, found that Pirozzoli was not liable to Parente, and held that Pirozzoli could keep the $138,000 windfall.

Case Questions

Critical Legal Thinking What is an illegal contract? Explain.

Business Ethics Did Parente act ethically in this case? Was it honorable for Pirozzoli to argue that his partnership agreement with Parente was an illegal contract?

Contemporary Business What is the result of a court finding that a contract is illegal? Explain. Was it fair for Pirozzoli to receive the windfall in this case?

Gambling Statutes

gambling statutes
Statutes that make certain forms of gambling illegal.

All states either prohibit or regulate gambling, wagering, lotteries, and games of chance via **gambling statutes**. States provide various criminal and civil penalties for illegal gambling. There are many exceptions to wagering laws. Many states have enacted statutes that permit games of chance under a certain dollar amount, bingo games, lotteries conducted by religious and charitable organizations, and the like. Many states also permit and regulate horse racing, harness racing, dog racing, and state-operated lotteries.

Effect of Illegality

effect of illegality
A doctrine which states that the courts will refuse to enforce or rescind an illegal contract and will leave the parties where it finds them.

Because illegal contracts are void, the parties cannot sue for nonperformance. Further, if an illegal contract is executed, the court will generally leave the parties where it finds them.

Certain situations are exempt from the general rule of the effect of finding an illegal contract. If an exception applies, the innocent party may use the court system to sue for damages or to recover consideration paid under the illegal contract. Persons who can assert an exception are:

- Innocent persons who were justifiably ignorant of the law or fact that made the contract illegal.

Example A person who purchases insurance from an unlicensed insurance company may recover insurance benefits from the unlicensed company.

- Persons who were induced to enter into an illegal contract by fraud, duress, or undue influence.

Example A shop owner who pays $5,000 "protection money" to a mobster so that his store will not be burned down by the mobster can recover the $5,000.

- Persons who entered into an illegal contract who withdraw before the illegal act is performed.

Example If the president of New Toy Corporation pays $10,000 to an employee of Old Toy Corporation to steal a trade secret from his employer but reconsiders and tells the employee not to do it before he has done it, the New Toy Corporation may recover the $10,000.

- Persons who were less at fault than the other party for entering into the illegal contract. At common law, parties to an illegal contract were considered ***in pari delicto*** (in equal fault). Some states have changed this rule and permit the less-at-fault party to recover restitution of the consideration they paid under an illegal contract from the more-at-fault party.

in pari delicto
A situation in which both parties are equally at fault in an illegal contract.

ETHICS SPOTLIGHT

Illegal Gambling Contract

"The trial court could not have compelled Ryno to honor his wager by delivering the BMW to Tyra. However, Ryno did deliver the BMW to Tyra and the facts incident to that delivery are sufficient to establish a transfer by gift of the BMW from Ryno to Tyra."

—Judge Farris

R. D. Ryno, Jr., owned Bavarian Motors, an automobile dealership in Fort Worth, Texas. One day, Lee Tyra discussed purchasing a BMW M-1 from Ryno for $125.000. Ryno then suggested a double-or-nothing coin flip, to which Tyra agreed. If the Ryno won the coin flip, Tyra would have to pay $250,000 for the car; if Tyra won the coin flip, he would get the car for free. The coin was flipped, and Tyra won the coin flip. Ryno said, "It's yours," and handed Tyra the keys, title, and possession to the car. Tyra drove away in the BMW. A lawsuit ensued as to the ownership of the car.

The court held that when Tyra won the coin toss and Ryno voluntarily gave the keys, title, and possession of the BMW to Tyra, this was a performed illegal gambling contract. There was sufficient evidence to find that Ryno intended to transfer to Tyra his ownership interest in the BMW at the time he delivered the documents, keys, and possession of the automobile to Tyra. The court left the parties where it found them: Tyra had the keys, title, and possession of the BMW; Ryno did not have either the car or payment for the car.

Note: If, when Tyra won the coin toss, Ryno had refused to give the BMW to Tyra, the result of this case would have been different. Tyra could not have compelled Ryno to honor his wager. This is because courts will not enforce an executory illegal gambling contract. The court would again have left the parties where it found them: Ryno would have had ownership and possession of the car and refused to honor the wager; Tyra would have won the coin toss but could not obtain the car from Ryno. *Ryno v. Tyra*, 752 S.W.2d 148, **Web** 1988 Tex. App. Lexis 1646 (Court of Appeals of Texas)

Business Ethics Did Ryno act ethically in this case? Did Tyra act ethically in this case? Should the court have lent its help to Ryno to recover the BMW from Tyra? Why or why not?

Kewadin Casino, Michigan *This sign advertises an Indian gaming casino operated in the Upper Peninsula of Michigan. In 1988, Congress enacted the* ***Indian Gaming Regulatory Act (IGRA)***[1] *that established the framework for permitting and regulating Indian gaming. There are more than 400 Indian gaming establishments in the country operated by more than 200 federally recognized tribes. Federal law permits Indian casino gambling only if the state permits such gambling. The Kewadin Casino in Brevort Township, Michigan, is operated by the Sault Ste. Marie Tribe of Chippewa Indians.*

Contracts Contrary to Public Policy

contract contrary to public policy
A contract that has a negative impact on society or that interferes with the public's safety and welfare.

immoral contract
A contract whose objective is the commission of an act that is society considers immoral.

Certain contracts are illegal because they are **contrary to public policy**. Such contracts are void. Although *public policy* eludes precise definition, the courts have held contracts to be contrary to public policy if they have a negative impact on society or interfere with the public's safety and welfare.

Immoral contracts—that is, contracts whose objective is the commission of an act that society considers immoral—may be found to be against public policy. Judges are not free to define morality based on their individual views. Instead, they must look to the practices and beliefs of society when defining immoral conduct.

Example A contract that is based on sexual favors is an immoral contract and void as against public policy.

ETHICS SPOTLIGHT

Murder, She Wrote

Ellen and Richard Alvin Flood, who were married, lived in a mobile home in Louisiana. Richard worked as a maintenance man, and Ellen was employed at an insurance agency. Ellen was unhappy with her marriage. Ellen took out a life insurance policy on the life of her husband and named herself as beneficiary. The policy was issued by Fidelity & Guaranty Life Insurance Company (Fidelity).

Thereafter, Richard became unexpectedly ill. He was taken to the hospital, where his condition improved. After a visit at the hospital from his wife, however, Richard died. Ellen was criminally charged with the murder of her husband by poisoning. Evidence showed that six medicine bottles at the couple's home, including Tylenol and paregoric bottles, contained arsenic. The court found that Ellen had fed Richard ice cubes laced with arsenic at the hospital. Ellen was tried and convicted of the murder of her husband.

Subsequently, Ellen, as the beneficiary of Richard's life insurance policy, requested Fidelity to pay her the benefits. Fidelity refused to pay the benefits and returned all premiums paid on the policy. A lawsuit followed. Does Fidelity have to pay Ellen the life insurance proceeds for Richard's death?

The court held that Fidelity did not have to pay Ellen the life insurance proceeds from her husband Richard's death because a beneficiary named in a life insurance policy is not entitled to the proceeds of the insurance if the beneficiary kills the insured. The enforcement of such a contract would violate public policy. The court stated, "Louisiana follows the majority rule that holds, as a matter of public policy, that a beneficiary named in a life insurance policy is not entitled to the proceeds of the insurance if the beneficiary feloniously kills the insured." *Flood v. Fidelity & Guaranty Life Insurance Company*, 394 So.2d 1311, **Web** 1981 La.App. Lexis 3538 (Court of Appeal of Louisiana)

Business Ethics Did Ellen Flood act ethically by trying to recover the life insurance proceeds from her husband's death? What would be the consequences if persons could recover insurance proceeds for losses caused by their illegal activities, such as murder?

▶ SPECIAL BUSINESS CONTRACTS

The issue of the lawfulness of contracts applies to several special business contracts. These include contracts that restrain trade; contracts to provide services that require a government license, exculpatory clauses, and covenants not to compete. These contracts are discussed in the following paragraphs.

Contract in Restraint of Trade

contract in restraint of trade
A contract that unreasonably restrains trade.

The general economic policy of this country favors competition. At common law, **contracts in restraint of trade**—that is, contracts that unreasonably restrain trade—are held to be unlawful.

Example It would be an illegal restraint of trade for Toyota, General Motors, and Ford Motor to agree to fix the prices of the automobiles they sell. Their contract would be void and could not be enforced by any of the parties against the other parties.

Licensing Statute

All states have **licensing statutes** that require members of certain professions and occupations to be licensed by the state in which they practice. Lawyers, doctors, real estate agents, insurance agents, certified public accountants, teachers, contractors, hairdressers, and such are among them. In most instances, a license is granted to a person who demonstrates that he or she has the proper schooling, experience, and moral character required by the relevant statute. Sometimes, a written examination is also required.

licensing statute
A statute that requires a person or business to obtain a license from the government prior to engaging in a specified occupation or activity.

Problems arise if an unlicensed person tries to collect payment for services provided to another under a contract. Some statutes expressly provide that unlicensed persons cannot enforce contracts to provide these services. If the statute is silent on the point, enforcement depends on whether it is a *regulatory statute* or a *revenue-raising statute*:

- **Regulatory statute.** Licensing statutes enacted to protect the public are called **regulatory statutes.** Generally, unlicensed persons cannot recover payment for services that a regulatory statute requires a licensed person to provide.

regulatory statute
A licensing statute enacted to protect the public.

Example State law provides that legal services can be provided only by lawyers who have graduated from law school and passed the appropriate bar exam. Nevertheless, suppose Marie, a first-year law student, agrees to draft a will for Randy for a $350 fee. Because Marie is not licensed to provide legal services, she has violated a regulatory statute. She cannot enforce the contract and recover payment from Randy. Randy, even though receiving services by having his will drafted, does not have to pay Marie $350.

- **Revenue-raising statute.** Licensing statutes enacted to raise money for the government are called **revenue-raising statutes.** A person who provides services pursuant to a contract without the appropriate license required by such a statute can enforce the contract and recover payment for services rendered.

revenue-raising statute
A licensing statute with the primary purpose of raising revenue for the government.

Example A state licensing statute requires licensed attorneys to pay an annual $500 renewal fee without requiring continuing education or other new qualifications. If a lawyer provides legal services but has not paid the annual licensing fee, the lawyer can still recover for her services.

Exculpatory Clause

An **exculpatory clause** (also called a **release of liability clause**) is a contractual provision that relieves one (or both) of the parties to a contract from tort liability. An exculpatory clause can relieve a party of liability for ordinary negligence. It cannot be used in a situation involving willful conduct, intentional torts, fraud, recklessness, or gross negligence. Exculpatory clauses are often found in leases, sales contracts, sporting event ticket stubs, parking lot tickets, service contracts, and the like. Such clauses do not have to be reciprocal (i.e., one party may be relieved of tort liability, whereas the other party is not).

exculpatory clause
A contractual provision that relieves one (or both) of the parties to a contract from tort liability for ordinary negligence. Also known as a *release of liability clause*.

Example Jim Jackson voluntarily enrolled in a parachute jump course and signed a contract containing an exculpatory clause that relieved the parachute center of liability. After receiving proper instruction, he jumped from an airplane. Unfortunately, Jim was injured when he could not steer his parachute toward the target area. He sued the parachute center for damages. Here, the court would usually enforce the exculpatory clause, reasoning that parachute jumping was a voluntary choice and did not involve an essential service.

Exculpatory clauses that either affect the public interest or result from superior bargaining power are usually found to be void as against public policy. Although the outcome varies with the circumstances of the case, the greater the degree to which the party serves the general public, the greater the chance that the exculpatory clause will be struck down as illegal. The courts will consider such factors as the type of activity involved; the relative bargaining power, knowledge, experience, and sophistication of the parties; and other relevant factors.

Covenant Not to Compete

covenant not to compete
A contract which provides that a seller of a business or an employee will not engage in a similar business or occupation within a specified geographical area for a specified time following the sale of the business or termination of employment. Also called a *noncompete clause*.

Entrepreneurs and others often buy and sell businesses. The sale of a business includes its "goodwill," or reputation. To protect this goodwill after the sale, the seller often enters into an agreement with the buyer not to engage in a similar business or occupation within a specified geographic area for a specified period of time following the sale. This agreement is called a **covenant not to compete**, or a **noncompete clause**.

Employers often do not want an employee who resigns or is terminated to work in a position that competes with the employer for a certain length of time after the employee is gone from the employer. Employers often require an employee, usually before he or she is hired, to sign a noncompete clause, agreeing not to work for another employer or for themselves in a position that would compete with their prior employer for a certain period of time after the employee has left or been terminated by the employer.

Covenants not to compete that are *ancillary* to a legitimate sale of a business or employment contract are lawful if they are reasonable in three aspects: (1) the line of business protected, (2) the geographic area protected, and (3) the duration of the restriction. A covenant that is found to be unreasonable is not enforceable as written. The reasonableness of covenants not to compete is examined on a case-by-case basis. If a covenant not to compete is unreasonable, the courts may either refuse to enforce it or change it so that it is reasonable. Usually, the courts choose the first option.

Examples Stacy is a certified public accountant (CPA) with a lucrative accounting practice in Providence, Rhode Island. Her business includes a substantial amount of goodwill with her clients. Stacy sells her accounting practice to Gregory. When she sells her practice to Gregory, Stacy agrees not to open another accounting practice in the state of Rhode Island for a 20-year period. This covenant not to compete is reasonable in the line of business protected but is unreasonable in geographic scope and duration. It will not be enforced by the courts as written. The covenant not to compete would be reasonable and enforceable if it prohibited Stacy only from practicing as a CPA in the city of Providence for 3 years.

▶ UNCONSCIONABLE CONTRACTS

The general rule of freedom of contract holds that if the object of a contract is lawful and the other elements for the formation of a contract are met, the courts will enforce a contract according to its terms. Although it is generally presumed that parties are capable of protecting their own interests when contracting, it is a fact of life that dominant parties sometimes take advantage of weaker parties.

In addition, many contracts that consumers sign are **contracts of adhesion**—that is, they are preprinted forms whose terms the consumer cannot negotiate and which they must sign in order to obtain a product or service. Most adhesion contracts are lawful even though there is a disparity in power of contracting.

Examples Automobile sales contracts and leases, mortgages, and apartment leases are usually contracts of adhesion.

However, when a contract is so oppressive or manifestly unfair as to be unjust, the law has developed the equity doctrine of unconscionability to prevent the enforcement of such contracts. The doctrine of unconscionability is based on public policy. A contract found to be unconscionable under this doctrine is called an **unconscionable contract**.

unconscionable contract
A contract that courts refuse to enforce in part or at all because it is so oppressive or manifestly unfair as to be unjust.

The courts are given substantial discretion in determining whether a contract or contract clause is unconscionable. There is no single definition of *unconscionability*. This doctrine may not be used merely to save a contracting party from a bad bargain.

Elements of Unconscionability

The following elements must be shown to prove that a contract or a clause in a contract is unconscionable:

A good judge decides fairly, preferring equity to strict law.

Legal maxim

- The parties possessed severely unequal bargaining power.
- The dominant party unreasonably used its unequal bargaining power to obtain oppressive or manifestly unfair contract terms.
- The adhering party had no reasonable alternative.

Unconscionable contracts are sometimes found where there is a consumer contract that takes advantage of uneducated, poor, or elderly people who have been persuaded to enter into an unfair contract. This often involves door-to-door sales and sales over the telephone. If the court finds that a contract or contract clause is unconscionable, it may (1) refuse to enforce the contract, (2) refuse to enforce the unconscionable clause but enforce the remainder of the contract, or (3) limit the applicability of any unconscionable clause so as to avoid any unconscionable result. The appropriate remedy depends on the facts and circumstances of each case. Note that because unconscionability is a matter of law, the judge may opt to decide the case without a jury trial.

Example Suppose a door-to-door salesperson sells a poor family a freezer full of meat and other foods for $3,000, with monthly payments for 60 months at 20 percent interest. If the actual cost of the freezer and the food is $1,000, this contract could be found to be unconscionable. The court could either find the entire contract unenforceable or rewrite the contract so that it has reasonable terms.

In the following case, the court found a contract clause to be unconscionable.

CASE 2 Unconscionable Contract

Muhammad, on Her Own Behalf and All Others Similarly Situated v. County Bank of Rehoboth Beach

189 N.J. 1, 912 A.2d 88, Web 2006 N.J. Lexis 1154 (2006)
Supreme Court of New Jersey

"By permitting claimants to band together, class actions equalize adversaries and provide a procedure to remedy a wrong that might otherwise go unredressed."

—Judge LaVecchia

Facts

Jaliyah Muhammad was a part-time student at Berkeley College in Paramus, New Jersey. Muhammad obtained a short-term single advance, unsecured loan of $200 from County Bank of Rehoboth Beach (County Bank). County Bank charged a finance charge of $60 for the loan. The loan rate was 608.33 percent. The loan was due in 21 days. Muhammad obtained two similar loans from County Bank.

To obtain the loans, Muhammad had to complete and sign three pages of standard form contracts. These loan documents contained an agreement that all disputes regarding the loan were subject to arbitration and could not be brought in court and that the borrower could not bring, join, or participate in class actions as to any disputes regarding the loans. The agreement to arbitrate and the agreement not to bring, join, or participate in class actions were conspicuously stated in capital letters in the loan documents.

Muhammad filed a class action lawsuit in New Jersey superior court against County Bank, alleging that County Bank charged illegal rates of interest, in violation of New Jersey law. Muhammad sought restitution, damages, penalties, and costs from County Bank. Muhammad argued that the arbitration agreement was unconscionable based on the class action waiver. County Bank made a motion to compel arbitration. The trial court and the appellate court held that Muhammad's claims were subject to arbitration. Muhammad appealed.

Issue

Was the class action waiver in the arbitration agreement unconscionable?

Language of the Court

It is well settled that courts may refuse to enforce contracts that are unconscionable. The unconscionability issue in this matter centers on access to class-action proceeding in the

(case continues)

arbitral setting. By permitting claimants to band together, class actions equalize adversaries and provide a procedure to remedy a wrong that might otherwise go unredressed. If each victim were remitted to an individual suit, the remedy would be illusory, for the individual loss may be too small to warrant a suit. A class-action proceeding can aid the efficient administration of justice by avoiding the expense, in both time and money, of relitigating similar claims. In sum, the class-action mechanism is recognized to be valuable to litigants, to the courts, and to the public interest.

We hold, therefore, that the presence of the class-action waiver in Muhammad's consumer arbitration agreement renders that agreement unconscionable. As a matter of generally applicable state contract law, it was unconscionable for County Bank to deprive Muhammad of the mechanism of a class-wide action, whether in arbitration or in court litigation. Finally, although we find that the class-arbitration waivers in Muhammad's arbitration agreements are unconscionable, we find that the waivers are severable. Once the waivers are removed, the remainder of the arbitration agreement is enforceable.

Decision

The supreme court of New Jersey held that the class action waiver clause in County Bank's arbitration agreement was unconscionable. The court further held that this clause could be severed from the arbitration clause and that Muhammad's class action would be heard by an arbitration panel.

Case Questions

Critical Legal Thinking What is a contract of adhesion? Have you ever signed one? What is an unconscionable contract? Explain.

Business Ethics Did County Bank act ethically in placing the class action waiver in its loan documents? Why do you think County Bank included the class action waiver clause in its loan documents?

Contemporary Business Were the terms of the loans—the interest rate and finance charge—for County Bank's loans unconscionable?

Web Exercise Go to **www.bankrate.com/brm/news/cc/20020320a.asp** to read about credit card interest rates.

China *Since 1976, Chinese leaders have opened the country to economic reform. Since taking over the island of Macau from the Portuguese in 1999, China has made Macau into one of the world's premiere gambling centers. Gambling revenues from Macau's casinos now exceed those of Las Vegas casinos. The Sands Macau, Wynn Macau, Venetian Macau, and MGM Grand Macau have opened on the island.*

TEST REVIEW TERMS AND CONCEPTS

Adjudged insane
Age of majority
Competent party's duty of restitution
Contract contrary to public policy
Contract in restraint of trade
Contract of adhesion
Contractual capacity
Covenant not to compete (noncompete clause)
Disaffirm
Effect of illegality
Emancipation
Exculpatory clause (release of liability clause)

Gambling statute
Illegal contract
Immoral contract
Indian Gaming Regulatory Act (IGRA)
Infancy doctrine
In pari delicto
Insane but not adjudged insane
Intoxicated person
Lawful contract
Legal insanity
Licensing statute
Minor
Minor's duty of restitution
Minor's duty of restoration
Necessaries of life
Period of minority
Quasi-contract
Ratification
Regulatory statute
Revenue-raising statute
Unconscionable contract
Usury law
Void
Voidable contract

CASE PROBLEMS

1 Infancy Doctrine James Halbman, Jr., a minor, entered into a contract to purchase an Oldsmobile from Michael Lemke. Halbman paid $1,000 cash and agreed to make weekly payments until the full purchase price was paid. Five weeks later, a connecting rod on the vehicle's engine broke, and Halbman took the car to a garage, where it was repaired at a cost of $637.40. Halbman refused to pay for the repairs, disaffirmed the contract with Lemke, and notified Lemke where the car was located. When Lemke refused to pick up the car and pay the repair bill, the garage legally satisfied its garageman's lien by removing the vehicle's engine. It then towed the car to Halbman's residence. Halbman notified Lemke to remove the car, but Lemke refused to do so. The car was subsequently vandalized, making it worthless and unsalvageable. Halbman sued to disaffirm the contract and recover the consideration from Lemke. Lemke argued that Halbman must make full restitution. Who is correct? *Halbman v. Lemke*, 99 Wis.2d 241, 298 N.W.2d 562, **Web** 1980 Wisc. Lexis 2825 (Supreme Court of Wisconsin)

2 Ratification Charles Edwards Smith, a minor, purchased an automobile from Bobby Floars Toyota (Toyota). Smith executed a security agreement to finance part of the balance due on the purchase price, agreeing to pay off the balance in 30 monthly installments. Smith turned 18, which was the age of majority in his state. Smith made 10 monthly payments after turning 18. He then decided to disaffirm the contract and stopped making the payments. Smith claims that he may disaffirm the contract entered into when he was a minor. Toyota argues that Smith has ratified the contract since attaining the age of majority. Who is correct? *Bobby Floars Toyota, Inc. v. Smith*, 48 N.C.App. 580, 269 S.E.2d 320, **Web** 1980 N.C.App. Lexis 3263 (Court of Appeals of North Carolina)

3 Adjudged Insane Manzelle Johnson, who had been adjudicated insane, executed a quitclaim and warranty deed conveying real estate she owned to her guardian, Obbie Neal. Neal subsequently conveyed the real estate to James R. Beavers by warranty deed. Charles L. Weatherly, Johnson's present guardian, brought this action, seeking a decree of the court that title to the real estate be restored to Johnson because of her inability to contract. Should Johnson be allowed to void the contract? *Beavers v. Weatherly*, 250 Ga. 546, 299 S.E.2d 730, **Web** 1983 Ga. Lexis 581 (Supreme Court of Georgia)

4 Intoxication Betty Galloway, an alcoholic, signed a settlement agreement upon her divorce from her husband, Henry Galloway. Henry, in Betty's absence in court, stated that she had lucid intervals from her alcoholism, had been sober for two months, and was lucid when she signed the settlement agreement. Betty moved to vacate the settlement agreement, after she had retained present legal counsel. Four months later, Betty was declared incompetent to handle her person and her affairs, and a guardian and conservator was appointed. Betty, through her guardian, sued to have the settlement agreement voided. Who wins? *Galloway v. Galloway*, 281 N.W.2d 804, **Web** 1979 N.D. Lexis 279 (Supreme Court of North Dakota)

5 Licensing Statute The state of Hawaii requires a person who wants to practice architecture to meet certain educational requirements and to pass a written examination before being granted a license to practice. After receiving the license, an architect must pay an annual license fee of $15. Ben Lee Wilson satisfied the initial requirements and was granted an architecture license. Four years later, Wilson failed to renew his license by paying the required annual fee. Wilson contracted with Kealakekua Ranch, Ltd., and Gentry Hawaii (defendants) to provide architectural services for the Kealakekua Ranch Center project. Wilson provided $33,994 of architectural services to the defendants. The defendants refused to pay this fee because Wilson did not have an architectural license. Wilson sued to collect his fees. Who wins? *Wilson v. Kealakekua Ranch, Ltd., and Gentry Hawaii*, 57 Haw. 124, 551 P.2d 525, **Web** 1976 Haw. Lexis 119 (Supreme Court of Hawaii)

6 Covenant Not to Compete Gerry Morris owned a silk screening and lettering shop in Tucson, Arizona. Morris entered into a contract to sell the business to Alfred and Connie Gann. The contract contained the following covenant not to compete: "Seller agrees not to enter into silk screening or lettering shop business within Tucson and a 100-mile radius of Tucson, for a period of ten (10) years from the date of this agreement and will not compete in any manner whatsoever with buyers, and seller further agrees that he will refer all business contracts to buyers." Morris opened a silk screening and lettering business in competition with the Ganns and in violation of the noncompete clause. The Ganns brought this action against Morris for breach of contract and to enforce the covenant not to compete. Is the covenant not to compete valid and enforceable in this case? *Gann v. Morris*,

122 Ariz. 517, 596 P.2d 43, **Web** 1979 Ariz.App. Lexis 487 (Court of Appeals of Arizona)

7 Exculpatory Clause Grady Perkins owned the Raleigh Institute of Cosmetology (Institute), and Ray Monk and Rovetta Allen were employed as instructors there. The school trained students to do hair styling and coloring, cosmetology, and other beauty services. The students received practical training by providing services to members of the public under the supervision of the instructors. Francis I. Alston went to Institute to have her hair colored and styled by a student who was under the supervision of Monk and Allen. Before receiving any services, Alston signed a written release form that released Institute and its employees from liability for their negligence. While coloring Alston's hair, the student negligently used a chemical that caused Alston's hair to fall out. Alston sued Institute, Perkins, Monk, and Allen for damages. The defendants asserted that the release form signed by Alston barred her suit. Is the exculpatory clause valid? *Alston v. Monk*, 92 N.C.App.59, 373 S.E.2d 463, **Web** 1988 N.C. App. Lexis 987 (Court of Appeals of North Carolina)

8 Exculpatory Clause Wilbur Spaulding owned and operated the Jacksonville racetrack at the Morgan Country Fairgrounds, where automobile races were held. Lawrence P. Koch was a flagman at the raceway. One day when Koch arrived at the pit shack at the raceway, he was handed a clipboard on which was a track release and waiver of liability form that released the racetrack from liability for negligence. Koch signed the form and took up his position as flagman. During the first race, the last car on the track lost control and slid off the end of the track, striking Koch. Koch suffered a broken leg and other injuries and was unable to work for 14 months. Koch sued Spaulding for damages for negligence. Spaulding asserted that the release form signed by Koch barred his suit. Is the exculpatory clause valid against Koch? *Koch v. Spaulding*, 174 Ill.App.3d 692, 529 N.E.2d. 19, **Web** 1988 Ill. App. Lexis 1427 (Appellate Court of Illinois)

BUSINESS ETHICS CASES

9 Business Ethics Joe Plumlee owned and operated an ambulance company. He alleged that the law firm Paddock, Loveless & Roach agreed to pay him an up-front fee and a percentage of the law firm's fees generated from personal injury case referrals. When the law firm did not pay Plumlee, he sued to recover damages for breach of contract. Texas law prohibits lawyers from sharing fees with laypersons [Tex. Penal Code Section 38.12; supreme court of Texas]. A disciplinary rule also forbids such activity [State Bar Rules Art. X, Section 9]. The law firm asserted that the contract could not be enforced because it would be an illegal contract. Who wins? Did Plumlee act ethically in this case? If the contract existed, did the lawyers act ethically? *Plumlee v. Paddock, Loveless, and Roach*, 832 S.W.2d 757, **Web** 1992 Tex.App. Lexis 1544 (Court of Appeals of Texas)

10 Business Ethics Richard Zientara was friends with Chester and Bernice Kaszuba. All three were residents of Indiana. Bernice, who was employed in an Illinois tavern where Illinois state lottery tickets were sold, had previously obtained lottery tickets for Zientara because Indiana did not have a state lottery. One day, Zientara requested that Kaszuba purchase an Illinois lottery ticket for him. He gave Kaszuba the money for the ticket and the numbers 6–15–16–23–24–37. Kaszuba purchased the ticket, but when it turned out to be the winning combination worth $1,696,800, she refused to give the ticket to Zientara and unsuccessfully tried to collect the money. Zientara filed suit against Kaszuba in Indiana, claiming the ticket and proceeds thereof. Was the contract legal? Did the Kaszubas act ethically in this case? *Kaszuba v. Zientara*, 506 N.E.2d 1, **Web** 1987 Ind. Lexis 874 (Supreme Court of Indiana)

ENDNOTE

1. 25 U.S.C. Section 2701 et seq.

GENUINENESS OF ASSENT AND UNDUE INFLUENCE

FOTOG/Getty Images, Inc. Tetra Images

▲ **Used Car Dealership** *The history of car sales has generated many cases of contracts tainted by mistakes and fraud.*

CHAPTER OBJECTIVES

After studying this chapter, you should be able to:

1. Explain genuineness of assent.
2. Explain how mutual mistake of fact excuses performance.
3. Describe intentional misrepresentation (fraud).
4. Describe duress.
5. Define *equitable doctrine of undue influence.*

CHAPTER CONTENTS

"Freedom of contract begins where equality of bargaining power begins."

—Oliver Wendell Holmes, Jr.
June 4, 1928

▶ INTRODUCTION TO GENUINENESS OF ASSENT AND UNDUE INFLUENCE

Voluntary *assent* by the parties is necessary to create an enforceable contract. Assent is determined by the relevant facts surrounding the negotiation and formation of a contract. Assent may be manifested in any manner sufficient to show agreement, including express words or conduct of the parties.

A contract may not be enforced if the assent of one or both of the parties to the contract was not genuine or real. *Genuine assent* may be missing because a party entered into a contract based on mistake, fraudulent misrepresentation, or duress. A court may permit the rescission of a contract based on the equitable doctrine of *undue influence*. Problems concerning **genuineness of assent** are discussed in this chapter.

genuineness of assent
The requirement that a party's assent to a contract be genuine.

▶ MISTAKE

A **mistake** occurs where one or both of the parties to a contract have an erroneous belief about the subject matter, value, or some other aspect of the contract. Mistakes may be either *unilateral* or *mutual*. The law permits **rescission** of some contracts made in mistake.

rescission
An action to undo a contract.

Unilateral Mistake

Unilateral mistakes occur when only one party is mistaken about a material fact regarding the subject matter of the contract. In most cases of unilateral mistake, the mistaken party will not be permitted to rescind the contract. The contract will be enforced on its terms.

unilateral mistake
A mistake in which only one party is mistaken about a material fact regarding the subject matter of a contract.

There are three types of situations in which a contract may not be enforced due to a unilateral mistake:

1. One party makes a unilateral mistake of fact, and the other party knew (or should have known) that a mistake was made.
2. A unilateral mistake occurs because of a clerical or mathematical error that is not the result of gross negligence.
3. The mistake is so serious that enforcing the contract would be unconscionable.[1]

Words are chameleons, which reflect the color of their environment.

Justice L. Hand
Commissioner v. National Carbide Co. (1948)

Example Suppose Trent wants to purchase a new car from the showroom floor. He looks at several models. Although he decides to purchase a car with a sunroof, he does not tell the salesperson about his preference. The model named in the contract he signs does not have this feature, although he believes it does. Trent's unilateral mistake will not relieve him of his contractual obligation to purchase the car.

In the following case, the court had to decide whether to allow a party to rescind a contract because of the party's unilateral mistake.

CASE 1 Unilateral Mistake

Wells Fargo Credit Corporation v. Martin

650 So.2d 531, Web 1992 Fla.App. Lexis 9927 (1992)
Court of Appeal of Florida

"We accept the trial court's conclusion that the amount of the sale was grossly inadequate. This inadequacy, however, occurred due to an avoidable, unilateral mistake by an agent of Wells Fargo."

—Judge Altenbernd

Facts

Wells Fargo Credit Corporation (Wells Fargo) obtained a judgment of foreclosure on a house owned by Mr. and Mrs. Clevenger. The total indebtedness stated in the judgment was $207,141. The foreclosure sale was scheduled for

11:00 A.M. July 12, 1991, at the west front door of the Hillsborough County Courthouse.

Wells Fargo was represented by a paralegal, who had attended more than 1,000 similar sales. Wells Fargo's handwritten instruction sheet informed the paralegal to make one bid at $115,000, the tax-appraised value of the property. Because the first "1" in the number was close to the "$," the paralegal misread the bid instruction as $15,000 and opened the bidding at that amount.

Harley Martin, who was attending his first judicial sale, bid $20,000. The county clerk gave ample time for another bid and then announced, "$20,000 going once, $20,000 going twice, sold to Harley. . . ." The paralegal screamed, "Stop, I'm sorry. I made a mistake!" The certificate of sale was issued to Martin. Wells Fargo filed suit to set aside the judicial sale based on its unilateral mistake. The trial court held for Martin. Wells Fargo appealed.

Issue

Does Wells Fargo's unilateral mistake constitute grounds for setting aside the judicial sale?

Language of the Court

We accept the trial court's conclusion that the amount of the sale was grossly inadequate. This inadequacy, however, occurred due to an avoidable, unilateral mistake by an agent of Wells Fargo. As between Wells Fargo and a good faith purchaser at the judicial sale, the trial court had the discretion to place the risk of this mistake upon Wells Fargo.

Thus, we affirm the trial court's orders denying relief to Wells Fargo. We are certain that this result seems harsh to Wells Fargo. Nevertheless, Mr. Martin's bid was accepted when the clerk announced "sold." Without ruling that a unilateral mistake by the complaining party could never justify relief, we hold that the trial court had the discretion under these facts to make Wells Fargo suffer the loss.

Decision

The appellate court held that Wells Fargo's unilateral mistake did not entitle it to relief from the judicial sale.

Case Questions

Critical Legal Thinking What is a unilateral mistake? Explain.

Business Ethics Did Martin act ethically in trying to enforce the judicial sale after being informed of the mistake? What would you have done in similar circumstances?

Contemporary Business Should a contract be allowed to be rescinded because of a unilateral mistake? What would be the danger if the assertion of unilateral mistakes could undo contracts?

Mutual Mistake of Fact

A party may rescind a contract if there has been a **mutual mistake of a past or existing material fact.**[2] A **material fact** is a fact that is important to the subject matter of a contract. An ambiguity in a contract may constitute a mutual mistake of a material fact. An ambiguity occurs where a word or term in the contract is susceptible to more than one logical interpretation. If there has been a mutual mistake, the contract may be rescinded on the grounds that no contract has been formed because there has been no "meeting of the minds" between the parties.

mutual mistake of fact
A mistake made by both parties concerning a material fact that is important to the subject matter of a contract.

Example In the celebrated case *Raffles v. Wichelhaus*,[3] which has become better known as the case of the good ship *Peerless*, the parties agreed on a sale of cotton that was to be delivered from Bombay by the ship. There were two ships named *Peerless*, however, and each party, in agreeing to the sale, was referring to a different ship. Because the sailing time of the two ships was materially different, neither party was willing to agree to shipment by the other *Peerless*. The court ruled that there was no binding contract because each party had a different ship in mind when the contract was formed.

Mutual Mistake of Value

A **mutual mistake of value** exists if both parties know the object of the contract but are mistaken as to its value. Here, the contract remains enforceable by either party because the identity of the subject matter of the contract is not at issue. If the rule were different, almost all contracts could later be rescinded by the party who got the "worst" of the deal.

mutual mistake of value
A mistake that occurs if both parties know the object of the contract but are mistaken as to its value.

Example Helen cleans her attic and finds a red and green silkscreen painting of a tomato soup can. She has no use for the painting, so she offers to sell it to Qian for $100. Qian, who thinks that the painting is "cute," accepts the offer and pays Helen $100. It is latter discovered that the painting is worth $2 million because it was painted by the famous American pop artist Andy Warhol. Neither party knew this at the time of contracting. It is a mistake of value. Helen cannot recover the painting.

▶ FRAUD

A misrepresentation occurs when an assertion is made that is not in accord with the facts.[4] An intentional misrepresentation occurs when one person consciously decides to induce another person to rely and act on a misrepresentation. Intentional misrepresentation is commonly referred to as **fraudulent misrepresentation**, or **fraud**. When fraudulent misrepresentation is used to induce another to enter into a contract, the innocent party's assent to the contract is not genuine, and the contract is voidable by the innocent party.[5] The innocent party can either rescind the contract and obtain restitution or enforce the contract and sue for contract damages.

fraudulent misrepresentation
An event that occurs when one person consciously decides to induce another person to rely and act on a misrepresentation. Also called *fraud*.

Proving Fraud

To prove fraud, the following elements must be shown:

- The wrongdoer made a false representation of material fact.
- The wrongdoer intended to deceive the innocent party.
- The innocent party justifiably relied on the misrepresentation.
- The innocent party was injured.

Each of these elements is discussed in the following paragraphs.

Material Misrepresentation of Fact A **misrepresentation** may occur by words (oral or written) or by the conduct of a party. To be actionable as fraud, the misrepresentation must be of a past or existing *material fact*. This means that the misrepresentation must have been a significant factor in inducing the innocent party to enter into the contract. It does not have to have been the sole factor. Statements of opinion or predictions about the future generally do not form the basis for fraud.

Intent to Deceive To prove fraud, the person making the misrepresentation must have either had knowledge that the representation was false or made it without sufficient knowledge of the truth. This is called **scienter** (**"guilty mind"**). The misrepresentation must have been made with the **intent to deceive** the innocent party. Intent can be inferred from the circumstances.

scienter
Knowledge that a representation is false or that it was made without sufficient knowledge of the truth.

A charge of fraud is such a terrible thing to bring against a man that it cannot be maintained in any court unless it is shown that he had a wicked mind.

M. R. Lord Esher
Le Lievre v. Gould (1732)

Reliance on the Misrepresentation A misrepresentation is not actionable unless the innocent party to whom the misrepresentation was directed acted on it. Further, an innocent party who acts in **reliance on a misrepresentation** must justify his or her reliance. Justifiable reliance is generally found unless the innocent party knew that the misrepresentation was false or was so extravagant as to be obviously false.

Injury to the Innocent Party To recover damages, the innocent party must prove that the fraud caused him or her economic **injury**. The measure of damages is the difference between the value of the property as represented and the actual value of the property. This measure of damages gives the innocent party the "benefit of the bargain." In the alternative, the buyer can rescind the contract and recover the purchase price.

Individuals must be on guard in their commercial and personal dealings not to be taken by fraud. Basically, something sounding "too good to be true" is a signal that the situation might be fraudulent. Although the law permits a victim of fraud to rescind the contract and recover damages from the wrongdoer, often the wrongdoer cannot be found or the money has been spent.

Fraud in the Inception

Fraud in the inception, or **fraud in the factum**, occurs if a person is deceived as to the nature of his or her act and does not know what he or she is signing. Contracts involving fraud in the inception are void rather than just voidable.

fraud in the inception
Fraud that occurs if a person is deceived as to the nature of his or her act and does not know what he or she is signing. Also known as fraud in the factum.

Example Heather brings her professor a grade card to sign. The professor signs the grade card on the front without reading the grade card. On the front, however, are contract terms that transfer all of the professor's property to Heather. Here, there is fraud in the inception. The contract is void.

Fraud in the Inducement

Many fraud cases concern **fraud in the inducement**. Here, the innocent party knows what he or she is signing or doing but has been fraudulently induced to enter into the contract. Such contracts are voidable by the innocent party.

fraud in the inducement
Fraud that occurs when the party knows what he or she is signing but has been fraudulently induced to enter into the contract.

Example Lyle tells Candice that he is forming a partnership to invest in drilling for oil in an oil field and invites her to invest in this venture. In reality, though, there is no oil field, and Lyle intends to use whatever money he receives from Candice for his personal expenses. Candice relies on Lyle's statements and invests $30,000 with Lyle. Lyle absconds with Candice's $30,000 investment. Here, there has been fraud in the inducement. Candice has been induced to give Lyle $30,000 based on Lyle's misrepresentation of fact. Candice can rescind the contract and recover the money from Lyle, if she can find him and locate his money or property.

Fraud by Concealment

Fraud by concealment occurs when one party takes specific action to conceal a material fact from another party.[6]

fraud by concealment
Fraud that occurs when one party takes specific action to conceal a material fact from another party.

Example Steel Inc. contracts to buy used manufacturing equipment from United Inc. United Inc. does not show Steel Inc. the repair invoices for repairs to the equipment even though Steel Inc. has asked to see all of the repair invoices for the equipment. Relying on the knowledge that the equipment is in good condition and has never had been repaired, Steel Inc. purchases the equipment from United Inc. If Steel Inc. subsequently discovers that a significant repair record has been concealed by United Inc., Steel Inc. can sue United Inc. for fraud by concealment.

Silence as Misrepresentation

Generally, neither party to a contract owes a duty to disclose all the facts to the other party. Ordinarily, such **silence** is not a misrepresentation unless (1) nondisclosure would cause bodily injury or death, (2) there is a fiduciary relationship (i.e., a relationship of trust and confidence) between the contracting parties, or (3) federal and state statutes require disclosure. The *Restatement (Second) of Contracts* specifies a broader duty of disclosure: Nondisclosure is a misrepresentation if it would constitute a failure to act in "good faith."[7]

Misrepresentation of Law

Usually, a **misrepresentation of law** is not actionable as fraud. The innocent party cannot generally rescind the contract because each party to a contract is assumed to know the law that applies to the transaction, either through his or her own investigation or by hiring a lawyer. There is one major exception to this rule: The misrepresentation will be allowed as grounds for rescission of the contract if one party to the contract is a professional who should know what the law is and intentionally misrepresents the law to a less sophisticated contracting party.[8]

Whoever is detected in a shameful fraud is ever after not believed even if they speak the truth.

Phaedrus (Thrace of Macedonia)

Innocent Misrepresentation

innocent misrepresentation
Fraud that occurs when a person makes a statement of fact that he or she honestly and reasonably believes to be true even though it is not.

An **innocent misrepresentation** occurs when a person makes a statement of fact that he or she honestly and reasonably believes to be true even though it is not. Innocent misrepresentation is not fraud. If an innocent misrepresentation has been made, the aggrieved party may rescind the contract but may not sue for damages. Often, innocent misrepresentation is treated as a mutual mistake.

In the following case, the court found fraud and awarded punitive damages.

CASE 2 Fraud

Krysa v. Payne

176 S.W.3d 150, Web 2005 Mo.App. Lexis 1680 (2005)
Court of Appeals of Missouri

"Punitive damages differ from compensatory damages in that compensatory damages are intended to redress the concrete loss that the plaintiff has suffered by reason of the defendant's wrongful conduct, while the well-established purpose of punitive damages is to inflict punishment and to serve as an example and a deterrent to similar conduct."

—Judge Ellis

Facts

Frank and Shelly Krysa were shopping for a truck to pull their 18-foot trailer. During the course of their search, they visited Payne's Car Company, a used car dealership owned by Emmett Payne. Kemp Crane, a used car salesman, showed the Krysas around the car lot. The Krysas saw an F-350 truck that they were interested in purchasing. Crane told the Krysas that the truck would tow their trailer, that the truck would make it to 400,000 miles, and that it was "a one-owner trade-in." The Krysas took the truck for a test drive and decided to purchase the truck. The Krysas, who had to borrow some of the money from Mrs. Krysas's mother, paid for the truck and took possession.

Later that day, the Krysas noticed that the power locks did not work on the truck. A few days later, the truck took three hours to start. The heater was not working. Mr. Krysa tried to fix some problems and noticed that the radiator was smashed up, the radiator cap did not have a seal, and the thermostat was missing. Mr. Krysa noticed broken glass on the floor underneath the front seats and that the driver's side window had been replaced. Shortly thereafter, Mr. Krysa attempted to tow his trailer, but within 2 miles, he had his foot to the floor trying to get the truck to pull the trailer. A large amount of smoke was pouring out of the back of the truck. Mr. Krysa also noticed that the truck was consuming a lot of oil. Mr. Krysa obtained a CARFAX report for the truck, which showed that the truck had had 13 prior owners. Evidence proved that the truck was actually two halves of different trucks that had been welded together. An automobile expert told the Krysas not to drive the truck because it was unsafe.

Mr. Krysa went back to the dealership to return the truck and get his money back. Payne told Krysa that he would credit the purchase price of the truck toward the purchase of one of the other vehicles on the lot but that he would not give Krysa his money back. Krysa could not find another vehicle on Payne's used car lot that would suit his needs. The Krysas sued Payne for fraudulent nondisclosure and fraudulent misrepresentation, and they sought to recover compensatory and punitive damages. The jury returned a verdict for the Krysas and awarded them $18,449 in compensatory damages and $500,000 in punitive damages. Payne appealed the award of punitive damages.

Issue

Did Payne engage in fraudulent nondisclosure, fraudulent misrepresentation, and reckless disregard for the safety of the Krysas and the public to support the award of $500,000 in punitive damages?

Language of the Court

Punitive damages differ from compensatory damages in that compensatory damages are intended to redress the concrete loss that the plaintiff has suffered by reason of the defendant's wrongful conduct, while the well-established purpose of punitive damages is to inflict punishment and to serve as an example and a deterrent to similar conduct. While the damage actually sustained by the Krysas was relatively small and was economic in nature, the record clearly supports a finding that Payne acted indifferently to or in reckless disregard of the safety of the Krysas in selling them a vehicle that he knew or should have known was not safe to drive and that the potential harm to the Krysas was much greater than the harm that was actually incurred.

The evidence also supported a finding that the harm sustained by Krysas was the result of intentional malice, trickery, or deceit, and was not merely an accident. Payne had a significant amount of work done to the vehicle to make it appear to be in good shape. This included, among numerous other repairs, straightening both the bed and cab of the truck. Payne's salesman, Crane, lied to the Krysas on several occasions about the condition of the truck, its origin, and its capabilities. This evidence, in addition to other evidence previously described, sufficiently established that Payne affirmatively misrepresented the condition of the F-350 to the Krysas in an attempt to trick them into buying the vehicle.

In sum, while the harm actually sustained by the Krysas in this case was economic as opposed to physical, Payne's conduct did pose a significant risk to the physical welfare of Respondents and evinced an indifference to or reckless disregard of the health or safety of Krysas and the general public as well. Furthermore, the conduct was consistent with Payne's regular business practices and was not an isolated incident, involved acts of intentional trickery and deceit, and targeted victims that were financially vulnerable. Thus, in society's eyes, viewing the totality of the circumstances, Payne's conduct can only be seen as exhibiting a very high degree of reprehensibility.

Payne contends that the ratio between the actual damages awarded, $18,449.53, and the punitive award, $500,000, is grossly excessive, in that the ratio of punitive to actual damages is approximately 27:1. The initial problem with Payne's argument is that it fails to consider the evidence of the potential harm that could have been sustained by the Krysas. In this case, given the relatively small amount of actual damages awarded, the egregious nature of Payne's acts, Payne's open refusal to alter his behavior, and the magnitude of the potential harm that could have been sustained had the structural problems with the truck not been discovered by the Krysas's expert, the ratio of the punitive to actual damages does not, in and of itself, offend due process.

Decision

The court of appeals found that Payne's fraudulent concealment, fraudulent misrepresentation, and reckless disregard for the safety of the Krysas and the public justified the award of $500,000 of punitive damages to the Krysas.

Case Questions

Critical Legal Thinking What is fraudulent concealment? What is fraudulent misrepresentation?

Business Ethics Did Payne, the used car dealer, act ethically in this case? Should punitive damages have been awarded in this case? Why or why not?

Contemporary Business Do you have any apprehension about purchasing a car from a used car dealership? Why or why not?

CONCEPT SUMMARY

TYPES OF MISREPRESENTATION

	Legal Party May: Consequences—Innocent for	
Type of Misrepresentation	**Sue for Damages**	**Rescind Contract**
Fraud in the inception	Yes	Yes
Fraud in the inducement	Yes	Yes
Fraud by concealment	Yes	Yes
Silence as misrepresentation	Yes	Yes
Misrepresentation of law	Usually no	Usually no
Innocent misrepresentation	No	Yes

▶ DURESS

Duress occurs when one party threatens to do some wrongful act unless the other party enters into a contract. If a party to a contract has been forced into making the contract, the assent is not voluntary. Such a contract is not enforceable against the innocent party. If someone threatens to physically harm another person unless that person signs a contract, this is *physical duress*. If the victim of the duress signs the contract, it cannot be enforced against the victim.

duress
A situation in which one party threatens to do a wrongful act unless the other party enters into a contract.

The threat to commit extortion unless someone enters into a contract constitutes duress. So does a threat to bring (or not drop) a criminal lawsuit. Such threats are duress even if the criminal lawsuit is well founded.[9] A threat to bring (or not drop) a civil lawsuit, however, does not constitute duress unless such a suit is frivolous or brought in bad faith.

EQUITY: UNDUE INFLUENCE

undue influence
A situation in which one person takes advantage of another person's mental, emotional, or physical weakness and unduly persuades that person to enter into a contract; the persuasion by the wrongdoer must overcome the free will of the innocent party.

The courts may permit the rescission of a contract based on the equitable doctrine of **undue influence**. Undue influence occurs when one person (the **dominant party**) takes advantage of another person's mental, emotional, or physical weakness and unduly persuades that person (the **servient party**) to enter into a contract. The persuasion by the wrongdoer must overcome the free will of the innocent party. A contract that is entered into because of undue influence is voidable by the innocent party.[10]

The following elements must be shown to prove undue influence:

- A fiduciary or confidential relationship must have existed between the parties.
- The dominant party must have unduly used his or her influence to persuade the servient party to enter into a contract.

The meaning of words varies according to the circumstances of and concerning which they are used.

Justice Blackburn
Allgood v. Blake (1873)

If there is a confidential relationship between persons—such as a lawyer and a client, a doctor and a patient, a psychiatrist and a patient—any contract made by the servient party that benefits the dominant party is presumed to be entered into under undue influence. This rebuttable presumption can be overcome through proper evidence.

Example Mr. Johnson, 70 years old, has a stroke and is partially paralyzed. He is required to use a wheelchair, and he needs constant nursing care. Prior to his stroke, Mr. Johnson had executed a will, leaving his property upon his death equally to his four grandchildren. Edward, a licensed nurse, is hired to care for Mr. Johnson on a daily basis, and Mr. Johnson relies on Edward's care. Edward works for Mr. Johnson for 2 years before Mr. Johnson passes away. It is later discovered that Mr. Johnson had executed a written contract with Edward three months before he died, deeding a valuable piece of real estate to Edward. If it is shown that Edward has used his dominant and fiduciary position to unduly influence Mr. Johnson to enter into this contract, then the contract is invalid. If no undue influence is shown, the contract with Edward is valid, and Edward will receive the property deeded to him by Mr. Johnson.

Mongolia *In Mongolia, many contracts are oral agreements where a person's word is as good as a bond. In countries where the nomadic form of living is prevalent, herders graze their animals on land owned by the government. Mongolia is a country where a large proportion of the country's residents still live the nomadic lifestyle. They have little access to lawyers or courts, so contract disputes are settled by members of the nomadic society.*

TEST REVIEW TERMS AND CONCEPTS

Dominant party
Duress
Fraud by concealment
Fraud in the inception (fraud in the factum)
Fraud in the inducement
Fraudulent misrepresentation (fraud)
Genuineness of assent
Injury to the innocent party
Innocent misrepresentation
Intent to deceive
Material fact
Material misrepresentation of fact
Misrepresentation of law
Mistake
Mutual mistake of a past or existing material fact
Mutual mistake of value
Reliance on a misrepresentation
Rescission
Scienter ("guilty mind")
Servient party
Silence as misrepresentation
Undue influence
Unilateral mistake

CASE PROBLEMS

1 Unilateral Mistake Mrs. Chaney died, leaving a house in Annapolis, Maryland. The representative of her estate listed the property for sale with a real estate broker, stating that the property was approximately 15,650 square feet. Drs. Steele and Faust made an offer of $300,000 for the property, which was accepted by the estate. A contract for the sale of the property was signed by all the parties. When a subsequent survey (done before the deed was transferred) showed that the property had an area of 22,047 square feet, the estate requested the buyers to pay more money for the property. When the estate refused to transfer the property to the buyers, they sued for specific performance. Can the estate rescind the contract? *Steele v. Goettee*, 313 Md. 11, 542 A.2d 847, **Web** 1988 Md. Lexis 91 (Court of Appeals of Maryland)

2 Unilateral Mistake The County of Contra Costa, California, held a tax sale in which it offered for sale a vacant piece of property located in the city of El Cerrito. Richard J. Schultz, a carpenter, saw the notice of the pending tax sale and was interested in purchasing the lot to build a house. Prior to attending the tax sale, Schultz visited and measured the parcel, examined the neighborhood and found the houses there to be "very nice," and had a title search done that turned up no liens or judgments against the property. Schultz did not, however, check with the city zoning department regarding the zoning of the property.

Schultz attended the tax sale and, after spirited bidding, won with a bid of $9,100 and received a deed to the property. Within one week of the purchase, Schultz discovered that the city's zoning laws prevented building a residence on the lot. In essence, the lot was worthless. Schultz sued to rescind the contract. Can the contract be rescinded? *Schultz v. County of Contra Costa, California*, 157 Cal.App.3d 242, 203 Cal.Rptr. 760, **Web** 1984 Cal.App. Lexis 2198 (Court of Appeal of California)

3 Mutual Mistake Ron Boskett, a part-time coin dealer, purchased a dime purportedly minted in 1916 at the Denver Mint; he paid nearly $450. The fact that the "D" on the coin signified Denver mintage made the coin rare and valuable. Boskett sold the coin to Beachcomber Coins, Inc. (Beachcomber), a retail coin dealer, for $500. A principal of Beachcomber examined the coin for 15 to 45 minutes prior to its purchase. Soon thereafter, Beachcomber received an offer of $700 for the coin, subject to certification of its genuineness by the American Numismatic Society. When this organization labeled the coin counterfeit, Beachcomber sued Boskett to rescind the purchase of the coin. Can Beachcomber rescind the contract? *Beachcomber Coins, Inc. v. Boskett*, 166 N.J. Super. 442, 400 A.2d 78, **Web** 1979 N.J. Super Lexis 659 (Superior Court of New Jersey)

4 Fraud Robert McClure owned a vehicle salvage and rebuilding business. He listed the business for sale and had a brochure printed that described the business and stated that the business grossed $581,117 and netted $142,727 the prior year. Fred H. Campbell saw the brochure and inquired about buying the business. Campbell hired a CPA to review McClure's business records and tax returns, but the CPA could not reconcile them with the income claimed for the business in the brochure. When Campbell asked McClure about the discrepancy, McClure stated that the business records did—and tax returns did not—accurately reflect the cash flow or profits of the business because it was such a high-cash operation, with much of the cash not being reported to the Internal Revenue Service on tax returns. McClure signed a warranty which stated that the true income of the business was as represented in the brochure.

Campbell bought the business based on McClure's representations. However, the business, although operated in substantially the same manner as when owned by McClure, failed to yield a net income similar to that warranted by McClure. Evidence showed that McClure's representations were substantially overstated. Campbell sued McClure for damages for fraud. Who wins? *Campbell v. McClure*, 182 Cal.App.3d 806, 227 Cal.Rptr. 450, **Web** 1986 Cal. App.Lexis 1751 (Court of Appeal of California)

5 Fraud James L. "Skip" Deupree, a developer, was building a development of townhouses called Point South in Destin, Florida. All the townhouses in the development were to have individual boat slips. Sam and Louise Butner, husband and wife, bought one of the townhouses. The sales contract between Deupree and the Butners provided that a boat slip would be built and was included in the price of the townhouse. The contract stated that permission from the Florida

Department of Natural Resources (DNR) had to be obtained to build the boat slips. It is undisputed that a boat slip adds substantially to the value of the property and that the Butners relied on the fact that the townhouse would have a boat slip.

Prior to the sale of the townhouse to the Butners, the DNR had informed Deupree that it objected to the plan to build the boat slips and that permission to build them would probably not be forthcoming. Deupree did not tell the Butners this information but instead stated that there would be "no problem" getting permission from the state to build the boat slips. The Butners purchased the townhouse. When the DNR would not approve the building of the boat slips for the Butners' townhouse, they sued for damages for fraud. Who wins? *Deupree v. Butner*, 522 So.2d 242, **Web** 1988 Ala. Lexis 55 (Supreme Court of Alabama)

6 Innocent Misrepresentation W. F. Yost, who owned the Red Barn Barbecue Restaurant (Red Barn), listed it for sale. Richard and Evelyn Ramano of Rieve Enterprises, Inc. (Rieve), were interested in buying the restaurant. After visiting and conducting a visual inspection of the premises, Rieve entered into a contract to purchase the assets and equipment of Red Barn, as well as the five-year lease of, and option to buy, the land and the building. Prior to the sale, the restaurant had been cited for certain health violations that Yost had corrected. In the contract of sale, Yost warranted that "the premises will pass all inspections" to conduct the business.

Rieve took possession immediately after the sale and operated the restaurant. After two weeks, when the Board of Health conducted a routine inspection, it cited 52 health code violations and thereupon closed the restaurant. Rieve sued to rescind the purchase agreement. Evidence established that Yost's misrepresentations were innocently made. Can Rieve rescind the contract? *Yost v. Rieve Enterprises, Inc.*, 461 So.2d 178, **Web** 1984 Fla.App. Lexis 16490 (Court of Appeals of Florida)

7 Duress Judith and Donald Eckstein were married and had two daughters. Years later, Judith left the marital abode in the parties' jointly owned Volkswagen van with only the clothes on her back. She did not take the children, who were six and eight years old at the time. She had no funds, and the husband promptly closed the couple's bank account. The wife was unemployed. Shortly after she left, the husband discovered her whereabouts and the location of the van and seized and secreted the van. The husband refused the wife's request to visit or communicate with her children and refused to give her clothing. He told her that she could see the children and take her clothes only if she signed a separation agreement prepared by his lawyer. The wife contacted Legal Aid but was advised that she did not qualify for assistance.

The wife was directed to go to her husband's lawyer's office. A copy of a separation agreement was given to her to read. The separation agreement provided that the wife (1) give custody of the children to her husband, (2) deed her interest in their jointly owned house to the husband, (3) assign her interest in a jointly owned new Chevrolet van to her husband, and (4) waive alimony, support, maintenance, court costs, attorneys' fees, and any right to inheritance in her husband's estate. By the agreement, she was to receive $1,100 cash, her clothes, the Volkswagen van, and any furniture she desired. The wife testified that her husband told her over an interoffice phone in the lawyer's office that if she did not sign the separation agreement, he would get her for desertion, that she would never see her children again, and that she would get nothing—neither her clothes nor the van—unless she signed the agreement. The wife signed the separation agreement. Immediately thereafter, her clothes were surrendered to her, and she was given $1,100 cash and the keys to the Volkswagen van. The husband filed for divorce. The wife filed an answer seeking to rescind the separation agreement. Can she rescind the separation agreement? *Eckstein v. Eckstein*, 38 Md.App. 506, 379 A.2d 757, **Web** 1978 Md.App. Lexis 324. (Court of Special Appeals of Maryland)

8 Undue Influence Conrad Schaneman, Sr., had eight sons and five daughters. He owned an 80-acre farm in the Scotts Bluff area of Nebraska. Conrad was born in Russia and could not read or write English. All of his children had frequent contact with Conrad and helped with his needs. Subsequently, however, his eldest son, Lawrence, advised the other children that he would henceforth manage his father's business affairs. After much urging by Lawrence, Conrad deeded the farm to Lawrence for $23,500. Evidence showed that at the time of the sale, the reasonable fair market value of the farm was between $145,000 and $160,000.

At the time of the conveyance, Conrad was over 80 years old, had deteriorated in health, suffered from heart problems and diabetes, had high and uncontrollable blood sugar levels, weighed almost 300 pounds, had difficulty breathing, could not walk more than 15 feet, and had to have a jackhoist lift him in and out of the bathtub. He was for all purposes an invalid, relying on Lawrence for most of his personal needs, transportation, banking, and other business matters. After Conrad died, the conservators of the estate brought an action to cancel the deed transferring the farm to Lawrence. Can the conservators cancel the deed? *Schaneman v. Schaneman*, 206 Neb. 113, 291 N.W.2d 412, **Web** 1980 Neb. Lexis 823 (Supreme Court of Nebraska)

BUSINESS ETHICS CASES

9 Business Ethics The First Baptist Church of Moultrie, Georgia, invited bids for the construction of a music, education, and recreation building. The bids were to be accompanied by a bid bond of five percent of the bid amount. Barber Contracting Company (Barber Contracting) submitted a bid in the amount of $1,860,000. A bid bond in the amount of five percent of the bid—$93,000—was issued by The American Insurance Company. The bids were opened by the church, and Barber Contracting was the lowest bid.

On the next day, Albert W. Barber, the president of Barber Contracting, informed the church that his company's bid was in error and should have been $143,120 higher. The error was caused in totaling the material costs on Barber Contracting's estimate worksheets. The church had not been provided these worksheets. Barber Contracting sent a letter to the church, stating that it was withdrawing its bid. The next day, the church sent a construction contract to Barber Contracting, containing the original bid amount. When Barber Contracting refused to sign the contract and refused to do the work for the original contract price, the church signed a contract with the second-lowest bidder, H & H Construction and Supply Company, Inc., to complete the work for $1,919,272. The church sued Barber Contracting and The American Insurance Company, seeking to recover the amount of the bid bond. Who wins? Did Barber act ethically in trying to get out of the contract? Did the church act ethically in trying to enforce Barber's bid? *First Baptist Church of Moultrie v. Barber Contracting Co.*, 189 Ga.App. 804, 377 S.E.2d 717, **Web** 1989 Ga.App. Lexis 25 (Court of Appeals of Georgia)

10 Business Ethics Lockheed Missiles & Space Company, Inc. (Lockheed), sent out a request to potential subcontractors, seeking bids for the manufacture of 124 ballast cans for the Trident II nuclear submarines it was building for the U.S. Navy. In February 1989, Lockheed received eight bids, including one from Sulzer Bingham Pumps, Inc. (Sulzer). Sulzer was the lowest bidder, at $6,544,055. The next lowest bid was $10,176,670, and the bids ranged up to $17,766,327. Lockheed itself estimated that the job would cost at least $8.5 million. Lockheed's employees were shocked by Sulzer's bid and thought it was surprisingly low.

Lockheed then inspected Sulzer's Portland facility to evaluate Sulzer's technical capabilities. The inspection revealed that Sulzer would have to make many modifications to its existing facility in order to complete the contract.

Lockheed did not reveal its findings to Sulzer. In addition, it never notified Sulzer that its bid was significantly lower than the next lowest bid and lower than Lockheed's own estimate of the cost of the job as well. Finally, Sulzer was never told that Lockheed suspected that the contract could not be completed at the bid price.

Lockheed accepted Sulzer's bid, and Sulzer started work. Nine months later, Sulzer revised its estimate of the cost of the job and asked Lockheed for an additional $2,110,000 in compensation. When Lockheed rejected this request, Sulzer sued Lockheed, asking the court to either increase the price of the contract to $8,645,000 or, alternatively, to rescind its bid. Did Lockheed act ethically in this case by not notifying Sulzer of the suspected mistake? Did Sulzer act ethically by trying to get out of the contract because of its own economic misjudgments? Legally, who wins? *Sulzer Bingham Pumps, Inc. v. Lockheed Missiles & Space Company, Inc.*, 947 F.2d 1362, **Web** 1991 U.S. App. Lexis 24966 (United States Court of Appeals for the Ninth Circuit)

ENDNOTES

1. *Restatement (Second) of Contracts*, Section 153.
2. *Restatement (Second) of Contracts*, Section 152.
3. 59 Eng. Rep. 375 (1864).
4. *Restatement (Second) of Contracts*, Section 159.
5. *Restatement (Second) of Contracts*, Sections 163 and 164.
6. *Restatement (Second) of Contracts*, Section 160.
7. *Restatement (Second) of Contracts*, Section 161.
8. *Restatement (Second) of Contracts*, Section 170.
9. *Restatement (Second) of Contracts*, Section 177.
10. *Restatement (Second) of Contracts*, Section 176.

STATUTE OF FRAUDS AND EQUITABLE EXCEPTIONS

STATUTE OF FRAUDS AND EQUITABLE EXCEPTIONS

Roger Dixon © Dorling Kindersley

▲ **Contract Signing** *Even written contracts can be subject to interpretation.*

CHAPTER OBJECTIVES

After studying this chapter, you should be able to:

1. List the contracts that must be in writing under the Statute of Frauds.
2. Explain the effect of noncompliance with the Statute of Frauds.
3. Describe how the Statute of Frauds is applicable to the sale of goods.
4. Describe the formality of the writing of contracts and the parol evidence rule.
5. Apply the equity doctrines of *part performance* and *promissory estoppel*.

CHAPTER CONTENTS

"A verbal contract isn't worth the paper it's written on."
—Samuel Goldwyn

INTRODUCTION TO STATUTE OF FRAUDS AND EQUITABLE EXCEPTIONS

Certain types of contracts must be in writing pursuant to the Statute of Frauds. Other issues regarding the form of a contract may arise, such as the form of signature that is required on a written contract, whether a contract can be created by the integration of several documents, whether any previous oral or written agreements between the parties can be given effect, and how contract language should be interpreted. Also, there are several equitable exceptions to the Statute of Frauds—namely the part performance exception and the doctrine of promissory estoppel.

Issues regarding the Statute of Frauds, the formality of the writing of contracts and equitable doctrines that allow exceptions to the Statute of Frauds are discussed in this chapter.

STATUTE OF FRAUDS

In 1677, the English Parliament enacted a statute called "An Act for the Prevention of Frauds and Perjuries." This act required that certain types of contracts had to be in writing and signed by the party against whom enforcement was sought. Today, every U.S. state has enacted a **Statute of Frauds** that requires certain types of contracts to be in *writing*. This statute is intended to ensure that the terms of important contracts are not forgotten, misunderstood, or fabricated. One court stated about the Statute of Frauds, "It is the purpose of the Statute of Frauds to suppress fraud, i.e., cooked-up claims of agreement, sometimes fathered by wish, sometimes imagined in the light of subsequent events, and sometimes simply conjured up."[1]

Statute of Frauds
A state statute that requires certain types of contracts to be in writing.

Writing Requirement

Although the statutes vary slightly from state to state, most states require the following types of contracts to be in writing.[2]

- Contracts involving interests in real property
- Contracts that by their own terms cannot possibly be performed within one year
- Collateral contracts in which a person promises to answer for the debt or duty of another
- Promises made in consideration of marriage
- Contracts for the sale of goods for $500 or more
- Contracts for the lease of goods with payments of $1,000 or more
- Real estate agents' contracts
- Agents' contracts where the underlying contract must be in writing
- Promises to write a will
- Contracts to pay debts barred by the statute of limitations or discharged in bankruptcy
- Contracts to pay compensation for services rendered in negotiating the purchase of a business
- Finder's fee contracts

Statute of Frauds: That unfortunate statute, the misguided application of which has been the cause of so many frauds.

Bacon, Viscount
Morgan v. Worthington (1878)

Generally, an **executory contract** that is not in writing even though the Statute of Frauds requires it to be is unenforceable by either party. The Statute of Frauds is usually raised by one party as a defense to the enforcement of the contract by the other party.

If an oral contract that should have been in writing under the Statute of Frauds is already executed, neither party can seek to **rescind** the contract on the ground of noncompliance with the Statute of Frauds. That is, the contract may be voluntarily performed by the parties.

Don't get it right, just get it written.

James Thurber

Generally, contracts listed in the Statute of Frauds must be in writing to be enforceable. There are several equity exceptions to this rule. The contracts that must be in writing pursuant to the Statute of Frauds and the exceptions to this rule are discussed in the following paragraphs.

Contracts Involving Interests in Real Property

real property
The land itself, as well as buildings, trees, soil, minerals, timber, plants, crops, fixtures and other things permanently affixed to the land or buildings.

Under the Statute of Frauds, any contract that transfers an ownership interest in **real property** must be in writing to be enforceable. Real property includes the land itself, buildings, trees, soil, minerals, timber, plants, crops, fixtures, and things permanently affixed to the land or buildings. Certain items of personal property that are permanently affixed to the real property are fixtures that become part of the real property.

Example Built-in cabinets in a house are *fixtures* that become part of the real property.

Other contracts that transfer an ownership interest in land must be in writing under the Statute of Frauds. These interests include the following:

mortgage
An interest in real property given to a lender as security for the repayment of a loan.

- **Mortgages.** Borrowers often give a lender an interest in real property as security for the repayment of a loan. This action must be done through the use of a written **mortgage** or **deed of trust**.

Example Ida purchases a house for $1 million. She pays $400,000 toward the payment of the house and borrows $600,000 of the purchase price from CityBank. CityBank requires that the house be collateral for the loan and takes a mortgage on the house. Here, the mortgage between Ida and CityBank must be in writing to be enforceable.

lease
The transfer of the right to use real property for a specified period of time.

life estate
An interest in real property for a person's lifetime; upon that person's death, the interest will be transferred to another party.

easement
A right to use someone else's land without owning or leasing it.

- **Leases.** A **lease** is the transfer of the right to use real property for a specified period of time. Most Statutes of Frauds require leases for a term over one year to be in writing.
- **Life estates.** On some occasions, a person is given a **life estate** in real property. In other words, the person has an interest in the real property for the person's lifetime, and the interest will be transferred to another party on that person's death. A life estate is an ownership interest that must be in writing under the Statute of Frauds.
- **Easements.** An **easement** is a given or required right to use another person's land without owning or leasing it. Easements may be either express or implied. Express easements must be in writing to be enforceable, while implied easements need not be written.

One-Year Rule

one-year rule
A rule which states that an executory contract that cannot be performed by its own terms within one year of its formation must be in writing.

According to the Statute of Frauds, an executory contract that cannot be performed by its own terms within one year of its formation must be in writing.[3] This **one-year rule** is intended to prevent disputes about contract terms that may otherwise occur toward the end of a long-term contract. If the performance of the contract is possible within the one-year period, the contract may be oral.

The extension of an oral contract might cause the contract to violate the Statute of Frauds if the original term and the extension period exceed one year.

Example Frederick, the owner of a store, hires Anna as the store manager for 6 months. Assume that after 3 months Frederick and Anna agree to extend the contract for an additional 11 months. At the time of the extension, the contract would be for 14 months (the 3 left on the original contract plus 11 months added by the extension). The modification would have to be in writing because it exceeds the one-year rule.

In the following case, the court held that the one-year rule prohibited the enforcement of an oral contract.

CASE 1 One-Year Rule

Sawyer v. Mills

Web 2007 Ky.App. Lexis 92 Court of Appeals of Kentucky (2007)

"The end result may not seem 'fair' to Sawyer. The Statute of Frauds, by its own terms, can be considered 'harsh' in that it will bar oral agreements between parties under certain conditions. This is simply the nature of the beast."

—Trial Court Judge Ishmael

Facts

Barbara Lucinda Sawyer worked as a paralegal for Melbourne Mills, Jr., an attorney at a law firm. Sawyer proposed that Mills and the law firm become engaged in class action lawsuits. Mills agreed to pay Sawyer an unspecified bonus when "the ship comes in." After Sawyer's assistance and persistence, the law firm became involved in class action litigation—primarily the Fen-Phen class action litigation. After the law firm received millions of dollars in fees from the Fen-Phen class action lawsuits, Sawyer and her husband Steve met with Mills to discuss Sawyers' bonus. Mills orally agreed to pay Sawyer $1,065,000 as a bonus to be paid in monthly installments over 107 months. Sawyer secretly tape recorded the conversation. Mills later refused to sign a written contract conveying the terms of the oral agreement.

After Mills had paid $165,000, he quit making further payments. Sawyer sued Mills to collect the remaining $900,000. Mills defended, arguing that the oral contract exceeded one year and was therefore unenforceable because it was not in writing, as required by the Statute of Frauds. The jury ruled in favor of Sawyer. Mills made a motion to the trial court judge to refuse to enforce the oral contract against him. The trial court heard and decided the motion.

Language of the Court

Sawyer produced no writing signed by Mills consistent with the oral discussions of the parties. Sawyer argues that the "writing" requirement of the Statute of Frauds has been satisfied in this case because of the cassette tape which was played to the jury and which surreptitiously recorded the discussions between Sawyer, her husband, and Mills, taken together with the several checks written by Mills and signed by him totaling $165,000. The Court cannot accept this argument. First of all, the cassette tape recording is not a "writing signed by the party to be charged" as required by the Statute of Frauds. The checks signed by Mills are, at best, evidence confirming the agreement of the parties, i.e., that the total amount of the bonus would be paid out in monthly installments of $10,000 on the first of each month for 107 months. These checks, at best, merely confirm the oral agreement of the parties.

The Court is aware of the apparent harshness of this ruling. The trial jury found, and the Court heard Mills state on the tape recording, that he agreed to make monthly payments to Sawyer which would eventually total over One Million Dollars. Honoring that oral agreement would be the "moral" and "right" thing for Mills to do. However, this Court is obligated by Oath of Office and Kentucky law, to consider cases based on the facts presented and the applicable law. The end result may not seem "fair" to Sawyer. The Statute of Frauds, by its own terms, can be considered "harsh" in that it will bar oral agreements between parties under certain conditions. This is simply the nature of the beast.

Decision

The trial court held that the Statute of Frauds required the bonus agreement between Sawyer and Mills to be in writing to be enforceable. Because the oral agreement exceeded one year, it did not meet the requirements of the Statute of Frauds and is therefore unenforceable. The court of appeals of Kentucky affirmed the trial court's decision.

Case Questions

Critical Legal Thinking What does the one-year rule provide? Explain.

Business Ethics Should Mills do the "moral" and "right" thing and pay the remainder of the money to Sawyer?

Contemporary Business Does the adage "Get it in writing!" mean anymore to you now that you have read this case?

Guaranty Contract

A **guaranty contract** occurs when one person agrees to answer for the debts or duties of another person. Guaranty contracts are required to be in writing under the Statute of Frauds.[4]

In a guaranty situation, there are at least three parties and two contracts (see Exhibit 1). The *first contract*, which is known as the **original contract**, or **primary contract**, is

guaranty contract
A promise in which one person agrees to answer for the debts or duties of another person. It is a contract between the guarantor and the original creditor.

between the debtor and the creditor. It does not have to be in writing (unless another provision of the Statute of Frauds requires it to be). The *second contract*, called the *guaranty contract*, is between the person who agrees to pay the debt if the primary debtor does not (i.e., the **guarantor**) and the original creditor. The guarantor's liability is secondary because it does not arise unless the party primarily liable fails to perform.

guarantor
A person who agrees to pay a debt if the primary debtor does not.

▶ Exhibit 1 GUARANTY CONTRACT

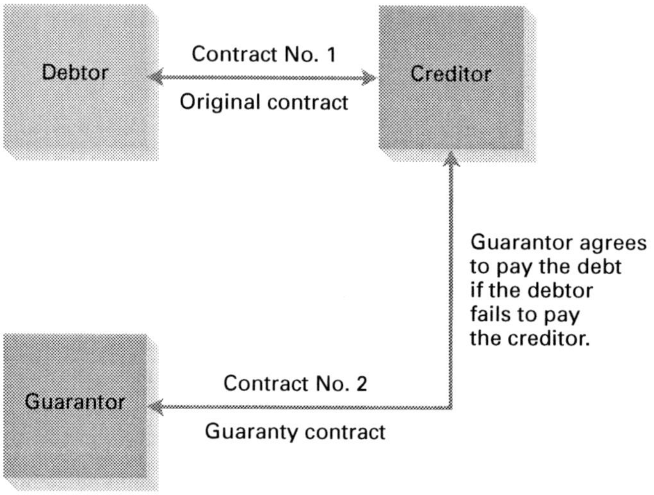

Example Wei, a recent college graduate, offers to purchase a new automobile on credit from a Mercedes-Benz automobile dealership. Because Wei does not have a credit history, the dealer will agree to sell the car to her only if there is a guarantor. If Wei's father signs a written guaranty contract, he becomes responsible for any payments his daughter fails to make. If Wei's father only orally guaranteed Wei's contract, he would not be bound to the guaranty because it was oral.

The "Main Purpose" Exception If the main purpose of a transaction and an oral collateral contract is to provide pecuniary (i.e., financial) benefit to the guarantor, the collateral contract is treated like an original contract and does not have to be in writing to be enforced.[5] This exception is called the **main purpose exception**, or **leading object exception**, to the Statute of Frauds. This exception is intended to ensure that the primary benefactor of the original contract (i.e., the guarantor) is answerable for the debt or duty.

main purpose exception
An exception to the Statute of Frauds which states that if the main purpose of a transaction and an oral collateral contract is to provide pecuniary benefit to the guarantor, the collateral contract does not have to be in writing to be enforced. Also known as the *leading object exception*.

Example Ethel is president and sole shareholder of Computer Corporation, Inc. Assume that (1) the corporation borrows $100,000 from CityBank for working capital, and (2) Ethel orally guarantees to repay the loan if the corporation fails to pay it. CityBank can enforce the oral guaranty contract against Ethel if the corporation does not meet its obligation because the main purpose of the loan was to benefit her as the sole shareholder of the corporation.

In the following case, the court refused to enforce an oral guaranty contract.

CASE 2 Guaranty Contract

Page v. Gulf Coast Motors

903 So.2d 148, Web 2004 Ala. Civ. App. Lexis 982 (2004) Court of Civil Appeal of Alabama

"A promise to pay the debt of another is barred by the Statute of Frauds unless it is in writing."

—Judge Murdock

Facts

Glenn A. Page (Glenn) had a long-term friendship with Jerry Sellers, an owner of Gulf Coast Motors. Glenn began borrowing money from Gulf Coast Motors on a recurring basis during a two-year period. The loan process was informal: Gulf Coast Motors set up a ledger account and recorded each loan made to Glenn, and Glenn would sign the ledger "I agree to pay Jerry Sellers as above." At various times, Glenn would make small payments toward his account, but he would thereafter borrow more money. At the times the loans were made, Glenn was not working and had no assets in his own name. There was no evidence as to what Glenn used the loan proceeds for, but evidence showed that he had a gambling problem.

Sellers testified that toward the end of the two-year period of making loans to Glenn, he telephoned Mary R. Page, Glenn's wife, and Mary orally guaranteed to repay Glenn's loans. Mary had significant assets of her own. Mary denied that she had promised to pay any of Glenn's debt, and she denied that Sellers had asked her to pay Glenn's debt. Gulf Coast Motors sued Glenn and Mary to recover payment for the unpaid loans. The trial court entered judgment in the amount of $23,020 in favor of Gulf Coast Motors. Mary appealed.

Issue

Was Mary's alleged oral promise to guarantee her husband's debts an enforceable guaranty contract?

Language of the Court

> *A promise to pay the debt of another is barred by the Statute of Frauds unless it is in writing. It is not disputed that Mary did not sign a note, guaranty, or any other writing promising to pay any part of Glenn's debts. Therefore, if the purported agreement to pay Glenn's debt is within the Statute of Frauds, Mary is not liable even if the trial court found Seller's testimony to be credible. Mary's alleged oral promises are not enforceable under the Statute of Frauds. We conclude that Mary's alleged promises to guaranty or repay Glenn's debts were within the Statute of Frauds and, therefore, were not enforceable.*

Decision

The court of civil appeals held that Mary's alleged oral promises to guarantee her husband's debts were not in writing, as required by the Statute of Frauds. The court remanded the case to the trial court to enter judgment in Mary's favor.

Case Questions

Critical Legal Thinking What is a guaranty contract? Explain.

Business Ethics Did Glenn act ethically in this case? Would Mary have acted unethically if she had actually orally guaranteed to repay her husband's debts and then raised the Statute of Frauds to prevent enforcement of the oral promises?

Contemporary Business Are guaranty contracts often used in business? Can you think of a situation in which a guaranty contract would be required?

Contract for the Sale of Goods

Section 2-201(1) of the Uniform Commercial Code (UCC) is the basic Statute of Frauds provision for **sales contracts**. It states that contracts for the sale of goods costing *$500 or more* must be in writing to be enforceable. If the contract price of an original sales contract is below $500, it does not have to be in writing under the **UCC Statute of Frauds**. However, if a modification of the sales contract increases the sales price to $500 or more, the *modification* has to be in writing to be enforceable.

UCC Statute of Frauds Section 2-201(1)
A section of the Uniform Commercial Code which states that sales contracts for the sale of goods costing $500 or more must be in writing.

Example Echo enters into an oral contract to sell James her used car for $10,000, with the delivery date to be May 1. When May 1 comes and James tenders $10,000 to Echo, Echo refuses to sell her car to James. The contract will not be enforced against Echo because it was an oral contract for the sale of goods costing $500 or more, and it should have been in writing.

The most recent revision to UCC 2-201 requires that contracts for the sale of goods costing *$5,000 or more* must be in writing to be enforceable. A state must adopt this amendment for it to become effective.

> *To break an oral agreement which is not legally binding is morally wrong.*
>
> Bava Metzi'a
> *The Talmud*

Contract for the Lease of Goods

Section 2A-201(1) of the Uniform Commercial Code (UCC) is the Statute of Frauds provision that applies to the lease of goods. It states that **lease contracts** involving payments of $1,000 or more must be in writing. If a lease payment of an original lease contract is below $1,000, it does not have to be in writing under the UCC Statute of Frauds. However, if a modification of the lease contract increases the lease payment to $1,000 or more, the *modification* has to be in writing to be enforceable.

UCC Statute of Frauds Section 2A-201(1)
A section of the Uniform Commercial Code which states that lease contracts involving payments of $1,000 or more must be in writing.

Agents' Contracts

Many state Statutes of Frauds require that **agents' contracts** to sell real property covered by the Statute of Frauds be in writing to be enforceable. The requirement is often referred to as the **equal dignity rule**.

equal dignity rule
A rule which says that agents' contracts to sell property covered by the Statute of Frauds must be in writing to be enforceable.

Example Barney hires Cynthia, a licensed real estate broker, to sell his house. Because a contract to sell real estate must be in writing pursuant to the Statute of Frauds, the equal dignity rule requires that the real estate agents' contract be in writing as well. Some state Statutes of Frauds expressly state that the real estate broker and agents' contracts must be in writing.

Promises Made in Consideration of Marriage

Under the Statute of Frauds, a unilateral promise to pay money or property in consideration for a promise to marry must be in writing.

Example A **prenuptial agreement**, which is a contract entered into by parties prior to marriage that defines their ownership rights in each other's property, must be in writing.

EQUITY: PART PERFORMANCE

If an oral contract for the sale of land or transfer of another interest in real property has been partially performed, it may not be possible to return the parties to their *status quo*. To solve this problem, the courts have developed the equitable doctrine of **part performance**. This doctrine allows the court to order such an oral contract to be specifically performed if performance is necessary to avoid injustice. For this performance exception to apply, most courts require that the purchaser either pay part of the purchase price and take possession of the property or make valuable improvements on the property.

part performance
An equitable doctrine that allows the court to order an oral contract for the sale of land or transfer of another interest in real property to be specifically performed if it has been partially performed and performance is necessary to avoid injustice.

ETHICS SPOTLIGHT

Equity: Part Performance

"The doctrine of part performance by the purchaser is a well-recognized exception to the Statute of Frauds as applied to contracts for the sale of real property."

—Judge Kline, P. J.

Arlene and Donald Warner inherited a home at 101 Molimo Street in San Francisco. The Warners obtained a $170,000 loan on the property. Donald Warner and Kenneth Sutton were friends. Donald Warner proposed that Sutton and his wife purchase the residence. His proposal included a $15,000 down payment toward the purchase price of $185,000. The Suttons were to pay all the mortgage payments and real estate taxes on the property for five years, and at any time during the five-year period, they could purchase the house. All this was agreed to orally.

The Suttons paid the down payment and cash payments equal to the monthly mortgage to the Warners. The Suttons paid the annual property taxes on the house. The Suttons also made improvements to the property. Four and one-half years later, the Warners reneged on the oral sales/option agreement. At that time, the house had risen in value to between $250,000 and $320,000. The Suttons sued for specific performance of the sales agreement. The Warners defended, alleging that the oral promise to sell real estate had to be in writing under the Statute of Frauds and was therefore unenforceable.

The trial court applied the equitable doctrine of part performance and ordered the Warners to specifically perform the oral contract. The court of appeal, which agreed, stated:

> *The doctrine of part performance by the purchaser is a well-recognized exception to the Statute of Frauds as applied to contracts for the sale of real property. The actions taken by the Suttons in reliance upon the oral agreement, when considered together with the Warners' admission that there was an oral agreement of some duration, satisfy the elements of the part performance doctrine.*

The court of appeal held that the equitable doctrine of part performance made the oral contract for the sale of real property in this case enforceable. *Sutton v. Warner*, 12 Cal.App.4th 415, 15 Cal.Rptr.2d 632, **Web** 1993 Cal.App. Lexis 22 (Court of Appeal of California)

Business Ethics What does the equitable doctrine of part performance provide? Did the Statute of Frauds give the Warners a justifiable reason not to go through with the deal?

FORMALITY OF THE WRITING

Some written commercial contracts are long, detailed documents that have been negotiated by the parties and drafted and reviewed by their lawyers. Others are preprinted forms with blanks that can be filled in to fit the facts of a particular situation.

Most of the disputes in the world arise from words.

Lord Mansfield, C. J.
Morgan v. Jones (1773)

A written contract does not, however, have to be either drafted by a lawyer or formally typed to be legally binding. Generally, the law only requires a writing containing the essential terms of the parties' agreement. Thus, any writing—including letters, telegrams, invoices, sales receipts, checks, and handwritten agreements written on scraps of paper—can be an enforceable contract under this rule.

Required Signature

The Statute of Frauds and the UCC require a written contract, whatever its form, to be signed *by the party against whom enforcement is sought*. The signature of the person who is enforcing the contract is not necessary. Thus, a written contract may be enforceable against one party but not the other party.

Generally, the signature may appear anywhere on the writing. In addition, it does not have to be a person's full legal name. The person's last name, first name, nickname, initials, seal, stamp, engraving, or other symbol or mark (e.g., an *X*) that indicates the person's intent can be binding. The signature may be affixed by an authorized agent.

If a signature is suspected of being forged, the victim can hire handwriting experts and use modern technology to prove it is not his or her signature.

Integration of Several Writings

Both the common law of contracts and the UCC permit several writings to be **integrated** to form a single written contract. That is, the entire writing does not have to appear in one document to be an enforceable contract.

integration of several writings
The combination of several writings to form a single contract.

Integration may be by an *express reference* in one document that refers to and incorporates another document within it. This procedure is called **incorporation by reference**. Thus, what may often look like a simple one-page contract may actually be hundreds of pages long when all of the documents incorporated by reference are considered.

incorporation by reference
Integration made by express reference in one document that refers to and incorporates another document within it.

Example Credit card contracts often incorporate by express reference such documents as the master agreement between the issuer and cardholders, subsequent amendments to the agreement, and such.

Several documents may be integrated to form a single written contract if they are somehow physically attached to each other to indicate a party's intent to show integration. Attaching several documents together with a staple, paper clip, or some other means may indicate integration. Placing several documents in the same container (e.g., an envelope) may also indicate integration. Such an action is called *implied integration*.

Interpreting Contract Words and Terms

When contracts are at issue in a lawsuit, courts are often called upon to interpret the meaning of certain contract words or terms. The parties to a contract may define the words and terms used in their contract. Many written contracts contain a detailed definition section—usually called a **glossary**—that defines many of the words and terms used in the contract.

If the parties have not defined the words and terms of a contract, the courts apply the following **standards of interpretation**:

- *Ordinary* words are given their usual meaning according to the dictionary.
- *Technical words* are given their technical meaning, unless a different meaning is clearly intended.

Counsel Randle Jackson: In the book of nature, my lords, it is written—
—Lord Ellenborough: Will you have the goodness to mention the page, sir, if you please?

Lord Campbell
Lives of the Chief Justices (1857)

- *Specific terms* are presumed to qualify *general terms*. For example, if a provision in a contract refers to the subject matter as "corn," but a later provision refers to the subject matter as "feed corn" for cattle, this specific term qualifies the general term.
- If both parties are members of the same trade or profession, words will be given their meaning as used in the trade (i.e., *usage of trade*). If the parties do not want trade usage to apply, the contract must indicate that.
- Where a preprinted form contract is used, *typed words* in a contract prevail over *preprinted words*. *Handwritten words* prevail over both preprinted and typed words.
- If there is an ambiguity in a contract, the ambiguity will be resolved against the party who drafted the contract.

PAROL EVIDENCE RULE

By the time a contract is reduced to writing, the parties usually have engaged in prior or contemporaneous discussions and negotiations or exchanged prior writings. Any oral or written words outside the *four corners* of the written contract are called **parol evidence**. *Parol* means "word."

parol evidence
Any oral or written words outside the four corners of a written contract.

The **parol evidence rule** was originally developed by courts as part of the common law of contracts. The UCC has adopted the parol evidence rule for sales and lease contracts.[6] The parol evidence rule states that if a written contract is a complete and final statement of the parties' agreement (i.e., a **complete integration**), any prior or contemporaneous oral or written statements that alter, contradict, or are in addition to the terms of the written contract are inadmissible in any court proceeding concerning the contract.[7] In other words, a completely integrated contract is viewed as the best evidence of the terms of the parties' agreement.

parol evidence rule
A rule that says if a written contract is a complete and final statement of the parties' agreement, any prior or contemporaneous oral or written statements that alter, contradict, or are in addition to the terms of the written contract are inadmissible in court regarding a dispute over the contract. There are several exceptions to this rule.

Merger, or Integration, Clause

The parties to a written contract may include a clause stipulating that the contract is a complete integration and the exclusive expression of their agreement and that parol evidence may not be introduced to explain, alter, contradict, or add to the terms of the contract. This type of clause, called a **merger clause**, or an **integration clause**, expressly reiterates the parol evidence rule.

merger clause
A clause in a contract that stipulates that it is a complete integration and the exclusive expression of the parties' agreement. Also known as an *integration clause*.

Exceptions to the Parol Evidence Rule

There are several major exceptions to the parol evidence rule. Parol evidence may be admitted in court if it:

- Shows that a contract is void or voidable (e.g., evidence that the contract was induced by fraud, misrepresentation, duress, undue influence, or mistake).
- Explains ambiguous language.
- Concerns *a prior course of dealing or course of performance* between the parties or a *usage of trade*.[8]
- *Fills in the gaps* in a contract (e.g., if a price term or time of performance term is omitted from a written contract, the court can hear parol evidence to imply the reasonable price or time of performance under the contract).
- Corrects an obvious clerical or typographical error. The court can *reform* the contract to reflect the correction.

The meaning of words varies according to the circumstances of and concerning which they are used.

Justice Blackburn
Allgood v. Blake (1873)

EQUITY: PROMISSORY ESTOPPEL

The doctrine of **promissory estoppel**, or **equitable estoppel**, is another equitable exception to the strict application of the Statute of Frauds. The version of promissory estoppel in the *Restatement (Second) of Contracts* provides that if parties enter into an oral contract that should be in writing under the Statute of Frauds, the oral promise is enforceable against the promisor if three conditions are met: (1) The promise induces action or forbearance of action by another, (2) the reliance on the oral promise was foreseeable, and (3) injustice can be avoided only by

promissory estoppel
An equitable doctrine that permits enforcement of oral contracts that should have been in writing. It is applied to avoid injustice. Also known as *equitable estoppel*.

enforcing the oral promise.[9] Where this doctrine applies, the promisor is *estopped* (*prevented*) from raising the Statute of Frauds as a defense to the enforcement of the oral contract.

Impression Made by an Eighteenth-Century Chinese Civil Service Seal *In China, Vietnam, Japan, and other countries of Asia, individuals often follow the age-old tradition of using a stamp as their signature. Government organizations and businesses have to use stamps on contracts and other documents of official business. The stamp is a character or set of characters carved onto one end of a cylinder-shaped piece—made out of ivory, jade, agate, gold, animal's horn, wood, or plastic. The owner places the end bearing the characters in ink and then applies this end to the document to be signed, leaving an ink imprint that serves as the owner's signature. The ink is red—thus the saying "red head" document. In China it is called a chop, in Japan it is called a hanko, and in Vietnam it is called a seal. These seals are registered with the government. Younger persons in these countries are increasingly using hand-applied signatures instead of traditional seals.*

TEST REVIEW TERMS AND CONCEPTS

Agents' contract
Complete integration
Easement
Equal dignity rule
Executory contract
Glossary
Guarantor
Guaranty contract
Incorporation by reference
Integration of several writings
Lease
Lease contract
Life estate
Main purpose exception (leading object exception)
Merger clause (integration clause)
Mortgage (deed of trust)
One-year rule
Original contract (primary contract)
Parol evidence
Parol evidence rule
Part performance
Prenuptial agreement
Promissory estoppel (equitable estoppel)
Real property
Rescission
Sales contract
Section 2-201(1) of the Uniform Commercial Code (UCC)
Section 2A-201(1) of the Uniform Commercial Code (UCC)
Standards of interpretation
Statute of Frauds
UCC Statute of Frauds

CASE PROBLEMS

1 Statute of Frauds Fritz Hoffman and Fritz Frey contracted the Sun Valley Company (Company) about purchasing a 1.64-acre piece of property known as the "Ruud Mountain Property," located in Sun Valley, Idaho, from Company. Mr. Conger, a representative of Company, was authorized to sell the property, subject to the approval of the executive committee of Company. Conger reached an agreement on the telephone with Hoffman and Frey, whereby they would purchase the property for $90,000, payable at 30 percent down, with the balance to be payable quarterly at an annual interest rate of 9.25 percent. The next day, Hoffman sent Conger a letter confirming the conversation.

The executive committee of Company approved the sale. Sun Valley Realty prepared the deed of trust, note, seller's closing statement, and other loan documents. However, before the documents were executed by either side, Sun Valley Company sold all its assets, including the Ruud Mountain property, to another purchaser. When the new owner refused to sell the Ruud Mountain lot to Hoffman and Frey, they brought this action for specific performance of the oral contract. Who wins? *Hoffman v. Sun Valley Company*, 102 Idaho 187, 628 P.2d 218, **Web** 1981 Ida. Lexis 320 (Supreme Court of Idaho)

2 Real Property Robert Briggs and his wife purchased a home located at 167 Lower Orchard Drive, Levittown, Pennsylvania. They made a down payment and borrowed the balance on a 30-year mortgage. Six years later, when Mr. and Mrs. Briggs were behind on their mortgage payments, they entered into an oral contract to sell the house to Winfield and Emma Sackett if the Sacketts would pay the three months' arrearages on the loan and agree to make the future payments on the mortgage. Mrs. Briggs and Mrs. Sackett were sisters. The Sacketts paid the arrearages, moved into the house, and continued to live there. Fifteen years later, Robert Briggs filed an action to void the oral contract as in violation of the Statute of Frauds and evict the Sacketts from the house. Who wins? *Briggs v. Sackett*, 275 Pa. Super. 13, 418 A.2d 586, **Web** 1980 Pa.Super. Lexis 2034 (Superior Court of Pennsylvania)

3 One-Year Contract Robert S. Ohanian was vice president of sales for the West Region of Avis Rent a Car System, Inc. (Avis). Officers of Avis testified that Ohanian's performance in the West Region was excellent, and, in a depressed economic period, Ohanian's West Region stood out as the one region that was growing and profitable. In the fall of 1980, when Avis's Northeast Region was doing badly, the president of Avis asked Ohanian to take over that region. Ohanian was reluctant to do so because he and his family liked living in San Francisco, and he had developed a good team in the West Region, was secure in his position, and feared the politics of the Northeast Region. Ohanian agreed to the transfer only after the general manager of Avis orally told him "unless you screw up badly, there is no way you are going to get fired— you will never get hurt here in this company." Ohanian did a commendable job in the Northeast Region. Approximately one year later, at the age of 47, Ohanian was fired without cause by Avis. Ohanian sued Avis for breach of the oral lifetime contract. Avis asserted the Statute of Frauds against this claim. Who wins? *Ohanian v. Avis Rent a Car System, Inc.*, 779 F.2d 101, **Web** 1985 U.S. App. Lexis 25456 (United States Court of Appeals for the Second Circuit)

4 Guaranty Contract David Brown met with Stan Steele, a loan officer with the Bank of Idaho (now First Interstate Bank) to discuss borrowing money from the bank to start a new business. After learning that he did not qualify for the loan on the basis of his own financial strength, Brown told Steele that his former employers, James and Donna West of California, might be willing to guarantee the payment of the loan. Steele talked to Mr. West, who orally stated on the telephone that he would personally guarantee the loan to Brown. Based on this guaranty, the bank loaned Brown the money. The bank sent a written guarantee to Mr. and Mrs. West for their signatures, but it was never returned to the bank. When Brown defaulted on the loan, the bank filed suit against the Wests to recover on their guaranty contract. Are the Wests liable? *First Interstate Bank of Idaho, N.A. v. West*, 107 Idaho 851, 693 P.2d 1053, **Web** 1984 Ida. Lexis 600 (Supreme Court of Idaho)

5 Guaranty Contract Six persons, including Benjamin Rosenbloom and Alfred Feiler, were members of the board of directors of the Togs Corporation. A bank agreed to loan the corporation $250,000 if the members of the board would personally guarantee the payment of the loan. Feiler objected to signing the guaranty to the bank because of other pending personal financial negotiations that the contingent liability of the guaranty might adversely affect. Feiler agreed with Rosenbloom and the other board members that if they were held personally liable on the guaranty, he would pay his one-sixth share of that amount to them directly. Rosenbloom and the other members of the board signed the personal guaranty with the bank, and the bank made the loan to the corporation. When the corporation defaulted on the loan, the five guarantors had to pay the loan amount to the bank. When they attempted to collect a one-sixth share from Feiler, he refused to pay, alleging that his oral promise had to be in writing under the Statute of Frauds. Does Feiler have to pay the one-sixth share to the other board members? *Feiler V. Rosenbloom*, 46 Md.App. 297, 416 A.2d 1345, **Web** 1980 Md.App. Lexis 328 (Court of Special Appeals of Maryland)

6 Agent's Contract Paul L. McGirr operated an Enco service station in Los Angeles that sold approximately 25,000 to 35,000 gallons of gasoline a month. McGirr telephoned Gulf Oil Corporation (Gulf) regarding an advertisement for dealers. McGirr met with Theodore Marks, an area representative of Gulf, to discuss the possibility of McGirr's operating a Gulf service station. McGirr asked Marks if Gulf had any good, high-producing units available. Marks replied that he had a station at the corner of Figueroa and Avenue 26 that sold about 200,000 gallons of gasoline a month. Marks told McGirr that this station would not be available for about 90 days because Gulf had to terminate the arrangement with the current operator of the station. Marks told McGirr that he could have the Figueroa station only if he also took a "dog" station on Garvey Avenue. Marks agreed to take this station only if he also was assured he would get the Figueroa station. Marks assured him he would. When McGirr asked Marks for this assurance in writing, Marks stated that he did not have to put it in writing because he was the "kingpin in his territory." So they shook hands on the deal.

McGirr terminated his arrangement with Enco and moved to the Garvey Avenue station. He signed a written lease for the Garvey station, which was signed by Max Reed, Gulf's regional sales manager. Under the Statute of Frauds, the lease for a service station must be in writing. Nothing in writing was ever signed by the parties regarding the Figueroa station. A few months later, Marks was transferred to a different territory, and Gulf refused to lease the Figueroa station to McGirr. McGirr sued Marks and Gulf for breach of an oral contract. Is Marks or Gulf liable? *McGirr v. Gulf Oil Corporation*, 41 Cal.App. 3d 246, 115 Cal.Rptr. 902, **Web** 1974 Cal.App. Lexis 783 (Court of Appeal of California)

7 Promissory Estoppel The Atlantic Wholesale Co., Inc. (Atlantic), located in Florence, South Carolina, was in the business of buying and selling gold and silver for customers' accounts. Gary A. Solondz, a New York resident, became a customer of Atlantic and thereafter made several purchases through Atlantic. One day, Solondz telephoned Atlantic and received a quotation on silver bullion. Solondz then bought 300 ounces of silver for a total price of $12,978. Atlantic immediately contracted United Precious Metals in Minneapolis and purchased the silver for Solondz. The silver was shipped to Atlantic, which paid for it.

Atlantic placed the silver in its vault while it waited for payment from Solondz. When Atlantic telephoned Solondz about payment, he told Atlantic to continue to hold the silver in its vault until he decided whether to sell it. Meanwhile, the price of silver had fallen substantially and continued to fall. When Solondz refused to pay for the silver, Atlantic sold it for $4,650, sustaining a loss of $8,328. When Atlantic sued Solondz to recover this loss, Solondz asserted that the Statute of Frauds prevented enforcement of his oral promise to buy the silver. Does the doctrine of promissory estoppel prevent the application of the Statute of Frauds in this case? *Atlantic Wholesale Co., Inc. v. Solondz*, 283 S.C. 36, 320 S.E.2d 720, **Web** 1984 S.C. App. Lexis 555 (Court of Appeals of South Carolina)

8 Sufficiency of a Writing Irving Levin and Harold Lipton owned the San Diego Clippers Basketball Club, a professional basketball franchise. Levin and Lipton met with Philip Knight to discuss the sale of the Clippers to Knight. After the meeting, they all initialed a three-page handwritten memorandum that Levin had drafted during the meeting. The memorandum outlined the major terms of their discussion, including subject matter, price, and the parties to the agreement. Levin and Lipton forwarded to Knight a letter and proposed sale agreement. Two days later, Knight informed Levin that he had decided not to purchase the Clippers. Levin and Lipton sued Knight for breach of contract. Knight argued in defense that the handwritten memorandum was not enforceable because it did not satisfy the Statute of Frauds. Is he correct? *Levin v. Knight*, 865 F.2d 1271, **Web** 1989 U.S. App. Lexis 458 (United States Court of Appeals for the Ninth Circuit)

BUSINESS ETHICS CASES

9 Business Ethics American Broadcasting Company Merchandising, Inc., a subsidiary of American Broadcasting Company, Inc. (collectively, ABC), entered into a written contract with model Cheryl Tiegs, whereby ABC would pay Tiegs $400,000 per year for the right to be the exclusive agent to license the merchandising of goods under her name. When ABC was unsuccessful in attracting licensing arrangements for Tiegs, a representative of ABC contacted Paul Sklar, who had previous experience in marketing apparel and licensing labels. Sklar enlisted the help of Mark Blye, and together they introduced ABC and Tiegs to Sears, Roebuck and Company (Sears). This introduction led to an agreement between Sears, ABC, and Tiegs, whereby Sears marketed a line of "Cheryl Tiegs" female apparel through Sears department stores and catalog sales. Blye and Sklar sued ABC for a finder's fee for introducing ABC and Tiegs to Sears. Because there was no express written or oral contract between ABC and Blye and Sklar, they alleged that there was an implied-in-fact contract between the parties. Section 5-701(a)(10) of the New York Statute of Frauds requires a finder's fee contract of the type in this case to be in writing. Who wins? Did ABC act ethically in this case? *Blye v. American Broadcasting Company Merchandising, Inc.*, 102 A.D.2d 297, 476 N.Y.S.2d 874, **Web** 1984 N.Y. App. Div. Lexis 18341 (Supreme Court of New York)

10 Business Ethics Adolfo Mozzetti, who owned a construction company, orally promised his son, Remo, that if Remo would manage the family business for their mutual benefit and would take care of him for the rest of his life, he would leave the family home to Remo. Section 2714 of the Delaware Code requires contracts for the transfer of land to be in writing. Section 2715 of the Delaware Code requires testamentary transfers of real property to be in writing. Remo performed as requested: He managed the family business and took care of his father until the father died. When the father died, his will devised the family home to his daughter, Lucia M. Shepard. Remo brought an action to enforce his father's oral promise that the home belonged to him. The daughter argued that the will should be upheld. Who wins? Did the daughter act ethically in trying to defeat the father's promise to leave the property to the son? Did the son act ethically in trying to defeat his father's will? *Shepard v. Mozzetti*, 545 A.2d 621, **Web** 1988 Del. Lexis 217 (Supreme Court of Delaware)

ENDNOTES

1. *Elias v. George Sahely & Co.*, 1983 App. Cas. (P.C.) 646, 655.
2. *Restatement (Second) of Contracts*, Section 110.
3. *Restatement (Second) of Contracts*, Section 130.
4. *Restatement (Second) of Contracts*, Section 112.
5. *Restatement (Second) of Contracts*, Section 116.
6. UCC Section 2-202 and UCC Section 2A-202.
7. *Restatement (Second) of Contracts*, Section 213.
8. UCC Sections 1-205, 2-202, and 2–208.
9. *Restatement (Second) of Contracts*, Section 139.

THIRD-PARTY RIGHTS AND DISCHARGE

Photodisc/Getty Images

▲ **Professional Baseball Player** *Professional athletes' contracts often provide that their personal service can be assigned.*

CHAPTER OBJECTIVES

After studying this chapter, you should be able to:

1. Describe assignment of contract rights and what contract rights are assignable.
2. Define *intended beneficiary* and describe this person's rights under a contract.
3. Define *covenant.*
4. Distinguish between conditions precedent, conditions subsequent, and concurrent conditions.
5. Explain when the performance of a contract is excused because of objective impossibility or commercial impracticability.

CHAPTER CONTENTS

- **INTRODUCTION TO THIRD-PARTY RIGHTS AND DISCHARGE**
- **ASSIGNMENT OF A RIGHT**
  Ethics Spotlight · *Successive Assignment of the Same Right*
- **DELEGATION OF A DUTY**
- **THIRD-PARTY BENEFICIARY**
- **COVENANT**
- **CONDITIONS**
  Contemporary Environment · *"Time Is of the Essence"*
- **DISCHARGE OF PERFORMANCE**
  Case 1 · Parker v. Arthur Murray, Inc.

"An honest man's word is as good as his bond."

—Don Quixote

From Chapter 15 of *Business Law: Legal Environment, Online Commerce, Business Ethics, and International Issues,* 7/e.

INTRODUCTION TO THIRD-PARTY RIGHTS AND DISCHARGE

privity of contract
The state of two specified parties being in a contract.

The parties to a contract are said to be in **privity of contract**. Contracting parties have a legal obligation to perform the duties specified in their contract. A party's duty of performance may be discharged by agreement of the parties, excuse of performance, or operation of law. If one party fails to perform as promised, the other party may enforce the contract and sue for breach.

With two exceptions, third parties do not acquire any rights under other people's contracts. The exceptions are (1) *assignees* to whom rights are subsequently transferred and (2) *intended third-party beneficiaries* to whom the contracting parties intended to give rights under the contract at the time of contracting.

This chapter discusses the rights of third parties under a contract, conditions to performance, and ways of discharging the duty of performance.

ASSIGNMENT OF A RIGHT

assignment
The transfer of contractual rights by an obligee to another party.

In many cases, the parties to a contract can transfer their rights under the contract to other parties. The transfer of contractual rights is called an **assignment of rights** or just an **assignment**.

Form of Assignment

assignor
An obligee who transfers a right.

assignee
A party to whom a right has been transferred.

A party who owes a duty of performance is called the **obligor**. A party who is owed a right under a contract is called the **obligee**. An obligee who transfers the right to receive performance is called an **assignor**. The party to whom the right has been transferred is called the **assignee**. The assignee can assign the right to yet another person (called a **subsequent assignee**, or **subassignee**). Exhibit 1 illustrates these relationships.

Exhibit 1
ASSIGNMENT OF A RIGHT

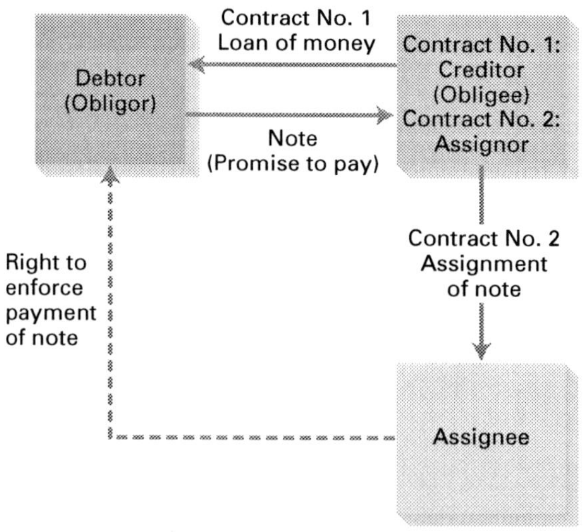

Generally, no formalities are required for a valid assignment of rights. Although the assignor often uses the word *assign*, other words or terms, such as *sell*, *transfer*, *convey*, and *give*, are sufficient to indicate intent to transfer a contract right.

Example A retail clothing store purchases $5,000 worth of goods on credit from a manufacturer. Payment is due in 120 days. If the manufacturer needs cash before the 120-day period expires, the manufacturer (assignor) can sell its right to collect the money to another party (assignee) for some price, let's say $4,000. If the retail store is given proper notice of the assignment, it must pay $5,000 to the assignee when the 120-day period is reached.

In the United States, public policy favors a free flow of commerce. Hence, most contract rights are assignable, including sales contracts and contracts for the payment of money. The following paragraphs discuss types of contracts that present special problems for assignment.

Personal Service Contract

Contracts for the provision of personal services are generally not assignable.[1]

Example If Angie Warhol, a famous artist, contracts to paint Jay-Z's portrait, Angie cannot assign this contract to another artist and send that artist to do the painting without the prior approval of Jay-Z. Jay-Z can reject this assignment and refuse to have his painting done by any artist except Angie Warhol.

The parties may agree that a **personal service contract** may be assigned.

Example Professional athletes often sign contracts with professional teams which provide that their personal service contract can be assigned.

Assignment of a Future Right

Usually, a person cannot assign a currently nonexistent right that he or she expects to have in the future (i.e., a **future right**).

Example Henrietta, an heiress worth millions of dollars, signs a will, leaving all her property to her granddaughter Brittany. Brittany has only an expected future right, and not a current right, to the money. Brittany cannot lawfully assign her expected future right to receive her inheritance. The assignment would be invalid.

If a man will improvidently bind himself up by a voluntary deed, and not reserve a liberty to himself by a power of revocation, this court will not loose the fetters he hath put upon himself, but he must lie down under his own folly.

Lord Chancellor Lord Nottingham
Villers v. Beaumont (1682)

Contract Where an Assignment Would Materially Alter the Risk

A contract cannot be assigned if the assignment would materially alter the risk or duties of the obligor.

Example Laura, who has a safe driving record, purchases automobile insurance from an insurance company. Laura cannot assign her rights to be insured to another driver because the assignment would materially alter the risk and duties of the insurance company.

Assignment of Legal Action

The right to sue another party for a violation of personal rights cannot usually be assigned.

Example Donald is severely injured by Alice in an automobile accident caused by Alice's negligence. Donald can sue Alice for the tort of negligence to recover monetary damages for his injuries. Donald's right to sue Alice is a personal right that cannot be assigned to another person.

A legal right that arises out of a breach of contract may be assigned.

Example Andrea borrows $10,000 from Country Bank with an 8% interest rate. The loan is to be repaid in equal monthly installments over a five-year period. If Andrea defaults on the loan, Country Bank may sue Andrea to collect the unpaid amount of the loan. Instead, Country Bank may sell (assign) its legal right to a collection agency to recover the money Andrea still owes on the loan. In this case, Country Bank is the assignor, and the collection agency is the assignee.

Effect of an Assignment of a Right

Make fair agreements and stick to them.

Confucius

Where there has been a valid assignment of rights, the assignee "stands in the shoes of the assignor." That is, the assignor is entitled to performance from the obligor. The unconditional assignment of a contract right extinguishes all the assignor's rights, including the right to sue the obligor directly for nonperformance.[2] An assignee takes no better rights under the contract than the assignor had.

Example If the assignor has a right to receive $10,000 from a debtor, the right to receive this $10,000 is all that the assignor can assign to the assignee.

An obligor can assert any defense he or she had against the assignor or the assignee. An obligor can raise the defenses of fraud, duress, undue influence, minority, insanity, illegality of the contract, mutual mistake, or payment by worthless check of the assignor, against enforcement of the contract by the assignee. The obligor can also raise any personal defenses (e.g., participation in the assignor's fraudulent scheme) he or she may have directly against the assignee.

Notice of Assignment

When an assignor makes an assignment of a right under a contract, the assignee is under a duty to notify the obligor that (1) the assignment has been made and (2) performance must be rendered to the assignee. If the assignee fails to provide **notice of assignment** to the obligor, the obligor may continue to render performance to the assignor, who no longer has a right to it. The assignee cannot sue the obligor to recover payment because the obligor has performed according to the original contract. The assignee's only course of action is to sue the assignor for damages.

That what is agreed to be done, must be considered as done.

Lord Chancellor Lord Hardwicke
Guidot v. Guidot (1745)

The result changes if the obligor is notified of the assignment but continues to render performance to the assignor. In such situations, the assignee can sue the obligor and recover payment. The obligor will then have to pay twice: once wrongfully to the assignor and then rightfully to the assignee. The obligor's only recourse is to sue the assignor for damages.

Anti-Assignment Clause

anti-assignment clause
A clause that prohibits the assignment of rights under the contract.

Some contracts contain an **anti-assignment clause** that prohibits the assignment of rights under the contract. Such clauses may be used if the obligor does not want to deal with or render performance to an unknown third party. Anti-assignment clauses are usually given effect.

Approval Clause

Some contracts contain an **approval clause**. Such clauses require that the obligor approve any assignment of a contract. Where there is an approval clause, many states prohibit the obligor from unreasonably withholding approval.

ETHICS SPOTLIGHT

Successive Assignment of the Same Right

An obligee (the party who is owed performance, money, a right, or another thing of value) has the right to assign a contract right or a benefit to another party. If the obligee fraudulently or mistakenly makes successive assignments of the same right to a number of assignees, which assignee has the legal right to the assigned right? To answer this question, the following rules apply:

American rule (New York Rule)
The **American rule** (or **New York Rule**) provides that the first assignment *in time* prevails, regardless of notice. Most states follow this rule.

English rule
The **English rule** provides that the first assignee to *give notice* to the obligor (the person who owes the

performance, money, duty, or other thing of value) prevails.

Possession of Tangible Token Rule
The **possession of tangible token rule** provides that under either the American or English rule, if the assignor makes successive assignments of a contract right that is represented by a tangible token, such as a stock certificate or a savings account passbook, the first assignee who receives delivery of the tangible token prevails over subsequent assignees.

Business Ethics Why does an assignor attempt to assign a contract right more than once? How can a first assignee protect his rights?

DELEGATION OF A DUTY

Unless otherwise agreed, the parties to a contract can generally transfer the performance of their duties under the contract to other parties. This transfer is called the **delegation of a duty**, or just **delegation**.

An obligor who transfers his or her duty is called a **delegator**. The party to whom the duty is transferred is the **delegatee**. The party to whom the duty is owed is the *obligee*. Generally, no special words or formalities are required to create a delegation of duties. Exhibit 2 illustrates the parties to a delegation of a duty.

delegation of duties
A transfer of contractual duties by an obligor to another party for performance.

delegator
An obligor who has transferred his or her duty.

delegatee
A party to whom a duty has been transferred.

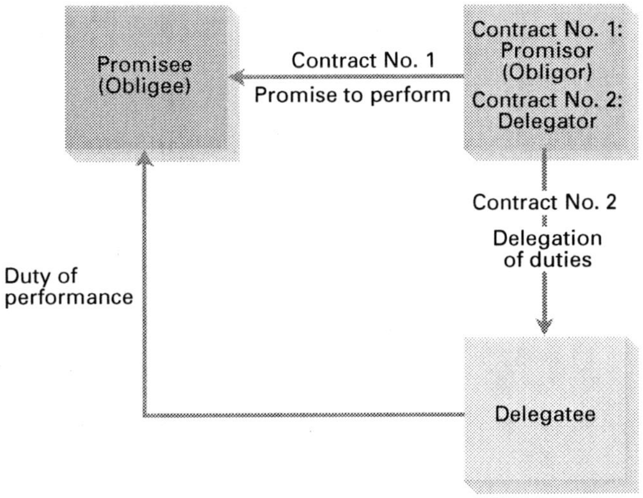

Exhibit 2 DELEGATION OF A DUTY

Duties That Can and Cannot Be Delegated

If an obligee has a substantial interest in having an obligor perform the acts required by a contract, these duties cannot be transferred.[3] This restriction includes obligations under the following types of contracts:

1. Personal service contracts calling for the exercise of personal skills, discretion, or expertise

   Example If P Diddy is hired to give a concert on a college campus, the Dixie Chicks cannot appear in his place.

2. Contracts whose performance would materially vary if the obligor's duties were delegated

   Example If a person hires an experienced surgeon to perform a complex surgery, a recent medical school graduate cannot be substituted to perform the operation.

"If there's no meaning in it," said the King, "that saves a world of trouble, you know, we needn't try to find any."
Lewis Carroll
Alice in Wonderland, Chapter 12

Often, contracts are entered into with companies or firms rather than with individuals. In such cases, a firm may designate any of its qualified employees to perform the contract.

Example If a client retains a firm of lawyers to represent her, the firm can **delegate** the duties under the contract to any qualified member of the firm.

Effect of Delegation of Duties

assumption of duties
A situation in which a delegation of duties contains the term *assumption*, *I assume the duties*, or other similar language. In such a case, the delegatee is legally liable to the obligee for nonperformance.

Where a valid delegation of duties contains the term *assumption* or other similar language, there is an **assumption of duties** by the delegatee. Here, the obligee can sue the delegatee and recover damages for nonperformance or negligent performance by the delegatee. In addition, the delegator remains legally liable for the performance of the contract. Thus, if the delegatee does not perform properly, the obligee can sue the obligor-delegator for any resulting damages caused by the delegatee's nonperformance or negligent conduct.

Anti-Delegation Clause

anti-delegation clause
A clause that prohibits the delegation of duties under the contract.

The parties to a contract can include an **anti-delegation clause** indicating that the duties cannot be delegated. Anti-delegation clauses are usually enforced. Some courts, however, have held that duties that are totally impersonal in nature—such as the payment of money—can be delegated despite such clauses.

Assignment and Delegation

An **assignment and delegation** occurs when there is a transfer of both rights and duties under a contract. If the transfer of a contract to a third party contains only language of assignment, the modern view holds that there is corresponding delegation of the duties of the contract.[4]

Morocco *The negotiation and enforcement of contracts differs in various cultures of the world.*

▶ THIRD-PARTY BENEFICIARY

Third parties sometimes claim rights under others' contracts; these parties are called **third-party beneficiaries**. Such third parties are either *intended* or *incidental beneficiaries*. Each of these designations is discussed here.

Intended Beneficiary

intended third-party beneficiary
A third party who is not in privity of contract but who has rights under the contract and can enforce the contract against the promisor.

When parties enter into a contract, they can agree that the performance of one of the parties should be rendered to or directly benefit a third party. Under such circumstances, the third party is called an **intended third-party beneficiary**. An intended third-party beneficiary can enforce the contract against the party who promised to render performance.[5]

Examples The beneficiary may be expressly named in a contract from which he or she is to benefit ("I leave my property to my son Ben") or may be identified by another means ("I leave my property to all my children, equally").

Intended third-party beneficiaries may be classified as either *donee* or *creditor* beneficiaries. These terms are defined in the following paragraphs. The *Restatement (Second) of Contracts* and many state statutes have dropped this distinction, however, and now refer to both collectively as *intended beneficiaries*.[6]

Donee Beneficiary The first type of intended beneficiary is the *donee beneficiary*. When a person enters into a contract with the intent to confer a benefit or gift on an intended third party, the contract is called a **donee beneficiary contract**. The three persons involved in such a contract are:

donee beneficiary contract
A contract entered into with the intent to confer a benefit or gift on an intended third party.

1. The **promisee** (the contracting party who directs that the benefit be conferred on another)
2. The **promisor** (the contracting party who agrees to confer performance for the benefit of the third person)
3. The **donee beneficiary** (the third person on whom the benefit is to be conferred)

donee beneficiary
A third party on whom a benefit is to be conferred.

If the promisor fails to perform the contract, the donee beneficiary can sue the promisor directly.

He who derives the advantage ought to sustain the burden.

Legal maxim

Example Nina goes to Life Insurance Company and purchases a $2 million life insurance policy on her life. Nina names her husband John as the beneficiary of the life insurance policy—that is, he is to be paid the $2 million if Nina dies. John is an intended beneficiary of the Nina–Life Insurance Company contract. Nina makes the necessary premium payments to Life Insurance Company. She dies in an automobile accident. Life Insurance Company does not pay the $2 million life insurance benefits to John. John, as an intended beneficiary, can sue Life Insurance Company to recover the life insurance benefits. Here, John has rights as an intended third-party beneficiary to enforce the Nina–Life Insurance Company contract. (See Exhibit 3.)

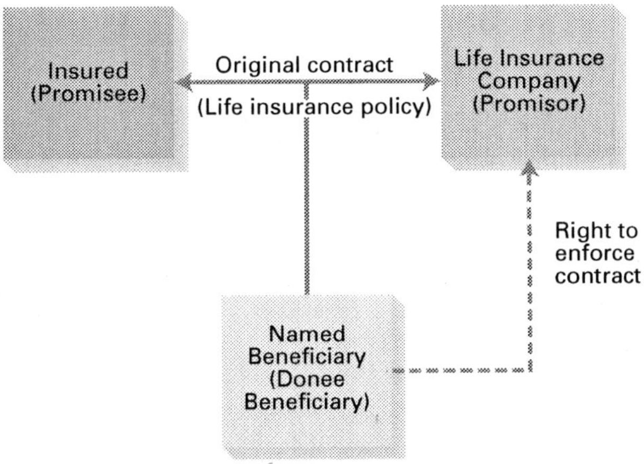

Exhibit 3 DONEE BENEFICIARY CONTRACT

Creditor Beneficiary The second type of intended beneficiary is the *creditor beneficiary*. A **creditor beneficiary contract** usually arises in the following situation:

creditor beneficiary contract
A contract that arises in the following situation: (1) a debtor borrows money, (2) the debtor signs an agreement to pay back the money plus interest, (3) the debtor sells the item to a third party before the loan is paid off, and (4) the third party promises the debtor that he or she will pay the remainder of the loan to the creditor.

1. A debtor (promisor) borrows money from a creditor (promisee) to purchase some item.
2. The debtor signs an agreement to pay the creditor the amount of the loan plus interest.
3. The debtor sells the item to another party before the loan is paid.
4. The new buyer (new promisor) promises the original debtor (new promisee) that he will pay the remainder of the loan amount to the original creditor.

The original creditor is now the creditor beneficiary of this second contract.[7] The parties to the second contract are the original debtor (promisee of the second contract) and the

creditor beneficiary
An original creditor who becomes a beneficiary under the debtor's new contract with another party.

new party (promisor of the second contract). The original creditor is the **creditor beneficiary** of the second contract. (See Exhibit 4.)

If the new debtor (promisor) fails to perform according to the second contract, the creditor beneficiary may either (1) enforce the original contract against the original debtor-promisor or (2) enforce the new contract against the new debtor-promisor. However, the creditor can collect only once.

Exhibit 4 CREDITOR BENEFICIARY CONTRACT

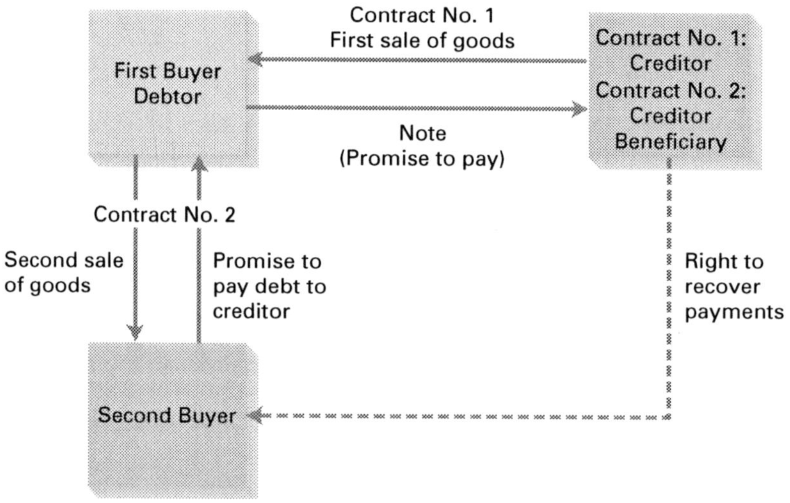

Example Big Hotels obtains a loan from City Bank to build an addition to a hotel it owns in Atlanta, Georgia. The parties sign a promissory note requiring Big Hotels (promisor) to pay off the loan in equal monthly installments over a period of 10 years to City Bank (promisee). With six years left before the loan would be paid, Big Hotels sells the hotel to Palace Hotels, another chain of hotels. Palace Hotels (new promisor) agrees with Big Hotels (new promisee) to complete the payments due to City Bank on the loan. If Palace Hotels fails to pay the loan, City Bank has two options: It can sue Big Hotels on the original promissory note to recover the unpaid loan amount, or it can use its status as a creditor beneficiary to sue and recover the unpaid loan amount from Palace Hotels.

Incidental Beneficiary

incidental beneficiary
A party who is unintentionally benefited by other people's contracts.

In many instances, the parties to a contract unintentionally benefit a third party when a contract is performed. In such situations, the third party is referred to as an **incidental beneficiary**. An incidental beneficiary has no rights to enforce or sue under other people's contracts.

Example Heather owns a house on Residential Street. Her house, which is somewhat older, needs a new exterior coat of paint. Her neighbor John owns the house next door. If Heather has her house painted, John will benefit by having a nicer-looking house next door that may actually raise housing values on the street. Heather contracts with George, a painting contractor, to paint her house. George breaches the contract and does not paint Heather's house. Although John may have benefitted if Heather's house had been painted, he is merely an incidental beneficiary to the Heather–George contract and has no cause of action to sue George for not painting Heather's house. Heather, of course, can sue George for breach of contract.

Generally, the public and taxpayers are only incidental beneficiaries to contracts entered into by the government on their behalf. As such, they acquire no right to enforce government contracts or to sue parties who breach these contracts.

COVENANT

In contracts, parties make certain promises to each other. A **covenant** is an *unconditional* promise to perform. Nonperformance of a covenant is a breach of contract that gives the other party the right to sue. The majority of provisions in contracts are covenants.

covenant
An unconditional promise to perform.

Example Seed Company borrows $400,000 from Rural Bank and signs a promissory note to repay the $400,000 plus 10 percent interest in one year. This promise is a covenant. That is, it is an unconditional promise to perform.

CONDITIONS

Some contract provisions are conditions rather than covenants. A **conditional promise** (or qualified promise) is not as definite as a covenant. The promisor's duty to perform or not perform arises only if the **condition** does or does not occur.[8] It becomes a covenant if the condition is met, however.

condition
A qualification of a promise that becomes a covenant if it is met. There are three types of conditions: conditions precedent, conditions subsequent, and concurrent conditions.

Generally, contractual language such as *if, on condition that, provided that, when, after*, and *as soon as* indicates a condition. A single contract may contain numerous conditions that trigger or excuse performance.

There are three primary types of conditions: *conditions precedent, conditions subsequent*, and *concurrent conditions*. Each of these are discussed in the following paragraphs.

Condition Precedent

If a contract requires the occurrence (or nonoccurrence) of an event *before* a party is obligated to perform a contractual duty, this is a **condition precedent**. The happening (or nonhappening) of the event triggers the contract or duty of performance. If the event does not occur, no duty to perform the contract arises because there is a failure of condition.

condition precedent
A condition that requires the occurrence of an event before a party is obligated to perform a duty under a contract.

Condition Precedent Based on Satisfaction Some contracts reserve the right to a party to pay for services provided by the other only if the services meet the first party's "satisfaction." The courts have developed two tests—the *personal satisfaction test* and the *reasonable person test*—to determine whether this special form of condition precedent has been met:

1. **Personal satisfaction test.** The **personal satisfaction test** is a *subjective* test that applies if the performance involves personal taste and comfort (e.g., contracts for interior decorating, contracts for tailoring clothes). The only requirement is that the person given the right to reject the contract acts in good faith.

   personal satisfaction test
   A subjective test that applies to contracts involving personal taste and comfort.

   Example Gretchen employs an artist to paint her daughter's portrait. The contract provides that Gretchen does not have to accept and pay for the portrait unless she is personally satisfied with it. This is a condition precedent based upon the personal satisfaction test. Gretchen rejects the painting because she personally dislikes it. This rejection is lawful because it is based on the personal satisfaction test.

2. **Reasonable person test.** The **reasonable person test** is an *objective* test that is used to judge contracts involving mechanical fitness and most commercial contracts. Most contracts that require the work to meet the satisfaction of a third person (e.g., engineer, architect) are judged by this standard.

   reasonable person test
   An objective test that applies to commercial contracts and contracts involving mechanical fitness.

   Example E-Commerce Company hires Einstein to install a state-of-the-art Internet webpage ordering system that will handle its order entry and record-keeping functions. Einstein installs a state-of-the-art Internet webpage ordering system that meets current industry standards. E-Commerce Company rejects the contract as not meeting its personal satisfaction. This is a breach of contract because the personal satisfaction test does not apply to this contract. Instead, the objective reasonable person test applies, and a reasonable e-commerce company in the same situation would have accepted the system.

CONTEMPORARY ENVIRONMENT

"Time Is of the Essence"

Generally, there is a breach of contract if a contract is not performed when due. Nevertheless, if the other party is not jeopardized by the delay, most courts treat the delay as a minor breach and give the nonperforming party additional time to perform.

Conversely, if a contract expressly provides that **"time is of the essence"** or similar language, performance by the stated time is an express condition. There is a breach of contract if the contracting party does not perform by the stated date.

Freedom of contracts begins where equality of bargaining power begins.

Oliver Wendell Holmes, Jr. (1928)

Condition Subsequent

A **condition subsequent** exists when there is a condition in a contract which provides that the occurrence or nonoccurrence of a specific event automatically excuses the performance of an existing duty to perform. That is, failure to meet the condition subsequent relieves the other party from obligation under the contract.

Note that the *Restatement (Second) of Contracts* eliminates the distinction between conditions precedent and conditions subsequent. Both are referred to as "conditions."[9]

condition subsequent
A condition whose occurrence or nonoccurrence of a specific event automatically excuses the performance of an existing contractual duty to perform.

Concurrent Conditions

Concurrent conditions arise when the parties to a contract agree to render performance simultaneously—that is, when each party's absolute duty to perform is conditioned on the other party's absolute duty to perform.

concurrent condition
A condition that exists when the parties to a contract must render performance simultaneously; each party's absolute duty to perform is conditioned on the other party's absolute duty to perform.

Example A contract by Samantha's Club to purchase goods from Kid's Toys Inc. provides that payment is due upon delivery of the goods. In other words, Samantha's Club's duty to pay and Kid's Toys Inc.'s duty to deliver the goods are concurrent conditions. Recovery of damages is available if one party fails to respond to the other party's performance.

Implied Condition

Any of the previous types of conditions may be further classified as either express or implied conditions. An *express condition* exists if the parties expressly agree on it. An **implied-in-fact-condition** is one that can be implied from the circumstances surrounding a contract and the parties' conduct.

implied-in-fact condition
A condition that can be implied from the circumstances surrounding a contract and the parties' conduct.

Example A contract in which a buyer agrees to purchase grain from a farmer implies that there are proper street access to the delivery site, proper unloading facilities, and the like.

CONCEPT SUMMARY

TYPES OF CONDITIONS

Type of Condition	Description
Condition precedent	A specified event must occur or not occur before a party is obligated to perform contractual duties.
Condition subsequent	The occurrence or nonoccurrence of a specified event excuses the performance of an existing contractual duty to perform.
Concurrent condition	The parties to a contract are obligated to render performance simultaneously. Each party's duty to perform is conditioned on the other party's duty to perform.
Implied condition	An implied-in-fact condition is implied from the circumstances surrounding a contract and the parties' conduct.

DISCHARGE OF PERFORMANCE

A party's duty to perform under a contract may be discharged by *mutual agreement* of the parties, by *impossibility of performance*, or by *operation of law*. These methods of discharge are discussed in the paragraphs that follow.

Men keep agreements when it is to the advantage of neither to break them.

Solon

Discharge by Agreement

In many situations, the parties to a contract mutually decide to **discharge** their contractual duties. The parties can do so by *mutual rescission*, *substituted contract*, *novation*, and *accord and satisfaction*. The different types of mutual agreement are discussed in the following paragraphs:

Mutual Rescission If a contract is wholly or partially executory on both sides, the parties can agree to rescind (i.e., cancel) the contract. **Mutual rescission** requires parties to enter into a second agreement that expressly terminates the first one.

Unilateral rescission of a contract by one of the parties without the other party's consent is not effective. Unilateral rescission of a contract constitutes a breach of that contract.

Substituted Contract The parties to a contract may enter into a new contract that revokes and discharges an existing contract. The new contract is called a **substituted contract**.

If one of the parties fails to perform his or her duties under a substituted contract, the nonbreaching party can sue to enforce its terms against the breaching party. The prior contract cannot be enforced against the breaching party because it has been discharged.

Novation A **novation agreement** (commonly called **novation**) substitutes a third party for one of the original contracting parties. The new substituted party is obligated to perform the contract. All three parties must agree to the substitution. In a novation, the exiting party is relieved of liability on the contract.

novation agreement
An agreement that substitutes a new party for one of the original contracting parties and relieves the exiting party of liability on the contract. Also known as simply a *novation*.

Accord and Satisfaction The parties to a contract may agree to settle a contract dispute by an **accord and satisfaction**. The agreement whereby the parties agree to accept something different in satisfaction of the original contract is called an *accord*.[10] The performance of an accord is called a *satisfaction*.

An accord does not discharge the original contract. It only suspends it until the accord is performed. Satisfaction of the accord discharges both the original contract and the accord. If an accord is not satisfied when it is due, the aggrieved party may enforce either the accord or the original contract.

accord and satisfaction
The settlement of a contract dispute.

Discharge by Impossibility

Under certain circumstances, the nonperformance of contractual duties is excused—that is, discharged—because of *impossibility of performance*. **Impossibility of performance** (or **objective impossibility**) occurs if a contract becomes impossible to perform.[11] The impossibility must be objective impossibility ("it cannot be done") rather than subjective impossibility ("I cannot do it"). The following types of objective impossibility excuse nonperformance:

impossibility of performance
Nonperformance that is excused if a contract becomes impossible to perform. It must be objective impossibility, not subjective.

- The death or incapacity of the promisor prior to the performance of a personal service contract[12]

Example If a professional athlete dies prior to or during a contract period, his or her contract with the team is discharged.

- The destruction of the subject matter of a contract prior to performance[13]

Example If a building is destroyed by fire, the lessees are discharged from further performance unless otherwise provided in the lease.

- A supervening illegality that makes performance of the contract illegal[14]

Example An art dealer contracts to purchase native art found in a foreign country. The contract is discharged if the foreign country enacts a law forbidding native art from being exported from the country before the contract is performed.

In the following case, the court had to decide whether impossibility existed that excused performance.

CASE 1 Impossibility of Performance

Parker v. Arthur Murray, Inc.

295 N.E.2d 487, Web 1973 Ill.App. Lexis 2760 (1973)
Appellate Court of Illinois

"Although neither party to a contract should be relieved from performance on the ground that good business judgment was lacking, a court will not place upon language a ridiculous construction."

—Judge Stamos

Facts

Ryland S. Parker, a 37-year-old college-educated bachelor, went to the Arthur Murray Studios (Arthur Murray) in Oak Park, Illinois, to redeem a certificate entitling him to three free dancing lessons. At that time, he lived alone in a one-room attic apartment. During the free lessons, the instructor told Parker that he had "exceptional potential to be a fine and accomplished dancer." Parker thereupon signed a contract for more lessons. Parker attended lessons regularly and was praised and encouraged by his instructors despite his lack of progress. Contract extensions and new contracts for additional instructional hours were executed, which Parker prepaid. Each written contract contained the bold-type words "NONCANCELABLE CONTRACT." Two years after having started to take dancing lessons, Parker was severely injured in an automobile accident, rendering him incapable of continuing his dancing lessons. At that time, he had contracted for a total of 2,734 hours of dance lessons, for which he had prepaid $24,812. When Arthur Murray refused to refund any of the money, Parker sued to rescind the outstanding contracts. The trial courts held in favor of Parker and ordered Arthur Murray to return the prepaid contract payments. Arthur Murray appealed.

Issue

Does the doctrine of impossibility excuse Parker's performance of the personal service contracts?

Language of the Court

Plaintiff was granted rescission on the grounds of impossibility of performance. Defendants do not deny that the doctrine of impossibility of performance is generally applicable to the case at bar. Rather they assert that certain contract provisions bring the case within the Restatement's limitation that the doctrine is inapplicable if "the contract indicates a contrary intention." It is contended that such bold-type phrases as "NON-CANCELLABLE CONTRACT," NON-CANCELLABLE NEGOTIABLE CONTRACT," and "I UNDERSTAND THAT NO REFUNDS WILL BE MADE UNDER THE TERMS OF THIS CONTRACT" manifest the parties' mutual intent to waive their respective rights to invoke the doctrine of impossibility.

This is a construction that we find unacceptable. Courts engage in the construction and interpretation of contracts with the sole aim of determining the intention of the parties. We need rely on no construction aids to conclude that plaintiff never contemplated that by signing a contract with such terms as "NON-CANCELLABLE" and "NO REFUNDS," he was waiving a remedy expressly recognized by Illinois courts. Although neither party to a contract should be relieved from performance on the ground that good business judgment was lacking, a court will not place upon language a ridiculous construction. We conclude that plaintiff did not waive his right to assert the doctrine of impossibility.

Suffice it to say that overwhelming evidence supported plaintiff's contention that he was incapable of continuing his lessons.

Decision

The appellate court held that the doctrine of impossibility of performance excused Parker's performance of the personal service contracts. The appellate court affirmed the trial court's judgment that ordered Arthur Murray to return the prepaid contract payments.

Case Questions

Critical Legal Thinking What does the doctrine of impossibility of performance provide? Explain.

Business Ethics Did Arthur Murray act ethically in not returning Parker's money? Did Arthur Murray act ethically by allowing Parker to sign up for and prepay for over 2,700 hours of dance lessons?

Contemporary Business Should the doctrine of impossibility excuse parties from performance of their contracts? Why or why not?

Force Majeure Clause

The parties may agree in a contract that certain events will excuse nonperformance of the contract. These clauses are called ***force majeure* clauses.**

force majeure **clause**
A clause in a contract in which the parties specify certain events that will excuse nonperformance.

Example A *force majeure* clause usually excuses nonperformance caused by natural disasters such as floods, tornadoes, earthquakes, and such. Modern clauses also often excuse performance due to labor strikes, shortages of raw materials, and the like.

Commercial Impracticability

Many states recognize the doctrine of **commercial impracticability** as an excuse for nonperformance of contracts. Commercial impracticability excuses performance if an unforeseeable event makes it impractical for the promisor to perform. This doctrine has not yet been fully developed by the courts. It is examined on a case-by-case basis.

commercial impracticability
Nonperformance that is excused if an extreme or unexpected development or expense makes it impractical for the promisor to perform.

Example A utility company enters into a contract to purchase uranium for its nuclear-powered generator from a uranium supplier at a fixed price of $1 million per year for five years. Suppose a new uranium cartel is formed worldwide, and the supplier must pay $5 million for uranium to supply the utility with each year's supply. It is not impossible for the supplier to satisfy the contract: The supplier can purchase the uranium for $5 million and resell it to the utility company for $1 million (losing $4 million per year). However, in this situation, the court would likely allow the supplier to rescind its contract with the utility based on commercial impracticability.

Statute of Limitations

Certain legal rules discharge parties from performing contractual duties. Every state has a **statute of limitations** that applies to contract actions. Although the time periods vary from state to state, the usual period for bringing a lawsuit for breach of contract is one to five years. The UCC provides that a cause of action based on a breach of sales or lease contract must be brought within four years after the cause of action accrues.[15]

statute of limitations
A statute that establishes the time period during which a lawsuit must be brought; if the lawsuit is not brought within this period, the injured party loses the right to sue.

Bankruptcy

Bankruptcy, which is governed by federal law, is a means of allocating the debtor's nonexempt property to satisfy his or her debts. Debtors may also reorganize in bankruptcy. In most cases, the debtor's assets are insufficient to pay all the creditors' claims. In this case, the debtor receives a **discharge** of the unpaid debts. The debtor is then relieved of legal liability to pay the discharged debts.

TEST REVIEW TERMS AND CONCEPTS

Accord and satisfaction
American rule (New York Rule)
Anti-assignment clause
Anti-delegation clause
Approval clause
Assignee
Assignment and delegation
Assignment of future right
Assignment of right (assignment)
Assignor
Assumption of duties
Commercial impracticability
Concurrent condition
Condition
Conditional promise
Condition precedent
Condition subsequent

Covenant
Creditor beneficiary
Creditor beneficiary contract
Delegate
Delegatee
Delegator
Delegation of a duty (delegation)
Discharge by agreement
Discharge in bankruptcy
Donee beneficiary
Donee beneficiary contract
English rule
Force majeure clause
Implied-in-fact-condition
Impossibility of performance (objective impossibility)
Incidental beneficiary
Intended third-party beneficiary
Mutual rescission
Notice of assignment
Novation agreement (novation)
Obligee
Obligor
Personal satisfaction test
Personal service contract
Possession of tangible token rule
Privity of contract
Promisee
Promisor
Reasonable person test
Statute of limitation
Subsequent assignee (subassignee)
Substituted contract
Third-party beneficiary
"Time is of the essence"

CASE PROBLEMS

1 Third-Party Beneficiary Eugene H. Emmick hired L. S. Hamm, an attorney, to draft his will. The will named Robert Lucas and others (Lucas) as beneficiaries. When Emmick died, it was discovered that the will was improperly drafted, violated state law, and was therefore ineffective. Emmick's estate was transferred pursuant to the state's intestate laws. Lucas did not receive the $75,000 he would have otherwise received had the will been valid. Lucas sued Hamm for breach of the Emmick–Hamm contract to recover what he would have received under the will. Who wins? *Lucas v. Hamm*, 56 Cal.2d 583, 364 P.2d 685, 15 Cal.Rptr. 821, **Web** 1961 Cal. Lexis 321 (Supreme Court of California)

2 Third-Party Beneficiary Angelo Boussiacos hired Demetrios Sofias, a general contractor, to build a restaurant for him. Boussiacos entered into a loan agreement with Bank of America (B of A) whereby B of A would provide the construction financing to build the restaurant. The loan agreement provided that loan funds would be periodically disbursed by B of A to Boussiacos at different stages of construction, as requested by Boussiacos. Problems arose in the progress of the construction. When Boussiacos did not pay Sofias for certain work that had been done, Sofias sued B of A for breach of contract to collect payment directly from B of A. Can Sofias maintain the lawsuit against B of A? *Sofias v. Bank of America*, 172 Cal.App.3d 583, 218 Cal.Rptr. 388, **Web** 1985 Cal.App. Lexis 2545 (Court of Appeal of California)

3 Assignment William John Cunningham, a professional basketball player, entered into a contract with Southern Sports Corporation, which owned the Carolina Cougars, a professional basketball team. The contract provided that Cunningham was to play basketball for the Cougars for a three-year period. The contract contained a provision that it could not be assigned to any other professional basketball franchise without Cunningham's approval. Subsequently, Southern Sports Corporation sold its assets, including its franchise and Cunningham's contract, to the Munchak Corporation (Munchak). There was no change in the location of the Cougars after the purchase. When Cunningham refused to play for the new owners, Munchak sued to enforce Cunningham's contract. Is Cunningham's contract assignable to the new owner? *Munchak Corporation v. Cunningham*, 457 F.2d 721, **Web** 1972 U.S. App. Lexis 10272 (United States Court of Appeals for the Fourth Circuit)

4 Assignment Berlinger Foods Corporation (Berlinger), pursuant to an oral contract, became a distributor for Häagen-Dazs ice cream. Over the next decade, both parties flourished as the marketing of high-quality, high-priced ice cream took hold. Berlinger successfully promoted the sale of Häagen-Dazs to supermarket chains and other retailers in the Baltimore–Washington, DC, area. Ten years later, the Pillsbury Company acquired Häagen-Dazs. Pillsbury adhered to the oral distribution agreement and retained Berlinger as a distributor for Häagen-Dazs ice cream. Two years later, Berlinger entered into a contract and sold its assets to Dreyers, a manufacturer of premium ice cream that competed with Häagen-Dazs. Dreyers ice cream had previously been sold primarily in the western part of the United States. Dreyers attempted to expand its market to the east by choosing to purchase Berlinger as a means to obtain distribution in the mid-Atlantic region. When Pillsbury learned of the sale, it advised Berlinger that its distributorship for Häagen-Dazs was terminated. Berlinger, which wanted to remain a distributor for Häagen-Dazs, sued Pillsbury for breach of contract, alleging that the oral distribution agreement with Häagen-Dazs and Pillsbury was properly assigned to Dreyers. Who wins? *Berlinger Foods Corporation v. The Pillsbury Company*, 633 F.Supp. 557, **Web** 1986 U.S. Dist. Lexis 26431 (United States District Court for the District of Maryland)

5 Anti-Assignment Clause The city of Vancouver, Washington, contracted with B & B Contracting Corporation (B & B) to construct a well pump at a city-owned water station. The contract contained the following anti-assignment clause: "The contractor shall not assign this contract or any part thereof, or any moneys due or to become due thereunder." The work was not completed on time, and the city withheld $6,510 as liquidated damages from the contract price. B & B assigned the claim to this money to Portland Electric and Plumbing Company (PEPCo). PEPCo, as the assignee, filed suit against the City of Vancouver, alleging that the city had breached its contract with B & B by wrongfully refusing to pay $6,510 to B & B. Can PEPCo maintain the lawsuit against the City of Vancouver? *Portland Electric and Plumbing Company v. City of Vancouver*, 29 Wn.App. 292, 627 P.2d 1350, **Web** 1981 Wash.App. Lexis 2295 (Court of Appeals of Washington)

6 Delegation of Duties C.W. Milford owned a registered Quarterhorse named Hired Chico. Milford sold the horse to Norman Stewart. Recognizing that Hired Chico was a good stud, Milford included the following provision in the written contract that was signed by both parties: "I, C.W. Milford, reserve 2 breedings each year on Hired Chico registration #403692 for the life of this stud horse regardless of whom the horse may be sold to." The agreement was filed with the County Court Clerk of Shelby County, Texas. Stewart later sold Hired Chico to Sam McKinnie. Prior to purchasing the horse, McKinnie read the Milford–Stewart contract and testified that he understood the terms of the contract. When McKinnie refused to grant Milford the stud services of Hired Chico, Milford sued McKinnie for breach of contract. Who wins? *McKinnie v. Milford*, 597 S.W.2d 953, **Web** 1980 Tex.App. Lexis 3345 (Court of Appeals of Texas)

7 Condition Shumann Investments, Inc. (Shumann), hired Pace Construction Corporation (Pace), a general contractor, to build "Outlet World of Pasco Country." In turn, Pace hired OBS Company, Inc. (OBS), a subcontractor, to perform the framing, drywall, insulation, and stucco work on the project. The contract between Pace and OBS stipulated: "Final payment shall not become due unless and until the following conditions precedent to final payment have been satisfied . . . (c) receipt of final payment for subcontractor's work by contractor from owner." When Shumann refused to pay Pace, Pace refused to pay OBS. OBS sued Pace to recover payment. Who wins? *Pace Construction Corporation v. OBS Company, Inc.*, 531 So.2d 737, **Web** 1988 Fla.App. Lexis 4020 (Court of Appeal of Florida)

8 Excuse of Condition Maco, Inc. (Maco), a roofing contractor, hired Brian Barrows as a salesperson. Barrows was assigned a geographical territory and was responsible for securing contracts for Maco within his territory. The employment contract provided that Barrows was to receive a 26 percent commission on the net profits from roofing contracts that he obtained. The contract contained the following provision: "To qualify for payment of the commission, the salesperson must sell and supervise the job; the job must be completed and paid for; and the salesperson must have been in the continuous employment of Maco, Inc., during the aforementioned period." Barrows obtained a $129,603 contract with the Board of Education of Cook County for Maco to make repairs to the roof of the Hoover School in Evanston, Illinois. During the course of the work, Barrows visited the site more than 60 times. Before the work was completed, Maco fired Barrows. Later, Maco refused to pay Barrows the commission when the project was completed and paid for. Barrows sued Maco to recover the commission. Who wins? *Barrows v. Maco, Inc.*, 94 Ill.App.3d 959, 419 N.E.2d 634, **Web** 1981 Ill. App. Lexis 2371 (Appellate Court of Illinois)

BUSINESS ETHICS CASES

9 Business Ethics Pabagold, Inc. (Pabagold), a manufacturer and distributor of suntan lotions, hired Mediasmith, an advertising agency, to develop an advertising campaign for Pabagold's Hawaiian Gold Pabatan suntan lotion. In the contract, Pabagold authorized Mediasmith to enter into agreements with third parties to place Pabagold advertisements for the campaign and to make payments to these third parties for the Pabagold account. Pabagold agreed to pay Mediasmith for its services and to reimburse it for expenses incurred on behalf of Pabagold. The Pabagold–Mediasmith contract provided for arbitration of any dispute arising under the contract.

Mediasmith entered into a contract with Outdoor Services, Inc. (Outdoor Services), an outdoor advertising company, to place Pabagold ads on billboards owned by Outdoor Services. Outdoor Services provided the agreed-upon work and billed Mediasmith $8,545 for its services. Mediasmith requested payment of this amount from Pabagold so it could pay Outdoor Services. When Pabagold refused to pay, Outdoor Services filed a demand for arbitration, as provided in the Pabagold–Mediasmith contract. Pabagold defended, asserting that Outdoor Services could not try to recover the money because it was not in privity of contract with Pabagold.

Did Pabagold act ethically in refusing to pay Outdoor Services? From an ethical perspective, does it matter that Outdoor Services and Pabagold were not in privity of contract? Who wins? *Outdoor Services, Inc. v. Pabagold, Inc.*, 185 Cal.App.3d 676, 230 Cal.Rptr. 73, **Web** 1986 Cal.App. Lexis 2030 (Court of Appeal of California)

10 Business Ethics Indiana Tri-City Plaza Bowl (Tri-City) leased a building from Charles H. Glueck for use as a bowling alley. The lease provided that Glueck was to provide adequate paved parking for the building. The lease gave Tri-City the right to approve the plans for the construction and paving of the parking lot. When Glueck submitted paving plans to Tri-City, it rejected the plans and withheld its approval. Tri-City argued that the plans were required to meet its personal satisfaction before it had to approve them.

Evidence showed that the plans were commercially reasonable in the circumstances. A lawsuit was filed between Tri-City and Glueck. Who wins? Was it ethical for Tri-City to reject the plans? *Indiana Tri-City Plaza Bowl, Inc. v. Estate of Glueck*, 422 N.E.2d 670, **Web** 1981 Ind.App. Lexis 1506 (Court of Appeals of Indiana)

ENDNOTES

1. *Restatement (Second) of Contracts*, Sections 311 and 318.
2. *Restatement (Second) of Contracts*, Section 317.
3. *Restatement (Second) of Contracts*, Section 318(2).
4. *Restatement (Second) of Contracts*, Section 328.
5. *Restatement (Second) of Contracts*, Section 302.
6. *Restatement (Second) of Contracts*, Section 302(1)(b).
7. *Restatement (Second) of Contracts*, Section 302(1)(a).
8. *The Restatement (Second) of Contracts*, Section 224, defines *condition* as "an event, not certain to occur, which must occur, unless its nonperformance is excused, before performance under a contract is due."
9. *Restatement (Second) of Contracts*, Section 224.
10. *Restatement (Second) of Contracts*, Section 281.
11. *Restatement (Second) of Contracts*, Section 261.
12. *Restatement (Second) of Contracts*, Section 262.
13. *Restatement (Second) of Contracts*, Section 263.
14. *Restatement (Second) of Contracts*, Section 264.
15. UCC Section 2-725 and UCC Section 2A-506.

REMEDIES FOR BREACH OF TRADITIONAL AND E-CONTRACTS

▲**Jewelry Store** *Many persons get engaged and most engagements result in a marriage. However, sometimes an engagement is broken off. Under the objective rule, the person who gave the engagement ring is entitled to the return of the ring and may bring a lawsuit to recover the ring if it is not voluntarily returned. Under the objective rule, the engagement ring must be returned, no matter which party broke off the engagement.*

CHAPTER OBJECTIVES

After studying this chapter, you should be able to:

1. Describe complete, substantial, and inferior performance of contractual duties.
2. Describe compensatory, consequential, and nominal damages awarded for the breach of traditional and e-contracts.
3. Explain rescission and restitution.
4. Define the equitable remedies of specific performance, reformation, and injunction.
5. Describe torts associated with contracts.

CHAPTER CONTENTS

"Contracts must not be sports of an idle hour, mere matters of pleasantry and badinage, never intended by the parties to have any serious effect whatsoever."

—Lord Stowell

Dalrymple v. Dalrymple, 2 Hag. Con. 54, at 105 (1811)

INTRODUCTION TO REMEDIES FOR BREACH OF TRADITIONAL AND E-CONTRACTS

There are three levels of performance of a contract: *complete*, *substantial*, and *inferior*. Complete (or strict) performance by a party discharges that party's duties under the contract. Substantial performance constitutes a minor breach of the contract. Inferior performance constitutes a material breach that impairs or destroys the essence of the contract. Various remedies may be obtained by a nonbreaching party if a **breach of contract** occurs—that is, if a contracting party fails to perform an absolute duty owed under a contract.[1]

breach of contract
A contracting party's failure to perform an absolute duty owed under a contract.

The most common remedy for a breach of contract is an award of *monetary damages*, often called the "law remedy." If a monetary award does not provide adequate relief, however, the court may order any one of several *equitable remedies*, including specific performance, reformation, and injunction. Equitable remedies are based on the concept of fairness.

This chapter discusses breach of contract and the remedies available to the nonbreaching party.

PERFORMANCE AND BREACH

Men keep their agreements when it is an advantage to both parties not to break them.

Solon
(c. 600 B.C.)

If a contractual duty has not been discharged (i.e., terminated) or excused (i.e., relieved of legal liability), the contracting party owes an absolute duty (i.e., covenant) to perform the duty. As mentioned in the chapter introduction, there are three types of performance of a contract: (1) *complete performance*, (2) *substantial performance* (or minor breach), and (3) *inferior performance* (or material breach). These concepts are discussed in the following paragraphs.

Complete Performance

complete performance
A situation in which a party to a contract renders performance exactly as required by the contract. Complete performance discharges that party's obligations under the contract.

Most contracts are discharged by the **complete performance**, or **strict performance**, of the contracting parties. Complete performance occurs when a party to a contract renders performance exactly as required by the contract. A fully performed contract is called an **executed contract**.

tender of performance
An unconditional and absolute offer by a contracting party to perform his or her obligations under a contract. Also known as *tender*.

Tender of performance also discharges a party's contractual obligations. **Tender** is an unconditional and absolute offer by a contracting party to perform his or her obligations under the contract.

Example Ashley, who owns a women's retail store, contracts to purchase high-fashion blue jeans from a manufacturer for $75,000. At the time of performance, Ashley tenders the $75,000. Ashley has performed her obligation under the contract once she tenders the $75,000 to the manufacturer. The manufacturer fails to deliver the blue jeans. There is no completed contract, and Ashley can sue the manufacturer for breach of contract.

substantial performance
Performance by a contracting party that deviates only slightly from complete performance.

minor breach
A breach that occurs when a party renders substantial performance of his or her contractual duties.

Substantial Performance: Minor Breach

Substantial performance occurs when there has been a **minor breach** of contract. In other words, it occurs when a party to a contract renders performance that deviates slightly from complete performance. The nonbreaching party may try to convince the breaching party to elevate his or her performance to complete performance. If the breaching party does not correct the breach, the nonbreaching party can sue to recover *damages* by (1) deducting the cost to repair the defect from the contract price and remitting the balance to the breaching party or (2) suing the breaching party to recover the cost to repair the defect if the breaching party has already been paid (see Exhibit 1).

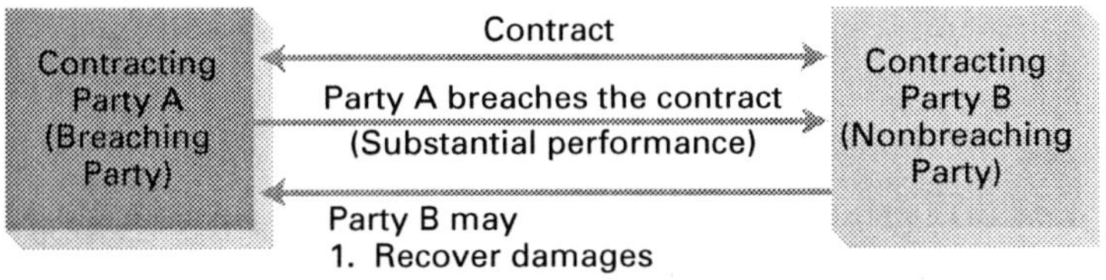

▶ Exhibit 1 REMEDY WHERE THERE HAS BEEN SUBSTANTIAL PERFORMANCE (MINOR BREACH)

Examples Donald Trump contracts with Big Apple Construction Co. to have Big Apple construct an office building for $100 million. The architectural plans call for installation of three-ply windows in the building. Big Apple constructs the building exactly to plan except that it installs two-ply windows. There has been substantial performance. It would cost $5 million to install the correct windows. If Big Apple agrees to replace the windows and does so, its performance is elevated to complete performance, and Trump must pay the entire contract price. However, if Trump has to hire someone else to replace the windows, he may deduct this cost of repair of $5 million from the contract price of $100 million and remit the difference of $95 million to Big Apple.

No cause of action arises from a bare promise.

Legal maxim

Inferior Performance: Material Breach

A **material breach** of a contract occurs when a party renders **inferior performance** of his or her contractual obligations that impairs or destroys the essence of the contract. There is no clear line between a minor breach and a material breach. A determination is made on a case-by-case basis.

Where there has been a material breach of contract, the nonbreaching party may *rescind* the contract and seek restitution of any compensation paid under the contract to the breaching party. The nonbreaching party is discharged from any further performance under the contract.[2] Alternatively, the nonbreaching party may treat the contract as being in effect and sue the breaching party to recover *damages* (see Exhibit 2).

material breach
A breach that occurs when a party renders inferior performance of his or her contractual duties.

inferior performance
A situation in which a party fails to perform express or implied contractual obligations and impairs or destroys the essence of a contract.

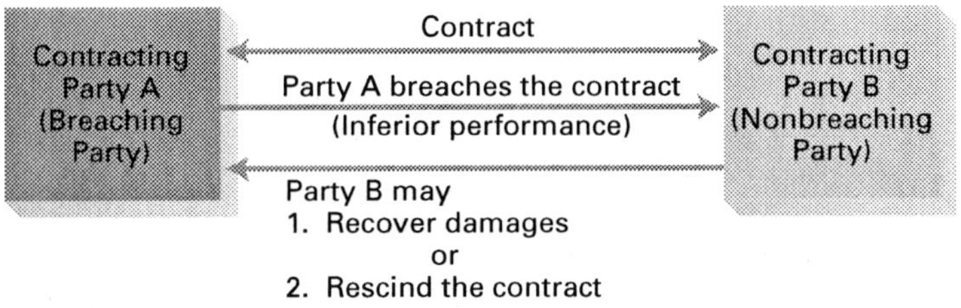

▶ Exhibit 2 REMEDIES WHERE THERE HAS BEEN INFERIOR PERFORMANCE (MATERIAL BREACH)

Example A university contracts with a general contractor to build a new three-story classroom building with classroom space for 1,000 students. The contract price is $100 million. However, the completed building cannot support more than 500 students because the contractor used inferior materials. The defect cannot be repaired without rebuilding the entire structure. Because this is a material breach, the university may rescind the contract, recover any money that it has paid to the contractor, and require the contractor to remove the building. The university is discharged of any obligations under the contract and is free to employ another contractor to rebuild the building. However, the building does meet building codes so that it can be used as an administration building of the university. Thus, as an alternative remedy, the university could accept the building as an administration building, which has a value of $20 million. The university would owe this amount—$20 million—to the contractor.

CONCEPT SUMMARY

TYPES OF PERFORMANCE

Type of Performance	Legal Consequence
Complete performance	The contract is discharged.
Substantial performance (minor breach)	The nonbreaching party may recover damages caused by the breach.
Inferior performance (material breach)	The nonbreaching party may either (1) rescind the contract and recover restitution or (2) affirm the contract and recover damages.

Anticipatory Breach

anticipatory breach
A breach that occurs when one contracting party informs the other that he or she will not perform his or her contractual duties when due.

Anticipatory breach (or **anticipatory repudiation**) of contract occurs when a contracting party informs the other party in advance that he or she will not perform his or her contractual duties when due. This type of material breach can be expressly stated or implied from the conduct of the repudiator. Where there is an anticipatory repudiation, the nonbreaching party's obligations under the contract are discharged immediately. The nonbreaching party also has the right to sue the repudiating party when the anticipatory breach occurs; there is no need to wait until performance is due.[3]

▶ MONETARY DAMAGES

monetary damages
An award of money.

A nonbreaching party may recover **monetary damages** from a breaching party. Monetary damages are available whether the breach was minor or material. Several types of monetary damages may be awarded. These include *compensatory*, *consequential*, *liquidated*, and *nominal damages*.

Compensatory Damages

compensatory damages
An award of money intended to compensate a nonbreaching party for the loss of the bargain. Compensatory damages place the nonbreaching party in the same position as if the contract had been fully performed by restoring the "benefit of the bargain."

Compensatory damages are intended to compensate a nonbreaching party for the loss of the bargain. In other words, they place the nonbreaching party in the same position as if the contract had been fully performed by restoring the "benefit of the bargain."

Examples Lederle Laboratories enters into a written contract to employ Wei as a chief operations officer (COO) of the company for three years, at a salary of $20,000 per month. After one year at work, Lederle informs Wei that her employment is terminated. This is a material breach of the contract. If Wei is unable to find a comparable job, Wei can sue Lederle Laboratiories and recover $480,000 (24 months × $20,000) as compensatory damages. If after six months Wei finds a comparable job that pays $20,000 per month, Wei can recover $360,000 from Laderle (18 months × $20,000) as compensatory damages. In these examples, the damages awarded to Wei place her in the same situation as if her contract with Lederle had been performed.

It is a vain thing to imagine a right without a remedy: for want of right and want of remedy are reciprocal.

Lord Chief Justice Holt
Ashby v. White (1703)

The amount of compensatory damages that will be awarded for breach of contract depends on the type of contract involved and which party breached the contract. The award of compensatory damages in some special types of contracts is discussed in the following paragraphs.

Sale of a Good Compensatory damages for a breach of a sales contract involving goods are governed by the Uniform Commercial Code (UCC). The usual measure of damages for a breach of a sales contract is the difference between the contract price and the market price of the goods at the time and place the goods were to be delivered.[4]

Example Revlon, Inc., contracts to buy a piece of equipment from Greenway Supply Co. for $80,000. Greenway does not deliver the equipment to Revlon when it is required to do so. Revlon purchases the equipment from another vendor but has to pay $100,000 because the current market price for the equipment has risen. Revlon can recover $20,000 from

Greenway—the difference between the market price paid ($100,000) and the contract price ($80,000)—in compensatory damages.

Construction Contract A construction contract arises when the owner of real property contracts to have a contractor build a structure or do other construction work. The compensatory damages recoverable for a breach of a construction contract vary with the stage of completion of the project when the breach occurs.

A contractor may recover the profits he or she would have made on the contract if the owner breaches the construction contract before construction begins.

Examples RXZ Corporation contracts to have Ace Construction Company build a factory building for $1,200,000. It will cost Ace $800,000 in materials and labor to build the factory for RXZ. If RXZ Corporation breaches the contract before construction begins, Ace can recover $400,000 in "lost profits" from RXZ as compensatory damages.

Example Entel Corporation contracts to have the Beta Construction Company build a factory building for Entel for $1,200,000. It will cost Beta Construction Company $800,000 to construct the building. Thus, Beta Corporation will make $400,000 profit on the contract. Beta begins construction and has spent $300,000 on materials and labor before Entel breaches the contract by terminating Beta. Here, Beta can recover $700,000, which is comprised of $400,000 lost profits ($1,200,000 – $800,000) plus $300,000 expended on materials and labor. The $700,000 of compensatory damages will make Beta Construction Company "whole."

Every unjust decision is a reproach to the law or the judge who administers it. If the law should be in danger of doing injustice, then equity should be called in to remedy it. Equity was introduced to mitigate the rigor of the law.

Lord Denning, Master of the Rolls
Re: Vandervell's Trusts (1974)

If the builder breaches a construction contract, either before or during construction, the owner can recover the increased cost above the contract price that he or she has to pay to have the work completed by another contractor.

Example Ethenol Corporation contracts to have the Sherry Construction Company build a factory building for Ethenol for $1,200,000. Just before Sherry Construction Company is to begin work, it breaches the contract by withdrawing from the project. Ethenol seeks new bids, and the lowest bid to construct the building is $1,700,000. Here, Ethenol can recover $500,000 in compensatory damages from Sherry Construction Company (the $1,700,000 new contract price – $1,200,000 Sherry Construction's original price).

Employment Contract An employee whose employer breaches an employment contract can recover lost wages or salary as compensatory damages. If the employee breaches the contract, the employer can recover the costs to hire a new employee plus any increase in salary paid to the replacement.

Mitigation of Damages

If a contract has been breached, the law places a duty on the innocent nonbreaching party to make reasonable efforts to **mitigate** (i.e., avoid or reduce) the resulting damages. The extent of mitigation required depends on the type of contract involved.

mitigation
A nonbreaching party's legal duty to avoid or reduce damages caused by a breach of contract.

If an employer breaches an employment contract, the employee owes a duty to mitigate damages by trying to find substitute employment. The employee is only required to accept *comparable employment*. The courts consider such factors as compensation, rank, status, job description, and geographical location in determining the comparability of jobs.

Consequential Damages

A nonbreaching party can sometimes recover **consequential damages**, or **special damages**, from the breaching party. Consequential damages are **foreseeable damages** that arise from circumstances outside a contract. To be liable for consequential damages, the breaching party must know or have reason to know that the breach will cause special damages to the other party.

consequential damages
Foreseeable damages that arise from circumstances outside a contract. To be liable for these damages, the breaching party must know or have reason to know that the breach will cause special damages to the other party.

Example W-Mart, a major retailer, contracts with Maytell, a major manufacturer of toys, to purchase 1,000,000 of the new "G.I. Barby Dolls" produced by Maytell at $20 per doll. W-Mart plans to sell these dolls in its stores nationwide at $50 per doll, and Maytell is aware that W-Mart intends to resell the dolls. The popularity of Barby Dolls guarantees that all the dolls purchased by W-Mart will be sold. If Maytell breaches this contract and fails to deliver the dolls to W-Mart, W-Mart cannot purchase the dolls elsewhere because Maytell holds the copyright and trademark on the doll. Therefore, W-Mart can recover the lost profits on each lost sale as consequential damages from Maytell—that is, the difference between the would-be sales price of the dolls ($50) and the purchase price of each doll ($20), or $30 lost profit per doll. In total, W-Mart can recover $30 million in consequential damages from Maytell ($50 – $20 = $30 × 1,000,000).

The very definition of a good award is that it gives dissatisfaction to both parties.

Sir Thomas Plumer, Master of the Rolls
Goodman v. Sayers (1820)

Liquidated Damages

Under certain circumstances, the parties to a contract may agree in advance to the amount of damages payable upon a breach of contract. These damages are called **liquidated damages**. To be lawful, the actual damages must be difficult or impracticable to determine, and the liquidated amount must be reasonable in the circumstances.[5] An enforceable liquidated damages clause is an exclusive remedy, even if actual damages are later determined to be different.

A liquidated damages clause is considered a **penalty** if actual damages are clearly determinable in advance or if the liquidated damages are excessive or unconscionable. If a liquidated damages clause is found to be a penalty, it is unenforceable. The nonbreaching party may then recover actual damages.

liquidated damages
Damages that parties to a contract agree in advance should be paid if the contract is breached.

ETHICS SPOTLIGHT

Liquidated Damages at Trump World Tower

"In his affidavit Donald Trump stated that he sought 25% down payments from preconstruction purchasers at the Trump World Tower because of the substantial length of time between contract signing and closing, and because of the obvious associated risks."

—Judge Mazzarelli

The Trump World Tower is a luxury condominium building constructed at 845 United Nations Plaza in Manhattan, New York. Donald Trump is managing general partner of the building, which is New York City's highest residential building. 845 UN Limited Partnership (845 UN) began selling condominiums at the building before the building was constructed. The condominium offering plan required a nonrefundable down payment of 25 percent of the purchase price. The purchase contract provided that if a purchaser defaulted and did not complete the purchase, 845 UN could keep the 25 percent down payment as liquidated damages.

Cem Uzan and Hakan Uzan, brothers and Turkish billionaires, each contracted to purchase two condominium units on the top floors of the building. Cem and Hakan were both represented by attorneys. Over the course of two years, while the building was being constructed, the brothers paid the 25 percent nonrefundable down payment of $8 million. On September 11, 2001, before the building was complete, terrorists attacked New York City by flying two planes into the World Trade Center, the city's two tallest buildings, murdering thousands of people. Cem and Hakan sent letters to 845 UN, rescinding their purchase agreements because of the terrorist attack that occurred on September 11.

That day, 845 UN sent Cem and Hakan default letters, notifying them that they had 30 days to cure their default. Upon the expiration of the cure period, 845 UN terminated the four purchase agreements and kept the 25 percent down payments on the four condominiums as liquidated damages. Cem and Hakan sued 845 UN, alleging that the 25 percent nonrefundable down payment liquidated damages clause was an unenforceable and unconscionable penalty and that the money should be returned to them. 845 UN defended, arguing that the 25 percent nonrefundable down payment was an enforceable liquidated damages clause. The issue for the court was: Is the 25 percent nonrefundable down payment an enforceable liquidated damages clause, or is it an unconscionable and unenforceable penalty?

The supreme court of New York, appellate division, sided with 845 UN and held that Cem and Hakan had breached their contract with 845 UN and that 845 UN was entitled to keep the 25 percent down payment as liquidated damages. The court stated:

It is clear that plaintiffs are not entitled to a return of any portion of their down payment. Here the 25% down payment was a specifically negotiated element of the contracts. There is no question that this was an arm's length transaction. The parties were sophisticated businesspeople, represented by counsel, who spent two months at the bargaining table before executing the amended purchase agreements. The detailed provision concerning the nonrefundable deposit was integral to the transaction. Clearly, plaintiffs were fully aware of and accepted the requirement of a nonrefundable 25%

down payment for these luxury preconstruction condominiums. If plaintiffs were dissatisfied with the 25% nonrefundable down payment provision in the purchase agreements, the time to have voiced objection was at the bargaining table.

The appellate court held that the 25 percent nonrefundable down payment was an enforceable liquidated damages clause and not an unconscionable penalty. The appellate court, as a matter of law, granted 845 UN's motion for summary judgment, allowing 845 UN to keep Cem and Hakan's down payments and dismissed their complaint. *Uzan v. 845 UN Limited Partnership*, 10 A.D.3d 230, 778 N.Y.S.2d 171, **Web** 2004 N.Y.App. Div. Lexis 8362 (Supreme Court of New York, Appellate Division)

Business Ethics Should sophisticated businesspersons be held to their bargains? Was it ethical for Cem and Hakan to try to back out of the purchase agreements and get their money back? Was it ethical for Donald Trump and 845 UN not to pay Cem and Hakan their money back?

Nominal Damages

A nonbreaching party can sue a breaching party to a contract for nominal damages even if no financial loss resulted from the breach. **Nominal damages** are usually awarded in a small amount, such as $1. Cases involving nominal damages are usually brought on principle. Most courts disfavor nominal damages lawsuits because they use valuable court time and resources.

nominal damages
Damages awarded when the nonbreaching party sues the breaching party even though no financial loss has resulted from the breach. Nominal damages are usually $1 or some other small amount.

Example Mary enters into an employment contract with Microhard Corporation. It is a three-year contract, and Mary is to be paid $100,000 per year. After Mary works for one year, Microhard Corporation fires Mary. The next day, Mary finds a better position at Microsoft Corporation, in the same city, paying $125,000 per year on a two-year contract. Mary has suffered no monetary damages but could bring a civil lawsuit against Microhard Corporation because of its breach and recover nominal damages ($1).

CONCEPT SUMMARY
TYPES OF MONETARY DAMAGES

Type of Damage	Description
Compensatory	Damages that compensate a nonbreaching party for the loss of a bargain. It places the nonbreaching party in the same position as if the contract had been fully performed.
Consequential	Damages that compensate a nonbreaching party for foreseeable special damages that arise from circumstance outside a contract. The breaching party must have known or should have known that these damages would result from the breach.
Liquidated	An agreement by the parties in advance that sets the amount of damages recoverable in case of breach. These damages are lawful if they do not cause a penalty.
Nominal	Damages awarded against the breaching party even though the nonbreaching party has suffered no financial loss because of the breach. A small amount (e.g., $1) is usually awarded.

Enforcement of Remedies

If a nonbreaching party brings a successful lawsuit against a breaching party to a contract, the court will enter a **judgment** in his or her favor. This judgment must then be collected. If the breaching party refuses to pay the judgment, the court may:

- **Issue a writ of attachment.** A **writ of attachment** orders the sheriff or other government officer to seize property in the possession of the breaching party that he or she owns and to sell the property at auction to satisfy the judgment.
- **Issue a writ of garnishment.** A **writ of garnishment** orders that wages, bank accounts, or other property of the breaching party that is in the hands of third parties be paid over to the nonbreaching party to satisfy the judgment. Federal and state laws limit the amount of the breaching party's wages or salary that can be garnished.

writ of attachment
An order of the court that enables a government officer to seize property of the breaching party and sell it at auction to satisfy a judgment.

writ of garnishment
An order of the court that orders that wages, bank accounts, or other property of the breaching party held by third persons be paid to the nonbreaching party to satisfy a judgment.

▶ RESCISSION AND RESTITUTION

rescission
An action to rescind (undo) a contract. Rescission is available if there has been a material breach of contract, fraud, duress, undue influence, or mistake.

restitution
The return of goods or property received from the other party to rescind a contract. If the actual goods or property are not available, a cash equivalent must be made.

Rescission is an action to undo a contract. It is available where there has been a material breach of contract, fraud, duress, undue influence, or mistake. Generally, to rescind a contract, the parties must make **restitution** of the consideration they received under the contract.[6] Restitution consists of returning the goods, property, money, or other consideration received from the other party. If possible, the actual goods or property must be returned. If the goods or property have been consumed or are otherwise unavailable, restitution must be made by conveying a cash equivalent. The rescinding party must give adequate notice of the rescission to the breaching party. Rescission and restitution restore the parties to the positions they occupied prior to the contract.

Example Pralene's Store contracts to purchase $1,000,000 of goods from a clothing manufacturer. Pralene's pays $100,000 as a down payment, and the first $200,000 of goods are delivered. The goods are materially defective, and the defect cannot be cured. This breach is a material breach. Pralene's can rescind the contract. Pralene's is entitled to receive its $100,000 down payment back from the manufacturer, and the manufacturer is entitled to receive the goods back from Pralene's.

In the following case, the court had to decide whether to order the rescission of a contract.

CASE 1 Rescission of a Contract

Hickman v. Bates

889 So.2d 1249, Web 2004 La.App. Lexis 3076 (2004)
Court of Appeal of Louisiana

"The Court finds that Keith's failure to inform his young, limited, first cousin was intentional and was done to obtain an advantage over her. That is, of divesting her interest in 45 acres in Bienville Parish and 236 acres in Madison Parish for a pittance."

—Judge Caraway

Facts

Patricia Dianne Hickman inherited one-half interests to two pieces of real property when her mother died. One of the properties, in Bienville Parish, Louisiana, contained 45 acres of woodland. The second property, in Madison Parish, Louisiana, contained approximately 236 acres of land and a house. Patricia was 20 years old and had a mental condition that required medication. Patricia, who lived separately from her parents, received a telephone call from her father, Joe Hickman, to come and visit him. Joe was ill with cancer and lived with his sister Christine Bates and her husband, who are parents of Keith Bates, Patricia's first cousin.

The day after Patricia arrived, Joe informed Patricia that an important concern of his was for her to sell her interests in the two pieces of property to Keith Bates and his wife Sheila (the Bates). Joe expressed his doubts that Patricia would be able to maintain the properties and his interest in keeping the property in the family. Patricia agreed to sell the properties to the Bates for $500. Patricia signed legal documents that had been drawn by an attorney prior to her arrival.

Subsequently, through a friend, Patricia sued the Bates to rescind the contracts that sold her interest in the two pieces of property to them, alleging fraud. Expert testimony at trial valued the Madison Parish property at $259,000 and the Bienville Parish property at $20,700. The trial court found fraud and rescinded the contracts. The trial court did not, however, award Patricia attorneys' fees. Both sides appealed.

Issue

Should the sales contracts be rescinded because of fraud, and should Patricia be awarded attorneys' fees?

Language of the Court

A contract is formed by the consent of the parties. However, consent may be vitiated by error, fraud, or duress. Fraud is a misrepresentation or a suppression of the truth made with the intention either to obtain an unjust advantage for one party or to cause a loss or inconvenience to the other. Fraud need only be proven by a preponderance of the evidence and may be established by circumstantial evidence. In its very thorough and well-reasoned oral ruling, the trial court made the following findings of fact concerning its determination of fraud:

> *The court finds that Patricia's intellectual abilities are limited, both from her lack of education and from her mental condition that requires medicine. Considering her situation, her youth, she was then*

20 years old, and her limited abilities, as well as her lack of prior knowledge of the purpose of the visit, and her father's illness, and the fact that she trusted her father and her cousin, the Court finds that Keith had a responsibility to make sure Patricia was informed fully about the transactions and make sure that she understood everything she was doing and the import of everything she was doing, including the fact that she would own nothing, and including the price considerations involved before she signed those documents. The Court finds that Keith's failure to inform his young, limited, first cousin was intentional and was done to obtain an advantage over her. That is, of divesting her interest in 45 acres in Bienville Parish and 236 acres in Madison Parish for a pittance.

We can discern no manifest error in these determinations. Accordingly, we find that the trial court committed no error in rescinding the sales on the ground of fraud.

Decision

The court of appeal affirmed the trial court's finding of fraud and its judgment rescinding the sales contracts by which Patricia sold her interests in the two properties to the Bates. The court of appeal reversed the trial court's denial of an award of attorneys' fees to Patricia and awarded $12,000 in attorneys' fees to Patricia.

Case Questions

Critical Legal Thinking Describe the rescission of a contract. When can a contract be rescinded? Explain.

Business Ethics Did Patricia's father, Joe Hickman, and her first cousin, Keith Bates, act ethically in this case? Did Patricia need the court's help in this case?

Contemporary Business Describe a fraud. Do you think people take advantage of their relatives very often?

▶ EQUITABLE REMEDIES

Equitable remedies are available if there has been a breach of contract that cannot be adequately compensated through a legal remedy. They are also available to prevent unjust enrichment. The most common equitable remedies are *specific performance*, *reformation*, and *injunction*, discussed in the following paragraphs.

Specific Performance

An award of **specific performance** orders the breaching party to perform the acts promised in a contract. The courts have the discretion to award this remedy if the subject matter of the contract is unique.[7] Specific performance is available to enforce land contracts because every piece of real property is considered to be unique. Works of art, antiques, and items of sentimental value, rare coins, stamps, heirlooms, and such also fit the requirement for uniqueness. Most other personal property does not.

specific performance
A remedy that orders the breaching party to perform the acts promised in the contract. Specific performance is usually awarded in cases in which the subject matter is unique, such as in contracts involving land, heirlooms, and paintings.

Specific performance of personal service contracts is not granted because the courts would find it difficult or impracticable to supervise or monitor performance of such a contract.

The court had to decide whether to issue an order of specific performance in the following case.

CASE 2 Specific Performance

Alba v. Kaufmann

27 A.D.3d 816, 810 N.Y.S.2d 539, Web 2006 N.Y.App. Div. Lexis 2321 (2006)
Supreme Court of New York, Appellate Division

"The case law reveals that the equitable remedy of specific performance is routinely awarded in contract actions involving real property, on the premise that each parcel of real property is unique."
—Judge Crew

Facts

Jean-Claude Kaufmann owned approximately 37 acres of real property located in the town of Stephentown, Rensselaer County, New York. The property is located in a wooded area and is improved with a nineteenth-century

(case continues)

farmhouse. Kaufmann and his spouse, Christine Cacace, reside in New York City and use the property as a weekend or vacation home. After Kaufmann and Cacace lost their jobs, their financial situation prompted Kaufmann to list the property for sale for $350,000.

Richard Alba and his spouse (Albas) looked at the property and offered Kaufmann the full asking price. The parties executed a contract for sale, and the Albas paid a deposit, obtained a mortgage commitment, and procured a satisfactory home inspection and title insurance. A date for closing the transaction was set. Prior to closing, Cacace sent the Albas an e-mail, indicating that she and Kaufmann had "a change of heart" and no longer wished to go forward with the sale. Albas sent a reply e-mail, stating their intent to go forward with the scheduled closing. Cacace responded with another e-mail, informing the Albas that she had multiple sclerosis and alleging that the "remorse and dread" over the impending sale was making her ill. When Kaufmann refused to close, the Albas sued, seeking specific performance, and moved for summary judgment. The supreme court denied the motion. The Albas appealed.

Issue

Was an order of specific performance of the real estate contract warranted in this case?

Language of the Court

> *In order to establish their entitlement to summary judgment, the Albas were required to demonstrate that they substantially performed their contractual obligations and were ready, willing and able to fulfill their remaining obligations, that Kaufmann was able but unwilling to convey the property and that there is no adequate remedy at law. The Albas plainly discharged that burden here. In short, the record demonstrates that the Albas were ready, willing and able to close and, but for Kaufmann's admitted refusal to do so, would have consummated the transaction.*
>
> *As to the remedy the Albas seek, the case law reveals that the equitable remedy of specific performance is routinely awarded in contract actions involving real property, on the premise that each parcel of real property is unique. Moreover, volitional unwillingness, as distinguished from good faith inability, to meet contractual obligations furnishes neither a ground for cancellation of the contract nor a defense against its specific performance.*
>
> *Even accepting, for purposes of this discussion, that the alleged exacerbation of Cacace's symptoms is both genuine and causally related to the proposed sale of property, as she is not a party to the contract, her connection to the transaction is simply too attenuated for Kaufmann to claim undue hardship. Simply put, permitting a defendant to raise an undue hardship defense under the circumstances present here would place a nearly impossible burden upon potential purchasers of real property namely, to ascertain whether any of the signatories' relatives had any potential objection to the sale in question.*

Decision

The appellate court reversed the supreme court's denial of Alba's motion for summary judgment. The appellate court, as a matter of law, granted the Albas' motion for summary judgment and ordered Kaufmann to specifically perform the real estate contract.

Case Questions

Critical Legal Thinking What does the doctrine of specific performance provide? Explain.

Business Ethics Was it ethical for Kaufman to try to back out of the contract? Once the Albas were aware of Cacace's health prroblems, should they have withdrawn their contract?

Contemporary Business Should a seller be permitted to cancel a contract for the sale of real estate because he or she has "seller's remorse"?

Reformation

reformation
An equitable doctrine that permits the court to rewrite a contract to express the parties' true intentions.

Reformation is an equitable doctrine that permits the court to rewrite a contract to express the parties' true intentions. Reformation is usually available to correct clerical errors in contracts. For example, suppose a clerical error is made during the typing of a contract, and both parties sign the contract without discovering the error. If a dispute later arises, the court can reform the contract to correct the clerical error to read as the parties originally intended.

Injunction

injunction
A court order that prohibits a person from doing a certain act.

An **injunction** is a court order that prohibits a person from doing a certain act. To obtain an injunction, the requesting party must show that he or she will suffer irreparable injury if the injunction is not issued.

CONCEPT SUMMARY

TYPES OF EQUITABLE REMEDIES

Type of Equitable Remedy	Description
Specific performance	A court orders the breaching party to perform the acts promised in the contract. The subject matter of the contract must be unique.
Reformation	A court rewrites a contract to express the parties' true intentions. This remedy is usually used to correct clerical errors.
Injunction	A court prohibits a party from doing a certain act. Injunctions are available in contract actions only in limited circumstances.

TORTS ASSOCIATED WITH CONTRACTS

The recovery for breach of contract is usually limited to contract damages. A party who can prove a contract-related **tort**, however, may also recover tort damages. Tort damages include compensation for personal injury, pain and suffering, emotional distress, and possibly punitive damages.

Generally, punitive damages are not recoverable for breach of contract. They are recoverable, however, for certain tortious conduct that may be associated with the non-performance of a contract.

The major torts associated with contracts are *intentional interference with contractual relations* and *breach of the implied covenant of good faith and fair dealing*. These torts are discussed in the following paragraphs.

Intentional Interference with Contractual Relations

A party to a contract may sue any third person who intentionally interferes with the contract and causes that party injury. The third party does not have to have acted with malice or bad faith. This tort, which is known as the tort of **intentional interference with contractual relations**, usually arises when a third party induces a contracting party to breach a contract with another party. The following elements must be shown:

1. A valid, enforceable contract between the contracting parties
2. Third-party knowledge of this contract
3. Third-party inducement to breach the contract

intentional interference with contractual relations
A tort that arises when a third party induces a contracting party to breach the contract with another party.

A third party can contract with the breaching party without becoming liable for this tort if a contracting party has already breached the contract and thus the third party cannot be held to have induced a breach of the other parties' contract.

Breach of the Implied Covenant of Good Faith and Fair Dealing

Several states have held that a **covenant of good faith and fair dealing** is implied in certain types of contracts. Under this covenant, the parties to a contract are not only held to the express terms of the contract but are also required to act in "good faith" and deal fairly in all respects in obtaining the objective of the contract. A breach of this implied covenant is a tort for which tort damages are recoverable. This tort, which is sometimes referred to as the **tort of bad faith**, is an evolving area of the law.

covenant of good faith and fair dealing
An implied covenant under which the parties to a contract not only are held to the express terms of the contract but are also required to act in "good faith" and deal fairly in all respects in obtaining the objective of the contract.

ETHICS SPOTLIGHT

Bad Faith Tort

"Where an insurer is pursued for its refusal to settle a claim, 'bad faith' lies in an insurer's failure to give at least equal consideration to the insured's interests when the insurer arrives at a decision on whether to settle the claim."

—Judge Clyde L. Kuehn

On Halloween Day, Christine Narvaez drove her automobile onto the parking lot of a busy supermarket. Narvaez had her two-year-old grandchild with her. The youngster was riding, unconstrained, in a booster seat. Narvaez saw a friend and decided to stop for a brief chat. She parked the car and exited the car, leaving the keys in the ignition and the motor running. The youngster crawled behind the wheel, slipped the car into gear, and set it in motion. The car struck Marguerite O'Neill, a woman in her 80s, pinned her between the Narvaez car and another car and slowly crushed the woman's trapped body.

O'Neill was pried loose and airlifted to a hospital trauma center. O'Neill suffered a crushed hip, a broken arm, and four cracked ribs, and she lost more than 40 percent of her blood supply as a result of internal bleeding. She spent one month in the hospital intensive care unit and had to be placed in a nursing home and was deprived of the ability to live independently.

Narvaez carried the $20,000 minimum amount of liability insurance allowed by law. She was insured by Gallant Insurance Company. O'Neill's medical bills totaled $105,000. O'Neill sued Narvaez and her insurance company, Gallant. O'Neill's attorney demanded the policy limit of $20,000 from Gallant in settlement of O'Neill's claim and offered a complete release from liability for Narvaez. Three Gallant insurance adjusters, its claims manager, and the lawyer of the law firm representing Gallant for the case all stated to John Moss, Gallant's executive vice president, that Gallant should accept the settlement offer. Moss rejected their advice and refused to settle the case.

One year later, on the eve of trial, Moss offered to settle for the $20,000 policy limit, but O'Neill then refused. The case went to trial, and the jury returned a verdict against Narvaez of $731,063. Gallant paid $20,000 of this amount, closed its file, and left Narvaez liable for the $711,063 excess judgment. To settle her debt to O'Neill, Narvaez assigned her claims against Gallant to O'Neill. O'Neill then sued Gallant for a bad faith tort for breaching the implied covenant of good faith and fair dealing that Gallant owed to Narvaez to settle the case. The jury found Gallant liable for a bad faith tort and awarded O'Neill $710,063 ($1,000 short of the judgment in the first trial) in actual damages and $2.3 million in punitive damages. The appellate court agreed. The court stated:

> *Where an insurer is pursued for its refusal to settle a claim, "bad faith" lies in an insurer's failure to give at least equal consideration to the insured's interests when the insurer arrives at a decision on whether to settle the claim. The jury's finding of bad faith was not against the manifest weight of the evidence. We must side with O'Neill and against Gallant on the extent to which the evidence established the existence of reprehensible conduct on the part of Narvaez's insurance provider.*

The appellate court held that Gallant was liable for a bad faith tort and upheld the trial court's judgment, awarding O'Neill $710,063 in actual damages and $2.3 million in punitive damages. *O'Neill v. Gallant Insurance Company*, 769 N.E.2d 100, **Web** 2002 Ill.App. Lexis 311 (Appellate Court of Illinois)

Business Ethics Did Gallant act ethically in this case? Will the implied covenant of good faith and fair dealing make insurance companies act more ethically toward their customers?

TEST REVIEW TERMS AND CONCEPTS

Anticipatory breach (anticipatory repudiation)
Breach of contract
Compensatory damages
Complete performance (strict performance)
Consequential damages (special damages or foreseeable damages)
Covenant of good faith and fair dealing
Equitable remedies
Executed contract
Inferior performance
Injunction
Intentional interference with contractual relations
Judgment
Liquidated damages
Material breach
Minor breach
Mitigation of damages
Monetary damages
Nominal damages
Penalty
Reformation
Rescission
Restitution
Specific performance
Substantial performance
Tender of performance (tender)
Tort
Tort of bad faith
Writ of attachment
Writ of garnishment

CASE PROBLEMS

1 Performance Louis Haeuser, who owned several small warehouses, contracted with Wallace C. Drennen, Inc. (Drennen), to construct a road to the warehouses. The contract price was $42,324. After Drennen completed the work, some cracks appeared in the road, causing improper drainage. In addition, "birdbaths" that accumulated water appeared in the road. When Haeuser refused to pay, Drennen sued to recover the full contract price. Haeuser filed a cross complaint to recover the cost of repairing the road. Who wins? *Wallace C. Drennen, Inc. v. Haeuser*, 402 So.2d 771, **Web** 1981 La. App. Lexis 4453 (Court of Appeal of Louisiana)

2 Anticipatory Repudiation Muhammad Ali (Ali), a professional heavyweight boxer, successfully defended his heavyweight boxing championship of the world by defeating Ken Norton. Shortly after the fight, Ali held a press conference and, as he had done on several occasions before, announced his retirement from boxing. At that time, Ali had beaten every challenger except Duane Bobick, whom he had not yet fought. Subsequently, Madison Square Garden Boxing, Inc. (MSGB), a fight promoter, offered Ali $2.5 million if he would fight Bobick. Ali agreed, stating, "We are back in business again." MSGB and Ali signed a fighters' agreement, and MSGB paid Ali a $125,000 advance payment. The fight was to take place in Madison Square Garden. Three months before the fight was to take place, Ali told MSGB that he was retiring from boxing and would not fight Bobick in February. Must MSGB wait until the date performance is due to sue Ali for breach of contract? *Madison Square Garden Boxing, Inc. v. Muhammad Ali*, 430 F.Supp. 679, **Web** 1977 U.S. Dist. Lexis 16101 (United States District Court for the Northern District of Illinois)

3 Damages Hawaiian Telephone Company entered into a contract with Microform Data Systems, Inc. (Microform), for Microform to provide a computerized assistance system that would handle 15,000 calls per hour with a one-second response time and with a "nonstop" feature to allow automatic recovery from any component failure. The contract called for installation of the host computer no later than mid-February of the next year. Microform was not able to meet the initial installation date, and at that time, it was determined that Microform was at least nine months away from providing a system that met contract specifications. Hawaiian Telephone canceled the contract and sued Microform for damages. Did Microform materially breach the contract? Can Hawaiian Telephone recover damages? *Hawaiian Telephone Co. v. Microform Data Systems Inc.*, 829 F.2d 919, **Web** 1987 U.S. App. Lexis 13425 (United States Court of Appeals for the Ninth Circuit)

4 Damages Raquel Welch was a movie actress who appeared in about 30 films over a 15-year period. She was considered a sex symbol, and her only serious dramatic role was as a roller derby queen in *Kansas City Bomber*. During that time period, Michael Phillips and David Ward developed a film package based on the John Steinbeck novella *Cannery Row*. Metro-Goldwyn-Mayer Film Company (MGM) accepted to produce the project and entered into a contract with Welch to play the leading female character, a prostitute named Suzy. At 40 years of age, Welch relished the chance to direct her career toward more serious roles. Welch was to receive $250,000 from MGM, with payment being divided into weekly increments during filming. Filming began, but three weeks later, MGM fired Welch and replaced her with another actress, Debra Winger. Welch sued MGM to recover the balance of $194,444 that remained unpaid under the contract. Who wins? *Welch v. Metro-Goldwyn-Mayer Film Co.*, 207 Cal.App.3d 164, 254 Cal.Rptr. 645, **Web** 1988 Cal.App. Lexis 1202 (Court of Appeal of California)

5 Damages Ptarmigan Investment Company (Ptarmigan), a partnership, entered into a contract with Gundersons, Inc. (Gundersons), a South Dakota corporation in the business of golf course construction. The contract provided that Gundersons would construct a golf course for Ptarmigan for a contract price of $1,294,129. Gundersons immediately started work and completed about one-third of the work by about three months later, when bad weather forced cessation of most work. Ptarmigan paid Gundersons for the work to that date. In the following spring, Ptarmigan ran out of funds and was unable to pay for the completion of the golf course. Gundersons sued Ptarmigan and its individual partners to recover the lost profits that it would have made on the remaining two-thirds of the contract. Can Gundersons recover these lost profits as damages? *Gundersons, Inc. v. Ptarmigan Investment Company*, 678 P.2d 1061, **Web** 1983 Colo.App. Lexis 1133 (Court of Appeals of Colorado)

6 Liquidated Damages H. S. Perlin Company, Inc. (Perlin), and Morse Signal Devices of San Diego (Morse) entered into a contract whereby Morse agreed to provide burglar and fire alarm service to Perlin's coin and stamp store. Perlin paid $50 per month for this service. The contract contained a liquidated damages clause limiting Morse's liability to $250 for any losses incurred by Perlin based on Morse's failure of service. Six years after the burglary system was installed, a burglary occurred at Perlin's store. Before entering the store, the burglars cut a telephone line that ran from the burglar system in Perlin's store to Morse's central location. When the line was cut, a signal indicated the interruption of service at Morse's central station. Inexplicably, Morse took no further steps to investigate the interruption of service at Perlin's store. The burglars stole stamps and coins with a wholesale value of $958,000, and Perlin did not have insurance against this loss. Perlin sued Morse to recover damages. Is the liquidated damages clause enforceable? *H. S. Perlin Company, Inc. v. Morse Signal Devices of San Diego*, 209

Cal.App.3d 1289, 258 Cal.Rptr. 1, **Web** 1989 Cal.App. Lexis 400 (Court of Appeal of California)

7 Liquidated Damages United Mechanical Contractors, Inc. (UMC), an employer, agreed to provide a pension plan for its unionized workers. UMC was to make monthly payments into a pension fund administered by the Idaho Plumbers and Pipefitters Health and Welfare Fund (Fund). Payments were due by the 15th of each month. The contract between UMC and Fund contained a liquidated damages clause which provided that if payments due from UMC were received later than the 20th of the month, liquidated damages of 20 percent of the required contribution would be assessed against UMC. In one month, Fund received UMC's payment on the 24th. Fund sued UMC to recover $9,245.23 in liquidated damages. Is the liquidated damages clause enforceable? *Idaho Plumbers and Pipefitters Health and Welfare Fund v. United Mechanical Contractors, Inc.*, 875 F.2d 212, **Web** 1989 U.S. App. Lexis 14528 (United States Court of Appeals for the Ninth Circuit)

8 Specific Performance Liz Claiborne, Inc. (Claiborne), is a large maker of sportswear in the United States and a well-known name in fashion, with sales of over $1 billion per year. Claiborne distributes its products through 9,000 retail outlets in the United States. Avon Products, Inc. (Avon), is a major producer of fragrances, toiletries, and cosmetics, with annual sales of more than $3 billion per year. Claiborne, which desired to promote its well-known name on perfumes and cosmetics, entered into a joint venture with Avon whereby Claiborne would make available its names, trademarks, and marketing experience and Avon would engage in the procurement and manufacture of the fragrances, toiletries, and cosmetics. The parties would equally share the financial requirements of the joint venture. During its first year of operation, the joint venture had sales of more than $16 million. In the second year, sales increased to $26 million, making it one of the fastest-growing fragrance and cosmetic lines in the country. One year later, Avon sought to "uncouple" the joint venture. Avon thereafter refused to procure and manufacture the line of fragrances and cosmetics for the joint venture. When Claiborne could not obtain the necessary fragrances and cosmetics from any other source for the fall/Christmas season, Claiborne sued Avon for breach of contract, seeking specific performance of the contract by Avon. Is specific performance an appropriate remedy in this case? *Liz Claiborne, Inc. v. Avon Products, Inc.*, 141 A.D.2d 329, 530 N.Y.S.2d 425, **Web** 1988 N.Y.App. Div. Lexis 6423 (Supreme Court of New York)

9 Injunction Anita Baker, a then-unknown singer, signed a multiyear recording contract with Beverly Glen Music, Inc. (Beverly Glen). Baker recorded for Beverly Glen a record album that was moderately successful. After having some difficulties with Beverly Glen, Baker was offered a considerably more lucrative contract by Warner Communications, Inc. (Warner). Baker accepted the Warner offer and informed Beverly Glen that she would not complete their contract because she had entered into an agreement with Warner. Beverly Glen sued Baker and Warner, and it sought an injunction to prevent Baker from performing as a singer for Warner. Is an injunction an appropriate remedy in this case? *Beverly Glen Music, Inc. v. Warner Communications, Inc.*, 178 Cal.App.3d 1142, 224 Cal.Rptr. 260, **Web** 1986 Cal.App. Lexis 2729 (Court of Appeal of California)

10 Intentional Interference with Contractual Relations Pacific Gas and Electric Company (PG & E) entered into a contract with Placer County Water Agency (Agency) to purchase hydroelectric power generated by Agency's Middle Fork American River Project. The contract was not terminable until 2013. As energy prices rose during the 1970s, the contract became extremely valuable to PG & E. The price PG & E paid for energy under the contract was much lower than the cost of energy from other sources. Ten year later, Bear Stearns & Company (Bear Stearns), an investment bank and securities underwriting firm, learned of Agency's power contract with PG & E. Bear Stearns offered to assist Agency in an effort to terminate the power contract with PG & E in exchange for a share of Agency's subsequent profits and the right to underwrite any new securities issued by Agency. Bear Stearns also agreed to pay the legal fees incurred by Agency in litigation concerning the attempt to get out of the PG & E contract. Who wins and why? *Pacific Gas and Electric Company v. Bear Stearns & Company*, 50 Cal.3d 1118, 791 P.2d 587, 270 Cal.Rptr. 1, **Web** 1990 Cal. Lexis 2119 (Supreme Court of California)

BUSINESS ETHICS CASES

11 Business Ethics Walgreen Company began operating a pharmacy in the Southgate Mall in Milwaukee when the mall opened. It had a lease for a 30-year term that contained an exclusivity clause in which the landlord, Sara Creek Property Company (Sara Creek), promised not to lease space in the mall to anyone else who wanted to operate a pharmacy or a store containing a pharmacy. With 11 years left on the Walgreen–Sara Creek lease, after its anchor tenant went broke, Sara Creek informed Walgreen that it intended to lease the anchor tenant space to Phar-Mor Corporation. Phar-Mor, a "deep discount" chain, would occupy 100,000 square feet, of which 12,000 square feet would be occupied by a pharmacy the same size as Walgreen's. The entrances to the two stores would be within a few hundred feet of each other. Walgreen sued Sara Creek for breach of contract and sought a permanent injunction against Sara Creek's leasing the anchor premises to Phar-Mor. Do the facts of this case justify the issuance of a permanent injunction? Did Sara Creek act ethically in not living up to the contract with Walgreen? *Walgreen Co. v. Sara Creek Property Co.*, 966 F.2d 273, **Web** 1992 U.S. App. Lexis 14847 (United States Court of Appeals for the Seventh Circuit)

12 Business Ethics Rosina Crisci owned an apartment building in which Mrs. DiMare was a tenant. One day while DiMare was descending a wooden staircase on the outside of the apartment building, she fell through the staircase and was left hanging 15 feet above the ground until she was rescued. Crisci had a $10,000 liability insurance policy on the building from the Security Insurance Company (Security) of New Haven, Connecticut. DiMare sued Crisci and Security for $400,000 for physical injuries and psychosis suffered from the fall. Prior to trial, DiMare agreed to take $10,000 in settlement of the case. Security refused this settlement offer. DiMare reduced her settlement offer to $9,000, of which Crisci offered to pay $2,500. Security again refused to settle the case. The case proceeded to trial, and the jury awarded DiMare and her husband $110,000. Security paid $10,000, pursuant to the insurance contract, and Crisci had to pay the difference. Crisci, a widow of 70 years of age, had to sell her assets, became dependent on her relatives, declined in physical health, and suffered from hysteria and suicide attempts. Crisci sued Security for tort damages for breach of the implied covenant of good faith and fair dealing. Did Security act in bad faith? *Crisci v. Security Insurance Company of New Haven, Connecticut*, 66 Cal.App.2d 425, 426 P.2d 173, 58 Cal.Rptr. 13, **Web** 1967 Cal. Lexis 313 (Supreme Court of California)

ENDNOTES

1. *Restatement (Second) of Contracts*, Section 235(2).
2. *Restatement (Second) of Contracts*, Section 241.
3. *Restatement (Second) of Contracts*, Section 253; UCC Section 2-610.
4. UCC Sections 2-708 and 2-713.
5. *Restatement (Second) of Contracts*, Section 356(1).
6. *Restatement (Second) of Contracts*, Section 370.
7. *Restatement (Second) of Contracts*, Section 359.

INTERNET LAW AND E-COMMERCE

INTERNET LAW AND E-COMMERCE

▲ **Internet Law** *The development of the Internet and electronic commerce has required courts to apply existing law to online commerce transactions and spurred the federal Congress and state legislatures to enact new laws that govern the formation and enforcement of e-contracts and protect Internet users from invasion of privacy and other cyber crimes.*

CHAPTER OBJECTIVES

After studying this chapter, you should be able to:

1. Describe Internet domain names and how domain names are protected by the Anticybersquatting Consumer Protection Act.
2. Define *e-contract* and a *software license*.
3. Describe the provisions of the Uniform Computer Information Transactions Act (UCITA).
4. Describe the provisions of the Electronic Signatures in Global and National Commerce Act (E-Sign Act).
5. Describe the federal laws that protect against cyber crimes.

CHAPTER CONTENTS

"Through the use of chat rooms, any person with a phone line can become a town crier with a voice that resonates farther than it could from any soapbox. Through the use of Web pages, mail exploders, and newsgroups, the same individual can become a pamphleteer."

—Justice Stevens
Reno v. American Civil Liberties Union, 521 U.S. 844 (1997)

▶ INTRODUCTION TO INTERNET LAW AND E-COMMERCE

The use of the Internet and the World Wide Web, and the sale of goods and services through **e-commerce**, have exploded. Large and small businesses sell goods and services over the Internet through **websites** and registered *domain names*. Consumers and businesses can purchase almost any good or service they want over the Internet, using such sites as Amazon.com, eBay, and others. Businesses and individuals may register domain names to use on the Internet. Anyone who infringes on these rights may be stopped from doing so and is liable for damages.

e-commerce
The sale of goods and services by computer over the Internet.

In addition, software and information may be licensed either by physically purchasing the software or information and installing it on a computer or by merely downloading the software or information directly into a computer.

Many legal scholars and lawyers argued that traditional rules of contract law do not adequately meet the needs of Internet transactions and software and information licensing. These concerns led to an effort to create new contract law for electronic transactions. After much debate, the National Conference of Commissioners on Uniform State Laws developed the *Uniform Computer Information Transactions Act (UCITA)*. This model act provides uniform and comprehensive rules for contracts involving computer information transactions and software and information licenses.

The federal government has also enacted many federal statutes that regulate the Internet and e-commerce. Federal law has been passed that regulates the Internet and protects personal rights while using the Internet. In addition, many new federal criminal statutes have been enacted to protect against cyber crimes.

This chapter covers Internet law, domain names, e-contracts, licensing of software, privacy laws, and criminal laws that regulate the Internet and online commerce.

▶ INTERNET

Internet
A collection of millions of computers that provide a network of electronic connections between the computers.

The **Internet**, or **Net**, is a collection of millions of computers that provide a network of electronic connections between the computers. Hundreds of millions of computers are connected to the Internet. The Internet's evolution helped usher in the Information Age. Individuals and businesses use the Internet for communication of information and data.

World Wide Web

World Wide Web
An electronic connection of millions of computers that support a standard set of rules for the exchange of information.

The **World Wide Web** consists of millions of computers that support a standard set of rules for the exchange of information called Hypertext Transfer Protocol (HTTP). Web-based documents are formatted using common coding languages. Businesses and individuals can access the web by registering with a service such as America Online (AOL).

Individuals and businesses can have their own websites. A website is composed of electronic documents known as webpages. Websites and webpages are stored on servers throughout the world, which are operated by **Internet service providers (ISPs)**. They are viewed by using web-browsing software such as Microsoft Internet Explorer and Netscape Navigator. Each website has a unique online address.

The web has made it extremely attractive to conduct commercial activities online. Companies such as Amazon.com and eBay are e-commerce powerhouses that sell all sorts of goods and services. Existing brick-and-mortar companies, such as Wal-Mart, Merrill Lynch, and Dell Computers, sell their goods and services online as well. E-commerce over the web will continue to grow dramatically each year.

E-MAIL AND WEBSITES

electronic mail (e-mail)
Electronic written communication between individuals using computers connected to the Internet.

Electronic mail, or **e-mail**, is one of the most widely used applications for communication over the Internet. Using e-mail, individuals around the world can instantaneously communicate in electronic writing with one another. Each person can have an e-mail address that identifies him or her by a unique address. E-mail will continue to grow in use in the future as it replaces some telephone and paper correspondence and increases new communication between persons.

INTERNET LAW & ONLINE COMMERCE

Controlling the Assault of Non-Solicited Pornography and Marketing Act (CAN-SPAM)

Americans are being bombarded in their e-mail accounts by "spam"—unsolicited commercial advertising. Spammers try to sell people literally anything. Spam accounts for approximately three-quarters of all business e-mail traffic. In addition, many spam messages are fraudulent and deceptive, including misleading subject lines. It takes time and money to sort through, review, and discard unwanted spam.

In 2003, Congress enacted the federal **Controlling the Assault of Non-Solicited Pornography and Marketing Act (CAN-SPAM Act)**.[1] The act (1) prohibits spammers from using falsified headers in e-mail messages, including the originating domain name and e-mail address, (2) prohibits deceptive subject lines that mislead a recipient of the contents or subject matter of the message, (3) requires that recipients of spam be given the opportunity to opt out and not have the spammer send e-mail to the recipient's address, and (4) requires spammers who send sexually oriented e-mail to properly label it as such. The Federal Trade Commission (FTC), a federal administrative agency, is empowered to enforce the CAN-SPAM Act.

In effect, the CAN-SPAM Act does not can spam but instead approves businesses to use spam as long as they do not lie. The act expressly provides that victims of spam do not have a right to bring civil lawsuits against spammers. The CAN-SPAM Act does not regulate spam sent internationally to Americans from other countries. In essence, the CAN-SPAM Act is very weak in helping consumers ward off the spam that deluges them daily.

In 2004, the FTC adopted a rule which requires that sexually explicit spam e-mail contain a warning on the subject line reading "SEXUALLY EXPLICIT." The FTC rule also prohibits the messages themselves from containing graphic material. The graphic material can appear only after the recipient has opened the e-mail message.

Internet Service Provider (ISP)

Internet service providers (ISP) are companies that provide consumers and businesses with access to the Internet. ISPs provide e-mail accounts to users, Internet access, and storage on the Internet. ISPs offer a variety of access devices and services, including dial-up, cable, DSL, broadband wireless, Ethernet, satellite Internet access, and other services to connect users to the Internet. There are also web-hosting services that allow users to create their own websites and provide storage space for website users.

A provision in the federal **Communications Decency Act** of 1996 provides: "No provider or user of an interactive computer service shall be treated as the publisher or speaker of any information provided by another information content provider."[2] Thus, ISPs are not liable for the content transmitted over their networks by e-mail users and websites.

INTERNET LAW & ONLINE COMMERCE

Electronic Communications Privacy Act (ECPA)

E-mail, computer data, and other electronic communications are sent daily by millions of people, using computers and the Internet. Recognizing that the use of computer and other electronic communications raise special issues of privacy, the federal government enacted the **Electronic Communications Privacy Act (ECPA)**.[3]

The ECPA makes it a crime to intercept an electronic communication at the point of transmission, while in transit, when stored by a router or server, or after receipt by the intended recipient. An electronic communication includes any transfer of signals, writings, images, sounds, data, or intelligence of any nature. The ECPA makes it illegal to access stored e-mail as well as e-mail in transmission.

The ECPA provides that stored electronic communications may be accessed without violating the law by the following:

1. The party or entity providing the electronic communication service. The primary example would be an employer who can access stored e-mail communications of employees using the employer's service.
2. Government and law enforcement entities that are investigating suspected illegal activity. Disclosure would be required only pursuant to a validly issued warrant.

The ECPA provides for criminal penalties. In addition, the ECPA provides that an injured party may sue for civil damages for violations of the ECPA.

DOMAIN NAMES

Most businesses conduct e-commerce by using websites on the Internet. Each website is identified by a unique Internet **domain name**.

domain name
A unique name that identifies an individual's or company's website.

Examples The domain name for the publisher of this book—Prentice Hall Publishing Company—is **www.prenhall.com.** The domain name for Microsoft Corporation is **www.microsoft.com.** The domain name for McDonald's Corporation is **www.mcdonalds.com.**

Domain names can be registered. The first step in registering a domain name is to determine whether any other party already owns the name. For this purpose, InterNIC maintains a "Whois" database that contains the domain names that have been registered. The InterNIC website is located online at **www.internic.net.**

Domain names can also be registered at Network Solutions, Inc.'s, website, which is located at **www.networksolutions.com**, as well as at other sites. An applicant must complete a registration form, which can be done online. It usually costs less than $50 to register a domain name for one year, and the fee may be paid by credit card online. Some country-specific domain names are more expensive to register.

The most commonly used top-level extensions for domain names are set forth in Exhibit 1.

▶ Exhibit 1 COMMONLY USED TOP-LEVEL EXTENSIONS FOR DOMAIN NAMES

It will be of little avail to the people, that the laws are made by men of their own choice, if the laws be so voluminous that they cannot be read, or so incoherent that they cannot be understood.

Alexander Hamilton
The Federalist Papers (1788)

.com	This extension represents the word *commercial* and is the most widely used extension in the world. Most businesses prefer a .com domain name because it is a highly recognized business symbol.
.net	This extension represents the word *network*, and it is most commonly used by ISPs, Web-hosting companies, and other business that are directly involved in the infrastructure of the Internet. Some businesses also choose domain names with a .net extension.
.org	This extension represents the word *organization* and is primarily used by nonprofit groups and trade associations.
.info	This extension signifies a resource website. It is an unrestricted global name that may be used by businesses, individuals, and organizations.
.biz	This extension is used for small-business websites.
.us	This extension is for U.S. websites. Many businesses choose this extension, which is a relatively new extension.
.cc	This extension was originally the country code for Coco Keeling Islands, but it is now unrestricted and may be registered by anyone from any country. It is often registered by businesses.
.bz	This extension was originally the country code for Belize, but it is now unrestricted and may be registered by anyone from any country. It is commonly used by small businesses.
.name	This extension is for individuals, who can use it to register personalized domain names.
.museum	This extension enables museums, museum associations, and museum professionals to register websites.
.coop	This extension represents the word *cooperative* and may be used by cooperative associations around the world.
.aero	This extension is exclusively reserved for the aviation community. It enables organizations and individuals in that community to reserve websites.
.pro	This extension is available to professionals, such as doctors, lawyers, and consultants.
.edu	This extension is for educational institutions.

There are other domain name extensions available. Countries have country-specific extensions assigned to the country. Some countries make these domain names extensions available for private purchase.

INTERNET LAW & ONLINE COMMERCE

Anticybersquatting Consumer Protection Act (ACPA)

In November 1999, the U.S. Congress enacted, and the president signed, the **Anticybersquatting Consumer Protection Act (ACPA)**.[4] The act was specifically aimed at cybersquatters who register Internet domain names of famous companies and people and hold them hostage by demanding ransom payments from the famous company or person.

In the past, trademark law was of little help in this area, either because the famous person's name was not trademarked or because, even if the name was trademarked, trademark laws required distribution of goods or services to find infringement, and most cybersquatters did not distribute goods or services but merely sat on the Internet domain names.

The 1999 act has two fundamental requirements: (1) The name must be famous and (2) the domain name must have been registered in bad faith. Thus, the law prohibits the act of cybersquatting itself if it is done in **bad faith**.

The first issue in applying the statute is whether the domain name is someone else's famous name. Trademarked names qualify; nontrademarked names—such as those of famous actors, actresses, singers, sports stars, politicians, and such—are also protected. In determining bad faith, the law provides that courts may consider the extent to which the domain name resembles the holder's name or the famous person's name, whether goods or services are sold under the name, the holder's offer to sell or transfer the name, and whether the holder has acquired multiple Internet domain names of famous companies and persons.

The act provides for the issuance of cease-and-desist orders and injunctions by the court. In addition, the law adds monetary penalties: A plaintiff has the option of seeking statutory damages in lieu of proving damages. The Anticybersquatting Consumer Protection Act gives owners of trademarks and persons with famous names a new weapon to attack the kidnapping of Internet domain names by cyberpirates.

Example The Academy Award–winning actress Julia Roberts won back the domain name **juliaroberts.com** because it had been registered in bad faith by another party not named Julia Roberts. The singer Sting was not so fortunate because the word *sting* is generic, allowing someone else to originally register and keep the domain name **sting.com**.

In the following case, the court applied the federal anticybersquatting act.

CASE 1 Domain Name

E. & J. Gallo Winery v. Spider Webs Ltd.

286 F.3d 270, Web 2002 U.S. App. Lexis 5928 (2002)
United States Court of Appeals for the Fifth Circuit

"Spider Webs has no intellectual property rights or trademark in the name 'ernestandjuliogallo,' aside from its registered domain name."

—Judge Jolly

Facts

Ernest & Julio Gallo Winery (Gallo) is a famous maker of wines that is located in California. The company registered the trademark "Ernest & Julio Gallo" in 1964 with the United States Patent and Trademark Office. The company has spent over $500 million promoting its brand name and has sold more than 4 billion bottles of wine. Its name has taken on a secondary meaning as a famous trademark name. Steve, Pierce, and Fred Thumann created Spider Webs Ltd., a limited partnership, to register Internet domain names. Spider Webs registered more than 2,000 Internet domain names, including **ernestandjuliogallo.com.** Spider Webs is in the business of selling domain names. Gallo filed suit against Spider Webs Ltd. and the Thumanns, alleging violation of the federal Anticybersquatting Consumer Protection Act (ACPA). The U.S. District Court held in favor of Gallo and ordered Spider Webs to transfer the domain name **ernestandjuliogallo.com** to Gallo. Spider Webs Ltd. appealed.

Issue

Did Spider Webs Ltd. and the Thumanns act in bad faith in registering the Internet domain name **ernestandjuliogallo.com?**

Language of the Court

Spider Webs does not appeal the holdings that Gallo had a valid registration in its mark, that the mark is famous and distinctive, and that the domain name registered by Spider Webs is identical or confusingly similar to Gallo's mark. However, Spider Webs argues that they did not act with a "bad faith intent to profit," as required by the ACPA.

Spider Webs has no intellectual property rights or trademark in the name "ernestandjuliogallo," aside from its registered domain name. The domain name does not contain the name of Spider Webs or any of the other defendants. Spider Webs had no prior use or any current use of the domain name in connection with the bona fide offering of goods or services. Steve Thumann admitted that the domain name was valuable and that they hoped Gallo would contact them so that they could "assist" Gallo in some way. There is uncontradicted evidence that Spider Webs was engaged in commerce in the selling of

(case continues)

domain names and that they hoped to sell this domain name some day.

There was evidence presented that Gallo's mark is distinctive and famous. Further, Gallo registered the mark, which is a family name, thirty-eight years ago, and other courts have found that "'Gallo' has clearly become associated with wine in the United States such that its evolution to 'secondary meaning' status may not be seriously questioned." The circumstances of this case all indicate that Spider Webs knew Gallo had a famous mark in which Gallo had built up goodwill, and that they hoped to profit from this by registering "ernestandjuliogallo.com" and waiting for Gallo to contact them so they could "assist" Gallo. In sum, the factors strongly support a finding of bad faith.

Decision

The U.S. Court of Appeals held that the name Ernest and Julio Gallo was a famous trademark name and that Spider Web Ltd. and the Thumanns acted in bad faith when they registered the Internet domain name **ernestandjuliogallo.com.** The U.S. Court of Appeals upheld the U.S. District Court's decision, ordering the defendants to transfer the domain name to plaintiff E. & J. Gallo Winery.

Case Questions

Critical Legal Thinking What does the Anticybersquatting Consumer Protection Act (ACPA) provide? Explain.

Business Ethics Did the defendants act ethically in registering so many Internet domain names? What was the motive of the defendants?

Contemporary Business How valuable is a company's trademark name? Does the ACPA protect that value? Explain.

INTERNET LAW & ONLINE COMMERCE

Domain Names Sold for Millions

What is a domain name worth? In some case, plenty. Take the case of the domain name **www.business.com**. This name, which was originally registered as a domain name for less than $50, was sold to another purchaser for $150,000 in 1996. Many people at the time thought this was an outrageous sum to pay for a domain name—that is, until the second purchaser turned around and resold the name to ECompanies for $7.5 million. Subsequently, **www.business.com** was sold to RH Donnelley for $350 million. RH Donnelly beat out the *New York Times* and Dow Jones in the bidding for the domain name. The sale was in stock.

Other domain names have been sold at high prices, too. The domain name **www.wine.com** sold for $3 million, **www.bingo.com** for $1.1 million, **www.wallstreet.com** for $1 million, **www.drugs.com** for $800,000, **www.pizza.com** for $2.6 million, and **www.vip.com** for $1.4 million. Gary Kremen, who had purchased the domain name **www.sex.com** in 1996 for next to nothing, sold the name to Escom in 2006 for $14 million.

As commerce over the Internet increases, unregistered memorable domain names become harder to find. The sale of the better domain names has increased, with multimillion-dollar price tags being paid for the most desirable names—which were originally registered for less than $50.

▶ E-CONTRACTS

e-mail and web contracts
Contracts that are entered into by e-mail and over the World Wide Web.

E-mail and the web have exploded as means of personal and business communication. In the business environment, e-mail and the web are sometimes the methods used to negotiate and agree on contract terms and to send and agree to an e-contract. Are e-contracts enforceable? Assuming that all the elements to establish a contract are present, an **e-mail contract** or **web contract** is valid and enforceable. The main problem in a lawsuit seeking to enforce an e-mail or web contract is evidence, but this problem, which exists in almost all lawsuits, can be overcome by printing out the e-mail or web contract and its prior e-mail or web negotiations, if necessary.

LANDMARK LAW

Electronic Signatures in Global and National Commerce Act (E-SIGN Act)

In 2000, the federal government enacted the **Electronic Signatures in Global and National Commerce Act (E-SIGN Act)**.[5] This act is a federal statute enacted by Congress and therefore has national reach. The act is designed to place the world of electronic commerce on a par with the world of paper contracts in the United States.

Writing Requirement of the Statute of Frauds Met

One of the main features of the E-SIGN Act is that it recognizes electronic contracts as meeting the writing requirement of the Statute of Frauds for most contracts. Statutes of Frauds are state laws that require certain types of contracts to be in writing. The 2000 federal act provides that electronically signed contracts cannot be denied effect because they are in electronic form or delivered electronically. The act also provides that record retention requirements are satisfied if the records are stored electronically.

The federal law was passed with several provisions to protect consumers. First, consumers must consent to receiving electronic records and contracts. Second, to receive electronic records, consumers must be able to demonstrate that they have access to the electronic records. Third, businesses must tell consumers that they have the right to receive hard-copy documents of their transaction.

E-Signatures Recognized as Valid

In the past, signatures have been hand-applied by the person signing a document. No more. In the electronic commerce world, it is now "What is your mother's maiden name?" "Slide your smart card in the sensor," or "Look into the iris scanner." But are electronic signatures sufficient to form an enforceable contract? The federal E-SIGN Act made the answer clear.

The E-SIGN Act recognizes an **electronic signature**, or **e-signature**. The act gives an e-signature the same force and effect as a pen-inscribed signature on paper. The act is technology neutral, however, in that the law does not define or decide which technologies should be used to create a legally binding signature in cyberspace. Loosely defined, a **digital signature** is some electronic method that identifies an individual. The challenge is to make sure that someone who uses a digital signature is the person he or she claims to be. The act provides that a digital signature can basically be verified in one of three ways:

1. By something the signatory knows, such as a secret password, pet's name, and so forth
2. By something a person has, such as a smart card, which looks like a credit card and stores personal information
3. By biometrics, which uses a device that digitally recognizes fingerprints or the retina or iris of the eye

The verification of electronic signatures is creating a need for the use of scanners and methods for verifying personal information.

E-LICENSING

Much of the new cyberspace economy is based on electronic contracts and the licensing of computer software and information. E-commerce created problems for forming contracts over the Internet, enforcing e-commerce contracts, and providing consumer protection. To address these problems, in 1999 the National Conference of Commissioners on Uniform State Laws (a group of lawyers, judges, and legal scholars) drafted the **Uniform Computer Information Transactions Act (UCITA)**.

Uniform Computer Information Transactions Act (UCITA)
A model state law that creates contract law for the licensing of information technology rights.

CONTEMPORARY ENVIRONMENT

Uniform Computer Information Transactions Act (UCITA)

The Uniform Computer Information Transactions Act (UCITA) is a model act that establishes a uniform and comprehensive set of rules that govern the creation, performance, and enforcement of computer information transactions. A computer information transaction is an agreement to create, transfer, or license computer information or information rights [UCITA § 102(a)(11)].

The UCITA does not become law until a state's legislature enacts it as a state statute. Most states have adopted e-commerce and licensing statutes that are similar to many of the provisions of the UCITA as their law for computer transactions and the licensing of software and informational rights. The UCITA will be used as the basis for discussing state laws that affect computer, software, and licensing contracts.

Unless displaced by the UCITA, state law and equity principles, including principal and agent law, fraud, duress, mistake, trade secret law, and other state laws, supplement the UCITA [UCITA § 114]. Any provisions of the UCITA that are preempted by federal law are unenforceable to the extent of the preemption [UCITA § 105(a)].

The unique provisions of the UCITA as they apply to e-licensing are discussed in the sections of this chapter and the special "Internet Law & Online Commerce" features that follow.

Licensing

Intellectual property and information rights are extremely important assets of many individuals and companies. Patents, trademarks, copyrights, trade secrets, data, software programs, and such constitute valuable intellectual property and information rights.

The owners of intellectual property and information rights often wish to transfer limited rights in the property or information to parties for specified purposes and limited duration. The agreement that is used to transfer such limited rights is called a **license**, which is defined as follows [UCITA § 102(a)(40)]:

license
A contract that transfers limited rights in intellectual property and informational rights.

License means a contract that authorizes access to, or use, distribution, performance, modification, or reproduction of, information or information rights, but expressly limits the access or uses authorized or expressly grants fewer than all rights in the information, whether or not the transferee has title to a licensed copy. The term includes an access contract, a lease of a computer program, and a consignment of a copy.

licensor
An owner of intellectual property or informational rights who transfers rights in the property or information to the licensee.

licensee
A party who is granted limited rights in or access to intellectual property or informational rights owned by a licensor.

The parties to a license are the licensor and the licensee. The **licensor** is the party who owns the intellectual property or information rights and obligates him- or herself to transfer rights in the property or information to the licensee. The **licensee** is the party who is granted limited rights in or access to the intellectual property or information [UCITA § 102(a)(41), (42)]. A **licensing** arrangement is illustrated in Exhibit 2.

Exhibit 2 LICENSING ARRANGEMENT

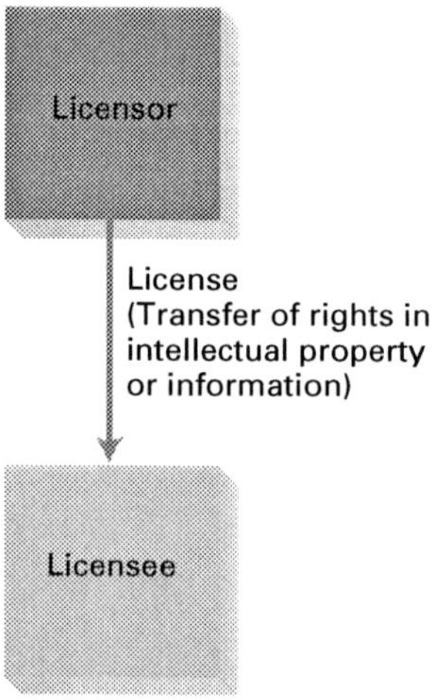

A license grants the contractual rights expressly described in the license and the right to use any information rights within the licensor's control that are necessary to exercise the expressly described rights [UCITA § 307(a)]. A license can grant the licensee the exclusive rights to use the information. An **exclusive license** means that for the specified duration of the license, the licensor will not grant to any other person rights in the same information [UCITA § 307(f)(2)].

exclusive license
A license that grants the licensee exclusive rights to use informational rights for a specified duration.

INTERNET LAW & ONLINE COMMERCE

Click-Wrap Licenses

In the past, most business and consumer contracts consisted of written agreements signed by both parties. With the advent of the Internet, many online contracts no longer fit this traditional mode. Take click-wrap licenses, for example. A **click-wrap license** is a contract used by many software companies to sell their software over the Internet or in physical packages where the software is later installed on a computer.

The software company, called the licensor, typically displays a series of dialog boxes on the computer screen that state the terms of the agreement before the software is downloaded or installed by the potential licensee. The terms of a software click-wrap license are typically not negotiable, and the licensee (the person who is granted the license) indicates his or her acceptance by clicking on a prompt button on the screen labeled "I accept" or "I agree." Click-wrap licenses contain terms of the agreement, disclaimers of warranties, guarantees for the protection of trademarks and trade secrets, and other provisions that would normally be contained in a paper license. Click-wrap agreements provide a fast, inexpensive, and convenient way for licensors to mass market their software to users without requiring paper contracts or physical signatures.

A question recently presented to the courts is whether click-wrap licenses are enforceable. The courts have held that a party is considered to have manifested her consent to enter into a contract by her physical action of using a mouse to click the "I Agree" prompt button for the click-wrap license.

The Uniform Computer Information Transactions Act (UCITA) specifically provides that a licensee who has the opportunity to review the terms of the license is bound by those terms if the licensee "manifests assent" before or during the party's initial use of or access to the licensor's software [UCITA § 210(a)]. Thus, under the modern e-commerce interpretation of the law of contracts, popular click-wrap licenses are enforceable contracts between software licensors and user licensees.

Licensing Agreement

A licensor and a licensee usually enter into a written **licensing agreement** that expressly states the terms of their agreement. Licensing agreements tend to be very detailed and comprehensive contracts. This is primarily because of the nature of the subject matter and the limited uses granted in the intellectual property or informational rights.

licensing agreement
A detailed and comprehensive written agreement between a licensor and a licensee that sets forth the express terms of their agreement.

Breach of License Agreement

The parties to a contract for the licensing of information owe a duty to perform the obligations stated in the contract. If a party fails to perform as required, there is a breach of the contract. Breach of contract by one party to a licensing agreement gives the non-breaching party certain rights, including the right to recover damages or other remedies [UCITA § 701].

Each party to a license agreement expects to receive due performance from the other party. If any reasonable grounds arise prior to the performance date that make one party think that the other party might not deliver performance when due, the aggrieved party may demand adequate assurance of due performance from the other party. Until such assurance is received, the aggrieved party may, if commercially reasonable, suspend performance until assurance is received. Failure to provide assurance within 30 days permits the aggrieved party to repudiate the contract [UCITA § 708].

If a licensor tenders a copy that is a material breach of the contract, the nonbreaching party to whom tender is made may either (1) refuse the tender, (2) accept the tender, or (3) accept any commercially reasonable units and refuse the rest [UCITA § 704].

If a licensee has accepted tender of a copy where the nonconformity is a material breach, the licensee may later revoke his or her acceptance if (1) acceptance was made because discovery was difficult at the time of tender but was then later discovered or (2) the nonconformity was discovered at the time of tender but the licensor agreed to cure the defect, and the defect has not been reasonably cured [UCITA § 707].

Our legal system faces no theoretical dilemma but a single continuous problem: how to apply to ever changing conditions the never changing principles of freedom.

Earl Warren
(1995)

INTERNET LAW & ONLINE COMMERCE

Consumers Saved from Electronic Errors

The UCITA provides that consumers are not bound by their unilateral **electronic errors** if a consumer:

1. Promptly upon learning of the error notifies the licensor of the error
2. Does not use or receive any benefit from the information or make the information or benefit available to a third party
3. Delivers all copies of the information to the licensor or destroys all copies of the information, pursuant to reasonable instructions from the licensor
4. Pays all shipping, reshipping, and processing costs of the licensor [UCITA § 217]

The UCITA does not relieve a consumer of his or her electronic error if the other party provides a reasonable method to detect and correct or avoid the error. Thus, many sellers establish methods whereby the buyer must verify the information and purchase order a second time before an electronic order is processed. This procedure strips the consumer of the defense of UCITA Section 217. Section 217 of the UCITA applies only to consumers who make electronic errors in contracting. Electronic errors by non-consumers are handled under the common law of contracts or the Uniform Commercial Code (UCC), whichever applies.

Example Kai, a consumer, intends to order 10 copies of a video game over the Internet from Cybertendo, a video game producer. In fact, Kai makes an error and orders 110 games. The electronic agent maintaining Cybertendo's website's ordering process electronically disburses 110 games. The next morning Kai discovers his mistake and immediately e-mails Cybertendo, describing the mistake and offering to return or destroy the copies at his expense. When Kai receives the games, he returns the 110 copies unused. Under the UCITA, Kai has no contract obligation for 110 copies but bears the cost of returning them to Cybertendo or destroying them if Cybertendo instructs him to do so. However, if Cybertendo's website's electronic ordering system had asked Kai to confirm his order of 110 copies of the purchase order, and Kai had confirmed the original order of 110 copies, Kai would have had to pay for the 110 copies, even if his confirmation had been in error.

Remedies

"You must remember that some things that are legally right are not morally right."

Abraham Lincoln (1840)

The UCITA provides certain *remedies* to an aggrieved party upon the breach of a licensing agreement. A party may not recover more than once for the same loss, and his or her remedy (other than liquidated damages) may not exceed the loss caused by the breach [UCITA § 801]. The UCITA provides that a cause of action must be commenced within one year after the breach was or should have been discovered but not more than five years after the breach actually occurred [UCITA § 805]. Remedies are discussed in the following paragraphs.

cancellation
The termination of a contract by a contracting party upon the material breach of the contract by the other party.

Cancellation If there has been a material breach of a contract that has not been cured or waived, the aggrieved party may cancel the contract. **Cancellation** is effective when the canceling party notifies the breaching party of the cancellation. Upon cancellation, the breaching party in possession or control of copies, information, documentation, or other materials that are the property of the other party must use commercially reasonable efforts to return them or hold them for disposal on instructions from the other party. All obligations that are executory on both sides at the time of cancellation are discharged [UCITA § 802(a) and (b)].

Upon cancellation of a license, the licensor has the right to have all copies of the licensed information returned by the licensee and to prevent the licensee from continuing to use the licensed information.

licensor's damages
Monetary damages that a licensor may recover from a licensee who breaches a contract.

Licensor's Damages If a licensee breaches a contract, the licensor may recover **licensor's damages.** The licensor may sue and recover from the licensee monetary damages caused by the breach, plus any consequential and incidental damages [UCITA § 808]. A licensor can recover *lost profits* caused by the licensee's failure to accept or complete performance of the contract. Lost profits is a proper measure of damages in this case because the licensor has effectively unlimited capability to make access available to others so there will be no license to substitute to reduce damages owed by the breaching licensee.

Example iSuperSoftware.com licenses a master disk of its software program to Distributors, Inc., to make and distribute 10,000 copies of the software. This is a nonexclusive license, and the license fee is $1 million. It costs iSuperSoftware.com $15 to produce the disk. If Distributors, Inc., refuses the disk and breaches the contract, iSuperSoftware.com can recover $1 million less $15 as damages for the profits lost on the transaction.

INTERNET LAW & ONLINE COMMERCE

Electronic Self-Help Permitted to Licensor

Just like normal contracts, electronic licenses can be breached by licensees. If such a breach occurs, the licensor can resort to remedies provided in the UCITA. Sections 815 and 816 of the UCITA provide that a licensor can resort to **electronic self-help** if a breach occurs—for example, if the licensee fails to pay the license fee. Such electronic self-help can consist of activating disabling bugs and time bombs that have been embedded in the software or information that will prevent the licensee from further using the software or information.

Section 816 provides that a licensor is entitled to use electronic self-help only if the following requirements are met:

1. The licensee must specifically agree to the inclusion in the license of self-help as a remedy. There must be a specific self-help option to which the licensee assents.
2. The licensor must give the licensee at least 15 days' notice prior to the disabling action. The notice period allows the licensee to make lawful adjustments to minimize the effects of the licensor's self-help or to seek a judicial remedy to combat the use of the self-help.
3. The licensor may not use self-help if doing so would cause a breach of the peace, risk personal injury, cause significant damage or injury to information other than the licensee's information, result in injury to the public health or safety, or cause grave harm to national security.

A licensor who violates these provisions and uses self-help improperly is liable for damages. This liability cannot be disclaimed.

Licensee's Damages When a licensor breaches a contract, the licensee may sue and recover monetary damages from the licensor. The amount of the damages depends on the facts of the situation. This is called the **licensee's damages**. Upon the licensor's breach, the licensee may either (1) cover by purchasing other electronic information from another source and recover the difference between the value of the promised performance from the licensor and the cost of cover or (2) not cover and recover the value of the performance from the licensor. **Cover** involves engaging in a commercially reasonable substitute transaction. The licensee may obtain an award of consequential and incidental damages in either case. A licensee cannot obtain excessive or double recovery [UCITA § 809].

licensee's damages
Monetary damages that a licensee may recover from a licensor who breaches a contract.

cover
A licensee's right to engage in a commercially reasonable substitute transaction after the licensor has breached the contract.

Limitation of Remedies The UCITA provides that the parties to an agreement may **limit the remedies** available for breach of the contract. This is done by including provisions in the contract. Remedies may be restricted to the return of copies and repayment of the licensing fee or limited to the repair or replacement of the nonconforming copies. Limitations of remedies in licenses subject to the UCITA are enforceable unless they are unconscionable [UCITA § 803].

The Net is a waste of time, and that's exactly what's right about it.

William Gibson

CYBER CRIMES

The advent of the computer and the Internet created an ability of persons to engage in a new form of crimes called *cyber crimes*. New technologies have allowed criminals to commit existing crimes using a new medium.

Fraud can now be perpetrated over the Internet. In addition, the Internet has allowed criminals to engage in new crimes. The police, law enforcement agencies, Congress, and the courts have had to address these new cyber crimes. In response, Congress has enacted several new federal statutes that define criminal behavior using computers and the Internet. The courts have had to interpret and apply these new statutes, as well as apply existing criminal statutes to this new medium of crime.

INTERNET LAW & ONLINE COMMERCE

Counterfeit Access Device and Computer Fraud and Abuse Act (CFAA)

The **Counterfeit Access Device and Computer Fraud and Abuse Act (CFAA)** of 1984, as amended, makes it a federal crime to access a computer knowingly to obtain (1) restricted federal government information, (2) financial records of financial institutions, and (3) consumer reports of consumer reporting agencies. The act also makes it a crime to use counterfeit or unauthorized access devices, such as cards or code numbers, to obtain things of value, transfer funds, or traffic in such devices.[6]

INTERNET LAW & ONLINE COMMERCE

Electronic Funds Transfer Act (EFTA)

The **Electronic Funds Transfer Act (EFTA)** regulates the payment and deposit of funds using electronic funds transfers, such as direct deposit of payroll and Social Security checks in financial institutions, transactions using automated teller machines (ATMs), and such. The act makes it a federal crime to use, furnish, sell, or transport a counterfeit, stolen, lost, or fraudulently obtained ATM card, code number, or other device used to conduct electronic funds transfers. The act imposes criminal penalties of imprisonment and the assessment of criminal fines.[7]

INTERNET LAW & ONLINE COMMERCE

Cyber Identity Fraud

For centuries, some people—for various purposes, mostly financial in nature—have attempted to take the identities of other persons. Today, stealing the identity of another can be extremely lucrative, earning the spoils of another's credit cards, bank accounts, Social Security benefits, and such. The use of new technology—computers and the Internet—has made such "identity fraud" easier than ever before. But a victim of such fraud may be left with funds stolen, a dismantled credit history, and thousands of dollars in costs trying to straighten out the mess. Identity fraud is the fastest-growing financial fraud in America.

DETER·DETECT·DEFEND

AVOID THEFT

To combat identity fraud, Congress passed the **Identity Theft and Assumption Deterrence Act** of 1998.[8] This act criminalizes identity fraud, making it a federal felony punishable with prison sentences ranging from 3 to 25 years. The act also appoints a federal administrative agency, the Federal Trade Commission (FTC), to help victims restore their credit and erase the impact of the imposter.

Law enforcement officials suggest the following steps to protect against identity fraud: Never put your Social Security number on any document unless it is legally required, obtain and review copies of your credit report at least twice each year, and use safe passwords (e.g., other than family names and birthdays) on bank accounts and other accounts that require personal identification numbers (PINs).

INTERNET LAW & ONLINE COMMERCE

Information Infrastructure Protection Act (IIP Act)

The Internet and Information Age ushered in a whole new world for education, business and consumer transactions. But what followed was a rash of cyber crimes. Prosecutors and courts wrestled over how to apply existing laws written in a nondigital age to new Internet-related abuses.

In 1996, Congress responded by enacting the **Information Infrastructure Protection Act (IIP Act)**.[9] In this federal law, Congress addressed computer-related crimes as distinct offenses. The IIP Act provides protection for any computer attached to the Internet.

The IIP Act makes it a federal crime for anyone to intentionally access and acquire information from a protected computer without authorization. The IIP Act does not require that the defendant accessed a protected computer for commercial benefit. Thus, persons who transmit a computer virus over the Internet or hackers who trespass into Internet-connected computers may be criminally prosecuted under the IIP Act. Even merely observing data on a protected computer without authorization is sufficient to meet the requirement that the defendant has accessed a protected computer. Criminal penalties for violating the IIP Act include imprisonment and fines.

The IIP Act gives the federal government a much-needed weapon for directly prosecuting cyber-crooks, hackers, and others who enter, steal, destroy, or look at others' computer data without authorization.

State Criminal Laws

Often, larceny statutes cover only the theft of tangible property. Because computer software, programs, and data are intangible property, they are not covered by some existing state criminal statutes. To compensate for this, many states have either modernized existing laws to include computer crime or amended existing penal codes to make certain abuses of computers a criminal offense. Computer trespass, the unauthorized use of computers, tampering with computers, and the unauthorized duplication of computer-related materials are usually forbidden by these acts.[10]

Our growing reliance on computers has made us more aware of the risks associated with losing the data stored on them. As a result, it is likely that the safety of the nation's ever-expanding computer networks will be legislated even more in the future.

ETHICS SPOTLIGHT

Computer Hacker Found Guilty of Cyber Crime

In "techie" circles, Kevin D. Mitnick became the underground icon of computer hackers. During a decade's reign, Mitnick terrorized the federal government, universities, and such high-tech companies as Sun Microsystems, Novell Corporation, MCI Communications, Digital Equipment Corporation, and others by breaking into their computer systems. Mitnick used his computer skills to penetrate his victims' computer systems to steal secret information and wreak havoc with their software and data.

Mitnick, a self-taught computer user, has a history of computer-related crime. As a 17-year-old, he was placed on probation for stealing computer manuals from a Pacific Bell Telephone switching center in Los Angeles. Mitnick was next accused of breaking into federal government and military computers. He has also been accused of breaking into the nation's telephone and cellular telephone networks, stealing thousands of data files and trade secrets from corporate targets, obtaining at least 20,000 credit card numbers of some of the country's richest persons, and sabotaging government, university, and private computer systems around the nation. Mitnick was arrested and convicted of computer crimes and served time in prison.

Upon release from prison, he was put on probation and placed in a medical program to treat his compulsive addiction to computers, which included a court order to not touch a computer or modem. Mitnick dropped out of sight and evaded federal law enforcement officials for several years as he continued a life of computer crime.

Mitnick's next undoing came when he broke into the computer of Tsutomu Shimomura, a researcher at the San Diego Supercomputer Center. Shimomura, a cybersleuth who advises the FBI and major companies on computer and Internet security, made it his crusade to catch the hacker who broke into his computer. Shimomura watched electronically as Mitnick invaded other computers across the country, but he could not physically locate Mitnick because he disguised his whereabouts by breaking into telephone company computers and rerouting all his computer calls. Eventually, Shimomura's patient watching paid off, as he traced the electronic burglar to Raleigh, North Carolina. Shimomura flew to Raleigh, where he used a cellular-frequency-direction-finding antenna to locate Mitnick's apartment. The FBI was notified, and an arrest warrant was obtained from a judge at his home. The FBI arrested Mitnick at his apartment. Mitnick was placed in jail without bail, pending the investigation of his case.

Mitnick's computer crimes spree has been estimated to have cost his victims several hundreds of millions of dollars in losses. Mitnick has not been accused of benefiting financially from his deeds. Mitnick entered into a plea agreement with federal prosecutors. The U.S. District Court judge sentenced Kevin Mitnick to 46 months in prison, including time served, and ordered him to pay

$4,125 in restitution to the companies he victimized. The judge called this a token amount but did not order a larger restitution because she believed Mitnick would not be able to pay more. After serving his time in jail, Mitnick was released from prison. As part of the sentencing, Mitnick cannot use electronic devices, from PCs to cellular telephones, during an additional probationary period following his release from prison. Mitnick is now acting as a consultant to businesses, advising them how to protect themselves from computer hackers.

Business Ethics Do you think hackers cause much economic loss? Should Mitnick have been given a greater sentence in this case? Why or why not?

Siem Reap, Cambodia *The world is connected by the Internet and World Wide Web.*

TEST REVIEW TERMS AND CONCEPTS

Anticybersquatting Consumer Protection Act (ACPA)
Bad faith
Cancellation
Click-wrap license
Communications Decency Act
Controlling the Assault of Non-Solicited Pornography and Marketing Act (CAN-SPAM Act)
Counterfeit Access Device and Computer Fraud and Abuse Act (CFAA)
Cover
Digital signature
Domain name
Electronic commerce (E-commerce)
Electronic Communications Privacy Act (ECPA)
Electronic errors
Electronic Funds Transfer Act (EFTA)
Electronic mail (e-mail)
Electronic self-help
Electronic signature (e-signature)
Electronic Signatures in Global and National Commerce Act (E-SIGN Act)
E-mail contract
Exclusive license
Identity Theft and Assumption Deterrence Act
Information Infrastructure Protection Act (IIP Act)
Internet (Net)
Internet service provider (ISP)
License
Licensee
Licensee's damages
Licensing
Licensing agreement
Licensor
Licensor's damages
Limitation of remedies
Uniform Computer Information Transactions Act (UCITA)
Web contract
Website
World Wide Web

CASE PROBLEMS

1 Domain Name Francis Net, a freshman in college and a computer expert, browses websites for hours each day. One day, she thinks to herself, "I can make money registering domain names and selling them for a fortune." She has recently seen an advertisement for Classic Coke, a cola drink produced and marketed by Coca-Cola Company. Coca-Cola Company has a famous trademark on the term *Classic Coke* and has spent millions of dollars advertising this brand and making the term famous throughout the United States and the world. Francis goes to the website **www.networksolutions.com**, an

Internet domain name registration service, to see if the Internet domain name **classiccoke.com** has been taken. She discovers that it is available, so she immediately registers the Internet domain name **classiccoke.com** for herself and pays the $70 registration fee with her credit card. Coca-Cola Company decides to register the Internet domain name **classiccoke.com,** but when it checks at Network Solutions, Inc.'s, website, it discovers that Francis Net has already registered the Internet domain name. Coca-Cola Company contacts Francis, who demands $500,000 for the name. Coca-Cola Company sues Francis to prevent Francis from using the Internet domain name **classiccoke.com** and to recover it from her under the federal ACPA. Who wins?

2 E-Mail Contract The Little Steel Company is a small steel fabricator that makes steel parts for various metal machine shop clients. When Little Steel Company receives an order from a client, it must locate and purchase 10 tons of a certain grade of steel to complete the order. The Little Steel Company sends an e-mail message to West Coast Steel Company, a large steel company, inquiring about the availability of 10 tons of the described grade of steel. The West Coast Steel Company replies by e-mail that it has available the required 10 tons of steel and quotes $450 per ton. The Little Steel Company's purchasing agent replies by e-mail that the Little Steel Company will purchase the 10 tons of described steel at the quoted price of $450 per ton. The e-mails are signed electronically by the Little Steel Company's purchasing agent and the selling agent of the West Coast Steel Company. When the steel arrives at the Little Steel Company's plant, the Little Steel Company rejects the shipment, claiming the defense of the Statute of Frauds. The West Coast Steel Company sues the Little Steel Company for damages. Who wins?

3 Contract Einstein Financial Analysts, Inc. (EFA), has developed an electronic database that has recorded the number of plastic pails manufactured and sold in the United States since plastic was first invented. Using this data and a complicated patented software mathematical formula developed by EFA, a user can predict with 100 percent accuracy (historically) how the stock of each of the companies of the Dow Jones Industrial Average will perform on any given day of the year. William Buffet, an astute billionaire investor, wants to increase his wealth, so he enters into an agreement with EFA whereby he is granted the sole right to use the EFA data (updated daily) and its financial model for the next five years. Buffet pays EFA $100 million for the right to the data and mathematical formula. After using the data and software formula for one week, Buffet discovers that EFA has also transferred the right to use the EFA plastic pail database and software formula to his competitor. Buffet sues EFA. What type of arrangement has EFA and Buffet entered into? Who wins?

4 License An Internet firm called Info.com, Inc., licenses computer software and electronic information over the Internet. Info.com has a website, **Info.com**, where users can license Info.com software and electronic information. The website is operated by an electronic agent; a potential user enters Info.com's website and looks at available software and electronic information that is available from Info.com. Mildred Hayward pulls up the Info.com website on her computer and decides to order a certain type of Info.com software. Hayward enters the appropriate product code and description; her name, mailing address, and credit card information; and other data needed to complete the order for a three-year license at $300 per month. The electronic agent has Hayward verify all the information a second time. When Hayward has completed verifying the information, she types at the end of her order, "I accept this electronic software only if after I have used it for two months I still personally like it." Info.com's electronic agent delivers a copy of the software to Hayward, who downloads the copy of the software onto her computer. Two weeks later, Hayward sends the copy of the software back to Info.com, stating, "Read our contract: I personally don't like this software; cancel my license." Info.com sues Hayward to recover the license payments for three years. Who wins?

5 Electronic Signature David Abacus uses the Internet to place an order to license software for his computer from Inet.License, Inc. (Inet), through Inet's electronic website ordering system. Inet's webpage order form asks David to type in his name, mailing address, telephone number, e-mail address, credit card information, computer location information, and personal identification number. Inet's electronic agent requests that David verify the information a second time before it accepts the order, which David does. The license duration is two years, at a license fee of $300 per month. Only after receiving the verification of information does Inet's electronic agent place the order and send an electronic copy of the software program to David's computer, where he installs the new software program. David later refuses to pay the license fee due Inet because he claims his electronic signature and information were not authentic. Inet sues David to recover the license fee. Is David's electronic signature enforceable against him?

6 License Tiffany Pan, a consumer, intends to order three copies of a financial software program from iSoftware, Inc. Tiffany, using her computer, enters iSoftware's website **isoftware.com** and places an order with the electronic agent taking orders for the website. The license provides for a duration of three years at $300 per month for each copy of the software program. Tiffany enters the necessary product code and description; her name, mailing address, and credit card information; and other data necessary to place the order. When the electronic order form prompts Tiffany to enter the number of copies of the software program she is ordering, Tiffany mistakenly types in "30." iSoftware's electronic agent places the order and ships 30 copies of the software program to Tiffany. When Tiffany receives the 30 copies of the software program, she ships them back to iSoftware with a note stating, "Sorry, there has been a mistake. I only meant to order

3 copies of the software, not 30." When iSoftware bills Tiffany for the license fees for the 30 copies, Tiffany refuses to pay. iSoftware sues Tiffany to recover the license fees for 30 copies. Who wins?

7 License Silvia Miofsky licenses a software program from Accura.com, Inc., to sort information from a database to be used in Silvia's financial planning business. The license is for three years, and the license fee is $500 per month. The new software program from Accura.com will be run in conjunction with other software programs and databases used by Silvia in her business. The licensing agreement between Accura.com and Silvia and the label on the software package state that the copy of the licensed software program has been tested by Accura.com and will run without error. Silvia installs the copy of Accura.com's software, but every fifth or sixth time the program is run, it fails to operate properly and shuts down Silvia's computer and other programs. Silvia sends the software, marked *defective*, back to Accura.com. When Accura.com bills Silvia for the unpaid license fees for the three years of the license, Silvia refuses to pay. Accura.com sues Silvia to recover the license fees under the three year license. Who wins?

8 License Metatag, Inc., is a developer and distributor of software and electronic information rights over the Internet. Metatag produces a software program called Virtual 4-D Links; a user of the program merely types in the name of a city and address anywhere in the world, and the computer transports the user there and creates a four-dimensional space and a sixth sense unknown to the world before. The software license is nonexclusive, and Metatag licenses its Virtual 4-D Link to millions of users worldwide. Nolan Bates, who has lived alone with his mother too long, licenses the Virtual 4-D Link program for five years for a license fee of $350 per month. Bates uses the program for two months before his mother discovers why he has had a smile on his face lately. Bates, upon his mother's urging, returns the Virtual 4-D Link software program to Metatag, stating that he is canceling the license. Metatag sues Bates to recover the unpaid license fees. Who wins?

BUSINESS ETHICS CASES

9 Business Ethics BluePeace.org is a new environmental group that has decided that expounding its environmental causes over the Internet is the best and most efficient way to spend its time and money to advance its environmental causes. To draw attention to its websites, BluePeace.org comes up with catchy Internet domain names. One is **macyswearus.org,** another is **exxonvaldezesseals.org,** and another is **generalmotorscrashesdummies.org.** The **macyswearus.org** website first shows beautiful women dressed in mink fur coats sold by Macy's Department Stores and then goes into graphic photos of minks being slaughtered and skinned and made into the coats. The **exxonvaldezesseals.org** website first shows a beautiful, pristine bay in Alaska, with the *Exxon Valdez* oil tanker quietly sailing through the waters, and then it shows photos of the ship breaking open and spewing forth oil and then seals who are gooed with oil, suffocating and dying on the shoreline. The website **generalmotorscrashesdummies.org** shows a General Motors automobile involved in normal crash tests with dummies followed by photographs of automobile accident scenes where people and children lay bleeding and dying after an accident involving General Motors automobiles. Macy's Department Stores, the Exxon Oil Company, and the General Motors Corporation sue BluePeace.org for violating the federal ACPA. Who wins? Has BluePeace.org acted unethically in this case?

10 Business Ethics Apricot.com is a major software developer that licenses software to be used over the Internet. One of its programs, called Match, is a search engine that searches personal ads on the Internet and provides a match for users for potential dates and possible marriage partners. Nolan Bates subscribes to the Match software program from Apricot.com. The license duration is five years, with a license fee of $200 per month. For each subscriber, Apricot.com produces a separate webpage that shows photos of the subscriber and personal data. Bates places a photo of himself with his mother, with the caption, "Male, 30 years old, lives with mother, likes quiet nights at home." Bates licenses the Apricot.com Match software and uses it 12 hours each day, searching for his Internet match. Bates does not pay Apricot.com the required monthly licensing fee for any of the three months he uses the software. After using the Match software but refusing to pay Apricot.com its licensing fee, Apricot.com activates the disabling bug in the software and disables the Match software on Bates' computer. Apricot.com does this with no warning to Bates. It then sends a letter to Bates stating, "Loser, the license is canceled!" Bates sues Apricot.com for disabling the Match software program. Who wins? Did Bates act ethically? Did Apricot.com act ethically?

ENDNOTES

1. 15 U.S.C. Sections 7701-7713.
2. 47 U.S.C. Section 230 (c)(1).
3. 18 U.S.C. Section 2510.
4. 15 U.S.C. Section 1125(d).
5. 15 U.S.C. Chapter 96.
6. 18 U.S.C. Section 1030.
7. 15 U.S.C. Section 1693.
8. 18 U.S.C. Section 1028.
9. 18 U.S.C. Section 1030.
10. See New York Session Laws, 1986, Chapter 514.

FORMATION OF SALES AND LEASE CONTRACTS

From Chapter 18 of *Business Law: Legal Environment, Online Commerce, Business Ethics, and International Issues,* 7/e.

FORMATION OF SALES AND LEASE CONTRACTS

Jochen Sand/Getty Images/Digital Vision

▲ **Retail Store** *The sale and lease of goods—consumer goods, automobiles, computers, electronics, business equipment, and such—makes up a considerable part of the United States economy. A special law—the Uniform Commercial Code (UCC)—contains rules that apply to contracts for the sale and lease of goods. The UCC is a model act that many states have adopted in whole or in part as their commercial code. Article 2 of the UCC covers sales of goods and Article 2A of the UCC covers the lease of goods. Under the UCC, the sale of goods that exceeds $500 sales price must be in writing to be enforceable.*

CHAPTER OBJECTIVES

After studying this chapter, you should be able to:

1. Describe sales contracts governed by Article 2 of the UCC.
2. Describe lease contracts governed by Article 2A of the UCC.
3. Describe the formation of sales and lease contracts.
4. Define the UCC's firm offer rule, additional terms rule, and written confirmation rule.
5. Describe how Revised Article 2 (Sales) and Article 2A (Leases) permit electronic contracting.

CHAPTER CONTENTS

"Commercial law lies within a narrow compass, and is far purer and freer from defects than any other part of the system."

Henry Peter Brougham
House of Commons, February 7, 1828

▶ INTRODUCTION TO FORMATION OF SALES AND LEASE CONTRACTS

Most tangible items—such as books, clothing, and tools—are considered *goods.* In medieval times, merchants gathered at fairs in Europe to exchange such goods. Over time, certain customs and rules evolved for enforcing contracts and resolving disputes. These customs and rules, which were referred to as the *Law Merchant*, were enforced by "fair courts" established by the merchants. Eventually, the customs and rules of the Law Merchant were absorbed into the common law.

Toward the end of the 1800s, England enacted a statute (the Sales of Goods Act) that codified the common law rules of commercial transactions. In the United States, laws governing the sale of goods also developed. In 1906, the **Uniform Sales Act** was promulgated in the United States and enacted in many states. It was quickly outdated, however, as mass production and distribution of goods developed in the twentieth century.

In 1949, the National Conference of Commissioners on Uniform State Laws promulgated a comprehensive statutory scheme called the *Uniform Commercial Code (UCC).* The UCC covers most aspects of commercial transactions.

Article 2 (Sales) and *Article 2A (Leases)* of the UCC govern personal property sales and leases. These articles are intended to provide clear, easy-to-apply rules that place the risk of loss of the goods on the party most able to either bear the risk or insure against it. The common law of contracts governs if either Article 2 or Article 2A is silent on an issue. Article 2 (Sales) and Article 2A (Leases) have been revised. Revised Article 2 (Sales) and Revised Article 2A (Leases) recognize the importance of electronic contracting and have established rules for e-contracts for the sale and lease of goods.

This chapter discusses the formation of sales and lease contracts.

▶ UNIFORM COMMERCIAL CODE (UCC)

One of the major frustrations of businesspersons conducting interstate business is that they are subject to the laws of each state in which they operate. To address this problem, in 1949 the National Conference of Commissioners on Uniform State Laws promulgated the **Uniform Commercial Code (UCC).**

Uniform Commercial Code (UCC)
A model act that includes comprehensive laws that cover most aspects of commercial transactions. All the states have enacted all or part of the UCC as statutes.

LANDMARK LAW

The Uniform Commercial Code (UCC)

The UCC is a **model act** drafted by the American Law Institute and the National Conference of Commissioners on Uniform State Laws. This model act contains uniform rules that govern commercial transactions. For the UCC or any part of the UCC to become law in a state, that state needs to enact the UCC as its commercial law statute. Every state (except Louisiana, which has adopted only parts of the UCC) has enacted the UCC or the majority of the UCC as a commercial statute.

The UCC is divided into articles, with each article establishing uniform rules for a particular facet of commerce in this country. The articles of the UCC are:

Article 1	General Provisions
Article 2	Sales
Revised Article 2	Sales
Article 2A	Leases
Revised Article 2A	Leases
Article 3	Negotiable Instruments
Article 4	Bank Deposits and Collections
Article 4A	Funds Transfers
Article 5	Letters of Credit
Article 6	Bulk Transfers
Article 7	Documents of Title
Article 8	Investment Securities
Article 9	Secured Transactions
Revised Article 9	Secured Transactions

The UCC is continually being revised to reflect changes in modern commercial practices and technology. Article 2, which establishes rules that govern the sale of goods, was recently revised. Article 2A, which governs leases of personal property, was recently revised. Article 4A was added to regulate the use of wire transfers in the banking system. Articles 3 and 4, which cover the creation and transfer of negotiable instruments and the clearing of checks through the banking system, were substantially amended. Article 9, which covers secured transactions in personal property, was also revised.

ARTICLE 2 (SALES)

Article 2 (Sales)
An article of the UCC that governs sale of goods.

All states except Louisiana have adopted some version of **Article 2 (Sales)** of the UCC. Article 2 is also applied by federal courts to sales contracts governed by federal law. Article 2 has recently been revised. This article, referred to as *Revised Article 2*, has been adopted by some states.

What Is a Sale?

sale
The passing of title of goods from a seller to a buyer for a price.

Article 2 of the UCC applies to transactions in goods [UCC 2-102]. All states have held that Article 2 applies to the sale of goods. A **sale** consists of the passing of title of goods from a seller to a buyer for a price [UCC 2-106(1)].

Example The purchase of a computer is a sale subject to Article 2, whether the computer was paid for using cash, credit card, or another form of consideration (see Exhibit 1).

Exhibit 1 SALES TRANSACTION

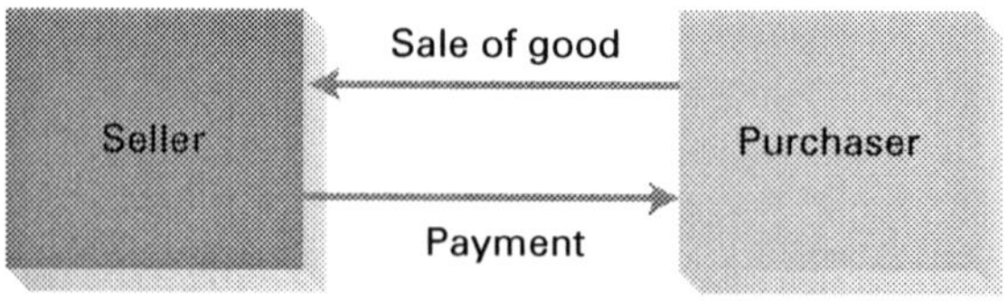

What Are Goods?

goods
Tangible things that are movable at the time of their identification to a contract.

Goods are defined as tangible things that are movable at the time of their identification to a contract [UCC 2-105(1)]. Specially manufactured goods and the unborn young of animals are examples of goods. Certain items are not considered goods and are not subject to Article 2. They include:

- Money and intangible items are not tangible goods.

Examples Stocks, bonds, and patents are not tangible goods.

- Real estate is not a tangible good because it is not movable [UCC 2-105(1)]. Minerals, structures, growing crops, and other things that are severable from real estate may be classified as goods subject to Article 2, however.

Examples The sale and removal of a chandelier in a house is a sale of goods subject to Article 2 because its removal would not materially harm the real estate. The sale and removal of the furnace, however, would be a sale of real property because its removal would cause material harm [UCC 2-107(2)].

Goods Versus Services

Contracts for the provision of services—including legal services, medical services, and dental services—are not covered by Article 2. Sometimes, however, a sale involves both the provision of a service and a good in the same transaction. This sale is referred to as a **mixed sale**. Article 2 applies to mixed sales only if the goods are the predominant part of the transaction. Whether the sale of goods is the predominant part of a mixed sale is decided by courts on a case-by-case basis.

mixed sale
A sale that involves the provision of a service and a good in the same transaction.

In the following case, the court had to decide whether a sale was of a good or a service.

CASE 1 Good or Service

Brandt v. Boston Scientific Corporation and Sarah Bush Lincoln Health Center

204 Ill.2d 640, 792 N.E.2d 296, Web 2003 Ill. Lexis 785 (2003)
Supreme Court of Illinois

"Where there is a mixed contract for goods and services, there is a transaction in goods only if the contract is predominantly for goods and incidentally for services."
—Justice Garman

Facts

Brenda Brandt was admitted to Sarah Bush Lincoln Health Center (Health Center) to receive treatment for urinary incontinence. During the course of an operation, the doctor surgically implanted a ProteGen Sling (sling) in Brandt. Subsequently, the manufacturer of the sling, Boston Scientific Corporation, issued a recall of the sling because it was causing medical complications in some patients. Brandt suffered serious complications and had the sling surgically removed.

Brandt sued Boston Scientific Corporation and the Health Center for breach of the implied warranty of merchantability included in Article 2 (Sales) of the Uniform Commercial Code (UCC). Health Center filed a motion with the court to have the case against it dismissed. Health Center argued that it was a provider of services and not a merchant that sold goods, and because the UCC (Sales) applies to the sale of goods, Health Center was not subject to the UCC. The trial court agreed with Health Center, found that the transaction was predominantly the provision of services and not the sale of goods, and dismissed Brandt's case against Health Center. The appellate court affirmed the decision. Brandt appealed.

Issue

Was the transaction between Brandt and Health Center predominantly the provision of services or the sale of goods?

Language of the Court

Article 2 of the UCC imposes the implied warranty of merchantability. To succeed on a claim of breach of implied warranty of merchantability, a plaintiff must allege and prove: (1) a sale of goods (2) by a merchant of those goods, and (3) the goods were not of merchantable quality. Where there is a mixed contract for goods and services, there is a transaction in goods only if the contract is predominantly for goods and incidentally for services.

We now apply the predominant purpose test to the facts of this case. In this case, Brandt's bill from the Health Center reflects that of the $11,174.50 total charge for her surgery, a charge of $1,659.50, or 14.9%, was for the sling and its surgical kit; a charge of $5,428.50, or 48.6%, was for all movable goods, including pharmaceuticals, medical supplies, and sterile supplies. The remainder of the charges were for various services, including the hospital and operating rooms and various kinds of medical testing and treatment. A charge for the implantation of the sling by the surgeon was not included in the bill. A majority of the charges, 51.4%, were for services rather than goods. Only a small fraction of the total charge was for the sling, the goods at issue in this case.

These services, the medical treatment, were the primary purpose of the transaction between Brandt and the

(case continues)

Health Center, and the purchase of the sling was incidental to the treatment. Brandt can seek recovery from the manufacturer of the sling.

Decision

The supreme court of Illinois held that the provision of services, and not the sale of goods, was the predominant feature of the transaction between Brandt and Health Center and that Health Center was not liable under Article 2 (Sales) of the UCC. The supreme court of Illinois affirmed the decision of the trial court and appellate court that dismissed Brandt's lawsuit against Health Center.

Case Questions

Critical Legal Thinking What is a good? Where there is a mixed contract for goods and services, what does the predominant purpose test provide?

Business Ethics Why do you think Brandt sued Health Center for violation of UCC Article 2 (Sales)?

Contemporary Business Is Boston Scientific Corporation subject to a UCC Article 2 lawsuit in this case? Why or why not?

Who Is a Merchant?

Generally, Article 2 of the UCC applies to all sales contracts, whether they involve merchants or not. However, Article 2 contains several provisions that either apply only to merchants or impose a greater duty on merchants. UCC 2-104(1) defines a **merchant** as (1) a person who deals in the goods of the kind involved in the transaction or (2) a person who by his or her occupation holds himself or herself out as having knowledge or skill peculiar to the goods involved in the transaction.

merchant
A person who (1) deals in the goods of the kind involved in a transaction or (2) by his or her occupation holds himself or herself out as having knowledge or skill peculiar to the goods involved in the transaction.

Examples A sporting goods dealer is a merchant with respect to the sporting goods he sells. This sporting goods dealer is not a merchant concerning the sale of his lawn mower to a neighbor.

Automobile Showroom
Many people and businesses lease their automobiles and other vehicles from dealers and other vehicle providers. Automobile and vehicle leases are subject to the rules of Article 2A (Leases) of the Uniform Commercial Code.

▶ ARTICLE 2A (LEASES)

Article 2A (Leases)
An article of the UCC that governs leases of goods.

Personal property leases are a billion-dollar industry. Consumer leases of automobiles or equipment and commercial leases of such items as aircraft and industrial machinery fall into this category. **Article 2A (Leases)** of the UCC directly addresses personal property leases [UCC 2A-101]. It establishes a comprehensive, uniform law covering the formation, performance, and default of leases in goods [UCC 2A-102, 2A-103(h)].

Article 2A is similar to Article 2. In fact, many Article 2 provisions were simply adapted to reflect leasing terminology and practices that carried over to Article 2A.

Definition of *Lease*

A **lease** is a transfer of the right to the possession and use of named goods for a set term in return for certain consideration [UCC 2A-103(1)(i)(x)]. Leased goods can be anything from a hand tool leased to an individual for a few hours to a complex line of industrial equipment leased to a multinational corporation for a number of years.

In an ordinary lease, the **lessor** is the person who transfers the right of possession and use of goods under the lease [UCC 2A-103(1)(p)]. The **lessee** is the person who acquires the right to possession and use of goods under a lease [UCC 2A-103(1)(n)].

lease
A transfer of the right to the possession and use of named goods for a set term in return for certain consideration.

lessor
A person who transfers the right of possession and use of goods under a lease.

lessee
A person who acquires the right to possession and use of goods under a lease.

Example Ingersoll-Rand Corporation, which manufactures robotic equipment, enters into a lease to lease robotic equipment to Dow Chemical. Ingersoll-Rand is the lessor, and Dow Chemical is the lessee (see Exhibit 2).

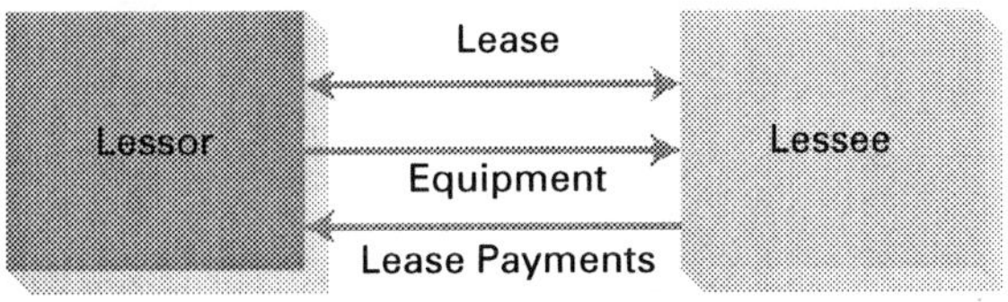

▶ **Exhibit 2 LEASE**

Finance Lease

A **finance lease** is a three-party transaction consisting of a lessor, a lessee, and a **supplier** (or vendor). The lessor does not select, manufacture, or supply the goods. Instead, the lessor acquires title to the goods or the right to their possession and use in connection with the terms of the lease [UCC 2A-103(1)(g)].

finance lease
A three-party transaction consisting of a lessor, a lessee, and a supplier.

Example JetGreen Airways, a commercial air carrier, decides to lease a new airplane that is manufactured by Boeing. To finance the airplane acquisition, JetGreen goes to City Bank. City Bank purchases the airplane from Boeing, and City Bank then leases the airplane to JetGreen. Boeing is the supplier, City Bank is the lessor, and JetGreen is the lessee. City Bank does not take physical delivery of the airplane; the airplane is delivered by Boeing directly to JetGreen (see Exhibit 3).

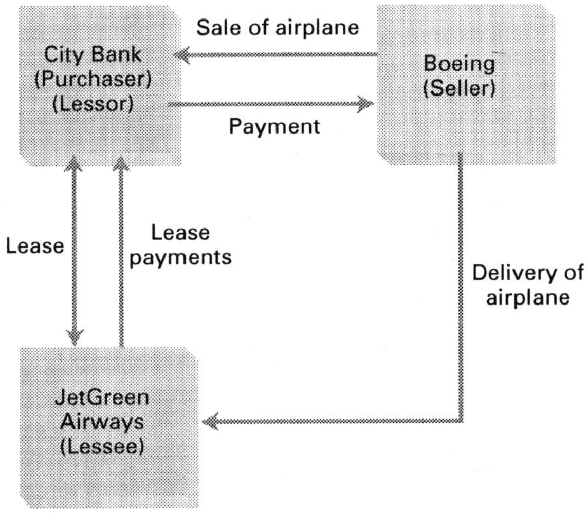

▶ **Exhibit 3 FINANCE LEASE**

LANDMARK LAW

Revised Article 2 (Sales) and Revised Article 2A (Leases)

After years of study and debate, in 2003 **Revised Article 2 (Sales)** and **Revised Article 2A (Leases)** were promulgated by the National Conference of Commissioners on Uniform State Laws and the American Law Institute.

The modifications to Article 2 and Article 2A include changes to provisions that have been controversial in the past, as well as the addition of new provisions to recognize changes in the commercial environment. The revised Articles 2 and 2A are considered to be the most modern and efficient rules governing the sales and leases of goods.

In addition, the revised Articles 2 and 2A contain many new provisions and rules that recognize the importance of electronic contracting for the sale and lease of goods. The revised articles provide rules for the creation and enforcement of electronic contracts for the sale and lease of goods.

Since the release of Revised UCC Article 2 (Sales) and Revised UCC Article 2A (Leases) in 2003, states have been studying whether to enact these revised articles as UCC statutes. It is expected that after sufficient study, many states will do so.

This chapter on sales and lease contracts notes the changes and differences that Revised Articles 2 and 2A have made to current UCC sales and lease laws.

FORMATION OF SALES AND LEASE CONTRACTS: OFFER

Laws made by common consent must not be trampled on by individuals.

George Washington

As with general contracts, the formation of sales and lease contracts requires an offer and an acceptance. The UCC-established rules for each of these elements often differ considerably from common law.

A contract for the sale or lease of goods may be made in any manner sufficient to show agreement, including conduct by both parties that recognizes the existence of a contract [UCC 2-204(1), 2A-204(1)]. Under the UCC, an agreement sufficient to constitute a contract for the sale or lease of goods may be found even though the moment of its making is undetermined [UCC 2-204(2), 2A-204(2)].

Open Terms

Sometimes the parties to a sales or lease contract leave open a major term in the contract. The UCC is tolerant of open terms. According to UCC 2-204(3) and 2A-204(3), a contract does not fail because of indefiniteness if (1) the parties intended to make a contract and (2) there is a reasonably certain basis for giving an appropriate remedy. In effect, certain **open terms** are permitted to be "read into" a sales or lease contract. This rule is commonly referred to as the **gap-filling rule**. Some examples of terms that are commonly left open are discussed in the following paragraphs.

gap-filling rule
A rule that says an open term can be "read into" a contract.

Open Price Term If a sales contract does not contain a specific price (**open price term**), a "reasonable price" is implied at the time of delivery.

Example A contract may provide that a price is to be fixed by a market rate, such as a commodities market rate.

Example A contract may provide that a price will be set or recorded by a third person or an agency, such as a government agency. For example, the federal government sets minimum prices for milk products.

A contract may provide that the price will be set by another standard, either upon delivery or on a set date. If the agreed-upon standard is unavailable when the price is to be set, a reasonable price is implied at the time of delivery of the goods [UCC 2-305(1)]. A seller or buyer who reserves the right to fix a price must do so in good faith [UCC 2-305(2)]. When one of the parties fails to fix an open price term, the other party may opt either (1) to treat the contract as canceled or (2) to fix a reasonable price for the goods [UCC 2-305(3)].

Open Payment Term If the parties to a sales contract do not agree on payment terms, payment is due at the time and place at which the buyer is to receive the goods.

If delivery is authorized and made by way of document of title, payment is due at the time and place at which the buyer is to receive the document of title, regardless of where the goods are to be received [UCC 2-310].

Open Delivery Term If the parties to a sales contract do not agree to the time, place, and manner of delivery of the goods, the place for delivery is the seller's place of business. If the seller does not have a place of business, delivery is to be made at the seller's residence.

If identified goods are located at some other place, and both parties know of this fact at the time of contracting, that place is the place of delivery [UCC 2-308].

If goods are to be shipped but the shipper is not named, the seller is obligated to make the shipping arrangements. Such arrangements must be made in good faith and within limits of commercial reasonableness [UCC 2-311(2)].

The foundation of justice is good faith.

Cicero
De Officiis, Book 1, Chapter VII

Open Time Term If the parties to a sales contract do not set a specific time of performance for any obligation under the contract, the contract must be performed within a reasonable time.

If a sales contract provides for successive performance over an unspecified period of time, the contract is valid for a reasonable time [UCC 2-309].

Open Assortment Term If the assortment of goods to a sales contract is left open, the buyer is given the option of choosing those goods. The buyer must make the selection in good faith and within limits set by commercial reasonableness [UCC 2-311(2)].

CONTEMPORARY ENVIRONMENT

UCC Firm Offer Rule

Recall that the common law of contracts allows the offeror to revoke an offer any time prior to its acceptance. The UCC recognizes an exception to this rule, which is called the **firm offer rule**. This rule states that a *merchant* who (1) offers to buy, sell, or lease goods and (2) gives a written and signed assurance on a separate form that the offer will be held open cannot revoke the offer for the time stated or, if no time is stated, for a reasonable time. The maximum amount of time permitted under this rule is three months [UCC 2-205, 2A-205].

Example On June 1, Sophisticated LLC, a BMW automobile dealer, offers to sell a BMW M3 coupe to Mandy for $60,000. Sophisticated LLC signs a written assurance to keep that offer open to Mandy until July 15. On July 5, Sophisticated LLC sells the car to another buyer. On July 15, Mandy tenders $60,000 for the car. Sophisticated LLC is a merchant subject to the firm offer rule. Sophisticated LLC is liable to Mandy for breach of contract. Thus, if Mandy has to pay $70,000 for the car at another dealership, she can recover $10,000 from Sophisticated LLC.

Consideration

The formation of sales and lease contracts requires consideration. However, the UCC changes the common law rule that requires the modification of a contract to be supported by new consideration. An agreement modifying a sales or lease contract needs no consideration to be binding [UCC 2-209(1), 2A-208(1)].

Modification of a sales or lease contract must be made in good faith [UCC 1-203]. As in the common law of contracts, modifications are not binding if they are obtained through fraud, duress, extortion, and such.

FORMATION OF SALES AND LEASE CONTRACTS: ACCEPTANCE

Both common law and the UCC provide that a contract is created when the offeree (i.e., the buyer or lessee) sends an acceptance to the offeror (seller or lessor), not when the offeror receives the acceptance.

Examples A sales or lease contract is made when the acceptance letter is delivered to the post office. The contract remains valid even if the post office loses the letter. An e-contract is made when the offeree sends an e-mail or another electronic document to the offeror.

Method and Manner of Acceptance

Law must be stable and yet it cannot stand still.

Roscoe Pound
Interpretations of Legal History (1923)

Unless otherwise unambiguously indicated by language or circumstance, an offer to make a sales or lease contract may be accepted in any manner and by any reasonable medium of acceptance [UCC 2-206(1)(a), 2A-206(1)].

Example A seller sends a telegram to a proposed buyer, offering to sell the buyer certain goods. The buyer responds by mailing a letter of acceptance to the seller. In most circumstances, mailing the letter of acceptance would be considered reasonable. If the goods were extremely perishable or if the market for the goods were very volatile, however, a faster means of acceptance (e.g., a telegram) might be warranted.

If an order or other offer to buy goods requires prompt or current shipment, the offer is accepted if the seller (1) promptly promises to ship the goods or (2) promptly ships either conforming or nonconforming goods [UCC 2-206(1)(b)]. The shipment of conforming goods signals acceptance of the buyer's offer.

Acceptance of goods occurs after the buyer or lessee has a reasonable opportunity to inspect them and signifies that (1) the goods are conforming, (2) he or she will take or retain the goods in spite of their nonconformity, or (3) he or she fails to reject the goods within a reasonable time after tender or delivery [UCC 2-513(1), 2A-515(1)].

CONTEMPORARY ENVIRONMENT

UCC Permits Additional Terms

Under common law's **mirror image rule**, an offeree's acceptance must be on the same terms as the offer. The inclusion of **additional terms** in the acceptance is considered a **counteroffer** rather than an acceptance. Thus, a counteroffer extinguishes the offeror's original offer.

UCC 2-207(1) is more liberal than the mirror image rule. It permits definite and timely expression of acceptance or written confirmation to operate as an acceptance even though they contain terms that are additional to or different from the offered terms, unless the acceptance is expressly conditional on assent to such terms. This rule differs for merchants and nonmerchants.

If one or both parties to a sales contract are nonmerchants, any additional terms are considered **proposed additions** to the contract. The proposed additions do not constitute a counteroffer or extinguish the original offer. If the offeree's proposed additions are accepted by the original offeror, they become part of the contract. If they are not accepted, the sales contract is formed on the basis of the terms of the original offer [UCC 2-207(2)].

Example A salesperson at a Lexus dealership offers to sell a coupe to a buyer for $65,000. The buyer replies, "I accept your offer, but I would like to have a satellite radio in the car." The satellite radio is a proposed addition to the contract. If the salesperson agrees, the contract between the parties consists of the terms of the original offer plus the additional term regarding the satellite radio. If the salesperson rejects the proposed addition, the sales contract consists of the terms of the original offer because the buyer made a definite expression of acceptance.

Accommodation Shipment

accommodation
A shipment that is offered to a buyer as a replacement for the original shipment when the original shipment cannot be filled.

A shipment of nonconforming goods does not constitute an acceptance if the seller reasonably notifies the buyer that the shipment is offered only as an **accommodation** to the buyer [UCC 2-206(1)(b)].

Example A buyer offers to purchase 500 red umbrellas from a seller. The seller's red umbrellas are temporarily out of stock. The seller sends the buyer 500 green umbrellas and notifies the buyer that these umbrellas are being sent as an accommodation. The seller did not accept (or breach) the contract. The accommodation is a counteroffer from the seller to the buyer. The buyer is free either to accept or to reject the counteroffer.

CONTEMPORARY ENVIRONMENT

"Battle of the Forms"

When merchants negotiate sales contracts, they often exchange preprinted forms. These "boilerplate" forms usually contain terms that favor the drafter. Thus, an offeror who sends a standard form contract as an offer to the offeree may receive an acceptance drafted on the offeree's own form contract. This scenario—commonly called the **battle of the forms**—raises important questions: Is there a contract? If so, what are its terms? The UCC provides guidance in answering these questions.

Under UCC 2-207(2), if both parties are merchants, any additional terms contained in an acceptance become part of the sales contract unless (1) the offer expressly limits acceptance to the terms of the offer, (2) the additional terms materially alter the terms of the original contract, or (3) the offeror notifies the offeree that he or she objects to the additional terms within a reasonable time after receiving the offeree's modified acceptance.

The most important point in the battle of the forms is that there is no contract if the additional terms so materially alter the terms of the original offer that the parties cannot agree on the contract. This fact-specific determination is made by the courts on a case-by-case basis.

UCC STATUTE OF FRAUDS

The UCC includes **Statute of Frauds** provisions that apply to all sales and lease contracts. These provisions are:

- All contracts for the *sale of goods* costing *$500 or more* must be in writing [UCC 2-201(1)].
- *Lease* contracts involving payments of *$1,000 or more* must be in writing [UCC 2A-201(1)].

UCC Statute of Frauds
A rule that requires all contracts for the sale of goods costing $500 or more and lease contracts involving payments of $1,000 or more to be in writing.

The writing must be sufficient to indicate that a contract has been made between the parties. Except as discussed in the paragraphs that follow, the writing must be signed by the party against whom enforcement is sought or by his or her authorized agent or broker. If a contract falling within these parameters is not written, it is unenforceable.

Example A seller orally agrees to sell her computer to a buyer for $550. When the buyer tenders the purchase price, the seller asserts the Statute of Frauds and refuses to sell the computer to him. The seller is correct. The contract must be in writing to be enforceable because the contract price for the computer exceeds $499.99.

Exceptions to the Statute of Frauds

In three situations, a sales or lease contract that would otherwise be required to be in writing is enforceable even if it is not in writing [UCC 2-201(3), UCC 2A-201(4)]:

The prince is not above the laws, but the laws above the prince.

Pliny the Younger
(Caius Caecilius Secundus)

1. **Specially manufactured goods.** Buyers and lessees often order **specially manufactured goods.** If a contract to purchase or lease such goods is oral, the buyer or lessee may not assert the Statute of Frauds against the enforcement of the contract if (1) the goods are not suitable for sale or lease to others in the ordinary course of the seller's or the lessor's business and (2) the seller or lessor has made either a substantial beginning of the manufacture of the goods or commitments for their procurement.
2. **Admissions in pleadings or court.** If the party against whom enforcement of an oral sales or lease contract is sought admits in pleadings, testimony, or otherwise in court that a contract for the sale or lease of goods was made, the oral contract is enforceable against that party. However, the contract is enforceable only as to the quantity of goods admitted.
3. **Part acceptance.** An oral sales or lease contract that should otherwise be in writing is enforceable to the extent to which the goods have been received and accepted by the buyer or lessee.

Example A lessor orally contracts to lease 20 automobiles to a lessee. The lessee accepts the first 8 automobiles tendered by the lessor. This action is part acceptance. The lessee refuses to take delivery of the remaining 12 automobiles. Here, the lessee must pay for the 8 automobiles it originally received and accepted. The lessee does not have to accept or pay for the remaining 12 automobiles.

CONTEMPORARY ENVIRONMENT

UCC Written Confirmation Rule

It both parties to an oral sales or lease contract are merchants, the Statute of Frauds writing requirement can be satisfied if (1) one of the parties to an oral agreement sends a written confirmation of the sale or lease within a reasonable time after contracting and (2) the other merchant does not give written notice of an objection to the contract within 10 days after receiving the confirmation. This situation is true even though the party receiving the written confirmation has not signed it. The only stipulations are that the confirmation is sufficient and that the party to whom it was sent has reason to know its contents [UCC 2-201(2)].

Example A merchant-seller in Chicago orally contracts by telephone to sell goods to a merchant-buyer in Phoenix for $100,000. Within a reasonable time after contracting, the seller sends a sufficient written confirmation to the buyer of the agreed-upon transaction. The buyer, who has reason to know the contents of the written confirmation, fails to object to the contents of the confirmation in writing within 10 days after receiving it. Under the UCC, the Statute of Frauds has been met, and the buyer cannot thereafter raise it against enforcement of the contract.

When Written Modification Is Required

Oral modification of a contract is not enforceable if the parties agree that any modification of the sales or lease contract must be signed in writing [UCC 2-209(2), 2A-208(2)]. In the absence of such an agreement, oral modifications to sales and lease contracts are binding if they do not violate the Statute of Frauds. If the oral modification brings the contract within the Statute of Frauds, it must be in writing to be enforceable.

Example A lessor and lessee enter into an oral lease contract for the lease of goods at a rent of $450. Subsequently, the contract is modified by raising the rent to $550. Because the modified contract rent is more than $499.99, the contract comes under the UCC Statute of Frauds, and the modification must be in writing to be enforceable.

Parol Evidence

parol evidence rule
A rule which says that if a written contract is a complete and final statement of the parties' agreement, any prior or contemporaneous oral or written statements that alter, contradict, or are in addition to the terms of the written contract are inadmissible in court regarding a dispute over the contract.

The **parol evidence rule** states that when a sales or lease contract is evidenced by a writing that is intended to be a final expression of the parties' agreement or a confirmatory memorandum, the terms of the writing may not be contradicted by evidence of (1) a prior oral or written agreement or (2) a contemporaneous oral agreement (i.e., parol evidence) [UCC 2-202, 2A-202]. This rule is intended to ensure certainty in written sales and lease contracts.

Occasionally, the express terms of a written contract are not clear on their face and must be interpreted. In such cases, reference may be made to certain sources outside the contract. These sources are construed together when they are consistent with each other. If that is unreasonable, they are considered in descending order of priority [UCC 2-208(2), 2A-207(2)]:

1. **Course of performance.** The previous conduct of the parties regarding the contract in question
2. **Course of dealing.** The conduct of the parties in prior transactions and contracts
3. **Usage of trade.** Any practice or method of dealing that is regularly observed or adhered to in a place, a vocation, a trade, or an industry

Example A cattle rancher contracts to purchase 3,000 bushels of "corn" from a farmer. The farmer delivers feed corn to the rancher. The rancher rejects this corn and demands delivery of corn that is fit for human consumption. If the parties did not have any prior course of performance or course of dealing that would indicate otherwise, usage of trade would be used to interpret the word *corn*. Thus, the delivery of feed corn would be assumed and become part of the contract.

CONCEPT SUMMARY

COMPARISON OF CONTRACT LAW AND THE LAW OF SALES

Topic	Common Law of Contract	UCC Law of Sales
Definiteness	Contract must contain all the material terms of the parties' agreement.	The UCC gap-filling rule permits terms to be implied if the parties intended to make a contract and there is a reasonably certain basis for giving an appropriate remedy [UCC 2-204].
Irrevocable offers	Option contracts.	Option contracts. Firm offers by merchants to keep an offer open are binding up to three months without any consideration [UCC 2-205].
Counteroffers	Acceptance must be a mirror image of the offer. A counteroffer rejects and terminates the offeror's original offer.	Additional terms of an acceptance become part of the contract if (1) they do not materially alter the terms of the offer and (2) the offeror does not object within a reasonable time after reviewing the acceptance [UCC 2-207].
Statute of Frauds	Writing must be signed by the party against whom enforcement is sought.	Writing may be enforced against a party who has not signed a contract if (1) both parties are merchants, (2) one party sends a written confirmation of oral agreement within a reasonable time after contracting, and (3) the other party does not give written notice of objection within 10 days after receiving the confirmation [UCC 2-201].
Modification	Consideration is required.	Consideration is not required [UCC 2-209].

INTERNET LAW & ONLINE COMMERCE

Revised Article 2 (Sales) and Article 2A (Leases) Recognize the Importance of Electronic Contracting

Revised Article 2 (Sales) and Revised Article 2A (Leases) contain provisions that recognize the importance of electronic contracting in sales and lease transactions. The revised articles contain new definitions that apply to sales and lease contracts. The following are some of the new definitions for electronic commerce and their implications:

- *Electronic* means relating to technology having electrical, digital, magnetic, wireless, optical, electromagnetic, or similar capabilities [Revised UCC 2-103(1)(f), Revised UCC 2A-103(1)(h)]. This term, as used throughout Revised Articles 2 and 2A, extends many of the provisions and rules of the UCC to cover electronic contracting of sales and lease contracts.
- *Electronic agent* means a computer program or an electronic or other automated means used independently to initiate an action or respond to electronic records or performances in whole or in part, without review or action by an individual [Revised UCC 2-103(1)(g), Revised UCC 2A-103(1)(i)]. This definition, as used in many of the provisions of UCC Article 2 and 2A, allows for the contracting for the sale and lease of goods over the Internet, using websites to order or lease goods.
- *Electronic record* means a record created, generated, sent, communicated, received, or stored by electronic means [Revised UCC 2-103(1)(h), Revised UCC 2A-103(1)(j)]. This term is often used in Revised Articles 2 and 2A to replace the word *writing* and thus recognizes that UCC contracts and other information may be sent or stored by electronic means rather than in tangible writings.
- *Record* means information that is inscribed on a tangible medium or that is stored in an electronic or other medium and is retrievable in perceivable form [Revised UCC 2-103(1)(m), Revised UCC 2A-103(1)(cc)]. The term *record* is now used in many of the provisions of Revised Article 2 and 2A in place of the term *writing* and thus further recognizes the importance of electronic contracting.

These terms are used throughout the provisions of Revised Article 2 (Sales) and Revised Article 2A (Leases). These definitions expand the coverage of the provisions of UCC Article 2 and Article 2A to electronic contracting of sales and lease contracts.

TEST REVIEW TERMS AND CONCEPTS

Accommodation
Additional terms
Article 2 (Sales)
Article 2A (Leases)
Battle of the forms
Counteroffer
Finance lease
Firm offer rule
Gap-filling rule
Goods
Lease
Lessee
Lessor
Merchant
Mirror image rule
Mixed sale
Model act
Open price term
Open term
Parol evidence
Parol evidence rule
Proposed additions
Revised Article 2 (Sales)
Revised Article 2A (Leases)
Sale
Specially manufactured goods
Supplier
UCC Statute of Frauds
Uniform Commercial Code (UCC)
Uniform Sales Act

CASE PROBLEMS

1 Merchant Mark Hemphill was a football player at Southern Illinois State University. As a member of the team, Hemphill was furnished with a uniform and helmet. He was injured while playing football for the school. Hemphill claimed that his helmet was defective and contributed to his injuries. Hemphill's attorneys suggested that he sue the university's athletic director, Sayers, and the head football coach, Shultz. The attorneys told Hemphill that he may be able to recover for his injuries based on several provisions of the Uniform Commercial Code. The attorneys specifically suggested that he use the UCC provisions that impose certain obligations upon merchants. Hemphill brought suit against Sayers and Shultz. Does Article 2 apply to this case? *Hemphill v. Sayers*, 552 F.Supp. 685, **Web** 1982 U.S. Dist. Lexis 16240 (United States District Court for the Southern District of Illinois)

2 Good or Service Mr. Gulash lived in Shelton, Connecticut. He wanted an above-ground swimming pool installed in his backyard. Gulash contacted Stylarama, Inc. (Stylarama), a company specializing in the sale and construction of pools. The two parties entered into a contract that called for Stylarama to "furnish all labor and materials to construct a Wavecrest brand pool, and furnish and install a pool with vinyl liners." The total cost for materials and labor was $3,690. There was no breakdown in the contract of costs between labor and materials. After the pool was installed, its sides began bowing out, the 2" × 4" wooden supports for the pool rotted and misaligned, and the entire pool became tilted. Gulash brought suit, alleging that Stylarama had violated several provisions of Article 2 of the UCC. Is this transaction one involving goods, making it subject to Article 2? *Gulash v. Stylarama*, 33 Conn.Supp. 108, 364 A.2d 1221, **Web** 1975 Conn.Super. Lexis 209 (Superior Court of Connecticut)

3 Unconscionable Contract Jane Wilson leased a Toyota pickup truck from World Omni Leasing, Inc. (Omni), Wilson had experience in business and had signed contracts before. In the past, Wilson had read the contracts before signing them. When signing the contract for the lease of the truck, however, Wilson did not take the opportunity to read the lease. However, she signed a statement declaring that she had read and understood the lease. The lease contained a provision that made Wilson responsible for payments on the truck even if the truck was destroyed. Several months after leasing the truck, Wilson was involved in a two-vehicle collision. The pickup truck was destroyed. Omni demanded to be paid for the balance of the lease. Wilson refused, claiming that the lease was unconscionable. Is the lease unconscionable? *Wilson v. World Omni Leasing, Inc.*, 540 So.2d 713, **Web** 1989 Ala. Lexis 41 (Supreme Court of Alabama)

4 Statute of Frauds St. Charles Cable TV (St. Charles) was building a new cable television system in Louisiana. It contacted Eagle Comtronics, Inc. (Eagle), by phone and began negotiating to buy descrambler units for its cable system. These units would allow St. Charles's customers to receive the programs they had paid for. Although no written contract was ever signed, St. Charles ordered several thousand descramblers. The descramblers were shipped to St. Charles, along with a sales acknowledgment form. St. Charles made partial payment for the descramblers before discovering that some of the units were defective. Eagle accepted a return of the defective scramblers. St. Charles then attempted to return all the descramblers, asking that they be replaced by a newer model. When Eagle refused to replace all the old descramblers, St. Charles stopped paying Eagle. Eagle sued St. Charles, claiming that no valid contract existed between the parties. Is there a valid sales contract? *St. Charles Cable TV v. Eagle Comtronics, Inc.*, 687 F.Supp. 820, **Web** 1988 U.S. Dist. Lexis 4566 (United States District Court for the Southern District of New York)

5 Firm Offer Gordon Construction Company (Gordon) was a general contractor in the New York City area. Gordon planned on bidding for the job of constructing two buildings for the Port Authority of New York. In anticipation of its own bid, Gordon sought bids from subcontractors.

E. A. Coronis Associates (Coronis), a fabricator of structured steel, sent a signed letter to Gordon. The letter quoted a price for work on the Port Authority project and stated that the price could change, based upon the amount of steel used. The letter contained no information other than the price Coronis would charge for the job. One month later, Gordon was awarded the Port Authority project. Four days later, Coronis sent Gordon a telegram, withdrawing its offer. Gordon replied that it expected Coronis to honor the price that it had previously quoted to Gordon. When Coronis refused, Gordon sued. Gordon claimed that Coronis was attempting to withdraw a firm offer. Who wins? *E. A. Coronis Associates v. Gordon Construction Co.*, 90 N.J.Super. 69, 216 A.2d 246, **Web** 1966 N.J.Super. Lexis 368 (Superior Court of New Jersey)

6 Battle of the Forms Dan Miller was a commercial photographer who had taken a series of photographs that had appeared in the *New York Times*. *Newsweek* magazine wanted to use the photographs. When a *Newsweek* employee named Dwyer phoned Miller, he was told that 72 images were available. Dwyer said that he wanted to inspect the photographs and offered a certain sum of money for each photo *Newsweek* used. The photos were to remain Miller's property. Miller and Dwyer agreed to the price and the date for delivery. *Newsweek* sent a courier to pick up the photographs. Along with the photos, Miller gave the courier a delivery memo that set out various conditions for the use of the photographs. The memo included a clause that required *Newsweek* to pay $1,500 each if any of the photos were lost or destroyed. After *Newsweek* received the package, it decided it no longer needed Miller's work. When Miller called to have the photos returned, he was told that they had all been lost. Miller demanded that *Newsweek* pay him $1,500 for each of the 72 lost photos. Assuming that the court finds Miller and *Newsweek* to be merchants, are the clauses in the delivery memo part of the sales contract? *Miller v. Newsweek, Inc.*, 660 F.Supp. 852, **Web** 1987 U.S. Dist. Lexis 4338 (United States District Court for the District of Delaware)

7 Open Terms Alvin Cagle was a potato farmer in Alabama who had had several business dealings with the H. C. Schmieding Produce Co. (Schmieding). Several months before harvest, Cagle entered into an oral sales contract with Schmieding. The contract called for Schmieding to pay the market price at harvest time for all the red potatoes that Cagle grew on his 30-acre farm. Schmieding asked that the potatoes be delivered during the normal harvest months. As Cagle began harvesting his red potatoes, he contacted Schmieding to arrange delivery. Schmieding told the farmer that no contract had been formed because the terms of the agreement were too indefinite. Cagle demanded that Schmieding buy his crop. When Schmieding refused, Cagle sued to have the contract enforced. Has a valid sales contract been formed? *H. C. Schmieding Produce Co. v. Cagle*, 529 So.2d 243, **Web** 1988 Ala. Lexis 284 (Supreme Court of Alabama)

8 Statute of Frauds Collins was a sales representative of Donzi Marine Corp. (Donzi), a builder of light speedboats. Collins met Wallach, the owner of a retail boat outlet, at a marine trade show. Collins offered him a Donzi dealership, which would include the right to purchase and then market Donzi speedboats. Wallach tendered a check for $50,000 to Collins. Collins accepted the check, but neither party ever signed a written contract. Wallach ordered several boats. Donzi terminated the dealership because it had found another boat dealer willing to pay more for the franchise. Wallach sued Donzi for breach of contract. Is the contract enforceable under the UCC? *Wallach Marine Corp. v. Donzi Marine Corp.*, 675 F.Supp. 838, **Web** 1987 U.S. Dist. Lexis 11762 (United States District Court for the Southern District of New York)

BUSINESS ETHICS CASES

9 Business Ethics Kurt Perschke was a grain dealer in Indiana. Perschke phoned Ken Sebasty, the owner of a large wheat farm, and offered to buy 14,000 bushels of wheat for $1.95 per bushel. Sebasty accepted the offer. Perschke said that he could send a truck for the wheat on a stated date six months later. On the day of the phone call, Perschke's office manager sent a memorandum to Sebasty, stating the price and quantity of wheat that had been contracted for. One month before the scheduled delivery, Perschke called Sebasty to arrange for the loading of the wheat. Sebasty stated that no contract had been made. When Perschke brought suit, Sebasty claimed that the contract was unenforceable because of the Statute of Frauds. Was it ethical for Sebasty to raise the Statute of Frauds as a defense? Assuming that both parties are merchants, who wins the suit? *Sebasty v. Perschke*, 404 N.E.2d 1200, **Web** 1980 Ind.App. Lexis 1489 (Court of Appeals of Indiana)

10 Business Ethics Alex Abatti was the sole owner of A&M Produce Company (A&M), a small farming company located in California's Imperial Valley. Although Abatti had never grown tomatoes, he decided to do so. He sought the advice of FMC Corporation (FMC), a large, diversified manufacturer of farming and other equipment, as to what kind of equipment he would need to process the tomatoes. An FMC representative recommended a certain type of machine, which A&M purchased from FMC pursuant to a form sales contract provided by FMC. Within the fine print, the contract contained one clause that disclaimed any warranty liability by FMC and a second clause that stated that FMC would not be liable for consequential damages if the machine malfunctioned.

A&M paid $10,680 down toward the $32,041 purchase price, and FMC delivered and installed the machine. A&M immediately began experiencing problems with the machine, which did not process the tomatoes quickly enough. Tomatoes began piling up in front of the belt that separated the tomatoes for weight-sizing. Overflow tomatoes had to be sent through the machine at least twice, causing damage to them. Fungus spread through the damaged crop. Because of these problems, the machine had to be continually started and stopped, which significantly reduced processing speed.

A&M tried on several occasions to get additional equipment from FMC, but on each occasion, its request was rejected. Because of the problems with the machine, A&M closed its tomato operation. A&M finally stated, "Let's call the whole thing off" and offered to return the machine if FMC would refund A&M's down payment. When FMC rejected this offer and demanded full payment of the balance due, A&M sued to recover its down payment and damages. It alleged breach of warranty caused by defect in the machine. In defense, FMC pointed to the fine print of the sales contract, stating that the buyer waived any rights to sue it for breach of warranty or to recover consequential damages from it.

Was it ethical for FMC to include waiver of liability and waiver of consequential damage clauses in its form contract? Did A&M act morally in signing the contract and then trying to get out from under its provisions? Legally, are the waiver clauses so unconscionable as to not be enforced? *A&M Produce Co. v. FMC Corp.*, 135 Cal.App.3d 473, 186 Cal.Rptr. 114, **Web** 1982 Cal.App. Lexis 1922 (Court of Appeal of California)

TITLE TO GOODS AND RISK OF LOSS

Dorling Kindersley © David Peart

▲ **A Couple Watches a Container Ship** *The title and risk of loss of the goods on this ship are governed by the shipping terms used by the parties to the international contract for the sale of the goods or as otherwise agreed to by the parties.*

CHAPTER OBJECTIVES

After studying this chapter, you should be able to:

1. Identify when title to goods passes in shipment and destination contracts.
2. Define shipment and delivery terms.
3. Describe who bears the risk of loss when goods are lost or damaged in shipment.
4. Identify who bears the risk of loss when goods are stolen and resold.
5. Define *good faith purchaser for value* and *buyer in the ordinary course of business.*

CHAPTER CONTENTS

From Chapter 19 of *Business Law: Legal Environment, Online Commerce, Business Ethics, and International Issues,* 7/e.

"A lawyer without history or literature is a mechanic, a mere working mason: if he possesses some knowledge of these, he may venture to call himself an architect."

—Sir Walter Scott
Guy Mannering, Chapter 37 (1815)

INTRODUCTION TO TITLE TO GOODS AND RISK OF LOSS

Under common law, the rights and obligations of the buyer, the seller, and third parties were determined based on who held technical title to the goods. Article 2 of the Uniform Commercial Code (UCC) establishes precise rules for determining the *passage of title* in sales contracts. Other provisions of Article 2 apply, irrespective of title, except as otherwise provided [UCC 2-401].

Common law placed the **risk of loss** to goods on the party who held title to the goods. Article 2 of the UCC rejects this notion and adopts concise rules for risk of loss that are not tied to title. It also gives the parties to a sales contract the right to *insure* the goods against loss if they have an "insurable interest" in the goods.

Article 2A (Leases) of the UCC establishes rules regarding title and risk of loss for leased goods. It also gives the parties to the lease contract the right to *insure* the goods against loss if they have an "insurable interest" in the goods.

Title, risk of loss, and insurable interest for the sale and lease of goods are discussed in this chapter.

IDENTIFICATION OF GOODS AND PASSAGE OF TITLE

Decided cases are the anchors of the law, as laws are of the state.

Francis Bacon

The *identification of goods* is rather simple. It means distinguishing the goods named in a contract from the seller's or lessor's other goods. The seller or lessor retains the risk of loss of the goods until he or she identifies them to a sales or lease contract. Further, UCC 2-401(1) and 2-501 prevent title to goods from passing from the seller to the buyer unless the goods are identified to the sales contract. In a lease transaction, title to the leased goods remains with the lessor or a third party. It does not pass to the lessee.

The identification of goods and passage of title are discussed in the following paragraphs.

Identification of Goods

identification of goods
Distinguishing the goods named in a contract from the seller's or lessor's other goods.

Identification of goods can be made at any time and in any manner explicitly agreed to by the parties of a contract. In the absence of such an agreement, the UCC mandates when identification occurs [UCC 2-501(1), 2A-217].

Already existing goods are identified when a contract is made and names the specific goods sold or leased.

Examples A piece of farm machinery, a car, or a boat is identified when its serial number is listed on a sales or lease contract.

Goods that are part of a larger mass of goods are identified when the specific merchandise is designated.

Example If a food processor contracts to purchase 150 cases of oranges from a farmer who has 1,000 cases of oranges, the buyer's goods are identified when the seller explicitly separates or tags the 150 cases for that buyer.

Future goods are goods not yet in existence.

Examples Unborn young animals (such as unborn cattle) are identified when the young are conceived. Crops to be harvested are identified when the crops are planted or otherwise become growing crops.

Future goods other than crops and unborn young are identified when the goods are shipped, marked, or otherwise designated by the seller or lessor as the goods to which the contract refers.

future goods
Goods not yet in existence (e.g., ungrown crops, unborn stock animals).

Passage of Title

Once the goods that are the subject of a contract exist and have been identified, title to the goods may be transferred from the seller to the buyer. Article 2 of the UCC establishes precise rules for determining the **passage of title** in sales contracts. (As mentioned earlier, lessees do not acquire title to the goods they lease.)

Under UCC 2-401(1), **title** to goods passes from the seller to the buyer in any manner and on any conditions explicitly agreed upon by the parties. If the parties do not agree to a specific time, title passes to the buyer when and where the seller's performance with reference to the physical delivery is completed. This point in time is determined by applying the rules discussed in the following paragraphs [UCC 2-401(2)].

title
Legal, tangible evidence of ownership of goods.

Shipment and Destination Contracts

A **shipment contract** requires the seller to ship the goods to the buyer via a common carrier. The seller is required to (1) make proper shipping arrangements and (2) deliver the goods into the carrier's hands. Title passes to the buyer at the time and place of shipment [UCC 2-401(2)(a)].

A **destination contract** requires the seller to deliver the goods either to the buyer's place of business or to another destination specified in the sales contract. Title passes to the buyer when the seller tenders delivery of the goods at the specified destination [UCC 2-401(2)(b)].

shipment contract
A contract that requires the seller to ship the goods to the buyer via a common carrier.

destination contract
A contract that requires the seller to deliver the goods either to the buyer's place of business or to another destination specified in the sales contract.

Delivery of Goods Without Moving Them

Sometimes a sales contract authorizes goods to be delivered without requiring the seller to move them. In other words, the buyer might be required to pick up goods from the seller. In such situations, the time and place of the passage of title depends on whether the seller is to deliver a **document of title** (i.e., a warehouse receipt or bill of lading) to the buyer. If a document of title is required, title passes when and where the seller delivers the document to the buyer [UCC 2-401(3)(a)].

document of title
An actual piece of paper, such as a warehouse receipt or bill of lading, that is required in some transactions of pickup and delivery.

Example If the goods named in a sales contract are located at a warehouse, title passes when the seller delivers to the buyer a warehouse receipt representing the goods.

If (1) no document of title is needed and (2) the goods are identified at the time of contracting, title passes at the time and place of contracting [UCC 2-401(3)(b)].

Example If a buyer signs a sales contract to purchase bricks from a seller, and the contract stipulates that the buyer will pick up the bricks at the seller's place of business, title passes when the contract is signed by both parties. This situation is true even if the bricks are not picked up until a later date.

CONTEMPORARY ENVIRONMENT

Shipping Terms

Often, goods subject to a sales contract are shipped by a common carrier such as a trucking company, a ship, or a railroad. Many sales contracts contain shipping terms that have different legal meanings and consequences. The following are commonly used shipping terms:

- **F.O.B. (free on board) *point of shipment*** requires the seller to arrange to ship the goods and put the goods in the carrier's possession. The buyer bears the shipping expense and risk of loss while the goods are in transit [UCC 2-319(1)(a)].

Example If a shipment contract specifies "F.O.B. Anchorage, Alaska," and the goods are shipped from New Orleans, Louisiana, the buyer bears the shipping expense and risk of loss while the goods are in transit to Anchorage, Alaska.

- **F.A.S. (free alongside ship)** or **F.A.S. (*vessel*) *port of shipment*** requires the seller to deliver and tender the goods alongside the named vessel or on the dock designated and provided by the buyer. The seller bears the expense and risk of loss until this is done [UCC 2-319(2)(a)]. The buyer bears shipping costs and the risk of loss during transport.

Example If a contract specifies "F.A.S. *The Gargoyle*, New Orleans," and the goods are to be shipped to Anchorage, Alaska, the seller bears the expense and risk of loss until it delivers the goods into the hands of the vessel *The Gargoyle* in New Orleans. Once this is done, the buyer pays the shipping costs and the risk of loss passes to the buyer during transport to Anchorage, Alaska.

- **C.I.F. (cost, insurance, and freight)** is a pricing term that means that the price includes the cost of the goods and the costs of insurance and freight. C.&F. (cost and freight) is a pricing term that means that the price includes the cost of the goods and the cost of freight. In both cases the seller must at his own expense and risk put the goods into the possession of a carrier. The buyer bears the risk of loss during transportation [UCC 2-320(1)(3)].

Example If a contract specifies "C.I.F. *The Gargoyle*, New Orleans, Louisiana" or "C.&F. *The Gargoyle*, New Orleans, Louisiana," and the goods are to be shipped to Anchorage, Alaska, the seller bears the expense and risk of loss until it delivers the goods into the hands of the vessel *The Gargoyle* in New Orleans. Once this is done, the risk of loss passes to the buyer during transport from New Orleans to Anchorage, Alaska.

- **F.O.B. (free on board) *place of destination*** requires the seller to bear the expense and risk of loss until the goods are tendered to the buyer at the place of destination [UCC 2-319(1)(b)].

Example If a destination contract specifies "F.O.B. Anchorage, Alaska," and the goods are shipped from New Orleans, Louisiana, the seller bears the expense and risk of loss before and while the goods are in transit until the goods are tendered to the buyer at the port of Anchorage, Alaska.

- **Ex-ship (from the carrying vessel)** requires the seller to bear the expense and risk of loss until the goods are unloaded from the ship at its port of destination [UCC 2-322(1)(b)].

Example If a contract specifies "Ex-ship, *The Gargoyle*, Anchorage, Alaska," and the goods are shipped from New Orleans, Louisiana, the seller bears the expense and risk of loss before and until the goods are unloaded from *The Gargoyle* at the port in Anchorage, Alaska.

- **No-arrival, no-sale contract** requires the seller to bear the expense and risk of loss of the goods during transportation. However, the seller is under no duty to deliver replacement goods to the buyer because there is no contractual stipulation that the goods will arrive at the appointed destination [UCC 2-324(a),(b)].

RISK OF LOSS: NO BREACH OF SALES CONTRACT

In the case of sales contracts, common law placed the risk of loss of goods on the party who had title to the goods. Article 2 of the UCC rejects this notion and allows the parties to a sales contract to agree among them who will bear the risk of loss if the goods subject to the contract are lost or destroyed. If the parties do not have a specific agreement concerning the assessment of the risk of loss, the UCC mandates who will bear the risk.

Where there has been no breach of the sales contract, the UCC provides the following rules regarding title and risk of loss.

Carrier Cases: Movement of Goods

Unless otherwise agreed, goods that are shipped via carrier (e.g., railroad, ship, truck) are considered to be sent pursuant to a *shipment contract* or a *destination contract*. Absent any indication to the contrary, sales contracts are presumed to be shipment contracts rather than destination contracts.

A **shipment contract** requires the seller to deliver goods conforming to the contract to a carrier. The risk of loss passes to the buyer when the seller delivers the conforming goods to the carrier. The buyer bears the risk of loss of the goods during transportation [UCC 2-509(1)(a)]. Shipment contracts are created in two ways. The first method requires the use of the term *shipment contract*. The second requires the use of one of the following delivery terms: F.O.B., point of shipment, F.A.S., C.I.F., or C.&F.

shipment contract
The buyer bears the risk of loss during transportation.

A sales contract that requires the seller to deliver conforming goods to a specific destination is a **destination contract**. Such a contract requires the seller to bear the risk of loss of the goods during their transportation. Thus, with the exception of a no-arrival, no-sale contract, the seller is required to replace any goods lost in transit. The buyer does not have to pay for destroyed goods. The risk of loss does not pass until the goods are tendered to the buyer at the specified destination [UCC 2-509(1)(b)].

destination contract
The seller bears the risk of loss during transportation.

Unless otherwise agreed, destination contracts are created in two ways. The first method requires the use of the term *destination contract*. The alternative method requires the use of the following delivery terms: F.O.B. *place of destination*, ex-ship, or no-arrival, no-sale contract.

Noncarrier Cases: No Movement of Goods

Sometimes a sales contract stipulates that the buyer is to pick up the goods at either the seller's place of business or another specified location. This type of arrangement raises a question: Who bears the risk of loss if the goods are destroyed or stolen after the contract date but before the buyer picks up the goods from the seller? The UCC provides two different rules for this situation. One applies to *merchant-sellers* and the other to *nonmerchant-sellers* [UCC 2-509(3)].

Merchant-Seller If the seller is a merchant, the risk of loss does not pass to the buyer until the goods are received. In other words, a merchant-seller bears the risk of loss between the time of contracting and the time the buyer picks up the goods.

The law is not a series of calculating machines where definitions and answers come tumbling out when the right levers are pushed.

William O. Douglas
The Dissent, A Safeguard of Democracy (1948)

Nonmerchant-Seller Nonmerchant-sellers pass the risk of loss to the buyer upon "tender of delivery" of the goods. Tender of delivery occurs when the seller (1) places or holds the goods available for the buyer to take delivery and (2) notifies the buyer of this fact.

Goods in the Possession of a Bailee

Goods sold by a seller to a buyer are sometimes in the possession of a **bailee** (e.g., a warehouse). If such goods are to be delivered to the buyer without the seller moving them, the risk of loss passes to the buyer when (1) the buyer receives a negotiable document of title (such as a warehouse receipt or bill of lading) covering the goods, or (2) the bailee acknowledges the buyer's right to possession of the goods, or (3) the buyer receives a nonnegotiable document of title or other written direction to deliver *and* has a reasonable time to present the document or direction to the bailee and demand the goods. If the bailee refuses to honor the document or direction, the risk of loss remains on the seller [UCC 2-509(2)].

bailee
A holder of goods who is not a seller or a buyer (e.g., a warehouse).

▶ RISK OF LOSS: CONDITIONAL SALES

Sellers often entrust possession of goods to buyers on a trial basis. These transactions are classified as *sales on approval*, *sales or returns*, and *consignment* transactions [UCC 2-326]. Title and risk of loss in these types of **conditional sales** are discussed in the following paragraphs.

Sale on Approval

In a **sale on approval**, there is no sale unless and until the buyer accepts the goods. A sale on approval occurs when a merchant allows a customer to take the goods for a specified

sale on approval
A type of sale in which there is no actual sale unless and until the buyer accepts the goods.

period of time to see if they fit the customer's needs. The prospective buyer may use the goods to try them out during this time.

Acceptance of the goods occurs if the buyer (1) expressly indicates acceptance, (2) fails to notify the seller of rejection of the goods within the agreed-upon trial period (or, if no time is agreed upon, a reasonable time), or (3) uses the goods inconsistently with the purpose of the trial (e.g., a customer resells a computer to another person).

In a sale on approval, the risk of loss and title to the goods remain with seller. They do not pass to the buyer until acceptance [UCC 2-327(1)]. The goods are not subject to the claims of the buyer's creditors until the buyer accepts them.

Sale or Return

sale or return contract
A contract in which the seller delivers goods to a buyer with the understanding that the buyer may return them if they are not used or resold within a stated or reasonable period of time.

In a **sale or return contract**, the seller delivers goods to a buyer with the understanding that the buyer may return them if they are not used or resold within a stated period of time (or within a reasonable time, if no specific time is stated). The sale is considered final if the buyer fails to return the goods within the specified time or within a reasonable time, if no time is specified. The buyer has the option of returning all the goods or any commercial unit of the goods.

Example Louis Vuitton delivers 10 women's handbags to a Fashion Boutique Store on a sale or return basis. The boutique pays $10,000 ($1,000 per handbag). If Fashion Boutique Store sells 6 handbags but fails to sell the other 4 handbags within a reasonable time, such as three months, it may return the unsold handbags to Louis Vuitton. Fashion Boutique Store can recover the compensation it paid to Louis Vuitton for the 4 returned handbags ($4,000).

In a sale or return contract, the risk of loss and title to the goods pass to the buyer when the buyer takes possession of the goods [UCC 2-327(2)]. Goods sold pursuant to a sale or return contract are subject to the claims of the buyer's creditors while the goods are in the buyer's possession.

Example In the previous example, title and risk of loss transferred to Fashion Boutique Store when it took possession of the Louis Vuitton handbags. If the Louis Vuitton handbags are destroyed while in the possession of Fashion Boutique Store, the store is responsible for their loss. It cannot recover the value of the handbags from Louis Vuitton.

Consignment

consignment
An arrangement in which a seller (the consignor) delivers goods to a buyer (the consignee) to sell.

In a **consignment**, a seller (the **consignor**) delivers goods to a buyer (the **consignee**) to sell. The consignee is paid a fee if he or she sells the goods on behalf of the consignor.

A consignment is treated as a sale or return under the UCC; that is, title and risk of loss of the goods pass to the consignee when the consignee takes possession of the goods.

Whether goods are subject to the claims of a buyer's creditors usually depends on whether the seller files a financing statement, as required by Article 9 of the UCC. If the seller files a financing statement, the goods are subject to the claims of the seller's creditors. If the seller fails to file such statement, the goods are subject to the claims of the buyer's creditors [UCC 2-326(3)].

RISK OF LOSS: BREACH OF SALES CONTRACT

Special risk of loss rules apply to situations in which there has been a breach of a sales contract [UCC 2-510]. These rules are discussed in the following paragraphs.

Seller in Breach of a Sales Contract

A seller breaches a sales contract if he or she tenders or delivers nonconforming goods to the buyer. If the goods are so nonconforming that the buyer has the right to reject them, the risk of loss remains on the seller until (1) the defect or nonconformity is cured or (2) the buyer accepts the nonconforming goods.

Laws are not masters but servants, and he rules them who obeys them.

Henry Ward Beecher
Proverbs from Plymouth Pulpit (1887)

Example A buyer orders 1,000 talking dolls from a seller. The contract is a shipment contract, which normally places the risk of loss during transportation on the buyer. However, the seller ships to the buyer totally nonconforming dolls that cannot talk. This switches the risk of loss to the seller during transit. The goods are destroyed in transit. The seller bears the risk of loss because he breached the contract by shipping nonconforming goods.

Buyer in Breach of a Sales Contract

A buyer breaches a sales contract if he or she (1) refuses to take delivery of conforming goods, (2) repudiates the contract, or (3) otherwise breaches the contract. A buyer who breaches a sales contract before the risk of loss would normally pass to him bears the risk of loss of any goods identified to the contract. The risk of loss rests on the buyer for only a commercially reasonable time. The buyer is liable only for any loss in excess of insurance recovered by the seller.

RISK OF LOSS: LEASE CONTRACTS

The parties to a lease contract are the party who leases the goods (the **lessor**) and the party who receives the goods (the **lessee**). The lessor and the lessee may agree as to who will bear the risk of loss of the goods if they are lost or destroyed. If the parties do not so agree, the UCC supplies the following risk of loss rules:

Faith, I have been a truant in the law
And never yet could frame my will to it,
And therefore frame the law unto my will.

William Shakespeare
King Henry the Sixth, Part I

1. In the case of an **ordinary lease**, if the lessor is a merchant, the risk of loss passes to the lessee on the receipt of the goods [UCC 2A-219].
2. If the lease is a **finance lease** and the supplier is a merchant, the risk of loss passes to the lessee on the receipt of the goods [UCC 2A-219]. A finance lease is a three-party transaction consisting of a lessor, a lessee, and a supplier (or vendor).
3. If a tender of delivery of goods fails to conform to the lease contract, the risk of loss remains with the lessor or supplier until cure or acceptance [UCC 2A-220(1)(a)].

CONTEMPORARY ENVIRONMENT

Insuring Against Loss of Goods

To protect against financial loss that would occur if goods were damaged, destroyed, lost, or stolen, the parties to sales and lease contracts should purchase insurance against such loss. If the goods are then lost or damaged, the insured party receives reimbursement from the insurance company for the loss.

To purchase insurance, a party must have an *insurable interest* in the goods. A seller has an insurable interest in goods as long as he or she retains title or has a security interest in the goods. A lessor retains an insurable interest in the goods during the term of the lease. A buyer or lessee obtains an insurable interest in the goods when they are identified in the sales or lease contract. Both the buyer and seller, or the lessee and lessor, can have an insurable interest in the goods at the same time [UCC 2-501, 2A-218].

To obtain and maintain proper insurance coverage on goods, a contacting party should:

- Determine the value of goods subject to the sales or lease contract.
- Purchase insurance from a reputable insurance company to cover the goods subject to the contract.
- Maintain the insurance by paying the premiums when they are due.
- Immediately file the proper claim and supporting documentation with an insurance company if the goods are damaged, destroyed, lost, or stolen.

void title
A situation in which a thief acquires no title to goods he or she steals. Also known as a *void leasehold interest.*

voidable title
A title that a purchaser has if the goods were obtained by (1) fraud, (2) a check that is later dishonored, or (3) impersonation of another person. Also known as *voidable leasehold interest.*

good faith purchaser for value
A person to whom good title can be transferred from a person with voidable title. The real owner cannot reclaim goods from a good faith purchaser for value.

good faith subsequent lessee
A person to whom a lease interest can be transferred from a person with voidable title. The real owner cannot reclaim the goods from the subsequent lessee until the lease expires.

buyer in the ordinary course of business
A person who in good faith and without knowledge that the sale violates the ownership or security interests of a third party buys goods in the ordinary course of business from a person in the business of selling goods of that kind. A buyer in the ordinary course of business takes the goods free of any third-party security interest in the goods.

SALES BY NONOWNERS

Sometimes people sell goods even though they do not hold valid title to them. The UCC anticipated many of the problems this situation could cause and established rules concerning the title, if any, that could be transferred to purchasers.

Stolen Goods: Void Title

In a case in which a buyer purchases goods or a lessee leases goods from a thief who has stolen them, the purchaser does not acquire title to the goods, and the lessee does not acquire any leasehold interest in the goods. The real owner can reclaim the goods from the purchaser or lessee [UCC 2-403(1)]. This is called **void title** or **void leasehold interest**.

Example Jack steals a truckload of Sony high-definition television sets that are owned by Electronics Store. The thief resells the televisions to City-Mart, which does not know that the goods were stolen. If Electronics Store finds out where the televisions are, it can reclaim them. This is because the thief had no title in the goods, so title was not transferred to City-Mart. There is void title. City-Mart's only recourse is against the thief, if he or she can be found.

Sales or Lease of Goods to Good Faith Purchasers for Value: Voidable Title

A seller or lessor has **voidable title**, or **voidable leasehold interest**, to goods if the goods were obtained by fraud, if a check is later dishonored, or if he or she impersonates another person.

A person with voidable title to goods can transfer good title to a **good faith purchaser for value** or a **good faith subsequent lessee**. A good faith purchaser or lessee for value is someone who pays sufficient consideration or rent for the goods to the person he or she honestly believes has good title to those goods [UCC 2-201(1), 1-201(44)(d)]. The real owner cannot reclaim goods from such a purchaser or lessee [UCC 2-403(1)].

Example Max buys a Rolex watch from his neighbor Dorothy for nearly fair market value. It is later discovered that Dorothy obtained the watch from Jewelry Store with a "bounced check"—that is, a check for which there were insufficient funds to pay for the Rolex watch. Jewelry Store cannot reclaim the watch from Max because Max, the second purchaser, purchased the watch in good faith and for value.

CONTEMPORARY ENVIRONMENT

Entrustment Rule

If an owner **entrusts** the possession of his or her goods to a merchant who deals in goods of that kind, the merchant has the power to transfer all rights (including title) in the goods to a **buyer in the ordinary course of business** [UCC 2-403(2)]. The real owner cannot reclaim the goods from this buyer. This is called the **entrustment rule**.

Example Kim brings her diamond ring to Ring Store to be repaired. Ring Store both sells and repairs jewelry. Kim leaves (entrusts) her ring at the store until it is repaired. Ring Store sells Kim's ring to Harold, who is going to propose marriage to Gretchen. Harold, a buyer in the ordinary course of business, acquires title to the ring. Kim cannot reclaim her ring from Harold (or Gretchen). Her only recourse is to sue Ring Store.

The entrustment rule also applies to leases. If a lessor entrusts the possession of his or her goods to a lessee who is a merchant who deals in goods of that kind, the merchant-lessee has the power to transfer all the lessor's and lessee's rights in the goods to a buyer or sublessee in the ordinary course of business [UCC 2A-305(2)].

In the following entrustment case, the court had to decide whether a purchaser was a buyer in the ordinary course of business.

CASE 1 Entrustment

Lindholm v. Brant

283 Conn. 65, 925 A.2d 1048, Web 2007 Conn. Lexis 264 (2007)
Supreme Court of Connecticut

"Any entrusting of possession of goods to a merchant who deals in goods of that kind gives him power to transfer all rights of the entruster to a buyer in ordinary course of business."

—Judge Rogers

Facts

In 1962, Andy Warhol, a famous artist, created a silkscreen on canvas titled *Red Elvis*. *Red Elvis* consists of 36 identical faces of Elvis Presley, with a red background, and is approximately 5.75 feet in height and 4.35 feet in width. Kerstin Lindholm was an art collector who, for 30 years, had been represented by Anders Malmberg, an art dealer. In 1987, with the assistance and advice of Malmberg, Lindholm purchased *Red Elvis* for $300,000

In 1996, the Guggenheim Museum in New York City decided to sponsor an Andy Warhol exhibition. The staff of the Guggenheim contacted Malmberg to see if Lindholm was willing to lend *Red Elvis* to the exhibition. Lindholm agreed, and *Red Elvis* was placed in the Guggenheim's exhibition. When the Guggenheim exhibition was completed in 2000, Malmberg told Lindholm that he could place *Red Elvis* on loan to the Louisiana Museum in Denmark if Lindholm agreed. By letter dated March 20, 2000, Lindholm agreed and gave permission to Malmberg to obtain possession of *Red Elvis* from the Guggenheim Museum and place it on loan to the Louisiana Museum. Instead of placing *Red Elvis* on loan to the Louisiana Museum, Malmberg, claiming ownership to *Red Elvis*, immediately contracted to sell *Red Elvis* to Peter M. Brant, an art collector, for $2.9 million. Brant had his lawyer do a UCC lien search and a search of the Art Loss Registry related to *Red Elvis*. These searches revealed no claims or liens against *Red Elvis*. Brant paid $2.9 million to Malmberg and received an invoice of sale and possession of *Red Elvis*.

Subsequently, Lindholm made arrangements to sell *Red Elvis* to a Japanese buyer for $4.6 million. Shortly thereafter, Lindholm discovered the fraud. Lindholm brought a civil lawsuit in the state of Connecticut against Brant to recover *Red Elvis*. Brant argued that he was a buyer in the ordinary course of business because he purchased *Red Elvis* from an art dealer to whom Lindholm had entrusted *Red Elvis*, and he had a claim that was superior to Lindholm's claim of ownership. The superior court of Connecticut issued a memorandum opinion that awarded *Red Elvis* to Brant.

Issue

Was Brant a buyer in the ordinary course of business who had a claim of ownership to *Red Elvis* that was superior to that of the owner Lindholm?

Language of the Court

The Brant defendants have pleaded a special defense to all counts that Brant is a buyer in the ordinary course pursuant to Conn. Gen. Stat. Sections 42a-2-403(2) and (3). A person with voidable title has power to transfer a good title to a good faith purchaser for value. Any entrusting of possession of goods to a merchant who deals in goods of that kind gives him power to transfer all rights of the entruster to a buyer in ordinary course of business. "Entrusting" includes any delivery and any acquiescence in retention of possession regardless of any condition expressed between the parties to the delivery or acquiescence and regardless of whether the procurement of the entrusting or the possessor's disposition of the goods have been such as to be larcenous under the criminal law.

That statutory provision sets forth the circumstances in which an innocent, good faith purchaser of goods who acquires them from a dealer in goods of that kind has a right to the goods superior to the rights of the owner/entrustor of the goods. This special defense requires the Brant defendants to show that Brant was a buyer in the ordinary course. K. Lindholm's March 20, 2000 letter constituted an entrustment of Red Elvis *to a merchant, Malmberg. Once K. Lindholm entrusted* Red Elvis *to Malmberg she gave him the power to transfer all of her rights as the entruster to a buyer in the ordinary course.*

After considering all of the evidence, the court finds that pursuant to Conn. Gen. Stat. Section 42a-2-403 Brant took good title to Red Elvis*. Specifically, Brant purchased* Red Elvis *from Malmberg in good faith and in the ordinary course of business. Brant honestly believed Malmberg owned* Red Elvis *when he purchased the painting from him. Brant also observed reasonable commercial standards of fair dealing in the art industry when he purchased* Red Elvis *from Malmberg. Accordingly, because Brant has proven his special defense of being a buyer in the ordinary course, judgment will enter in favor of the defendants on all counts.*

Decision

The trial court held that Brant was a buyer in the ordinary course of business who obtained ownership to *Red*

(case continues)

Elvis when he purchased the stolen *Red Elvis* from Malmberg. The court held that Brant's claim of ownership as a buyer in the ordinary course of business was superior to Lindholm's claim of ownership because she had entrusted *Red Elvis* to an art dealer who sold the stolen *Red Elvis* to Brant.

Note: Lindholm appealed the decision of the trial court to the supreme court of Connecticut, which affirmed the decision of the trial court and awarded the *Red Elvis* to Brant. A court in Sweden convicted Malmberg of criminal fraud and sentenced him to three years in prison. A Swedish court awarded Lindholm $4.6 in damages against Malmberg.

Case Questions

Critical Legal Thinking What is the entrustment rule? Explain. What does the rule of ordinary buyer in the course of business provide regarding the purchase of stolen property? Explain.

Business Ethics Did Malmberg act ethically in this case? Did he act criminally? Did Brandt have any ethical duty to return *Red Elvis* to its original owner, Lindholm?

Contemporary Business What are the possible consequences of an owner of a good entrusting the good to a merchant who sells the type of property that is entrusted to him?

CONCEPT SUMMARY

PASSAGE OF TITLE BY NONOWNER THIRD PARTIES

Type of Transaction	Title Possessed by Seller	Innocent Purchaser	Purchaser Acquires Title to Goods
Goods acquired by theft are resold.	Void title	Good faith purchaser for value	No. Original owner may reclaim the goods.
Goods acquired by fraud or dishonored check are resold.	Voidable title	Good faith purchaser for value	Yes. Purchaser takes goods, free of claim of original owner.
Goods entrusted by owner to merchant who deals in that type of good are resold.	No title	Buyer in the ordinary course of business	Yes. Purchaser takes goods, free of claim of original owner.

INTERNET LAW & ONLINE COMMERCE

Revised Article 2 (Sales) and Revised Article 2A (Leases) Establish Rules for Electronic Contracts and Signatures

Written contracts and written signatures are given effect by Article 2 (Sales) and Article 2A (Leases) of the UCC. The UCC has also established rules for written communications concerning contracts for the sale and lease of goods. Revised Article 2 (Sales) and Revised Article 2A (Leases) add new rules regarding the recognition of signatures and communications concerning electronic contracts. The following are several of these rules:

- A record or signature may not be denied legal effect or enforcement solely because it is in electronic form [Revised UCC 2-211(1), Revised UCC 2A-222(1)]. This provision states that electronic contracts and electronic signatures are to be given legal effect and can be enforced against contracting parties.
- An **electronic record** or **electronic signature** is attributable to a person if it was the act of the person or the person's **electronic agent** [Revised UCC 2-212, Revised UCC 2A-223]. This provision permits a person to conduct business himself or through electronic agents, using electronic records and electronic signatures.
- If the receipt of an **electronic communication** has a legal effect, it has that effect even if no individual is aware of its receipt [Revised UCC 2-213(1), Revised UCC 2A-224(1)]. This rule acknowledges the legal effect of electronic communications that are received by electronic agents such as Internet websites.

- Receipt of an **electronic acknowledgment** of an electronic communication establishes that the communication was received but, in itself, does not establish that the content sent corresponds to the content received [Revised UCC 2-213(2), Revised UCC 2A-224(2)]. Thus, an electronic acknowledgement of the receipt of an electronic communication proves that the electronic communication was received. This acknowledgment does not, in itself, establish what the content of the electronic communication was, however. That must come from other evidence.

These rules place electronic signatures on par with written signatures. They also establish special conditions regarding the receipt of electronic communications.

INTERNATIONAL LAW

Letters of Credit in International Trade

The major risks in any business transaction involving the sale of goods are (1) that the seller will not be paid after delivering the goods and (2) that the buyer will not receive the goods after paying for them. These risks are especially acute in international transactions, where the buyer and seller may not know each other, the parties are dealing at long distance, and the judicial systems of the parties' countries may not have jurisdiction to decide a dispute if one arises. The irrevocable **letter of credit** has been developed to manage these risks in international sales. The function of a letter of credit is to substitute the credit of a recognized international bank for that of the buyer.

Example Suppose a buyer in one country and a seller in another country enter into a contract for the sale of goods. The buyer goes to his or her bank and pays the bank a fee to issue a letter of credit in which the bank agrees to pay the amount of the letter (which is the amount of the purchase price of the goods) to the seller's bank if certain conditions are met. These conditions are usually the delivery of documents indicating that the seller has placed the goods in the hands of a shipper. The buyer is called the **account party**, the bank that issues the letter of credit is called the **issuing bank**, and the seller is called the **beneficiary** of the letter of credit.

Article 5 (Letters of Credit) of the Uniform Commercial Code governs letters of credit unless otherwise agreed by the parties. The International Chamber of Commerce has promulgated the **Uniform Customs and Practices for Documentary Credits (UCP)**, which contains rules governing the formation and performance of letters of credit. Although the UCP is neither a treaty nor a legislative enactment, most banks incorporate the terms of the UCP in letters of credit they issue.

Chas Howson © The British Museum

Japanese Currency *Japan and the United States have two of the largest economies in the world. There is significant trade between the two countries. Irrevocable letters of credit are used in conducting international trade to ensure that a seller located in one country will be paid for the goods it has sold to a buyer who is located in another country.*

TEST REVIEW TERMS AND CONCEPTS

Account party
Article 5 (Letters of Credit)
Bailee
Beneficiary
Buyer in the ordinary course of business
C.&F. (cost and freight)
C.I.F. (cost, insurance, and freight)
Conditional sale
Consignee
Consignment
Consignor
Destination contract
Document of title
Electronic acknowledgment
Electronic agent
Electronic communication
Electronic record (electronic signature)
Entrust
Entrustment rule
Ex-ship (from the carrying vessel)
F.A.S. (free alongside ship)
F.A.S. (*vessel*) *port of shipment*
Finance lease
F.O.B. (free on board) *place of destination*
F.O.B. (free on board) *point of shipment*
Future goods
Good faith purchaser for value
Good faith subsequent lessee
Identification of goods
Issuing bank
Lessee
Lessor
Letter of credit
No-arrival, no-sale contract
Ordinary lease
Passage of title
Risk of loss
Sale on approval
Sale or return contract
Shipment contract
Title
Uniform Customs and Practices for Documentary Credits (UCP)
Void title (void leasehold interest)
Voidable title (voidable leasehold interest)

CASE PROBLEMS

1 Identification of Goods The Big Knob Volunteer Fire Company (Fire Co.) agreed to purchase a fire truck from Hamerly Custom Productions (Hamerly), which was in the business of assembling various component parts into fire trucks. Fire Co. paid Hamerly $10,000 toward the price two days after signing the contract. Two weeks later, it gave Hamerly $38,000 more toward the total purchase price of $53,000. Hamerly bought an engine chassis for the new fire truck on credit from Lowe and Meyer Garage (Lowe and Meyer). After installing the chassis, Hamerly painted the Big Knob Fire Department's name on the side of the cab. Hamerly never paid for the engine chassis, and the truck was repossessed by Lowe and Meyer. Fire Co. sought to recover the fire truck from Lowe and Meyer. Although Fire Co. was the buyer of a fire truck, Lowe and Meyer questioned whether any goods had ever been identified in the contract. Are they? *Big Knob Volunteer Fire Co. v. Lowe and Meyer Garage*, 338 Pa.Super. 257, 487 A.2d 953, **Web** 1985 Pa.Super. Lexis 5540 (Superior Court of Pennsylvania)

2 Passage of Title New England Yacht Sales (Yacht Sales) sold a yacht to Robert Pease. Pease paid for the yacht in full, and Yacht Sales delivered to him a marine bill of sale. The marine bill of sale stated that Yacht Sales was transferring "all of its right, title, and interest" in the yacht to Pease. The yacht never left the Connecticut shipyard that Yacht Sales rented. During the winter, Yacht Sales did repair work on the yacht. In the spring, Yacht Sales delivered the yacht to Pease in Rhode Island. At issue in this case was when the sales tax was due to the state of Connecticut—on the date of sale or on the date of delivery. When does the title actually pass? *New England Yacht Sales v. Commissioner of Revenue Services*, 198 Conn. 624, 504 A.2d 506, **Web** 1986 Conn. Lexis 719 (Supreme Court of Connecticut)

3 Stolen Goods John Torniero was employed by Micheals Jewelers, Inc. (Micheals). During the course of his employment, Torniero stole pieces of jewelry, including several diamond rings, a sapphire ring, a gold pendant, and several loose diamonds. Over a period of several months, Torniero sold individual pieces of the stolen jewelry to G&W Watch and Jewelry Corporation (G&W). G&W had no knowledge of how Torniero obtained the jewels. Torniero was arrested when Micheals discovered the thefts. After Torniero admitted that he had sold the stolen jewelry to G&W, Micheals attempted to recover it from G&W. G&W claimed title to the jewelry as a good faith purchaser for value. Micheals challenged G&W's claim to title in court. Who wins? *United States v. Micheals Jewelers, Inc.*, 42 UCC Rep.Serv. 141, **Web** 1985 U.S. Dist. Lexis 15142 (United States District Court for the District of Connecticut)

4 Passage of Title J.A. Coghill owned a Rolls Royce Corniche automobile, which he sold to a man claiming to be Daniel Bellman. Bellman gave Coghill a cashier's check for $94,500. When Coghill tried to cash the check, his bank informed him that the check had been forged. Coghill reported the vehicle as stolen. Subsequently, Barry Hyken responded to a newspaper ad listing a Rolls Royce Corniche for sale. Hyken went to meet the seller of the car, the man who claimed to be Bellman, in a parking lot. When Hyken asked why the car was advertised as a 1980 model when it was in fact a 1979, Bellman replied that it was a newspaper mistake. Hyken agreed to pay $62,000 for the car. When Hyken asked to see Bellman's identification, Bellman provided documents with two different addresses. Bellman explained that he was in the process of moving. Although there seemed to be some irregularities in the title documents to the car, Hyken took possession anyway. Three weeks later, the Rolls Royce

Corniche was seized by the police. Hyken sued to get it back. Who wins? *Landshire Food Service, Inc. v. Coghill*, 709 S.W.2d 509, **Web** 1986 Mo.App. Lexis 3961 (Court of Appeals of Missouri)

5 Passage of Title Cherry Creek Dodge, Inc. (Cherry Creek), sold a 1985 Dodge Ramcharger to Executive Leasing of Colorado (Executive Leasing). Executive Leasing, which was in the business of buying and selling cars, paid for the Dodge with a draft. Cherry Creek maintained a security interest in the car until the draft cleared. The same day that Executive Leasing bought the Dodge, it sold the car to Bruce and Peggy Carter. The Carters paid in full for the Dodge with a cashier's check, and the vehicle was delivered to them. The Carters had no knowledge of the financial arrangement between Executive Leasing and Cherry Creek. The draft that Executive Leasing gave Cherry Creek was worthless. Cherry Creek attempted to recover the vehicle from the Carters. Who wins? *Cherry Creek Dodge, Inc. v. Carter*, 733 P.2d 1024, **Web** 1987 Wyo. Lexis 408 (Supreme Court of Wyoming)

6 Entrustment Rule Fuqua Homes, Inc. (Fuqua), is a manufacturer of prefabricated houses. MMM, a dealer of prefabricated homes, was a partnership created by two men named Kirk and Underhill. On seven occasions before the disputed transactions occurred, MMM had ordered homes from Fuqua. MMM was contacted by Kenneth Ryan, who wanted to purchase a 55-foot modular home. MMM called Fuqua and ordered a prefabricated home that met Ryan's specifications. Fuqua delivered the home to MMM and retained a security interest in it until MMM paid the purchase price. MMM installed the house on Ryan's property and collected full payment from Ryan. Kirk and Underhill then disappeared, taking Ryan's money with them. Fuqua was never paid for the prefabricated home it had manufactured. Ryan had no knowledge of the dealings between MMM and Fuqua. Fuqua claimed title to the house based upon its security interest. Who has title to the home? *Fuqua Homes, Inc. v. Evanston Bldg. & Loan Co.*, 52 OhioApp. 2d 399, 370 N.E.2d 780, **Web** 1977 OhioApp. Lexis 6968 (Court of Appeals of Ohio)

7 Risk of Loss All America Export-Import Corp. (All America) placed an order for several thousand pounds of yarn with A. M. Knitwear (Knitwear). On June 4, All America sent Knitwear a purchase order. The purchase order stated the terms of the sale, including language that stated that the price was F.O.B. the seller's plant. A truck hired by All America arrived at Knitwear's plant. Knitwear turned the yarn over to the carrier and notified All America that the goods were now on the truck. The truck left Knitwear's plant and proceeded to a local warehouse. Sometime during the night, the truck was hijacked, and all the yarn was stolen. All America had paid for the yarn by check but stopped payment on it when it learned that the goods had been stolen. Knitwear sued All America, claiming that it must pay for the stolen goods because it bore the risk of loss. Who wins? *A. M. Knitwear v. All America, Etc.*, 41 N.Y.2d 14, 359 N.E.2d 342, 390 N.Y.S.2d 832, **Web** 1976 N.Y. Lexis 3201 (Court of Appeals of New York)

8 Risk of Loss Mitsubishi International Corporation (Mitsubishi) entered into a contract with Crown Door Company (Crown) that called for Mitsubishi to sell 12 boxcar loads of plywood to Crown. According to the terms of the contract, Mitsubishi would import the wood from Taiwan and deliver it to Crown's plant in Atlanta. Mitsubishi had the wood shipped from Taiwan to Savannah, Georgia. At Savannah, the plywood was loaded onto trains and hauled to Atlanta. When the plywood arrived in Atlanta, it was discovered that the railroad had been negligent in loading the train. The negligent loading had caused the cargo to shift during the trip, and the shifting had caused extensive damage to the wood. Who bears the risk of loss? *Georgia Port Authority v. Mitsubishi International Corporation*, 156 Ga.App. 304, 274 S.E.2d 699, **Web** 1980 Ga.App. Lexis 2952 (Court of Appeals of Georgia)

9 Risk of Loss Martin Silver ordered two rooms of furniture from Wycombe, Meyer & Co., Inc. (Wycombe), a manufacturer and seller of custom-made furniture. On February 23, 1982, Wycombe sent invoices to Silver, advising him that the furniture was ready for shipment. Silver tendered payment in full for the goods and asked that one room of furniture be shipped immediately and that the other be held for shipment on a later date. Before any instructions were received as to the second room of furniture, it was destroyed in a fire. Silver and his insurance company attempted to recover the money he had paid for the destroyed furniture. Wycombe refused to return the payment, claiming that the risk of loss was on Silver. Who wins? *Silver v. Wycombe, Meyer & Co., Inc.*, 124 Misc.2d 717, 477 N.Y.S.2d 288, **Web** 1984 N.Y.Misc. Lexis 3319 (Civil Court of the City of New York)

10 Insurable Interest Donald Hayward signed a sales contract with Dry Land Marina, Inc. (Dry Land). The contract was for the purchase of a 30-foot Revel Craft Playmate Yacht for $10,000. The contract called for Dry Land to install a number of options on Hayward's yacht and then deliver it to him. Before taking delivery of the yacht, Hayward signed a security agreement in favor of Dry Land and a promissory note. Several weeks later, a fire swept through Dry Land's showroom. Hayward's yacht was among the goods destroyed in the fire. Who has an insurable interest in the yacht? *Hayward v. Potsma*, 31 Mich.App. 720, 188 N.W.2d 31, **Web** 1971 Mich.App. Lexis 2150 (Court of Appeals of Michigan)

BUSINESS ETHICS CASES

11 Business Ethics Raceway Auto Auction (Raceway), New York, sold an Oldsmobile automobile to Triangle Auto Sales (Triangle). Triangle paid for the car with a check. Raceway delivered possession of the car to Triangle. Thereafter, Triangle's check bounced because of insufficient funds. In the meantime, Triangle sold the car to Campus Auto Sales (Campus), Rhode Island, which sold it to Charles Motor Co., Inc. (Charles), Rhode Island, which sold it to Lee Oldsmobile-Cadillac, Inc. (Lee Oldsmobile), Maine, which sold it to Stephanie K. LeBlanc of Augusta, Maine. When Triangle's check bounced, Raceway reported the car as stolen. Four months after she purchased the car, Stephanie was stopped by the Maine police, who seized the car. To maintain good relations with its customer, Lee Oldsmobile paid Raceway to obtain the certificate of title to the automobile and then sued Charles to recover. Did Triangle Auto Sales act ethically in this case? Does Charles Motor Co. obtain valid title to the automobile? *Lee Oldsmobile-Cadillac, Inc. v. Labonte*, 30 UCC Rep.Serv. 74, **Web** 1980 R.I.Super. Lexis 190 (Superior Court of Rhode Island)

12 Business Ethics Executive Financial Services, Inc. (EFS), purchased three tractors from Tri-County Farm Company (Tri-County), a John Deere dealership owned by Gene Mohr and James Loyd. The tractors cost $48,000, $19,000, and $38,000. EFS did not take possession of the tractors but instead left the tractors on Tri-County's lot. EFS leased the tractors to Mohr-Loyd Leasing (Mohr-Loyd), a partnership between Mohr and Loyd, with the understanding and representation by Mohr-Loyd that the tractors would be leased out to farmers. Instead of leasing the tractors, Tri-County sold them to three different farmers. EFS sued and obtained judgment against Tri-County, Mohr-Loyd, and Mohr and Loyd personally for breach of contract. Because that judgment remained unsatisfied, EFS sued the three farmers who bought the tractors to recover the tractors from them. Did Mohr and Loyd act ethically in this case? Who owns the tractors, EFS or the farmers? *Executive Financial Services, Inc. v. Pagel*, 238 Kan. 809, 715 P.2d 381, **Web** 1986 Kan. Lexis 290 (Supreme Court of Kansas)

REMEDIES FOR BREACH OF SALES AND LEASE CONTRACTS

Vincent P. Walter/Pearson Education/PH College

▲ **Forklift** *A seller or lessor is under a duty to deliver conforming goods, but the UCC gives a seller or lessor who delivers nonconforming goods an opportunity to cure the nonconformity.*

CHAPTER OBJECTIVES

After studying this chapter, you should be able to:

1. Describe the performance of sales and lease contracts.
2. List and describe the seller's remedies for the buyer's breach of a sales contract.
3. List and describe the buyer's remedies for the seller's breach of a sales contract.
4. List and describe the lessor's remedies for the lessee's breach of a lease contract.
5. List and describe the lessee's remedies for the lessor's breach of a lease contract.

CHAPTER CONTENTS

From Chapter 20 of *Business Law: Legal Environment, Online Commerce, Business Ethics, and International Issues,* 7/e.

"Trade and commerce, if they were not made of Indian rubber, would never manage to bounce over the obstacles which legislators are continually putting in their way."

—Henry D. Thoreau
Resistance to Civil Government (1849)

INTRODUCTION TO REMEDIES FOR BREACH OF SALES AND LEASE CONTRACTS

obligation
An action a party to a sales or lease contract is required by law to carry out.

breach
Failure of a party to perform an obligation in a sales or lease contract.

Usually, the parties to a sales or lease contract owe a duty to perform the **obligations** specified in their agreement [UCC 2-301, 2A-301]. The seller's or lessor's general obligation is to transfer and deliver the goods to the buyer or lessee. The buyer's or lessee's general obligation is to accept and pay for the goods.

When one party **breaches** a sales or lease contract, the UCC provides the injured party with a variety of prelitigation and litigation remedies. These remedies are designed to place the injured party in as good a position as if the breaching party's contractual obligations were fully performed [UCC 1-106(1), 2A-401(1)]. The best remedy depends on the circumstances of the particular case.

The performance of obligations and remedies available for breach of sales and lease contracts are discussed in this chapter.

SELLER'S AND LESSOR'S PERFORMANCE

tender of delivery
The obligation of a seller to transfer and deliver goods to the buyer or lessee in accordance with a sales or lease contract.

The seller's or lessor's basic obligation is the **tender of delivery**, or the transfer and delivery of goods to the buyer or lessee in accordance with a sales or lease contract [UCC 2-301]. Tender of delivery requires the seller or lessor to (1) put and hold conforming goods at the buyer's or lessee's disposition and (2) give the buyer or lessee any notification reasonably necessary to enable delivery of goods. The parties may agree as to the time, place, and manner of delivery. If there is no special agreement, tender must be made at a reasonable hour, and the goods must be kept available for a reasonable period of time.

Example The seller cannot telephone the buyer at 12:01 A.M. and say that the buyer has 15 minutes to accept delivery [UCC 2-503(1), 2A-508(1)].

Unless otherwise agreed or unless the circumstances permit either party to request delivery in lots, the goods named in a contract must be tendered in a single delivery. Payment of a sales contract is due upon tender of delivery unless an extension of credit between the parties has been arranged. If the goods are rightfully delivered in lots, the payment is apportioned for each lot [UCC 2-307]. Lease payments are due in accordance with the terms of the lease contract.

Place of Delivery

Many sales and lease contracts state where the goods are to be delivered. Often, the contract will say that the buyer or lessee must pick up the goods from the seller or lessor. If the contract does not expressly state the **place of delivery**, the UCC stipulates place of delivery on the basis of whether a carrier is involved.

Noncarrier Cases

A legal decision depends not on the teacher's age, but on the force of his argument.

The Talmud

Unless otherwise agreed, the place of delivery is the seller's or lessor's place of business. If the seller or lessor has no place of business, the place of delivery is the seller's or lessor's residence. If the parties have knowledge at the time of contracting that identified goods are located in some other place, that place is the place of delivery.

Example If parties contract regarding the sale of wheat that is located in a silo, the silo is the place of delivery [UCC 2-308].

Sometimes goods are in the possession of a bailee (e.g., a warehouse) and are to be delivered without being moved. In such cases, tender of delivery occurs when the seller either (1) tenders to the buyer a negotiable document of title covering the goods, (2) produces acknowledgment from the bailee of the buyer's right to possession of the goods, or (3) tenders a nonnegotiable document of title or a written direction to the bailee to deliver the goods to a buyer. The seller must deliver all such documents in correct form [UCC 2-503(4), 2-503(5)].

Carrier Cases

Unless the parties have agreed otherwise, if delivery of goods to a buyer is to be made by carrier, the UCC establishes different rules for *shipment contracts* and *destination contracts*. These rules are described in the paragraphs that follow.

Shipment Contracts Sales contracts that require the seller to send the goods to the buyer, but not to a specifically named destination, are called **shipment contracts**. Under such contracts, the seller must do the following [UCC 2-504]:

1. Put the goods in the carrier's possession and contract for the proper and safe transportation of the goods.
2. Obtain and promptly deliver or tender in correct form any documents (a) necessary to enable the buyer to obtain possession of the goods, (b) required by the sales contract, or (c) required by usage of trade.
3. Promptly notify the buyer of the shipment.

shipment contract
A sales contract that requires the seller to send the goods to the buyer but not to a specifically named destination.

The buyer may reject the goods if a material delay or loss is caused by the seller's failure to make a proper contract for the shipment of goods or properly notify the buyer of the shipment. If a shipment contract involves perishable goods and the seller fails to ship the goods via a refrigerated carrier, the buyer may rightfully reject the goods if they spoil during transit.

Destination Contracts A sales contract that requires the seller to deliver goods to the buyer's place of business or another specified destination is a **destination contract**. Unless otherwise agreed, destination contracts require delivery to be tendered at the buyer's place of business or other location specified in the sales contract. Delivery must occur at a reasonable time, in a reasonable manner, and with proper notice to the buyer. Appropriate documents of title must be provided by the seller to enable the buyer to obtain the goods from the carrier [UCC 2-503].

destination contract
A sales contract that requires the seller to deliver the goods to the buyer's place of business or another specified destination.

Perfect Tender Rule

A seller or lessor is under a duty to deliver conforming goods. If the goods or tender of delivery fails in any respect to conform to the contract, the buyer or lessee may opt either (1) to reject the whole shipment, (2) to accept the whole shipment, or (3) to reject part and accept part of the shipment. This option is referred to as the **perfect tender rule** [UCC 2-601, 2A-509]. If a buyer accepts nonconforming goods, the buyer may seek remedies against the seller.

perfect tender rule
A rule that says if the goods or tender of a delivery fail in any respect to conform to the contract, the buyer may opt either (1) to reject the whole shipment, (2) to accept the whole shipment, or (3) to reject part and accept part of the shipment.

Example A sales contract requires the Lawn Mower Company to deliver 100 lawn mowers to Outdoor Store. When the buyer inspects the delivered goods, it is discovered that 80 lawn mowers conform to the contract, and 20 lawn mowers do not conform. Pursuant to the perfect tender rule, the buyer Outdoor Store may reject the entire shipment of lawn mowers. In the alternative, the buyer Outdoor Store can accept the 80 conforming lawn mowers and reject the 20 nonconforming lawn mowers. As another alternative, the buyer Outdoor Store may accept the whole shipment, both the conforming and nonconforming lawn mowers, and seek remedies from the seller Lawn Mower Company for the 20 nonconforming lawn mowers.

Exceptions to the Perfect Tender Rule

The UCC alters the perfect tender rule in the following situations:

The buyer needs a hundred eyes, the seller not one.

George Herbert
Jacula Prudentum (1651)

cure
An opportunity to repair or replace defective or nonconforming goods.

1. **Agreement of the parties.** The parties to a sales or lease contract may agree to limit the effect of the perfect tender rule. For example, they may decide that (1) only the defective or nonconforming goods may be rejected, (2) the seller or lessor may replace nonconforming goods or repair defects, or (3) the buyer or lessee will accept nonconforming goods with appropriate compensation from the seller or lessor.
2. **Substitution of carriers.** The UCC requires the seller to use a commercially reasonable substitute if (1) the agreed-upon manner of delivery fails or (2) the agreed-upon type of carrier becomes unavailable [UCC 2-614(1)].

CONTEMPORARY ENVIRONMENT

Opportunity to Cure

The UCC gives a seller or lessor who delivers nonconforming goods an opportunity to **cure** the nonconformity. Although the term *cure* is not defined by the UCC, it generally means an opportunity to repair or replace defective or nonconforming goods [UCC 2-508, 2A-513].

A cure may be attempted if the time for performance has not expired and the seller or lessor notifies the buyer or lessee of his or her intention to make a conforming delivery within the contract time.

Example A lessee contracts to lease a BMW 750i automobile from a lessor for delivery July 1. On June 15, the lessor delivers a BMW 550i to the lessee, and the lessee rejects it as nonconforming. The lessor has until July 1 to cure the nonconformity by delivering the BMW 750i specified in the contract.

A cure may also be attempted if the seller or lessor had reasonable grounds to believe the nonconforming delivery would be accepted. The seller or lessor may have a further reasonable time to substitute a conforming tender.

Example A buyer contracts to purchase 500 red dresses from a seller for delivery July 1. On July 1, the seller delivers 100 blue dresses to the buyer. In the past, the buyer has accepted different-colored dresses than those ordered. This time, though, the buyer rejects the blue dresses as nonconforming. The seller has a reasonable time after July 1 to deliver conforming red dresses to the buyer.

Installment Contracts

installment contract
A contract that requires or authorizes goods to be delivered and accepted in separate lots.

An **installment contract** is a contract that requires or authorizes goods to be delivered and accepted in separate lots. Such a contract must contain a clause that states "each delivery in a separate lot" or equivalent language.

Example A contract in which the buyer orders 1,000 widgets, to be delivered in four equal installments of 250 items, is an installment contract.

The UCC alters the perfect tender rule with regard to installment contracts. The buyer or lessee may reject the entire contract only if the nonconformity or default with respect to any installment or installments substantially impairs the value of the entire contract. The buyer or lessee may reject any nonconforming installment if the value of the installment is impaired and the defect cannot be cured. Thus, in each case, the court must determine whether the nonconforming installment impairs the value of the entire contract or only that installment [UCC 2-612, 2A-510].

This is the kind of order which makes the administration of justice stink in the nostrils of commercial men.

A. L. Smith
L. J. Graham v. Sutton, Carden & Company (1897)

Destruction of Goods

The UCC provides that if goods identified in a sales or lease contract are totally destroyed without the fault of either party before the risk of loss passes to the buyer or the lessee, the contract is void. Both parties are then excused from performing the contract.

If the goods are only partially destroyed, the buyer or lessee may inspect the goods and then choose either to treat the contract as void or to accept the goods. If the buyer or lessee opts to accept the goods, the purchase price or rent will be reduced to compensate for damages [UCC 2-613, 2A-221].

Example A buyer contracts to purchase a sofa from a seller. The seller agrees to deliver the sofa to the buyer's home. The truck delivering the sofa is hit by an automobile, and the sofa is totally destroyed. Because the risk of loss has not passed to the buyer, the contract is voided, and the buyer does not have to pay for the sofa.

ETHICS SPOTLIGHT

Good Faith and Reasonableness

Generally, the common law of contracts only obligates the parties to perform their contracts according to the **express terms** of their contract. There is no breach of contract unless the parties fail to meet these terms.

Recognizing that certain situations may develop that are not expressly provided for in a contract or that strict adherence to the terms of a contract without doing more may not be sufficient to accomplish the contract's objective, the Uniform Commercial Code (UCC) adopts two broad principles that govern the performance of sales and lease contracts: **good faith** and **reasonableness**.

UCC 1-203 states, "Every contract or duty within this Act imposes an obligation of good faith in its performance or enforcement." Thus, both parties owe a duty of good faith to perform a sales or lease contract. Nonmerchants are held to the subjective standard of honesty in fact. Merchants are held to a higher standard of good faith than nonmerchants. Merchants are held to the objective standard of fair dealing in the trade [UCC 2-103(1)(b)].

The words *reasonable* and *reasonably* are used throughout the UCC to establish the duties of performance by the parties to sales and lease contracts. For example, unless otherwise specified, the parties must act within a "reasonable" time [UCC 1-204(1)(2)]. As another example, if a seller does not deliver the goods as contracted, the buyer may make "reasonable" purchases to cover (i.e., obtain substitute performance) [UCC 2-712(1)]. The term **commercial reasonableness** is used to establish certain duties of merchants under the UCC. Articles 2 and 2A of the UCC do not specifically define the terms *reasonable* and *commercial reasonableness*. Instead, these terms are defined by reference to the course of performance or the course of dealing between the parties, usage of trade, and such.

Note that the concepts of good faith and reasonableness extend to the "spirit" of a contract as well as the contract terms. The underlying theory is that the parties are more apt to perform properly if their conduct is to be judged against these principles. This is a major advance in the law of contracts.

Business Ethics Do the concepts of *good faith* and *reasonableness* that are contained in the Uniform Commercial Code (UCC) promote ethical behavior?

BUYER'S AND LESSEE'S PERFORMANCE

The buyer or lessee to a sales or lease contract owes certain duties of performance under the contract. These duties are either specified in the contract itself or are created by UCC Articles 2 and 2A. Once the seller or lessor has properly tendered delivery, the buyer or lessee is obligated to accept and pay for the goods in accordance with the sales or lease contract. If there is no agreement, the provisions of the UCC control.

Right of Inspection

Unless otherwise agreed, the buyer or lessee has the **right to inspect** goods that are tendered, delivered, or identified in a sales or lease contract prior to accepting or paying for them. If the goods are shipped, the inspection may take place after their arrival. If the inspected goods do not conform to the contract, the buyer or lessee may reject them without paying for them [UCC 2-513(1), 2A-515(1)]. If the goods are rejected for nonconformance, the cost of inspection can be recovered from the seller [UCC 2-513(2)].

Nobody has a more sacred obligation to obey the law than those who make the law.

Sophocles

The parties may agree as to the time, place, and manner of inspection. If there is no such agreement, the inspection must occur at a reasonable time and place and in a reasonable manner. Reasonableness depends on the circumstances of the case, common usage of trade, prior course of dealing between the parties, and such. If the goods conform to the contract, the buyer pays for the inspection.

C.O.D. shipment
A type of shipment contract in which the buyer agrees to pay the shipper cash upon the delivery of the goods.

Buyers who agree to **C.O.D. (cash on delivery) shipments** are not entitled to inspect the goods before paying for them. In certain sales contracts (e.g., cost, insurance, and freight [C.I.F.] contracts), payment is due from the buyer upon receipt of documents of title, even if the goods have not yet been received. In such a case, the buyer is not entitled to inspect the goods before paying for them [UCC 2-513(3)].

A proceeding may be perfectly legal and may yet be opposed to sound commercial principles.

Lord Justice Lindley
Verner v. General and Commercial Trust (1894)

Payment

Goods that are accepted must be paid for [UCC 2-607(1)]. Unless the parties to a contract agree otherwise, **payment** is due from a buyer when and where the goods are delivered, even if the place of delivery is the same as the place of shipment. Buyers often purchase goods on credit extended by the seller. Unless the parties agree to other terms, the credit period begins to run from the time the goods are shipped [UCC 2-310]. A lessee must pay lease payments in accordance with the lease contract [UCC 2A-516(1)].

The goods can be paid for in any manner currently acceptable in the ordinary course of business (e.g., check, credit card) unless the seller demands payment in cash or unless the contract names a specific form of payment. If the seller requires cash payment, the buyer must be given an extension of time necessary to procure the cash. If the buyer pays by check, payment is conditional on the check being honored (paid) when it is presented to the bank for payment [UCC 2-511].

Acceptance

acceptance
An act that occurs when a buyer or lessee takes any of the following actions after a reasonable opportunity to inspect the goods: (1) signifies to the seller or lessor in words or by conduct that the goods are conforming or that the buyer or lessee will take or retain the goods despite their nonconformity or (2) fails to effectively reject the goods within a reasonable time after their delivery or tender by the seller or lessor. Acceptance also occurs if a buyer acts inconsistently with the seller's ownership rights in the goods.

Acceptance occurs when the buyer or lessee takes any of the following actions after a reasonable opportunity to inspect the goods: (1) signifies to the seller or lessor in words or by conduct that the goods are conforming or that the buyer or lessee will take or retain the goods despite their nonconformity or (2) fails to effectively reject the goods within a reasonable time after their delivery or tender by the seller or lessor. Acceptance also occurs if a buyer acts inconsistently with the seller's ownership rights in the goods. Acceptance occurs if the buyer resells the goods delivered by the seller [UCC 2-606(1), 2A-515(1)].

Buyers and lessees may only accept delivery of a *commercial unit*—a unit of goods that commercial usage deems is a single whole for purpose of sale. Acceptance of a part of any commercial unit is acceptance of the entire unit [UCC 2-606(2), 2A-515(2)].

Example A commercial unit may be a single article (e.g., a machine), a set of articles (e.g., a suite of furniture or an assortment of sizes), a quantity (e.g., a bale, a gross, or a carload), or any other unit treated in use or in the relevant market as a single whole.

Revocation of Acceptance

A buyer or lessee who has accepted goods may subsequently revoke his or her acceptance if (1) the goods are nonconforming, (2) the nonconformity substantially impairs the value of the goods to the buyer or lessee, and (3) one of the following factors is shown: (a) the seller's or lessor's promise to timely cure of the nonconformity is not met, (b) the goods were accepted before the nonconformity was discovered and the nonconformity was difficult to discover, or (c) the goods were accepted before the nonconformity was discovered and the seller or lessor assured the buyer or lessee that the goods were conforming.

revocation of acceptance
Reversal of acceptance.

Revocation of acceptance is not effective until the seller or lessor is so notified. In addition, the revocation must occur within a reasonable time after the buyer or lessee discovers or should have discovered the grounds for the revocation. The revocation, which must be of a lot or commercial unit, must occur before there is any substantial change in the condition of the goods (e.g., before perishable goods spoil) [UCC 2-608(1), 2A-517(1)].

Rodeo Drive, Beverly Hills, California *This is Rodeo Drive in Beverly Hills, California, one of the premiere shopping streets in the United States. The Uniform Commercial Code (UCC) provides for various remedies if a seller or buyer breaches a sales contract or if a lessor or lessee breaches a lease contract.*

SELLER'S AND LESSOR'S REMEDIES

Oftentimes, a buyer or lessee may breach a sales or lease contract. The UCC provides various remedies to sellers and lessors if a buyer or lessee *breaches a contract*. The remedies available to sellers and lessors if a buyer or lessee breaches a sales or lease contract are discussed in the following paragraphs.

Right to Withhold Delivery

A seller or lessor may withhold delivery of goods in his or her possession when the buyer or lessee breaches the contract. The **right to withhold delivery** is available if the buyer or lessee wrongfully rejects or revokes acceptance of the goods, fails to make a payment when due, or repudiates the contract. If part of the goods under the contract have been delivered when the buyer or lessee materially breaches the contract, the seller or lessor may withhold delivery of the remainder of the affected goods [UCC 2-703(a), 2A-523(1)(c)].

right to withhold delivery
A seller's or lessor's right to refuse to deliver goods to a buyer or lessee upon breach of a sales or lease contract by the buyer or lessee or the insolvency of the buyer or lessee.

A seller or lessor who discovers that the buyer or lessee is insolvent before the goods are delivered may refuse to deliver as promised unless the buyer or lessee pays cash for the goods [UCC 2-702(1), 2A-525(1)]. Under the UCC, a person is insolvent when he or she (1) ceases to pay his or her debts in the ordinary course of business, (2) cannot pay his or her debts as they become due, or (3) is insolvent within the meaning of federal bankruptcy law [UCC 1-201(23)].

Right to Stop Delivery of Goods in Transit

Often, sellers and lessors employ common carriers and other bailees (e.g., warehouses) to hold and deliver goods to buyers and lessees. The goods are considered to be *in transit* while they are in possession of these carriers or bailees.

A seller or lessor has the **right to stop delivery of goods in transit** if while the goods are in transit (1) the buyer or lessee repudiates the contract, (2) the buyer or lessee fails to make payment when due, or (3) the buyer or lessee otherwise gives the seller or lessor some other right to withhold or reclaim the goods. In these circumstances, the delivery can be stopped only if it constitutes a carload, a truckload, a planeload, or a larger express or freight shipment [UCC 2-705(1), 2A-526(1)]. A seller or lessor who learns of the buyer's or lessee's insolvency while the goods are in transit has the right to stop delivery of the goods transit, regardless of the size of the shipment. The seller or lessor is responsible for all expenses borne by the bailee in stopping the goods [UCC 2-705(3), 2A-526(3)].

right to stop delivery of goods in transit
The right of a seller or lessor to stop delivery of goods in transit if he or she learns of the buyer's or lessee's insolvency or if the buyer or lessee repudiates the contract, fails to make payment when due, or gives the seller or lessor some other right to withhold the goods.

The seller or lessor must give sufficient notice to allow the bailee, by reasonable diligence, to prevent delivery of the goods. After receipt of notice, the bailee must hold and deliver the goods according to the directions of the seller or lessor. Goods may be stopped in transit until the buyer or lessee obtains possession of the goods or the carrier or other bailee acknowledges that it is holding the goods for the buyer or lessee [UCC 2-705(2), 2A-526(2)].

Right to Reclaim Goods

right to reclaim goods
The right of a seller or lessor to demand the return of goods from the buyer or lessee under specified situations.

In certain situations, a seller or lessor may demand the return of the goods it sold or leased that are already in the possession of the buyer or lessee. In a sale transaction, the seller or lessor has the **right to reclaim goods** in two situations. If the goods are delivered in a credit sale and the seller then discovers that the buyer was insolvent, the seller has 10 days within which to demand that the goods be returned [UCC 2-507(2)]. If the buyer misrepresented his or her solvency in writing within three months before delivery [UCC 2-702(2)] or paid for goods in a cash sale with a check that bounces [UCC 2-507(2)], the seller may reclaim the goods at any time.

A lessor may reclaim goods in the possession of the lessee if the lessee is in default of the contract [UCC 2A-525(2)].

To exercise a right of reclamation, the seller or lessor must send the buyer or lessee a written notice demanding return of the goods. The seller or lessor may not use self-help to reclaim the goods if the buyer or lessee refuses to honor his or her demand. Instead, appropriate legal proceedings must be instituted.

Right to Dispose of Goods

right to dispose of goods
The right to dispose of goods in a good faith and commercially reasonable manner. A seller or lessor who is in possession of goods at the time the buyer or lessee breaches or repudiates a contract may in good faith resell, release, or otherwise dispose of the goods in a commercially reasonable manner and recover damages, including incidental damages, from the buyer or lessee.

incidental damages
Reasonable expenses incurred in stopping delivery, transportation charges, storage charges, sales commissions, and so on.

If a buyer or lessee breaches or repudiates a sales or lease contract before the seller or lessor has delivered the goods, the seller or lessor may resell or release the goods and recover damages from the buyer or lessee [UCC 2-703(d), 2-706(1), 2A-523(1)(e), 2A-527(1)]. The **right to dispose of goods** also arises if the seller or lessor has reacquired the goods after stopping them in transit.

The seller or lessor may recover any damages incurred on the disposition of the goods. In the case of a sales contract, damages are defined as the difference between the disposition price and the original contract price. In the case of a lease contract, damages are the difference between the disposition price and the rent the original lessee would have paid. Any profit made on the resale or release of the goods does not revert to the original buyer or lessee if the seller or lessor disposes of the goods at a higher price than the buyer or lessee contracted to pay.

The seller or lessor may also recover any **incidental damages** (reasonable expenses incurred in stopping delivery, transportation charges, storage charges, sales commission, and the like [UCC 2-710, 2A-530]) incurred on the disposition of the goods [UCC 2-706(1), 2A-527(2)].

The disposition of goods by the seller or lessor must be made in good faith and in a commercially reasonable manner. The goods may be disposed of as a unit or in parcels in a public or private transaction. The seller or lessor must give the buyer or lessee reasonable notification of his or her intention to dispose of goods unless the goods threaten to quickly decline in value or are perishable. The party who buys or leases the goods in good faith for value takes the goods, free of any rights of the original buyer or lessee [UCC 2-706(5), 2A-527(4)].

Unfinished Goods

Sometimes a sales or lease contract is breached or repudiated before the goods are finished. In a case of **unfinished goods**, the seller or lessor may choose either (1) to cease manufacturing the goods and resell them for scrap or salvage value or (2) to complete the manufacture of the goods and resell, release, or otherwise dispose of them to another party [UCC 2-704(2), 2A-524(2)]. The seller or lessor may recover damages from the breaching buyer or lessee.

Right to Recover the Purchase Price or Rent

In certain circumstances, the UCC provides that a seller or lessor may sue the buyer or lessee to recover the purchase price or rent stipulated in a sales or lease contract. The seller or lessor has the **right to recover the purchase price or rent** in the following situations:

right to recover the purchase price or rent
A seller's or lessor's right to recover the contracted-for purchase price or rent from the buyer or lessee (1) if the buyer or lessee fails to pay for accepted goods, (2) if the buyer or lessee breaches the contract and the seller or lessor cannot dispose of the goods, or (3) if the goods are damaged or lost after the risk of loss passes to the buyer or lessee.

1. The buyer or lessee accepts the goods but fails to pay for them when the price or rent is due.
2. The buyer or lessee breaches the contract after the goods have been identified in the contract and the seller or lessor cannot resell or dispose of them.
3. The goods are damaged or lost after the risk of loss passes to the buyer or lessee [UCC 2-709(1), 2A-529(1)].

To recover the purchase price or rent, the seller or lessor must hold the goods for the buyer or lessee. If resale or other disposition of the goods becomes possible prior to the collection of the judgment, however, the seller or lessor may resell or dispose of them. In such situations, the net proceeds of any disposition must be credited against the judgment [UCC 2-709(2), 2A-529(2), 2A-529(3)]. The seller or lessor may also recover incidental damages from the buyer or lessee.

Right to Recover Damages for Breach of Contract

If a buyer or lessee repudiates a sales or lease contract or wrongfully rejects tendered goods, the seller or lessor may sue to **recover the damages** caused by the buyer's or lessee's breach. Generally, the amount of damages is calculated as the difference between the contract price (or rent) and the market price (or rent) of the goods at the time and place the goods were to be delivered to the buyer or lessee plus incidental damages [UCC 2-708(1), 2A-528(1)].

right to recover damages for breach of contract
A seller's or lessor's right to recover damages measured as the difference between the contract price (or rent) and the market price (or rent) at the time and place the goods were to be delivered, plus incidental damages, from a buyer or lessee who repudiates the contract or wrongfully rejects tendered goods.

If the preceding measure of damages will not put the seller or lessor in as good a position as performance of the contract would have, the seller or lessor has the **right to recover any lost profits** that would have resulted from the full performance of the contract plus an allowance for reasonable overhead and incidental damages [UCC 2-708(2), 2A-528(2)].

Right to Cancel a Contract

A seller or lessor has the right to cancel a contract if the buyer or lessee breaches the contract by rejecting or revoking acceptance of the goods, failing to pay for the goods, or repudiating all or any part of the contract. The cancellation may refer only to the affected goods or to the entire contract if the breach is material [UCC 2-703(f), 2A-523(1)(a)].

seller's or lessor's cancellation
A seller or lessor has the right to cancel a sales or lease contract if the buyer or lessee rejects or revokes acceptance of the goods, fails to pay for the goods, or repudiates the contract in part or in whole.

A seller or lessor who rightfully cancels a sales or lease contract by notifying the buyer or lessee is discharged of any further obligations under that contract. The buyer's or lessee's duties are not discharged, however. The seller or lessor retains the right to seek damages for the breach [UCC 2-106(4), 2A-523(3)].

CONTEMPORARY ENVIRONMENT

Lost Volume Seller

Should a seller be permitted to recover the profits it lost on a sale to a defaulting buyer if the seller sold the goods to another buyer? It depends. If the seller had only one item or a limited number of items and could produce no more, the seller cannot recover lost profits from the defaulting buyer. This is because the seller made profits on the sale of the item to the new buyer.

If, however, the seller could have produced more of the item, the seller is a **lost volume seller**. In this situation, the seller can make the profit from the sale of the item to the new buyer and sue the defaulting buyer to recover the profit it would have made from that sale. This is because the seller would have realized profits from two sales—the sale to the first buyer who defaulted and the second sale to the new buyer.

CONCEPT SUMMARY
SELLER'S AND LESSOR'S REMEDIES

Possession of Goods at the Time of the Buyer's or Lessee's Breach	Seller's or Lessor's Remedies
Goods in the possession of the seller or lessor	1. Withhold delivery of the goods [UCC 2-703(a), 2A-523(1)(c)]. 2. Demand payment in cash if the buyer is insolvent [UCC 2-702(1), 2A-525(1)]. 3. Resell or release the goods and recover the difference between the contract or lease price and the resale or release price [UCC 2-706, 2A-527]. 4. Sue for breach of contract and recover as damages either of the following: a. The difference between the market price and the contract price [UCC 2-708(1), 2A-528(1)]. b. Lost profits [UCC 2-708(2), 2A-528(2)]. 5. Cancel the contract [UCC 2-703(f), 2A-523(1)(a)].
	1. Stop goods in transit [UCC 2-705(1), 2A-526(1)]. a. Carload, truckload, planeload, or larger shipment if the buyer is solvent. b. Any size shipment if the buyer is insolvent.
Goods in the possession of the buyer or lessee	1. Sue to recover the purchase price or rent [UCC 2-709(1), 2A-529(1)]. 2. Reclaim the goods [UCC 2-507(2), 2A-525(2)]. a. The seller delivers goods in cash sale, and the buyer's check is dishonored. b. The seller delivers goods in a credit sale, and the goods are received by an insolvent buyer.

▶ BUYER'S AND LESSEE'S REMEDIES

If a seller or lessor breaches a sales or lease contract, the UCC provides a variety of remedies to the buyer or lessee for the seller's or lessor's breach. These remedies are discussed in the following paragraphs.

Right to Reject Nonconforming Goods or Improperly Tendered Goods

If the contracted-for goods or the seller's or lessor's tender of delivery fails to conform to a sales or lease contract in any way, the buyer or lessee may (1) reject the whole, (2) accept the whole, or (3) accept any commercial unit and reject the rest. Nonconforming or improperly tendered goods must be rejected within a reasonable time after their delivery or tender. The seller or lessor must be notified of the **rejection**. The buyer or lessee must hold any rightfully rejected goods with reasonable care for a reasonable time [UCC 2-602(2), 2A-512(1)].

right to reject nonconforming goods or improperly tendered goods
A situation in which a buyer or lessee rejects goods that do not conform to the contract. If the goods or the seller's or lessor's tender of delivery fails to conform to the contract, the buyer or lessee may (1) reject the whole, (2) accept the whole, or (3) accept any commercial unit and reject the rest.

If the buyer or lessee chooses to reject the goods, he or she must identify defects that are ascertainable by reasonable inspection. Failure to do so prevents the buyer or lessee from relying on those defects to justify the rejection of the contract if the defect could have been cured had the seller or lessor received notification in a timely manner [UCC 2-601, 2A-509].

If a buyer or lessee is a merchant and the seller or lessor has no agent or place of business at the market where the goods are rejected, the merchant-buyer or merchant-lessee must follow any reasonable instructions received from the seller or lessor with respect to the rejected goods [UCC 2-603, 2A-511]. If the seller or lessor gives no instructions and the rejected goods are perishable or will quickly decline in value, the buyer or lessee may make reasonable efforts to sell them on the seller's or lessor's behalf [UCC 2-604, 2A-512].

Any buyer or lessee who rightfully rejects goods is entitled to reimbursement from the seller or lessor for reasonable expenses incurred in holding, storing, reselling, shipping, and otherwise caring for the rejected goods.

Right to Recover Goods from an Insolvent Seller or Lessor

If a buyer or lessee makes partial or full payment for goods before they are received and the seller or lessor becomes insolvent within 10 days after receiving the first payment, the buyer or lessee has the **right to recover the goods from the insolvent seller or lessor**. To do so, the buyer or lessee must tender the unpaid portion of the purchase price or rent due under the sales or lease contract. Only conforming goods that are identified in the contract may be recovered [UCC 2-502, 2A-522]. This remedy is often referred to as **capture**.

right to recover goods from an insolvent seller or lessor
The right of a buyer or lessee who has wholly or partially paid for goods before they are received to recover the goods from a seller or lessor who becomes insolvent within 10 days after receiving the first payment; the buyer or lessee must tender the remaining purchase price or rent due under the contract.

Right to Obtain Specific Performance

If goods are unique or the remedy at law is inadequate, a buyer or lessee has the **right to obtain specific performance** of a sales or lease contract. A decree of **specific performance** orders the seller or lessor to perform the contract. Specific performance is usually used to obtain possession of works of art, antiques, rare coins, and other unique items [UCC 2-716(1), 2A-521(1)].

Example A buyer enters into a sales contract to purchase a specific Rembrandt painting from a seller for $25 million. When the buyer tenders payment, the seller refuses to sell the painting to the buyer. The buyer may bring an equity action to obtain a decree of specific performance from the court, which orders the seller to sell the painting to the buyer.

specific performance
A decree of the court that orders a seller or lessor to perform his or her obligations under the contract; usually occurs when the goods in question are unique, such as art or antiques.

right to cover
The right of a buyer or lessee to purchase or lease substitute goods if a seller or lessor fails to make delivery of the goods or repudiates the contract or if the buyer or lessee rightfully rejects the goods or justifiably revokes their acceptance.

CONTEMPORARY ENVIRONMENT

Right to Cover

A buyer or lessee has the **right to cover** by purchasing or renting substitute goods if the seller or lessor fails to make delivery of the goods or repudiates the contract or if the buyer or lessee rightfully rejects the goods or justifiably revokes their acceptance. The buyer's or lessee's cover must be made in good faith and without unreasonable delay. If the exact commodity is not available, the buyer or lessee may purchase or lease any commercially reasonable substitute.

A buyer or lessee who rightfully covers may sue the seller or lessor to recover as damages the difference between the cost of cover and the contract price or rent. The buyer or lessee may also recover incidental and consequential damages, less expenses saved (such as delivery costs) [UCC 2-712, 2A-518].

Example University contracts to purchase 1,000 ePhones from Orange Store for $500 each to be used by its faculty members. Orange Store breaches the contract and does not deliver the ePhones to University. University covers and contracts with Apple Store to purchase 1,000 ePhones at the price of $600 per phone. Here, University may recover $100,000 from Orange Store ($600 cover price – $500 contract price = $100 × 1,000 phones).

The UCC does not require a buyer or lessee to cover when a seller or lessor breaches a sales or lease contract. Failure of the buyer or lessee to cover does not bar the buyer from other remedies against the seller.

Right to Replevy Goods

A buyer or lessee has the **right to replevy (recover) goods** from a seller or lessor who is wrongfully withholding the goods. The buyer or lessee must show that he or she was unable to cover or that attempts at cover will be unavailing. Thus, the goods must be scarce but not unique. **Replevin** actions are available only as to goods identified in a sales or lease contract [UCC 2-716(3), 2A-521(3)].

replevin
An action by a buyer or lessor to recover scarce goods wrongfully withheld by a seller or lessor.

buyer's or lessee's cancellation
A buyer or lessee has the right to cancel a sales or lease contract if the seller or lessor fails to deliver conforming goods or repudiates the contract or if the buyer or lessee rightfully rejects the goods or justifiably revokes acceptance of the goods.

Right to Cancel a Contract

If a seller or lessor fails to deliver conforming goods or repudiates the contract, the buyer or lessee may cancel the sales or lease contract. The buyer or lessee can also cancel a sales or lease contract if the buyer or lessee rightfully rejects the goods or justifiably revokes acceptance of the goods. The contract may be canceled with respect to the affected goods, or, if there is a material breach, the whole contract may be canceled. A buyer or lessee who rightfully cancels a contract is discharged from any further obligations on the contract and retains his or her rights to other remedies against the seller or lessor [UCC 2-711(1), 2A-508(1)(a)].

Right to Recover Damages for Nondelivery or Repudiation

damages
Damages a buyer or lessee recovers from a seller or lessor who fails to deliver the goods or repudiates the contract. Damages are measured as the difference between the contract price (or original rent) and the market price (or rent) at the time the buyer or lessee learned of the breach.

If a seller or lessor fails to deliver the goods or repudiates the sales or lease contract, the buyer or lessee has the **right to recover damages for nondelivery or repudiation**. The measure of **damages** is the difference between the contract price (or original rent) and the market price (or rent) at the time the buyer or lessee learned of the breach. Incidental and consequential damages, less expenses saved, can also be recovered [UCC 2-713, 2A-519].

Right to Recover Damages for Accepted Nonconforming Goods

A buyer or lessee may accept nonconforming goods from a seller or lessor. Even with acceptance, the buyer or lessee still has the **right to recover damages for accepted nonconforming goods** and any loss resulting from the seller's or lessor's breach. Incidental and consequential damages may also be recovered. The buyer or lessee must notify the seller or lessor of the nonconformity within a reasonable time after the breach was or should have been discovered. Failure to do so bars the buyer or lessee from any recovery. If the buyer or lessee accepts nonconforming goods, he or she may deduct all or any part of damages resulting from the breach from any part of the purchase price or rent still due under the contract [UCC 2-714(1), 2A-516(1)].

CONCEPT SUMMARY
BUYER'S AND LESSEE'S REMEDIES

Situation	Buyer's or Lessee's Remedy
Seller or lessor refuses to deliver the goods or delivers nonconforming goods that the buyer or lessee does not want.	1. Reject nonconforming goods [UCC 2-601, 2A-509]. 2. Revoke acceptance of nonconforming goods [UCC 2-608, 2A 517(1)]. 3. Cover [UCC 2-712, 2A-518]. 4. Sue for breach of contract and recover damages [UCC 2-713, 2A-519]. 5. Cancel the contract [UCC 2-711(1), 2A-508(1)(a)].
Seller or lessor tenders nonconforming goods and the buyer or lessee accepts them.	1. Sue for ordinary damages [UCC 2-714(1), 2A-516(1)]. 2. Deduct damages from the unpaid purchase or rent price [UCC 2-714(1), 2A-516(1)].
Seller or lessor refuses to deliver the goods and the buyer or lessee wants them.	1. Sue for specific performance [UCC 2-716(1), 2A-521(1)]. 2. Replevy the goods [UCC 2-716(3), 2A-521(3)]. 3. Recover the goods from an insolvent seller or lessor [UCC 2-502, 2A-522].

ADDITIONAL PERFORMANCE ISSUES

UCC Articles 2 (Sales) and 2A (Leases) contain several other provisions that affect the parties' performance of a sales or lease contract. These provisions are discussed in the following paragraphs.

Assurance of Performance

Each party to a sales or lease contract expects that the other party will perform his or her contractual obligations. If one party to a contract has reasonable grounds to believe that the other party either will not or cannot perform his or her contractual obligations, an **adequate assurance of performance** may be demanded in writing. If it is commercially reasonable to do so, the party making the demand may suspend his or her performance until adequate assurance of due performance is received from the other party [UCC 2-609, 2A-401].

adequate assurance of performance
Adequate assurance of performance from the other party if there is an indication that the contract will be breached by that party.

Example A buyer contracts to purchase 1,000 bushels of wheat from a farmer. The contract requires delivery on September 1. In July, the buyer learns that floods have caused substantial crop loss in the area of the seller's farm. The farmer receives the buyer's written demand for adequate assurance on July 15. The farmer fails to give adequate assurance of performance. The buyer may suspend performance and treat the sales contract as having been repudiated.

Anticipatory Repudiation

Occasionally, a party to a sales or lease contract repudiates the contract before his or her performance is due under the contract. If the repudiation impairs the value of the contract to the aggrieved party, it is called **anticipatory repudiation**. Mere wavering on performance does not meet the test for anticipatory repudiation.

anticipatory repudiation
The repudiation of a sales or lease contract by one of the parties prior to the date set for performance.

If an anticipatory repudiation occurs, the aggrieved party can (1) await performance by the repudiating party for a commercially reasonable time (e.g., until the delivery date or shortly thereafter) or (2) treat the contract as having been breached at the time of the anticipatory repudiation, which gives the aggrieved party an immediate cause of action. In either case, the aggrieved party may suspend performance of his or her obligations under the contract [UCC 2-610, 2A-402].

An anticipatory repudiation may be retracted before the repudiating party's next performance is due if the aggrieved party has not (1) canceled the contract, (2) materially changed his or her position (e.g., purchased goods from another party), or (3) otherwise indicated that the repudiation is considered final. The retraction may be made by any method that clearly indicates the repudiating party's intent to perform the contract [UCC 2-611, 2A-403].

Statute of Limitations

The **UCC statute of limitations** provides that an action for breach of any written or oral sales or lease contract must commence within four years after the cause of the action accrues. The parties may agree to reduce the limitations period to one year, but they cannot extend it beyond four years.

UCC statute of limitations
A rule which provides that an action for breach of any written or oral sales or lease contract must commence within four years after the cause of action accrues. The parties may agree to reduce the limitations period to one year.

Agreements Affecting Remedies

The parties to a sales or lease contract may agree on remedies in addition to or in substitution for the remedies provided by the UCC. The parties may limit the buyer's or lessee's remedies to repair and replacement of defective goods or parts or to the return of the goods and repayment (refund) of the purchase price or rent.

The remedies agreed upon by the parties are in addition to the remedies provided by the UCC unless the parties expressly provide that they are exclusive. If an exclusive remedy fails in its essential purpose (e.g., there is an exclusive remedy of repair, but there are no repair parts available), any remedy may be had, as provided in the UCC.

Convenience is the basis of mercantile law.

Lord Mansfield
Medcalf v. Hall (1782)

Liquidated Damages

The UCC permits parties to a sales or lease contract to establish in advance in their contract the damages that will be paid upon a breach of the contract. Such preestablished

liquidated damages
Damages that will be paid upon a breach of contract that are established in advance.

damages, called **liquidated damages**, substitute for actual damages. In a sales or lease contract, liquidated damages are valid if they are reasonable in light of the anticipated or actual harm caused by the breach, the difficulties of proof of loss, and the inconvenience or nonfeasibility of otherwise obtaining an adequate remedy [UCC 2-718(1), 2A-504].

ETHICS SPOTLIGHT

Unconscionable Contracts

UCC Article 2 (Sales) and Article 2A (Leases) have adopted the equity doctrine of **unconscionability**. Under this doctrine, a court may determine as a matter of law that a contract is unconscionable. To prove unconscionability, there must be proof that the parties had substantially unequal bargaining power, that the dominant party misused its power in contracting, and that it would be manifestly unfair or oppressive to enforce the contract. This sometimes happens where a dominant party uses a preprinted form contract and the terms of the contract are unfair or oppressive.

If a court finds that a contract or any clause in a contract is unconscionable, the court may refuse to enforce the contract, or it may enforce the remainder of the contract without the unconscionable clause, or it may so limit the application of any unconscionable clause as to avoid any unconscionable result [UCC 2-302, 2A-108]. Unconscionability is sometimes found in a consumer lease if the consumer has been induced by unconscionable conduct to enter into the lease. The doctrine of unconscionability applies to online contracts as well as traditional contracts.

Business Ethics What does the doctrine of unconscionability provide? Explain. Does the doctrine of unconscionability encourage ethical behavior?

TEST REVIEW TERMS AND CONCEPTS

Acceptance
Adequate assurance of performance
Anticipatory repudiation
Breach
Buyer's or lessee's cancellation
Capture
C.O.D. (cash on delivery) shipment
Commercial reasonableness
Cure
Damages
Destination contract
Express terms
Good faith
Incidental damages
Installment contract
Liquidated damages
Lost volume seller
Obligations
Payment
Perfect tender rule
Place of delivery
Reasonableness
Replevin
Revocation of acceptance
Right of inspection
Right to cancel a contract
Right to cover
Right to dispose of goods
Right to obtain specific performance
Right to reclaim goods
Right to recover damages for accepted nonconforming goods
Right to recover damages for nondelivery or repudiation
Right to recover goods from an insolvent seller or lessor
Right to recover lost profit
Right to recover the purchase price or rent
Right to reject nonconforming goods or improperly tendered goods
Right to replevy (recover) goods
Right to stop delivery of goods in transit
Right to withhold delivery
Seller's or lessor's cancellation
Shipment contract
Specific performance
Tender of delivery
UCC statute of limitations
Unconscionability
Unfinished goods

CASE PROBLEMS

1 Nonconforming Goods The Jacob Hartz Seed Company, Inc. (Hartz), bought soybeans for use as seed from E. R. Coleman. Coleman certified that the seed had an 80 percent germination rate. Hartz paid for the beans and picked them up from a warehouse in Card, Arkansas. After the seed was transported to Georgia, a sample was submitted for testing to the Georgia Department of Agriculture. When the department reported a germination level of only 67 percent, Coleman requested that the seed be retested. The second set of tests reported a germination rate of 65 percent. Hartz canceled the contract after the second test, and Coleman reclaimed the seed. Hartz sought a refund of the money it had paid for the seed, claiming that the soybeans were nonconforming goods. Who wins? *Jacob Hartz Seed Co. v. Coleman*, 271 Ark. 756, 612 S.W.2d 91, **Web** 1981 Ark. Lexis 1153 (Supreme Court of Arkansas)

2 Right to Cure Connie R. Grady purchased a new Chevrolet Chevette from Al Thompson Chevrolet (Thompson). Grady gave Thompson a down payment on the car and financed the remainder of the purchase price through General Motors Acceptance Corporation (GMAC). Grady picked up the Chevette. The next day, the car broke down and had to be towed back to Thompson. Grady picked up the repaired car one day later. The car's performance was still unsatisfactory in that the engine was hard to start, the transmission slipped, and the brakes had to be pushed to the floor to function. Two weeks later, Grady again returned the Chevette for servicing. When she picked up the car that evening, the engine started, but the engine and brake warning lights came on. This pattern of malfunction and repair continued for another two months. Grady wrote a letter to Thompson, revoking the sale. Thompson repossessed the Chevette. GMAC sued Grady to recover its money. Grady sued Thompson to recover her down payment. Thompson claimed that Grady's suit was barred because the company was not given adequate opportunity to cure. Who wins? *General Motors Acceptance Corp. v. Grady*, 27 OhioApp.3d 321, 501 N.E.2d 68, **Web** 1985 OhioApp. Lexis 10353 (Court of Appeals of Ohio)

3 Revocation of Acceptance Roy E. Farrar Produce Company (Farrar) was a packer and shipper of tomatoes in Rio Arribon County, New Mexico. Farrar contacted Wilson, an agent and salesman for International Paper Company (International), and ordered 21,500 tomato boxes for $0.64 per box. The boxes were to each hold between 20 and 30 pounds of tomatoes for shipping. When the boxes arrived at Farrar's plant, 3,624 of them were immediately used to pack tomatoes. When the boxes were stacked, they began to collapse and crush the tomatoes contained within them. The produce company was forced to repackage the tomatoes and store the unused tomato boxes. Farrar contacted International and informed it that it no longer wanted the boxes because they could not perform as promised. International claimed that Farrar had accepted the packages and must pay for them. Who wins? *International Paper Co. v. Farrar*, 102 N.M. 739, 700 P.2d 642, **Web** 1985 N.M. Lexis 2000 (Supreme Court of New Mexico)

4 Commercial Impracticality Charles C. Campbell was a farmer who farmed some 600 acres in the vicinity of Hanover, Pennsylvania. In the spring, Campbell entered into a contract with Hostetter Farms, Inc. (Hostetter), a grain dealer with facilities in Hanover. The sales agreement called for Campbell to sell Hostetter 20,000 bushels of No. 2 yellow corn at $1.70 per bushel. Delivery was made five months later, in the fall. Unfortunately, the summer was an unusually rainy one, and Campbell could not plant part of his crop because of the wet ground. After the corn was planted, part of the crop failed due to the excessive rain. As a result, Campbell delivered only 10,417 bushels. Hostetter sued Campbell for breach of contract. Campbell asserted the defense of commercial impracticability. Who wins? *Campbell v. Hostetter Farms, Inc.*, 251 Pa.Super. 232, 380 A.2d 463, **Web** 1977 Pa.Super. Lexis 2699 (Superior Court of Pennsylvania)

5 Right to Reclaim Goods Archer Daniels Midland Company (Archer) sold ethanol for use in gasoline. Archer sold 80,000 gallons of ethanol on credit to Charter International Oil Company (Charter). The ethanol was shipped to Charter's facility in Houston. Charter became insolvent sometime during that period. Archer sent a written notice to Charter, demanding the return of the ethanol. At the time Charter received the reclamation demand, it had only 12,000 gallons of ethanol remaining at its Houston facility. When Charter refused to return the unused ethanol, Archer sued to recover the ethanol. Who wins? *Archer Daniels Midland v. Charter International Oil Company*, 60 B.R. 854, **Web** 1986 U.S. Dist. Lexis 25828 (United States District Court for the Middle District of Florida)

6 Right to Resell Goods Meuser Material & Equipment Company (Meuser) was a dealer in construction equipment. Meuser entered into an agreement with Joe McMillan for the sale of a bulldozer to McMillan. The agreement called for Meuser to deliver the bulldozer to McMillan's residence in Greeley, Colorado. McMillan paid Meuser with a check. Before taking delivery, McMillan stopped payment on the check. Meuser entered into negotiations with McMillan in an attempt to get McMillan to abide by the sales agreement. During this period, Meuser paid for the upkeep of the bulldozer. When it became apparent that further negotiations would be fruitless, Meuser began looking for a new buyer. Fourteen months after the original sale was supposed to have taken place, the bulldozer was resold for less than the original contract price. Meuser sued McMillan to recover the difference between the contract price and the resale price as well as for the cost of upkeep on the bulldozer for 14 months. Who wins? *McMillan v. Meuser Material & Equipment Company*, 260 Ark. 422, 541 S.W.2d 911, **Web** 1976 Ark. Lexis 1814 (Supreme Court of Arkansas)

7 Right to Recover Purchase Price C. R. Daniels, Inc. (Daniels), entered into a contract for the design and sale of grass catcher bags for lawn mowers to Yazoo Manufacturing Company, Inc. (Yazoo). Daniels contracted to design grass catcher bags that would fit the "S" series mower made by Yazoo. Yazoo provided Daniels with a lawn mower to design the bag. After Yazoo approved the design of the bags, it issued a purchase order for 20,000 bags. Daniels began to ship the bags. After accepting 8,000 bags, Yazoo requested that the shipments stop. Officials of Yazoo told Daniels that it would resume accepting shipments in a few months. Despite several attempts, Daniels could not get Yazoo to accept delivery of the remaining 12,000 bags. Daniels sued Yazoo to recover the purchase price of the grass bags still in its inventory. Who wins? *C. R. Daniels, Inc. v. Yazoo Mfg. Co., Inc.*, 641 F.Supp. 205, **Web** 1986 U.S. Dist. Lexis 23550 (United States District Court for the Southern District of Mississippi)

8 Right to Recover Lost Profits Saber Energy, Inc. (Saber), entered into a sales contract with Tri-State Petroleum Corporation (Tri-State). The contract called for Saber to sell Tri-State 110,000 barrels of gasoline per month for six months. Saber was to deliver the gasoline through the colonial pipeline in Pasadena, Texas. The first 110,000 barrels were delivered on time. On August 1, Saber was informed that Tri-State was canceling the contract. Saber sued Tri-State for breach of contract and sought to recover its lost profits as damages. Tri-State admitted its breach but claimed that lost profits is an inappropriate measure of damages. Who wins? *Tri-State Petroleum Corporation v. Saber Energy, Inc.* 845 F.2d 575, **Web** 1988 U.S. App. Lexis 6819 (United States Court of Appeals for the Fifth Circuit)

9 Specific Performance Dr. and Mrs. Sedmak (Sedmaks) were collectors of Chevrolet Corvettes. The Sedmaks saw an article in *Vette Vues* magazine concerning a new limited-edition Corvette. The limited edition was designed to commemorate the selection of the Corvette as the official pace car of the Indianapolis 500. Chevrolet was manufacturing only 6,000 of these pace cars. The Sedmaks visited Charlie's Chevrolet, Inc. (Charlie's), a local Chevrolet dealer. Charlie's was to receive only one limited-edition car, which the sales manager agreed to sell to the Sedmaks for the sticker price of $15,000. When the Sedmaks went to pick up and pay for the car, they were told that because of the great demand for the limited edition, it was going to be auctioned to the highest bidder. The Sedmaks sued the dealership for specific performance. Who wins? *Sedmak v. Charlie's Chevrolet, Inc.*, 622 S.W.2d. 694, **Web** 1981 Mo.App. Lexis 2911 (Court of Appeals of Missouri)

10 Right to Cover Kent Nowlin Construction, Inc. (Nowlin), was awarded a contract by the state of New Mexico to pave a number of roads. After Nowlin was awarded the contract, it entered into an agreement with Concrete Sales & Equipment Rental Company, Inc. (C&E). C&E was to supply 20,000 tons of paving material to Nowlin. Nowlin began paving the roads, anticipating C&E's delivery of materials. On the delivery date, however, C&E shipped only 2,099 tons of paving materials. Because Nowlin had a deadline to meet, the company contracted with Gallup Sand and Gravel Company (Gallup) for substitute material. Nowlin sued C&E to recover the difference between the higher price it had to pay Gallup for materials and the contract price C&E had agreed to. C&E claims that it is not responsible for Nowlin's increased costs. Who wins? *Concrete Sales & Equipment Rental Company, Inc. v. Kent Nowlin Construction, Inc.*, 106 N.M. 539, 746 P.2d 645, **Web** 1987 N.M. Lexis 3808 (Supreme Court of New Mexico)

BUSINESS ETHICS CASES

11 Business Ethics Ruby and Carmen Ybarra purchased a new double-wide mobile home from Modern Trailer Sales, Inc. (Modern). Modern delivered the mobile home to the Ybarras. A few days after delivery, portions of the floor began to rise and bubble, creating an unsightly and troublesome situation for the Ybarras. The Ybarras complained to Modern about the floor as soon as they discovered the defects. Modern sent repairmen to cure the defective floor on at least three occasions, but each time they were unsuccessful. The Ybarras continued to complain about the defects. The Ybarras continued to rely on Modern's assurances that it was able and willing to repair the floor. After four years of complaints, the Ybarras sued to revoke their acceptance of the sales contract. Did the Ybarras properly revoke their acceptance of the sales contract? Did Modern act ethically in this case? Did the Ybarras? *Ybarras v. Modern Trailer Sales, Inc.*, 94 N.W. 249, 609 P.2d 331, **Web** 1980 N.M. Lexis 2676 (Supreme Court of New Mexico)

12 Business Ethics Allsopp Sand and Gravel (Allsopp) and Lincoln Sand and Gravel (Lincoln) were both in the business of supplying sand to construction companies. In March, Lincoln's sand dredge became inoperable. To continue in business, Lincoln negotiated a contract with Allsopp to purchase sand over the course of a year. The contract called for the sand to be loaded on Lincoln's trucks during Allsopp's regular operating season (March through November). Loading at other times was to be done by "special arrangement." By the following November, Lincoln had taken delivery of one-quarter of the sand it had contracted for. At that point, Lincoln requested that several trucks of sand be loaded in December. Allsopp informed Lincoln that it would have to pay extra for this special arrangement. Lincoln refused to pay extra, pointing out that the sand was already stockpiled at Allsopp's facilities. Allsopp also offered to supply an employee to supervise the loading. Negotiations between the parties broke down, and Lincoln informed Allsopp that it did not intend to honor the remainder of the contract. Allsopp sued Lincoln. Was it commercially reasonable for Lincoln to demand delivery of sand during December? Did Lincoln act ethically in this case? *Allsopp Sand and Gravel v. Lincoln Sand and Gravel*, 171 Ill.App.3d 532, 525 N.E.2d 1185, **Web** 1988 Ill.App. Lexis 939 (Appellate Court of Illinois)

SALES AND LEASE WARRANTIES

istockphoto.com

▲ **Warranty** *Many goods—automobiles, motorcycles, electronics, computers, business equipment, and consumer goods—come with manufacturers' warranties. The manufacturer's warranty usually warrants that the product will last a certain period of time or for a certain number of uses. If the warranty is not met the manufacturer will either repair the product, replace the product, or take some other action that it has warranted.*

CHAPTER OBJECTIVES

After studying this chapter, you should be able to:

1. Identify and describe express warranties.
2. Describe the implied warranty of merchantability.
3. Describe the implied warranty of fitness for a particular purpose.
4. Identify warranty disclaimers and determine when they are unlawful.
5. Describe the warranties of good title and no infringements.

CHAPTER CONTENTS

From Chapter 21 of *Business Law: Legal Environment, Online Commerce, Business Ethics, and International Issues*, 7/e.

"When a manufacturer engages in advertising in order to bring his goods and their quality to the attention of the public and thus to create consumer demand, the representations made constitute an express warranty running directly to a buyer who purchases in reliance thereon. The fact that the sale is consummated with an independent dealer does not obviate the warranty."

—Justice Francis
Henningsen v. Bloomfield Motors, Inc.

INTRODUCTION TO SALES AND LEASE WARRANTIES

warranty
A seller's or lessor's express or implied assurance to a buyer or lessee that the goods sold or leased meet certain quality standards.

The doctrine of ***caveat emptor***—"let the buyer beware"—governed the law of sales and leases for centuries. Finally, the law recognized that consumers and other purchasers and lessees of goods needed greater protection. Article 2 of the Uniform Commercial Code (UCC), adopted in whole or in part by all 50 states, establishes certain **warranties** that apply to the sale of goods. Article 2A of the UCC, adopted in almost all states, establishes warranties that apply to lease transactions.

Warranties are the buyer's or lessee's assurance that the goods meet certain standards. Warranties, which are based on contract law, may be either *expressly* stated or *implied* by law. If the seller or lessor fails to meet a warranty, the buyer or lessee can sue for breach of warranty.

Sales and lease warranties are discussed in this chapter.

EXPRESS WARRANTY

express warranty
A warranty that is created when a seller or lessor makes an affirmation that the goods he or she is selling or leasing meet certain standards of quality, description, performance, or condition.

Express warranties, which are the oldest form of warranty, are created when a seller or lessor affirms that the goods he or she is selling or leasing meet certain standards of quality, description, performance, or condition [UCC 2-313(1), 2A-210(1)]. Express warranties can be either written, oral, or inferred from the seller's conduct.

It is not necessary to use formal words such as *warrant* or *guarantee* to create an express warranty. Express warranties can be made by mistake because the seller or lessor does not have to specifically intend to make the warranty [UCC 2-313(2), 2A-210(2)].

Sellers and lessors are not required to make express warranties. Generally, express warranties are made to entice consumers and others to buy or lease their products. That is why these warranties are often found in advertisements, brochures, catalogs, pictures, illustrations, diagrams, blueprints, and so on.

An express warranty is created when a seller or lessor indicates that the goods will conform to:

1. All *affirmations of fact or promise* made about the goods.

   Examples Promises are statements such as "This car will go 100 miles per hour" or "This house paint will last at least five years."

2. Any *description* of the goods.

   Examples Descriptions of goods include terms such as *Idaho potatoes* and *Michigan cherries*.

3. Any *model* or *sample* of the goods.

   Example A model of an oil-drilling rig or a sample of wheat taken from a silo creates an express warranty.

Basis of the Bargain

Buyers and lessees can recover for a breach of an express warranty if the warranty was a contributing factor—not necessarily the sole factor—that induced the buyer to purchase the product or the lessee to lease the product. This is known as the **basis of the bargain** [UCC 2-313(1), 2A-210(1)]. The UCC does not define the term *basis of the bargain*, so this test is broadly applied by the courts. Generally, all statements by the seller or lessor prior to or at the time of contracting are presumed to be part of the basis of the bargain unless good reason is shown to the contrary. Postsale statements that modify the contract are part of the basis of the bargain.

Warranties are favored in law, being a part of a man's assurance.

Coke First Institute

Generally, a retailer is liable for the express warranties made by manufacturers of goods it sells. A manufacturer is not liable for express warranties made by wholesalers and retailers unless the manufacturer authorizes or ratifies a warranty.

Statement of Opinion

Many express warranties arise during the course of negotiations between a buyer and a seller or a lessor and a lessee. The seller's or lessor's **statement of opinion** (i.e., **puffing**) or commendation of the goods does not create an express warranty. It is often difficult to determine whether a seller's statement is an affirmation of fact (which creates an express warranty) or a statement of opinion (which does not create a warranty). An affirmation of the *value* of goods does not create an express warranty [UCC 2-313(2), 2A-210(2)].

statement of opinion
A commendation of goods, made by a seller or lessor, that does not create an express warranty. Also known as *puffing*.

Examples A used car salesperson's saying "This is the best used car available in town" does not create an express warranty because it is an opinion and mere puffing. However, a statement such as "This car has been driven only 20,000 miles" is an express warranty because it is a statement of fact.

Examples Statements such as "This painting is worth a fortune" or "Others would gladly pay $20,000 for this car" do not create an express warranty because these are statements of value and not statements of fact.

ETHICS SPOTLIGHT

Express Warranty

"We conclude that Ashe's description of the goods was more than his opinion; rather, he intended it to be a statement of a fact."

—Judge Whiting

W. Hayes Daughtrey consulted Sidney Ashe, a jeweler, about the purchase of a diamond bracelet as a Christmas present for his wife. Ashe showed Daughtrey a diamond bracelet that he had for sale for $15,000. When Daughtrey decided to purchase the bracelet, Ashe completed and signed an appraisal form that stated that the diamonds were "H color and v.v.s. quality." (v.v.s. is one of the highest ratings in a jeweler's quality classification.) After Daughtrey paid for the bracelet, Ashe put the bracelet and the appraisal form in a box. Daughtrey gave the bracelet to his wife as a Christmas present. One year later, when another jeweler looked at the bracelet, Daughtrey discovered that the diamonds were of substantially lower grade than v.v.s. Daughtrey filed a specific performance suit against Ashe to compel him to replace the bracelet with one mounted with v.v.s. diamonds or pay appropriate damages.

Was an express warranty made by Ashe regarding the quality of the diamonds in the bracelet? The trial court said no and held that the term *v.v.s. quality* was a mere opinion and not an express warranty. The supreme court of Virginia reversed, finding that the term *v.v.s. quality* created an express warranty that the jeweler gave when he sold the bracelet to Daughtrey. The supreme court stated:

> *The trial court contends that Ashe's statement of the grade of the diamonds is a mere opinion and, thus, cannot qualify as an express warranty. It is not necessary to the creation of an express warranty that the seller use formal words such as "warrant" or "guarantee" or that he have a specific intention to make a warranty. Here, Ashe did more than give a mere opinion of the value of the goods; he specifically described them as diamonds of "H color and v.v.s. quality." We conclude that Ashe's description of the goods was more than his opinion; rather, he intended it to be a statement of a fact.*

The supreme court of Virginia held that an express warranty had been created. The trial court's decision was reversed, and the case was remanded for a determination of appropriate damages to be awarded to Daughtrey. *Daughtrey v. Ashe*, 243 Va. 73, 413 S.E.2d 336, **Web** 1992 Va. Lexis 152 (Supreme Court of Virginia)

Business Ethics Do you think that Daughtrey relied on the term *v.v.s. quality* when he purchased the diamond bracelet? Did Ashe act ethically in denying that his statement created an express warranty?

Damages Recoverable for Breach of Warranty

compensatory damages
Damages that are generally equal to the difference between the value of the goods as warranted and the actual value of the goods accepted at the time and place of acceptance.

Where there has been a breach of warranty, the buyer or lessee may sue the seller or lessor to recover **compensatory damages**. The amount of recoverable compensatory damages is generally equal to the difference between (1) the value of the goods as warranted and (2) the actual value of the goods accepted at the time and place of acceptance [UCC 2-714(2), 2A-508(4)]. A purchaser or lessee can recover for personal injuries that are caused by a breach of warranty.

Example A used car salesperson warrants that a used car has been driven only 20,000 miles. If true, that would make the car worth $20,000. The salesperson gives the buyer a "good deal" and sells the car for $16,000. Unfortunately, the car was worth only $10,000 because it was actually driven 100,000 miles. The buyer discovers the breach of warranty and sues the salesperson for damages. The buyer can recover $10,000 ($20,000 warranted value minus $10,000 actual value). The contract price ($16,000) is irrelevant to this computation.

Example Frances purchases new tires for her car, and the manufacturer expressly warrants the tires against blowout for 50,000 miles. One of the tires blows out after being used only 20,000 miles, causing severe injury to Frances. She can recover personal injury damages from the manufacturer because of the breach of warranty.

▶ IMPLIED WARRANTY OF MERCHANTABILITY

In addition to express warranties made by a manufacturer or seller, the law sometimes *implies* warranties in the sale or lease of goods. Implied warranties are not expressly stated in the sales or lease contract but instead are **implied by law**. One such warranty is the *implied warranty of merchantability*.

implied warranty of merchantability
Unless properly disclosed, a warranty that is implied that sold or leased goods are fit for the ordinary purpose for which they are sold or leased, as well as other assurances.

Law should be like death, which spares no one.

Charles de Montesquieu

If a seller or lessor of a good is a merchant with respect to goods of that kind, the sales contract or lease contract contains an **implied warranty of merchantability** of the good unless this implied warranty is properly disclaimed [UCC 2-314(1), 2A-212(1)]. This implied warranty requires that the following standards be met:

- The goods must be fit for the ordinary purposes for which they are used.

Examples A chair must be able to safely perform the function of a chair. If a normal-sized person sits in a chair that has not been tampered with, and the chair collapses, there has been a breach of the implied warranty of merchantability. If, however, the same person is injured because he or she uses the chair as a ladder and it tips over, there is no breach of implied warranty because serving as a ladder is not the ordinary purpose of a chair.

- The goods must be adequately contained, packaged, and labeled.

Example The implied warranty of merchantability applies to a milk bottle as well as to the milk inside the bottle.

- The goods must be of an even kind, quality, and quantity within each unit.

Example All the goods in a carton, package, or box must be consistent.

- The goods must conform to any promise or affirmation of fact made on the container or label.

Example The goods must be capable of being used safely in accordance with the instructions on the package or label.

- The quality of the goods must pass without objection in the trade.

Example Other users of the goods would not object to quality of the goods.

- Fungible goods must meet a fair average or middle range of quality.

Example To be classified as a certain grade, such as pearl millet grain (*Pennisetum glaucum*) or iron ore (magnetite Fe_3O_4), goods must meet the average range of quality of that grade.

Note that the implied warranty of merchantability does not apply to sales or leases by nonmerchants or casual sales.

Examples The implied warranty of merchantability applies to the sale of a lawn mower that is sold by a merchant who is in the business of selling lawn mowers. The implied warranty of merchantability does not apply when one neighbor sells a lawn mower to another neighbor.

The following case raised the issue of implied warranty of merchantability.

CASE 1 Implied Warranty of Merchantability

Denny v. Ford Motor Company

87 N.Y.2d 248, 662 N.E.2d 730, 639 N.Y.S.2d 250, Web 1995 N.Y. Lexis 4445 (1995)
Court of Appeals of New York

"The law implies a warranty by a manufacturer that places its product on the market that the product is reasonably fit for the ordinary purpose for which it was intended."

—Judge Titone

Facts

Nancy Denny purchased a Bronco II, a small sport-utility vehicle (SUV) that was manufactured by Ford Motor Company. Denny testified that she purchased the Bronco for use on paved city and suburban streets and not for off-road use. When Denny was driving the vehicle on a paved road, she slammed on the brakes in an effort to avoid a deer that had walked directly into her SUV's path. The Bronco II rolled over, and Denny was severely injured. Denny sued Ford Motor Company to recover damages for breach of the implied warranty of merchantability.

Denny alleged that the Bronco II presented a significantly higher risk of occurrence of rollover accidents than did ordinary passenger vehicles. Denny introduced evidence at trial that showed that the Bronco II had a low stability index because of its high center of gravity, narrow tracks, and shorter wheelbase, as well as the design of its suspension system. Ford countered that the Bronco II was intended as an off-road vehicle and was not designed to be used as a conventional passenger automobile on paved streets. The trial court found Ford liable and awarded Denny $1.2 million in damages. Ford appealed.

Issue

Did Ford Motor Company breach the implied warranty of merchantability?

Language of the Court

Plaintiff introduced a Ford marketing manual that predicted many buyers would be attracted to the Bronco II because utility vehicles were suitable to "contemporary lifestyles" and were "considered fashionable" in some suburban areas. According to this manual, the sales presentation of the Bronco II should take into account the vehicle's "suitability for commuting and for suburban and city driving." Additionally, the vehicle's ability to switch between two-wheel and four-wheel drive would "be particularly appealing to women who may be concerned about driving in snow and ice with their children." Plaintiff testified that the perceived safety benefits of its four-wheel drive capacity was what attracted her to the Bronco II. She was not at all interested in its off-road use.

The law implies a warranty by a manufacturer that places its product on the market that the product is reasonably fit for the ordinary purpose for which it was intended. If it is, in fact, defective and not reasonably fit to be used for its intended purpose, the warranty is breached. Plaintiff's proof focused on the sale of the Bronco II for suburban driving and everyday road travel. Plaintiff also adduced proof that the Bronco II's design characteristics made it unusually susceptible to rollover accidents when used on paved roads. All of this evidence was useful in showing that routine highway and street driving was the "ordinary purpose" for which the Bronco II was sold and that it was not "fit"—or safe—for that purpose. Thus, under the evidence in this case, a rational fact finder could have concluded that the vehicle was not safe for the "ordinary purpose" of daily driving for which it was marketed and sold.

Decision

The court of appeals held that Ford had breached the implied warranty of merchantability and upheld the jury award for the plaintiff.

Case Questions

Critical Legal Thinking What is an implied warranty of merchantability? Explain.

Business Ethics Did Ford act ethically in defending that the Bronco II was sold only as an off-road vehicle? Was this argument persuasive?

Contemporary Business Do you think that SUVs such as the Bronco II have a higher rollover danger than normal passenger automobiles?

Implied Warranty of Fitness for Human Consumption

implied warranty of fitness for human consumption
A warranty that applies to food or drink consumed on or off the premises of restaurants, grocery stores, fast-food outlets, and vending machines.

The common law implied a special warranty—the **implied warranty of fitness for human consumption**—to food products. The UCC incorporates this warranty within the implied warranty of merchantability, and it applies to food and drink consumed on or off the seller's premises. Restaurants, grocery stores, fast-food outlets, and vending-machine operators are all subject to this warranty. States use one of the following two tests in determining whether there has been a breach of the implied warranty of fitness for human consumption:

foreign substance test
A test to determine merchantability based on foreign objects found in food.

1. **Foreign substance test.** Under the **foreign substance test**, a food product is unmerchantable if a foreign object in that product causes injury to a person.

   Examples Under this test, the implied warranty would be breached if a person were injured by eating a nail in a cherry pie. This is because a nail is a foreign object in the cherry pie. The implied warranty would not be breached if a person were injured by eating a cherry pit in the pie. This is because the cherry pit is not a foreign object in the cherry pie.

consumer expectation test
A test to determine merchantability based on what the average consumer would expect to find in food products.

2. **Consumer expectation test.** The majority of states have adopted the modern **consumer expectation test** to determine the merchantability of food products. Under this test, the court asks what a consumer would expect to find or not find in food or drink that he or she consumes.

   Examples Under this test, the implied warranty would be breached if a person were injured by a chicken bone while eating a chicken salad sandwich. This is because a consumer would expect that the food producer would have removed all bones from the chicken. Under this test, the implied warranty would not be breached if a person were injured by a chicken bone while eating fried chicken. This is because a consumer would expect to find bones in fried chicken.

Restaurant, Sault Ste. Marie, Michigan *The implied warranty of fitness for human consumption is an implied warranty that food and drink served by restaurants, bars, fast-food outlets, coffee shops, vending machines, and other purveyors of food and drink be safe for human consumption. Each state applies one of two tests in determining whether there has been a breach of the implied warranty of fitness for human consumption: (1) the foreign substance test or (2) the consumer expectation test. Most states use the consumer expectation test.*

▶ IMPLIED WARRANTY OF FITNESS FOR A PARTICULAR PURPOSE

implied warranty of fitness for a particular purpose
A warranty that arises where a seller or lessor warrants that the goods will meet the buyer's or lessee's expressed needs.

The UCC contains an **implied warranty of fitness for a particular purpose**. This implied warranty attaches to the sale or lease of goods if the seller or lessor has made statements that the goods will meet the buyer's or lessee's needs or purpose. This implied warranty is breached if the goods do not meet the buyer's or lessee's expressed needs. The warranty applies to both merchant and nonmerchant sellers and lessors.

The warranty of fitness for a particular purpose is implied at the time of contracting if [UCC 2-315, 2A-213]:

- The seller or lessor has reason to know the particular purpose for which the buyer is purchasing the goods or the lessee is leasing the goods.
- The seller or lessor makes a statement that the goods will serve this purpose.
- The buyer or lessee relies on the seller's or lessor's skill and judgment and purchases or leases the goods.

Example Susan wants to buy lumber to build a small deck in her backyard. She goes to Joe's Lumber Yard to purchase the lumber and describes to Joe, the owner of the lumber yard, the size of the deck she intends to build. Susan also tells Joe that she is relying on him to select the right lumber for the project. Joe selects the lumber and states that the lumber will serve Susan's purpose. Susan buys the lumber and builds the deck. Unfortunately, the deck collapses because the lumber was not strong enough to support it. Susan can sue Joe for breach of the implied warranty of fitness for a particular purpose.

CONCEPT SUMMARY
EXPRESS AND IMPLIED WARRANTIES OF QUALITY

Type of Warranty	How Created	Description
Express warranty	Made by the seller or lessor.	Affirms that the goods meet certain standards of quality, description, performance, or condition [UCC 2-313(1), 2A-210(1)].
Implied warranty of merchantability	Implied by law if the seller or lessor is a merchant.	Implies that the goods: 1. Are fit for the ordinary purposes for which they are used. 2. Are adequately contained, packaged, and labeled. 3. Are of an even kind, quality, and quantity within each unit. 4. Conform to any promise or affirmation of fact made on the container or label. 5. Pass without objection in the trade. 6. Meet a fair average, or middle range of quality for fungible goods [UCC 2-314(1), 2A-212(1)].
Implied warranty of fitness for a particular purpose	Implied by law.	Implies that the goods are fit for the purpose for which the buyer or lessee acquires the goods if: 1. The seller or lessor has reason to know the particular purpose for which the goods will be used. 2. The seller or lessor makes a statement that the goods will serve that purpose. 3. The buyer or lessee relies on the statement and buys or leases the goods [UCC 2-315, UCC 2A-213].

▶ WARRANTY DISCLAIMERS

Warranties can be **disclaimed**, or limited. If an *express warranty* is made, it can be limited only if the **warranty disclaimer** and the warranty can be reasonably construed with each

warranty disclaimer
A statement that negates express and implied warranties

other. All implied warranties of quality may be disclaimed. The rules for disclaiming implied warranties are:

- **"As is" disclaimer.** Expressions such as *as is*, *with all faults*, or other language that makes it clear to the buyer that there are no implied warranties disclaims all implied warranties. This type of disclaimer is often included in sales contracts for used products.
- **Disclaimer of the implied warranty of merchantability.** If the "as is" type of disclaimer is not used, disclaimers of the *implied warranty of merchantability* must specifically mention the term *merchantability* for the implied warranty of merchantability to be disclaimed. These disclaimers may be oral or written.
- **Disclaimer of the implied warranty of fitness for a particular purpose.** If the "as is" type of disclaimer is not used, the *implied warranty of fitness for a particular purpose* may be disclaimed in general language, without specific use of the term *fitness*. The disclaimer has to be in writing.

Conspicuous Display of Disclaimer

conspicuous
A requirement that warranty disclaimers be noticeable to the reasonable person.

Written disclaimers must be conspicuously displayed to be valid. The courts construe **conspicuous** as noticeable to a reasonable person [UCC 2-316, 2A-214]. A heading printed in uppercase letters or a typeface that is larger or in a different style than the rest of the body of a sales or lease contract is considered to be conspicuous. Different-color type is also considered conspicuous.

INTERNET LAW & ONLINE COMMERCE

Warranty Disclaimers in Software Licenses

Most software companies license their software to users. A software license is a complex contract that contains the terms of the license. Most software licenses contain warranty disclaimer and limitation on liability clauses that limit the licensor's liability if the software malfunctions. Disclaimer of warranty and limitation on liability clauses that are included in a typical software license appear below.

SOFTWARE.COM, INC.
LIMITATION AND WAIVERS OF WARRANTIES, REMEDIES, AND CONSEQUENTIAL DAMAGES

Limited Warranty. Software.com, Inc. warrants that (a) the software will perform substantially in accordance with the accompanying written materials for a period of 90 days from the date of receipt, and (b) any hardware accompanying the software will be free from defects in materials and workmanship under normal use and service for a period of one year from the date of the receipt. Any implied warranties on the software and hardware are limited to 90 days and one (1) year, respectively. Some states do not allow limitations on duration of an implied warranty, so the above limitation may not apply to you.

Customer Remedies. Software.com, Inc.'s entire liability and your exclusive remedy shall be, at Software.com, Inc.'s option, either (a) return of the price paid or (b) repair or replacement of the software or hardware that does not meet Software.com, Inc.'s Limited Warranty and that is returned to Software.com, Inc. with a copy of your receipt. This Limited Warranty is void if failure of the software or hardware has resulted from accident, abuse, or misapplication. Any replacement software will be warranted for the remainder of the original warranty or 30 days, whichever is longer. These remedies are not available outside the United States of America.

No Other Warranties. Software.com, Inc. disclaims all other warranties, either express or implied, including but not limited to implied warranties of merchantability and fitness for a particular purpose, with respect to the software, the accompanying written materials, and any accompanying hardware. This Limited Warranty gives you specific legal rights. You may have others, which vary from state to state.

No Liability for Consequential Damages. In no event shall Software.com, Inc. or its suppliers be liable for any damages whatsoever (including, without limitation, damages for loss of business profits, business interruption, loss of business information, or other pecuniary loss) arising out of the use of or inability to use this Software.com, Inc. product, even if Software.com, Inc. has been advised of the possibility of such damages. Because some states do not allow the exclusion or limitation of liability for consequential or incidental damages, the above limitation may not apply to you.

MAGNUSON-MOSS WARRANTY ACT

In 1975, Congress enacted the **Magnuson-Moss Warranty Act**, which covers written warranties related to *consumer products*.[1] This federal act is administered by the Federal Trade Commission (FTC). Consumer transactions, but not commercial and industrial transactions, are governed by the act.

Magnuson-Moss Warranty Act
A federal statute that regulates written warranties on consumer products.

LANDMARK LAW

Magnuson-Moss Warranty Act Protects Consumers

The Magnuson-Moss Warranty Act does not require a seller or lessor to make an *express* written warranty. However, sellers or lessors who do make express warranties are subject to the provisions of the act. If a warrantor chooses to make an express warranty, the Magnuson-Moss Warranty Act requires that the warranty be labeled as either "full" or "limited." The fact that a warranty is full or limited must be conspicuously displayed. The disclosures must be in "understandable language":

- **Full warranty.** For a warranty to qualify as a **full express warranty**, the warrantor must guarantee free repair or replacement of the defective product. The warrantor must indicate whether there is a time limit on the full warranty (e.g., "full 36-month warranty").
- **Limited warranty.** In a **limited express warranty**, the warrantor limits the scope of a full warranty in some way (e.g., a return of the purchase price).

Violations of the Magnuson-Moss Warranty Act

A consumer may bring a *civil action* against a defendant for violating the provisions of the Magnuson-Moss Warranty Act. A successful plaintiff can recover damages, attorneys' fees, and other costs incurred in bringing the action. The act authorizes warrantors to establish an informal dispute resolution procedure. The procedure must be conspicuously described in the written warranty. Aggrieved consumers must assert their claims through this procedure before they can take legal action.

Note that the act does not create any implied warranties. The act does, however, modify the state law of implied warranties in one crucial respect: Sellers or lessors who make express written warranties related to *consumer products* are forbidden from disclaiming or modifying the implied warranties of merchantability and fitness for a particular purpose. A seller or lessor may set a time limit on implied warranties, but this time limit must correspond to the duration of any express warranty.

In the following case, the court addressed the issue of a breach of an express warranty.

CASE 2 Magnuson-Moss Warranty Act

Milicevic v. Fletcher Jones Imports, Ltd. and Mercedes-Benz USA

402 F.3d 912, Web 2005 U.S. App. Lexis 4905 (2005)
United States Court of Appeals for the Ninth Circuit

"I feel like I am stranded. I cannot feel comfortable to take the car on a trip. I do not feel comfortable to drive because I don't know what next will come. Every day is a new problem."
—Marina Milicevic, consumer

Facts

Marina Milicevic purchased a new Mercedes-Benz S500 automobile from Fletcher Jones Imports, Ltd., a car dealership, for $98,722. The automobile had been imported into the United States by Mercedes-Benz USA. (Fletcher Jones and Mercedes-Benz are collectively referred to as Mercedes.) Mercedes advertised the car as the "best car in the world." Mercedes made a new car limited express warranty that warranted to the owner that authorized Mercedes-Benz Centers would make any repairs or replacements necessary to correct defects in material or workmanship for the duration of the warranty.

(case continues)

From day one, Milicevic's car exhibited a number of aesthetic and mechanical problems. Within the first seven months, the following repairs were made: All four brake rotors were warped and required replacement at 6,000 miles; after locking Milicevic out of the car, the remote entry system was replaced; the motor for the passenger side window was replaced; the passenger side mirror was replaced; and the rear window seal and molding were unsuccessfully repaired three times. All repairs were covered and paid for under the Mercedes-Benz limited warranty. By the end of seven months, the car had spent 55 days at the Fletcher Jones repair shop. The rear window deformity and the problem with the brakes were never corrected.

At that point, Milicevic notified Mercedes that she wanted Mercedes to replace the car or take the car back and reimburse her for the purchase price. When Mercedes did not respond, Milicevic sued Mercedes-Benz and Fletcher Jones for breach of an express limited warranty, to rescind the purchase of the automobile, and to recover the value of the car, damages, and attorneys' fees. Milicevic testified at trial: "I feel like I am stranded. I cannot feel comfortable to take the car on a trip. I do not feel comfortable to drive because I don't know what next will come. Every day is a new problem."

The U.S. District Court found that the defendants had breached the written warranty between the parties. Milicevic was awarded $93,423—the purchase price of the car, including taxes and fees, less an amount that represented her reasonable use of the automobile. The Court also awarded Milicevic costs and attorneys' fees. The defendants appealed.

Issue

Was there a breach of the express warranty by Mercedes that would permit Milicevic to rescind the purchase of the Mercedes-Benz automobile and recover the value of the car and damages?

Language of the Court

As defined in the Magnuson-Moss Warranty Act, a written warranty is a writing made by the supplier of a product relating to the nature of the material or workmanship of the product, which warranty promises that the product is defect free or will meet a certain level of performance for a given period of time, or a writing in which the supplier agrees to refund, repair, replace, or take other remedial action in the event that the product fails to meet its specifications. Here, Mercedes supplied such a limited written warranty which by its terms "warrants to the original and each subsequent owner of a new Mercedes-Benz passenger car that any authorized Mercedes-Benz Center will make any repairs or replacements necessary to correct defects in material or workmanship" at no charge for parts or labor.

The district court did not clearly err in finding that two significant nonconformities—the rear window seal and the brakes—were not corrected. Milicevic testified the brakes still did not work properly. The district court also found that all of the defects, conditions and nonconformities complained of by Milicevic, which Fletcher Jones was unable to repair, were covered by Mercedes-Benz's said warranty. Thus, when Mercedes failed to correct the defects in the rear window seal and brakes, Mercedes breached the terms of its limited written warranty. Having made out a claim for relief under the Magnuson-Moss Warranty Act, Milicevic may be awarded reasonable costs and attorneys' fees.

Decision

The U.S. Court of Appeals affirmed the U.S. District Court's judgment, which found that Mercedes had breach the express limited warranty, thus permitting Milicevic to rescind the contract and recover the value of the car, damages, costs, and attorneys' fees.

Case Questions

Critical Legal Thinking What types of contracts are covered by the Magnuson-Moss Warranty Act? What does the act provide if a dealer who made an express warranty cannot repair the defect in a reasonable time?

Business Ethics Did Mercedes-Benz or Fletcher Jones act ethically in this case? What do you think Mercedes-Benz and Fletcher Jones should have done in this case? Explain.

Contemporary Business Why do you think they fought this case to the appellate level? Was this "good business"? What do you think was the amount of Mercedes's legal fees?

SPECIAL WARRANTIES OF TITLE AND POSSESSION

No man is above the law and no man is below it; nor do we ask any man's permission when we ask him to obey it.

Theodore Roosevelt

The UCC imposes special warranties on sellers and lessors of goods. These include a *warranty of good title*, a *warranty of no security interests*, a *warranty against infringements*, and a *warranty of no interference*. These warranties are discussed in the following paragraphs.

Warranty of Good Title

Unless they properly disclaim warranties, sellers of goods warrant that they have valid title to the goods they are selling and that the transfer of title is rightful [UCC 2-312(1)(a)]. This is called the **warranty of good title**. Persons who transfer goods without proper title breach this warranty.

warranty of good title
A warranty in which the seller warrants that he or she has valid title to the goods being sold and that the transfer of title is rightful.

Example Ingersoll-Rand owns a heavy-duty crane. A thief steals the crane and sells it to Turner Construction. Turner Construction does not know that the crane is stolen. If Ingersoll-Rand discovers that Turner Construction has the equipment, it can reclaim it. Turner Construction, in turn, can recover against the thief for breach of the warranty of title. This is because the thief impliedly warranted that he had good title to the equipment and that the transfer of title to Turner Construction was rightful.

Warranty of No Security Interests

Under the UCC, sellers of goods automatically warrant that the goods they sell are delivered free from any third-party security interests, liens, or encumbrances that are unknown to the buyer [UCC 2-312(1)(b)]. This is called the **warranty of no security interests**.

warranty of no security interests
A warranty in which sellers of goods warrant that the goods they sell are delivered free from any third-party security interests, liens, or encumbrances that are unknown to the buyer.

Example Albert purchases a refrigerator on credit from Appliance World, an appliance store. The store takes back a security interest in the refrigerator. Before completely paying off the refrigerator, Albert sells it to Monica for cash. Monica has no knowledge of the store's security interest in the refrigerator. After Albert misses several payments, the appliance store discovers that Monica has the refrigerator and repossesses the refrigerator. Monica can recover against Albert based on his breach of warranty of no security interests in the goods [UCC 2-312(1)(b)].

The warranties of good title and no security interests may be excluded or modified by specific language [UCC 2-312(2)]. For example, specific language such as "seller hereby transfers only those rights, title, and interest as he or she has in the goods" is sufficient to disclaim these warranties. General language such as "as is" or "with all faults" is not specific enough to be a disclaimer to the warranties of good title and no security interests. The special nature of certain sales (e.g., sheriffs' sales) tells the buyer that the seller is not giving title warranties with the sale of the goods.

Warranty Against Infringements

Unless otherwise agreed, a seller or lessor who is a merchant regularly dealing in goods of the kind sold or leased automatically warrants that the goods are delivered free of any third-party patent, trademark, or copyright claim [UCC 2-312(3), 2A-211(2)]. This is called the **warranty against infringement**.

warranty against infringements
An automatic warranty of a seller or lessor who is a merchant who regularly deals in goods of the kind sold or leased which warrants that the goods are delivered free of any third-party patent, trademark, or copyright claim.

Example Adams Company, a manufacturer of machines that make shoes, sells a machine to Smith & Franklin, a shoe manufacturer. Subsequently, Nerdette claims that she has a patent on the machine. Nerdette proves her patent claim in court. Nerdette notifies Smith & Franklin that the machine can no longer be used without her permission and the payment of a fee to her. Smith & Franklin may rescind the sales contract with Adams Company based on the breach of the warranty against infringement.

Warranty of No Interference

When goods are leased, the lessor warrants that no person holds a claim or an interest in the goods that arose from an act or omission of the lessor that will interfere with the lessee's enjoyment of his leasehold interest [UCC 2A-211(1)]. This is referred to as the **warranty against interference** or the **warranty of quiet possession**.

warranty against interference
A warranty in which the lessor warrants that no person holds a claim or an interest in the goods that arose from an act or omission of the lessor that will interfere with the lessee's enjoyment of his or her leasehold interest. Also known as the *warranty of quiet possession*.

Example Occi-Petroleum, as lessor, leases a piece of heavy equipment to Aztec Drilling. Occi-Petroleum later gives a security interest in the equipment to CityBank as collateral for a loan. If Occi-Petroleum defaults on the loan to CityBank and CityBank repossesses the equipment from Aztec, Aztec can recover damages from Occi-Petroleum for breach of the warranty of no interference.

Delhi, India *Many countries have developed warranty law that applies to the sale or lease of goods. For example, India's Sale of Goods Act of 1930 includes laws regarding making express warranties, the creation of implied warranties, and disclaiming of warranties.*

Chris Stowers © Dorling Kindersley

TEST REVIEW TERMS AND CONCEPTS

Basis of the bargain
Caveat emptor
Compensatory damages
Conspicuous
Consumer expectation test
Disclaimed
Express warranty
Foreign substance test
Full express warranty
Implied by law
Implied warranty of fitness for human consumption
Implied warranty of fitness for a particular purpose
Implied warranty of merchantability
Limited express warranty
Magnuson-Moss Warranty Act
Statements of opinion (puffing)
Warranty
Warranty against infringement
Warranty against interference (warranty of quiet possession)
Warranty disclaimer
Warranty of good title
Warranty of no security interests

CASE PROBLEMS

1 Warranty of Title When James Redmond wanted to purchase an automobile, he spoke to a salesman at Bill Branch Chevrolet, Inc. (Bill Branch). The salesman offered to sell Redmond a blue Chevrolet Caprice for $6,200. The car was to be delivered to Redmond's residence. Redmond gave the salesman $1,000 cash and received a receipt in return. The next day, the salesman delivered the car to Redmond, and Redmond paid the remaining amount due. The salesman gave Redmond a printed sales contract that reflected the payments made, with no balance due. One month later, Redmond called Bill Branch and asked for the title papers to the car. Redmond was told that the car had been reported stolen prior to the sale and that he could not receive title until he contacted Bill Branch's insurance company. Redmond sued Bill Branch Chevrolet, Inc. Is Bill Branch liable? *Bill Branch Chevrolet v. Redmond*, 378 So.2d 319, **Web** 1980 Fla.App. Lexis 15413 (Court of Appeal of Florida)

2 Express Warranty Gloria Crandell purchased a used Coronado clothes dryer from Larkin and Jones Appliance

Company (Larkin and Jones). The dryer, which was displayed on the sales floor, had a tag affixed to it that described the machine as a "quality reconditioned unit" that was "tag tested" and "guaranteed." In addition to these written statements, a salesman assured Crandell that the dryer carried a 90-day guarantee for "workmanship, parts, and labor." Crandell bought the dryer because of the guarantee and the low price. Two weeks after the machine was delivered, Crandell asked her son to put a blanket in the dryer to dry. Twenty minutes later, she noticed smoke pouring into her bedroom. By the time Crandell reached the laundry room, the machine was engulfed in flames. A defect in the clothes dryer had caused the fire. Crandell sued Larkin and Jones for breach of an express warranty. Is there an express warranty? *Crandell v. Larkin and Jones Appliance Company*, 334 N.W.2d 31, **Web** 1983 S.D. Lexis 326 (Supreme Court of South Dakota)

3 Statement of Fact or Opinion Jack Crothers went to Norm's Auto Sales (Norm's) to buy a used car. Maurice Boyd, a salesman at Norm's, showed Crothers a Dodge automobile. While running the car's engine, Boyd told Crothers that the Dodge "had a rebuilt carburetor" and "was a good runner." After listening to the sales pitch, Crothers bought the car. As Crothers was driving the Dodge the next day, the car suddenly went out of control and crashed into a tree. Crothers was seriously injured. The cause of the crash was an obvious defect in the Dodge's accelerator linkage. Crothers sued Norm's. Who wins? *Crothers v. Norm's Auto Sales*, 384 N.W.2d 562, **Web** 1986 Minn.App. Lexis 4202 (Court of Appeals of Minnesota)

4 Implied Warranty of Merchantability Geraldine Maybank took a trip to New York City to visit her son and her two-year-old grandson. She borrowed her daughter's camera for the trip. Two days before leaving for New York, Maybank purchased a package of G. T. E. Sylvania Blue Dot flashcubes at a Kmart store, owned by the S. S. Kresge Company. On the carton of the package were words to the effect that each bulb was safety coated. Upon arriving in New York, Maybank decided to take a picture of her grandson. She opened the carton of flashcubes and put one on the camera. When Maybank pushed down the lever to take a picture, the flashcube exploded. The explosion knocked her glasses off and caused cuts to her left eye. Maybank was hospitalized for eight days. Maybank sued S. S. Kresge Company. Who wins? *Maybank v. S. S. Kresge Company*, 46 N.C.App. 687, 266 S.E.2d 409, **Web** 1980 N.C.App. Lexis 2927 (Court of Appeals of North Carolina)

5 Implied Warranty of Fitness for Human Consumption Tina Keperwes went to a Publix Supermarket (Publix) in Florida and bought a can of Doxsee brand clam chowder. Keperwes opened the can of soup and prepared it at home. While eating the chowder, she bit down on a clamshell and injured one of her molars. Keperwes filed suit against Publix and Doxsee for breach of an implied warranty. In the lawsuit, Keperwes alleged that the clam chowder "was not fit for use as food, but was defective, unwholesome, and unfit for human consumption" and "was in such condition as to be dangerous to life and health." At the trial, Doxsee's general manager testified as to the state-of-the-art methods Doxsee uses in preparing its chowder. Are Publix and Doxsee liable for the injury to Keperwes's tooth? *Keperwes v. Publix Supermarkets. Inc.*, 534 So.2d 872, **Web** 1988 Fla.App. Lexis 5306 (Court of Appeal of Florida)

6 Disclaimer of Warranty Automatic Sprinkler Corporation of America (Automatic Sprinkler) wished to purchase a dry chemical fire protection system from Ansul Company (Ansul). An Ansul representative gave Automatic Sprinkler a proposal on the company's behalf. The proposal was a document five pages long. Each page included printed information describing the fire extinguisher system. Only the fifth and last page had printing on the back. The information on the back of page 5 contained a limited five-year warranty that covered only the replacement of defective parts. The limited warranty concluded with this statement: "This warranty is in lieu of all other warranties express or implied."

Automatic Sprinkler purchased the system and installed it in a client's building. Several years later, a fire broke out in the building, and the Ansul fire extinguisher system failed to discharge. Automatic Sprinkler sued Ansul for a breach of an implied warranty of merchantability. Ansul claimed that all warranties except the limited five-year warranty were disclaimed. Is Ansul's disclaimer enforceable? *Insurance Company of North America v. Automatic Sprinkler*, 67 Ohio St.2d 91, 423 N.E.2d 151, **Web** 1981 Ohio Lexis 554 (Supreme Court of Ohio)

7 Disclaimer of Warranty Cole Energy Development Company (Cole Energy) wanted to lease a gas compressor for use in its business of pumping and selling natural gas and began negotiating with the Ingersoll-Rand Company (Ingersoll-Rand). On December 5, 1983, the two parties entered into a lease agreement for a KOA gas compressor. The lease agreement contained a section labeled "WARRANTIES." Part of the section read:

> *THERE ARE NO IMPLIED WARRANTIES OF MERCHANTABILITY OR FITNESS FOR A PARTICULAR PURPOSE CONTAINED HEREIN.*

The gas compressor that was installed failed to function properly. As a result, Cole Energy lost business. Cole Energy sued Ingersoll-Rand for the breach of an implied warranty of merchantability. Is Ingersoll-Rand liable? *Cole Energy Development Company v. Ingersoll-Rand Company*, 678 F.Supp. 208, **Web** 1988 U.S. Dist. Lexis 923 (United States District Court for the Central District of Illinois)

8 Disclaimer of Warranty Edward Cate owned and operated an automotive repair shop. Cate wanted to purchase a set of automotive lifts (i.e., the devices used to elevate vehicles for repair work). Cate purchased a set of Rotary Brand lifts, manufactured by Dover Corporation (Dover). The contract for the lifts contained a five-year written warranty covering the repair of all defective parts returned to the factory. The warranty section of the contract, printed in black ink, also contained a separate paragraph stating:

> *This warranty is exclusive and in lieu of all other warranties express or implied including any implied warranty of merchantability or implied warranty of fitness for a particular purpose.*

The entire warranty section was framed by double blue lines, and the word "Warranty" was printed in solid blue letters. After the lifts were installed in Cate's shop, they began to malfunction. Cars would suddenly fall off the lifts. Dover's employees made several unsuccessful repair attempts. Rather than send the lifts back to the factory, Cate sued Dover for breach of implied warranty of merchantability. Who wins? *Cate v. Dover Corporation*, 776 S.W.2d 680, **Web** 1989 Tex. App. Lexis 2086 (Court of Appeals of Texas)

BUSINESS ETHICS CASES

9 Business Ethics Brian Keith, an actor, attended a boat show in Long Beach, California. At the boat show, Keith obtained sales literature on a sailboat called the "Island Trader 41" from a sales representative of James Buchanan, a seller of sailboats. One sales brochure described the vessel as "a picture of sure-footed seaworthiness." Another brochure called the sailboat "a carefully well-equipped and very seaworthy live-aboard vessel." One month later, Keith purchased an Island Trader 41 sailboat from Buchanan for a total purchase price of $75,610. After delivery of the sailboat, a dispute arose in regard to the seaworthiness of the vessel. Keith sued Buchanan for breach of warranty. Buchanan defended, arguing that no warranty had been made. Is it ethical for Buchanan to try to avoid being held accountable for statements of quality about the product that were made in the sales brochures given to Keith? Should sales "puffing" be considered to create an express warranty? Why or why not? Who wins this case? *Keith v. Buchanan*, 173 Cal.App.3d 13, 220 Cal.Rptr. 392, **Web** 1985 Cal.App. Lexis 2603 (Court of Appeal of California)

10 Business Ethics Peter Troy, president and owner of Troy's Custom Smoking Co., Inc. (Troy's), contacted Peter Bader, president of Swan Island Sheet Metal Works, Inc. (Swan Island), and asked Bader if Swan Island could manufacture two stainless steel gas-burner crab cookers for Troy's. Troy explained to Bader the planned use of the cookers and some of the special needs a crab cooker must satisfy—that is, a crab is cooked by dropping it into boiling water, allowing the water to recover to a rolling boil, and boiling the crab for 10 minutes. If the recovery time exceeds 10 minutes, or if the cooker cannot sustain a rolling boil, the crab is immersed too long in hot water, and the finished product is unpalatable. Troy and Bader were equally unknowledgeable about gas-burner cookers, but Bader assured Troy that he would hire an expert to assist in manufacturing a crab cooker to meet Troy's needs.

Bader sent Troy a brochure illustrating the type of burner the expert had selected to meet Troy's needs. Troy ordered the cooker, which was delivered to Troy's Beaverton, Oregon, store. Within two weeks after delivery, Troy complained to Swan Island about the cooker's performance. The cooker cooked too slowly, and the pilot light and burner were difficult to light and keep lit. Swan Island attempted but could not correct the defects. For four months, Troy's cooked crab in the Swan Island cooker. Because of the poor performance of the cooker, Troy's ruined a substantial amount of crab and had to obtain cooked crab from another outlet to serve its customers. Troy's notified Swan Island to pick up the crab cooker. Swan Island sued Troy's to recover the purchase price of the cooker. Troy's filed a counterclaim against Swan Island to rescind the contract and recover damages. Did Swan Island breach an implied warranty of fitness for a particular purpose? Did Swan Island act ethically in denying liability in this case? *Swan Island Sheet Metal Works, Inc. v. Troy's Custom Smoking Co., Inc.*, 49 Ore.App. 469, 619 P.2d 1326, **Web** 1980 Ore.App. Lexis 3731 (Court of Appeals of Oregon)

ENDNOTE

1. 15 U.S.C. Sections 2301-2312.

AGENCY FORMATION AND TERMINATION

AGENCY FORMATION AND TERMINATION

Stewart Cohen/Getty Images/Digital Vision

▲ **Real Estate Agency** *Agency is governed by a large body of common law known as agency law. Most people are familiar with many types of agencies, such as those in real estate, insurance, and travel.*

CHAPTER OBJECTIVES

After studying this chapter, you should be able to:

1. Define *agency*.
2. Identify and define a principal–independent contractor relationship.
3. Describe how express and implied agencies are created.
4. Define *apparent agency*.
5. Describe how an agency is terminated.

CHAPTER CONTENTS

"Let every eye negotiate for itself, and trust no agent."

—William Shakespeare
Much Ado About Nothing

INTRODUCTION TO AGENCY FORMATION AND TERMINATION

If businesspeople had to personally conduct all their business, the scope of their activities would be severely curtailed. Partnerships would not be able to operate, corporations could not act through managers and employees, and sole proprietorships would not be able to hire employees. The use of agents (or agency), which allows one person to act on behalf of another, solves this problem.

Examples Examples of agency relationships include a salesperson selling goods for a store, an executive working for a corporation, a partner acting on behalf of a partnership, an attorney representing a client, and a real estate broker selling a house.

Agency is governed by a large body of common law known as **agency law**. The formation of agencies, the duties of principals and agents, and termination of agencies are discussed in this chapter.

agency law
The large body of common law that governs agency; a mixture of contract law and tort law.

AGENCY

Agency relationships are formed by the mutual consent of a principal and an agent. Section 1(1) of the ***Restatement (Second) of Agency*** defines **agency** as a **fiduciary relationship** "which results from the manifestation of consent by one person to another that the other shall act in his behalf and subject to his control, and consent by the other so to act." The *Restatement (Second) of Agency* is the reference source for the rules of agency. A party who employs another person to act on his or her behalf is called a **principal**. A party who agrees to act on behalf of another is called an **agent**. The principal–agent relationship is commonly referred to as an *agency*. This relationship is depicted in Exhibit 1.

agency
The principal–agent relationship; the fiduciary relationship "which results from the manifestation of consent by one person to another that the other shall act in his behalf and subject to his control, and consent by the other so to act" [*Restatement (Second) of Agency*].

principal
A party who employs another person to act on his or her behalf.

agent
A party who agrees to act on behalf of another.

Persons Who Can Initiate an Agency Relationship

Any person who has the capacity to contract can appoint an agent to act on his or her behalf. Generally, persons who lack **contractual capacity**, such as insane persons and minors, cannot appoint agents. However, the court can appoint legal guardians or other representatives to handle the affairs of insane persons, minors, and others who lack capacity to

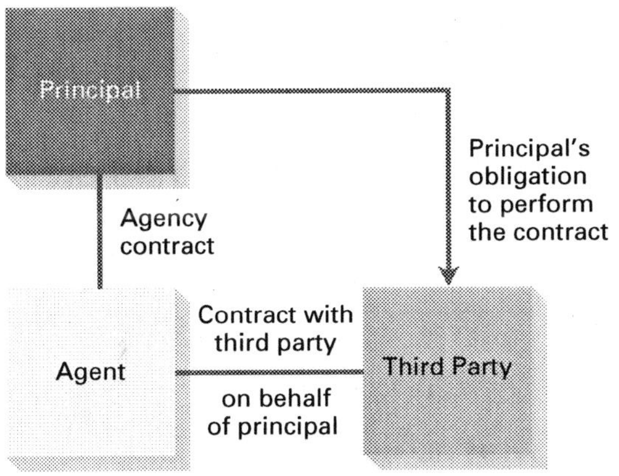

Exhibit 1
PRINCIPAL–AGENT RELATIONSHIP

It isn't the people you fire who make your life miserable, it's the people you don't.

Harvey MacKay

contract. With court approval, these representatives can enter into enforceable contracts on behalf of the persons they represent.

An agency can be created only to accomplish a lawful purpose. Agency contracts that are created for illegal purposes or are against public policy are void and unenforceable.

Example A principal cannot hire an agent to kill another person.

Some agency relationships are prohibited by law.

Example Unlicensed agents cannot be hired to perform the duties of certain licensed professionals (e.g., doctors, lawyers).

Principal–Agent Relationship

principal–agent relationship
A relationship formed when an employer hires an employee and gives that employee authority to act and enter into contracts on his or her behalf.

A **principal–agent relationship** is formed when an employer hires an employee and gives that employee authority to act and enter into contracts on his or her behalf. The extent of this authority is governed by any express agreement between the parties and implied from the circumstances of the agency.

Example The president of a corporation usually has the authority to enter into major contracts on the corporation's behalf, and a supervisor on the corporation's assembly line may have the authority only to purchase the supplies necessary to keep the line running.

Employer–Employee Relationship

employer–employee relationship
A relationship that results when an employer hires an employee to perform some task or service but the employee has not been authorized to enter into contracts on behalf of his employer.

An **employer–employee relationship** exists when an employer hires an employee to perform some task or service but the employee has not been authorized to enter into contracts on behalf of his employer.

Example A welder on General Motors Corporation's assembly line is employed in an employer–employee relationship if she is not authorized to enter into contracts on behalf of her employer. She has been employed to perform a task without being given agency authority.

An employee is an agent if he or she is empowered to enter into contracts on the employer's behalf.

Example The welder in the previous example is an agent if she is given authority to enter into contracts on behalf of General Motors Corporation.

CONCEPT SUMMARY
KINDS OF EMPLOYMENT RELATIONSHIPS

Type of Relationship	Description
Principal-agent	The agent has authority to act on behalf of the principal, as authorized by the principal and implied from the agency. An employee is often the agent of his employer.
Employer-employee	An employee is hired to perform a task or service. An employee cannot enter into contracts on behalf of the employer.

Principal–Independent Contractor Relationship

independent contractor
A person or business that is not an employee but is employed by a principal to perform a certain task on behalf of the principal.

Principals often employ outsiders—that is, persons and businesses that are not employees—to perform certain tasks on their behalf. These persons and businesses are called **independent contractors**.

Examples Doctors, dentists, consultants, stockbrokers, architects, certified public accountants, real estate brokers, and plumbers are examples of those in professions and trades who commonly act as independent contractors. An independent contractor who is a professional, such as a lawyer, is called a **professional agent**.

A principal can authorize an independent contractor to enter into contracts. Principals are bound by the authorized contracts of their independent contractors. For example, if a client authorizes an attorney to settle a case within a certain dollar amount and the attorney does so, the settlement agreement is binding.

FORMATION OF AN AGENCY

An agency and the resulting authority of an agent can arise in several ways, including express agency, implied agency, incidental authority, agency by ratification, and apparent agency. These types of agencies are discussed in the following paragraphs and material.

Express Agency

Express agency is the most common form of agency. In an express agency, the agent has the authority to contract or otherwise act on the principal's behalf, as expressly stated in the agency agreement. In addition, the agent may also possess certain implied or apparent authority to act on the principal's behalf (as discussed later in this chapter).

express agency
An agency that occurs when a principal and an agent expressly agree to enter into an agency agreement with each other.

Express agency occurs when a principal and an agent expressly agree to enter into an agency agreement with each other. Express agency contracts can be either oral or written, unless the Statute of Frauds stipulates that they must be written. For example, in most states, a real estate broker's contract to sell real estate must be in writing.

If a principal and an agent enter into an **exclusive agency contract**, the principal cannot employ any agent other than the exclusive agent. If the principal does so, the exclusive agent can recover damages from the principal. If an agency is not an exclusive agency, the principal can employ more than one agent to try to accomplish a stated purpose. When multiple agents are employed, the agencies with all the agents terminate when any one of the agents accomplishes the stated purpose.

exclusive agency contract
A contract a principal and agent enter into that says the principal cannot employ any agent other than the exclusive agent.

In the following case, the court had to decide whether an agency had been created.

CASE 1 Agency

Bosse v. Brinker Restaurant Corporation, d.b.a. Chili's Grill and Bar

Web 2005 Mass. Super. Lexis 372 (2005)
Superior Court of Massachusetts

"The evidence is insufficient to create a genuine issue whether Chili's appointed or authorized the patron to act as a posse to conduct the chase."

—Judge Sikora

Facts

Brendan Bosse and Michael Griffin were a part of a group of four teenagers eating a meal at a Chili's restaurant in Dedham, Massachusetts. Chili's is owned by Brinker Restaurant Corporation (collectively "Chili's"). The teenagers decided not to pay the $56 bill for their meal. They went out of the building, got in their car, and drove away, heading northward up Route 1.

A patron of the restaurant saw the teenagers leave without payment. He followed them in his white sport-utility vehicle (SUV). The teenagers saw him following them. A high-speed chase ensued through Dedham side streets. The patron used his cell phone to call the Chili's manager. The manager called 911 and reported the incident and the location of the car chase. The teenagers' car collided with a cement wall, and Bosse and Griffin were seriously injured. The Chili's patron drove past the crash scene and was never identified.

Bosse and Griffin sued Chili's for compensatory damages for their injuries. The plaintiffs argued that the patron was an agent of Chili's, and therefore Chili's was liable to the plaintiffs, based on the doctrine of *respondeat superior*, which holds a principal liable for the acts of its agents. Chili's filed a motion for summary judgment, arguing that the patron was not its agent.

Issue

Was the restaurant patron who engaged in the high-speed car chase an agent of Chili's?

(case continues)

Language of the Court

The plaintiffs sue under the theory of respondeat superior. *They contend that the Chili's patron converted to a Chili's servant; that he conducted the chase as an agent of the restaurant; and that the restaurant should be liable for the consequences of his negligent or reckless pursuit. An agency relationship will require three elements. Most obviously, Chili's must have consented to the action of the patron on its behalf. Second, Chili's must have retained control, or the right of control, over the physical conduct of the patron in the performance of the pursuit. Third, the conduct of the agent must serve the benefit or further the interest of the principal.*

The evidence is insufficient to create a genuine issue whether Chili's appointed or authorized the patron to act as a posse to conduct the chase. No information indicates any preliminary communication between the patron and restaurant manager. The events were spontaneous and fast breaking. No member of Chili's house staff joined in the pursuit. The plaintiffs argue that Chili's effectively assented to an agency relationship by acceptance of the patron's reconnaissance reports during the course of the chase; and by failure to instruct him to break off the chase. That circumstance is not enough. The patron need not have been an agent to engage in that conduct. He was pursuing petty crime. Chili's was reporting the petty crime to the police. No information indicates that Chili's had any effective control over the patron. The dominant purpose of Chili's relay of the patron's reports to the police appears to have been the public interest in the apprehension of petty criminals and not the private recovery of the unpaid bill.

Decision

The superior court held that the restaurant patron who engaged in the high-speed chase in which the plaintiffs were injured was not an agent of Chili's restaurant. The superior court granted summary judgment to Chili's.

Case Questions

Critical Legal Thinking What does the doctrine of *respondeat superior* provide? Explain.

Business Ethics Why do you think the plaintiffs sued Chili's? Do you think they had a very good chance of winning the lawsuit against Chili's?

Contemporary Business Did the elements exist to make the restaurant patron an agent of Chili's restaurant? Explain. Is the restaurant patron liable?

CONTEMPORARY ENVIRONMENT

Power of Attorney

A **power of attorney** is one of the most formal types of express agency agreements. It is often used by a principal to give an agent the power to sign legal documents, such as deeds to real estate, on behalf of the principal. There are two kinds of powers of attorney:

1. **General power of attorney**, which confers broad powers on the agent to act in any matters on the principal's behalf.
2. **Special power of attorney**, which limits the agent to those acts specifically enumerated in the agreement.

An agent with power of attorney is called an **attorney-in-fact** even though he or she does not have to be a lawyer. Powers of attorney must be written. Usually, they must also be notarized. Often, a principal makes a power of attorney a **durable power of attorney**. A durable power of attorney remains effective if the principal is incapacitated.

power of attorney
An express agency agreement that is often used to give an agent the power to sign legal documents on behalf of the principal.

implied agency
An agency that occurs when a principal and an agent do not expressly create an agency, but it is inferred from the conduct of the parties.

Implied Agency

In many situations, a principal and an agent do not expressly create an agency. Instead, the agency is implied from the conduct of the parties. This type of agency is referred to as an **implied agency**. The extent of the agent's authority is determined from the facts and circumstances of the particular situation. Implied authority can be conferred by either industry custom, prior dealing between the parties, the agent's position, acts deemed necessary to carry out the agent's duties, and other factors the court deems relevant. Implied authority cannot conflict with express authority or with stated limitations on express authority.

Incidental Authority

Often, even an express agency agreement does not provide enough detail to cover contingencies that may arise in the future regarding the performance of the agency. In such a case, the agent possesses certain implied authority to act beyond his express agency powers. This authority is sometimes referred to as **incidental authority**. Certain emergency situations may arise in the course of an agency. If the agent cannot contact the principal for instructions, the agent has incidental emergency powers to take all actions reasonably necessary to protect the principal's property and rights.

Example A homeowner employs a real estate broker to sell his house. The real estate broker's express powers are to advertise and market the house for sale, show the house to prospective buyers, and accept offers from persons who want to purchase the house. The homeowner goes away on a month long trip where he cannot be contacted. During this time a water pipe breaks and begins to leak water in the house. The real estate broker has incidental authority to hire a plumber to repair the pipe to stop the water leak. The homeowner is responsible for paying for the repairs.

An agent's scope of employment was at issue in the following case.

CASE 2 Scope of Employment

Keating v. Goldick and Lapp Roofing and Sheet Metal Company, Inc.

Web 2004 Del. Super. Lexis 102 (2004)
Superior Court of Delaware

"There comes a point in every litigation where common sense will make some conclusions obvious."

—Judge Carpenter

Facts

Lapp Roofing and Sheet Metal Company, Inc., is an Ohio corporation headquartered in Dayton, Ohio. The company provides construction services in several states. Lapp Roofing sent James Goldick and other Lapp Roofing employees to work on a roofing project in Wilmington, Delaware. Lapp Roofing's company policy prohibited employees from driving company vehicles for personal purposes. Lapp Roofing entrusted Goldick, as job foreman, with a white Ford van to transport the workers to the job site and to provide transportation to meals and other necessities.

While in Wilmington, Goldick and another Lapp Roofing employee, James McNees, went to Gators Bar and Restaurant. Goldick, after eating and drinking for several hours, was ejected from the bar. Shortly thereafter, Goldick drove the company van onto the curb in front of the bar, striking two people in the parking lot and seven individuals on the curb outside the bar. Subsequently, the police stopped the van and apprehended Goldick. Goldick was arrested and pleaded guilty to criminal assault charges. Christopher M. Keating and the other injured individuals filed a personal injury lawsuit against Goldick and Lapp Roofing. Lapp Roofing defended, alleging that it was not liable because Goldick's negligent conduct was committed outside the scope of his employment.

Issue

Was Goldick's negligent conduct committed within the scope of his employment for Lapp Roofing?

Language of the Court

There comes a point in every litigation where common sense will make some conclusions obvious. If the injured plaintiffs were not involved in this litigation and were simply asked whether they believe that an individual who used an employer's truck late at night to go to a bar and consume alcohol was acting within the scope of that employer's employment, they would without hesitation say no. Logic and common sense would lead any reasonable person to the same conclusion.

One could argue that sending a work crew from Ohio with only a work truck as transportation would be sufficient deviation. To a degree, the court agrees this allows the range of covered conduct to be explained. Obviously a crew who is assigned for several days or weeks to a remote location will need to utilize the company vehicle to get meals or other necessities associated with that stay. Therefore, if this event had occurred as the employees were leaving Happy Harry's after they obtained a needed prescription or from Denny's Restaurant after a meal, the court believes these foreseeable and logical consequences of a lengthy stay away from home would bring the conduct within the scope of employment under the dual purpose rationale.

However, no reasonable person could conclude this limitation on available transportation would provide the mechanism to expand the coverage to a drunken brawl that occurred after hours and was unassociated with the

(case continues)

employee's work or associated with his stay. Such conduct is so adverse to the employer that no conceivable benefit could be derived. It is completely unrelated to the employer's business and does not advance the work for which the employees were sent to this location. Here, Goldick used the van to go drinking with another employee and drove the van in the parking lot and on the curb injuring various individuals. No jury could reasonably conclude that Goldick's conduct was actuated, even in part, by a purpose to serve his employer. This incident did not occur during working hours and Goldick decided to go to Gators and become intoxicated for purely personal reasons and not to serve Lapp Roofing's interests whatsoever.

Decision

The superior court held that Goldick was not acting within the course and scope of his employment when his negligent conduct occurred. The superior court granted summary judgment to Lapp Roofing on this issue.

Case Questions

Critical Legal Thinking Define *scope of employment.* Why is this concept important in principal–agent relationships? Explain.

Contemporary Business Why was Lapp Roofing found not liable in this case? Explain. If the negligent conduct had occurred when Goldick was driving to a restaurant for a meal, would the decision have been the same?

Business Ethics Did Lapp Roofing act ethically in denying liability for the negligent conduct of one of its employees?

Agency by Ratification

agency by ratification
An agency that occurs when (1) a person misrepresents him- or herself as another's agent when in fact he or she is not and (2) the purported principal ratifies the unauthorized act.

Agency by ratification occurs when (1) a person misrepresents himself or herself as another's agent when in fact he or she is not and (2) the purported principal ratifies (accepts) the unauthorized act. In such cases, the principal is bound to perform, and the agent is relieved of any liability for misrepresentation.

Example Bill Levine sees a house for sale and thinks his friend Sherry Maxwell would want it. Bill Levine enters into a contract to purchase the house from the seller and signs the contract "Bill Levine, agent for Sherry Maxwell." Because Bill is not Sherry Maxwell's agent, she is not bound to the contract. However, if Sherry agrees to purchase the house, there is an agency by ratification. The ratification "relates back" to the moment Bill Levine entered into the contract. Upon ratification of the contract, Sherry Maxwell is obligated to purchase the house.

▶ APPARENT AGENCY

apparent agency
Agency that arises when a principal creates the appearance of an agency that in actuality does not exist.

Apparent agency (or **agency by estoppel**) arises when a principal creates the appearance of an agency that in actuality does not exist. Where an apparent agency is established, the principal is **estopped** (stopped) from denying the agency relationship and is bound to contracts entered into by the apparent agent while acting within the scope of the apparent agency. Note that the principal's actions—not the agent's—create an apparent agency.

Example Georgia Pacific, Inc., interviews Albert Iorio for a sales representative position. Mr. Iorio, accompanied by Jane Franklin, the national sales manager, visits retail stores located in the open sales territory. While visiting one store, Jane tells the store manager, "I wish I had more sales reps like Albert." Nevertheless, Albert is not hired. If Albert later enters into contracts with the store on behalf of Georgia Pacific and Jane has not controverted the impression of Albert she left with the store manager, the company will be bound to the contract.

CONCEPT SUMMARY

FORMATION OF AGENCY RELATIONSHIPS

Type of Agency	Formation	Enforcement of the Contract
Express	Authority is expressly given to the agent by the principal.	Principal and third party are bound to the contract.

Type of Agency	Formation	Enforcement of the Contract
Implied	Authority is implied from the conduct of the parties, custom and usage of trade, or act incidental to carrying out the agent's duties.	Principal and third party are bound to the contract.
Incidental	Authority that is implied to act beyond express agency powers to take all actions reasonably necessary to protect the principal's property and rights.	Principal and third party are bound to the contract.
Apparent	Authority is created when the principal leads a third party to believe that the agent has authority.	Principal and third party are bound to the contract.
By ratification	Acts of the agent are committed outside the scope of his or her authority.	Principal and third party are not bound to the contract unless the principal ratifies the contract.

PRINCIPAL'S DUTIES

A principal owes certain duties to an agent. These duties are discussed in the following paragraphs.

Principal's Duty to Compensate

A principal owes a **duty to compensate** an agent for services provided. Usually, the agency contract (whether written or oral) specifies the compensation to be paid. The principal must pay this amount either upon the completion of the agency or at some other mutually agreeable time.

duty to compensate
A duty that a principal owes to pay an agreed-upon amount to the agent either upon the completion of the agency or at some other mutually agreeable time.

If there is no agreement as to the amount of compensation, the law implies a promise that the principal will pay the agent the customary fee paid in the industry. If the compensation cannot be established by custom, the principal owes a duty to pay the reasonable value of the agent's services. There is no duty to compensate a gratuitous agent. However, gratuitous agents who agree to provide their services free of charge may be paid voluntarily.

Certain types of agents traditionally perform their services on a **contingency-fee basis**. Under this type of arrangement, the principal owes a duty to pay the agent the agreed-upon contingency fee only if the agency is completed. Real estate brokers, finders, lawyers, and salespersons often work on a contingency-fee basis.

Principal's Duties to Reimburse and to Indemnify

In carrying out an agency, an agent may spend his or her own money on the principal's behalf. Unless otherwise agreed, the principal owes a **duty to reimburse** the agent for all such expenses if they were (1) authorized by the principal, (2) within the scope of the agency, and (3) necessary to discharge the agent's duties in carrying out the agency.

Example A principal must reimburse an agent for authorized business trips taken on the principal's behalf.

A principal also owes a **duty to indemnify** the agent for any losses the agent suffers because of the principal. This duty usually arises where an agent is held liable for the principal's misconduct.

Example An agent enters into an authorized contract with a third party on the principal's behalf, the principal fails to perform on the contract, and the third party recovers a judgment against the agent. The agent can recover indemnification of this amount from the principal.

Principal's Duty to Cooperate

Unless otherwise agreed, a principal owes a **duty to cooperate** with and assist an agent in the performance of the agent's duties and the accomplishment of the agency.

Example Unless otherwise agreed, a principal who employs a real estate agent to sell her house owes a duty to allow the agent to show the house to prospective purchasers during reasonable hours.

AGENT'S DUTIES

An agent owes certain duties to a principal. These duties are discussed in the following paragraphs.

Agent's Duty to Perform

An agent who enters into a contract with a principal has two distinct obligations: (1) to perform the lawful duties expressed in the contract and (2) to meet the standards of reasonable care, skill, and diligence implicit in all contracts. Collectively, these duties are referred to as the agent's **duty to perform**. Normally, an agent is required to render the same standard of care, skill, and diligence that a fictitious reasonable agent in the same occupation would render in the same locality and under the same circumstances.

duty to perform
An agent's duty to a principal that includes (1) performing the lawful duties expressed in the contract and (2) meeting the standards of reasonable care, skill, and diligence implicit in all contracts.

Examples A general medical practitioner in a rural area would be held to the standard of a reasonable general medical practitioner in rural areas. The standard might be different for a general medical practitioner in a big city. In some professions, such as accounting, a national standard of performance (e.g., "generally accepted accounting principles") is imposed. If an agent holds himself or herself as possessing higher-than-customary skills, the agent is held to that higher standard of performance. For example, a lawyer who claims to be a specialist in securities law will be held to a reasonable specialist-in-securities-law standard.

An agent who does not perform his or her express duties or fails to use the standard degree of care, skill, or diligence is liable to the principal for breach of contract. An agent who has negligently or intentionally failed to perform properly is also liable in tort to the principal.

Agent's Duty to Notify

In the course of an agency, the agent usually learns information that is important to the principal. This information may come from third parties or other sources. The agent's duty to notify the principal of such information is called the **duty to notify**. The agent is liable to the principal for any injuries resulting from a breach of this duty. Most information learned by an agent in the course of an agency is **imputed** to the principal. This means that the principal is assumed to know what the agent knows. This is so even if the agent does not tell the principal certain relevant information.

imputed knowledge
Information that is learned by an agent that is attributed to the principal.

Agent's Duty to Account

Unless otherwise agreed, an agent owes a duty to maintain an accurate accounting of all transactions undertaken on the principal's behalf. This **duty to account** (sometimes called the **duty of accountability**) includes keeping records of all property and money received and expended during the course of the agency. A principal has a right to demand an accounting from the agent at any time, and the agent owes a legal duty to make the accounting. This duty also requires the agent to (1) maintain a separate account for the principal and (2) use the principal's property in an authorized manner.

duty to account
A duty that an agent owes to maintain an accurate accounting of all transactions undertaken on the principal's behalf. Also known as the *duty of accountability*.

Any property, money, or other benefit received by the agent in the course of an agency belongs to the principal. For example, all secret profits received by an agent are the property of the principal. If an agent breaches the agency contract, the principal can sue the agent to recover damages caused by breach. The court can impose a *constructive trust* for the benefit of the principal on any property purchased with secret profits.

TERMINATION OF AN AGENCY BY ACTS OF THE PARTIES

An agency contract is similar to other contracts in that it can be terminated by an act of the parties. Note that once an agency relationship is terminated, the agent can no longer represent the principal or bind the principal to contracts. The parties to an agency contract can terminate the agency contract either by agreement or by their actions. The four methods of **termination of an agency relationship by acts of the parties** are:

The way to wealth is as plain as the way to market. It depends chiefly on two words, industry and frugality: that is, waste neither time nor money, but make the best use of both. Without industry and frugality nothing will do, and with them everything.

Benjamin Franklin

1. **Mutual agreement.** As with any other contract, the parties to an agency contract can mutually agree to terminate their agreement. By doing so, the parties relieve each other of any further rights, duties, obligations, or powers provided for in the agency contract. Either party can propose the termination of an agency contract.
2. **Lapse of time.** Agency contracts are often written for a specific period of time. When this is the case, the agency terminates when the specified time period elapses. If an agency contract does not set forth a specific termination date, the agency terminates after a reasonable time has elapsed. The courts often look to the custom of an industry in determining the reasonable time for the termination of the agency.

   Example A principal and an agent enter into an agency contract "beginning January 1, 2011, and ending December 31, 2014." The agency automatically terminates on December 31, 2014.

3. **Purpose achieved.** A principal can employ an agent for the time it takes to accomplish a certain task, purpose, or result. Such agencies automatically terminate when they are completed.

   Example A principal employs a licensed real estate broker to sell his house. The agency terminates when the house is sold and the principal pays the broker the agreed-upon compensation.

4. **Occurrence of a specified event.** An agency contract can specify that the agency exists until a specified event occurs. The agency terminates when the specified event happens.

   Example A principal employs an agent to take care of her dog until she returns from a trip. The agency terminates when the principal returns from the trip.

Notification Required at the Termination of an Agency

If an agency is terminated by agreement between the parties, the principal is under a **duty of notification of the termination of the agency to third parties**. Unless otherwise required, the notice can be from the principal or some other source (e.g., the agent). If an agency terminates by operation of law, there is no duty to notify third parties about the termination, however.

Shortly his fortune shall be lifted higher;
True industry doth kindle honour's fire.

William Shakespeare

The termination of an agency extinguishes an agent's actual authority to act on the principal's behalf. However, if the principal fails to give the proper notice of termination to a third party, the agent still has apparent authority to bind the principal to contracts with these third parties. If this happens, the contract is enforceable against the principal. The principal's only recourse is against the agent to recover damages caused by these unauthorized contracts.

The following notification requirements must be met:

- **Parties who dealt with the agent.** Direct notice of termination must be given to all persons with whom the agent dealt. Although the notice may be either written or oral, it is better practice to give written notice.
- **Parties who have knowledge of the agency.** The principal must give direct or constructive notice to any third party who has knowledge of the agency but with whom the agent has not dealt. Direct notice is often in the form of a letter. Constructive notice usually consists of placing a notice of the termination of the agency in a newspaper serving the relevant community. This notice is effective even against persons who do not see it.
- **Parties who have no knowledge of the agency.** Generally, a principal is not obligated to give notice of termination to strangers who have no knowledge of the agency. However, a principal who has given the agent written authority to act but fails to

recover the writing upon termination of the agency may be liable to strangers who later rely on the writing and deal with the agent. The laws of most states provide that this liability can be avoided by giving constructive notice (e.g., newspaper announcement) of the termination of the agency.

CONTEMPORARY ENVIRONMENT

Agency Coupled with an Interest

An **agency coupled with an interest** is a special type of agency relationship that is created for the agent's benefit. This type of agency is **irrevocable** by the principal (i.e., the principal cannot terminate it). An agency coupled with an interest is commonly used in security agreements to secure loans. An agency coupled with an interest is not terminated by the death or incapacity of either the principal or the agent. It terminates only when the agent's obligations are performed. However, the parties can expressly agree that an agency coupled with an interest is terminated.

Example Heidi owns a piece of real estate. She goes to Wells Fargo Bank to obtain a loan on the property. The bank makes the loan but requires her to sign a security agreement (e.g., a mortgage) pledging the property as collateral for the loan. The security agreement contains a clause that appoints that bank as Heidi's agent and permits the bank to sell the property and recover the amount of the loan from the sale proceeds if she defaults on her payments. This agency is irrevocable by Heidi, the principal.

agency coupled with an interest
A special type of agency that is created for the agent's benefit and that the principal cannot revoke.

Wrongful Termination of an Agency or Employment Contract

Generally, agency and employment contracts that do not specify a definite time for their termination can be terminated at will by either the principal or the agent, without liability to the other party. When a principal terminates an agency contract, it is called a **revocation of authority**. When an agent terminates an agency, it is called a **renunciation of authority**.

Unless an agency is irrevocable, both the principal and the agent have individual power to unilaterally terminate any agency contract. Note that having the power to terminate an agency agreement is not the same as having the right to terminate it. The unilateral termination of an agency contract may be wrongful. If a principal's or an agent's termination of an agency contract breaches the contract, the other party can sue for damages for **wrongful termination**.

wrongful termination
The termination of an agency contract in violation of the terms of the agency contract. The nonbreaching party may recover damages from the breaching party.

Example A principal employs a licensed real estate agent to sell his house. The agency contract gives the agent an exclusive listing for three months. After one month, the principal unilaterally terminates the agency. The principal has the power to do so, and the agent can no longer act on behalf of the principal. However, because the principal did not have the right to terminate the contract, the agent can sue him and recover damages (i.e., lost commission) for wrongful termination.

TERMINATION OF AN AGENCY BY OPERATION OF LAW

The crowning fortune of a man is to be born to some pursuit which finds him employment and happiness, whether it be to make baskets, or broad swords, or canals, or statues, or songs.

Ralph Waldo Emerson

Agency contracts can be **terminated by operation of law** as well as by agreement. The five methods of terminating an agency relationship by operation of law are:

1. **Death.** The death of either the principal or the agent terminates an agency relationship. This rule is based on the old legal principle that because a dead person cannot act, no one can act for him or her. Note that an agency terminates even if one party is unaware of the other party's death. An agent's actions that take place after the principal's death do not bind the principal's estate.

2. **Insanity.** The insanity of either the principal or the agent generally terminates an agency relationship. A few states have modified this rule to provide that a contract entered into by an agent on behalf of an insane principal is enforceable if (1) the insane person has not been adjudged insane, (2) the third party does not have knowledge of the principal's insanity at the time of contracting, and (3) the enforcement of the contract will prevent injustice.
3. **Bankruptcy.** An agency relationship is terminated if the principal is declared bankrupt. Bankruptcy requires the filing of a petition for bankruptcy under federal bankruptcy law. With few exceptions, neither the appointment of a state court receiver nor the principal's financial difficulties or insolvency terminates the agency relationship. The agent's bankruptcy usually does not terminate an agency unless the agent's credit standing is important to the agency relationship.
4. **Changed circumstances.** An agency terminates when there is an unusual change in circumstances that would lead the agent to believe that the principal's original instructions should no longer be valid.

   Example A principal employs a licensed real estate agent to sell a farm for $100,000. The agent thereafter learns that oil has been discovered on the property and makes it worth $1 million. The agency terminates because of this change in circumstances.

5. **War.** The outbreak of a war between the principal's country and the agent's country terminates an agency relationship between the parties. Such an occurrence usually makes the performance of the agency contract impossible.

Most are engaged in business the greater part of their lives, because the soul abhors a vacuum and they have not discovered any continuous employment for man's nobler faculties.

Henry David Thoreau

Termination by Impossibility

An agency relationship terminates if a situation arises that makes its fulfillment impossible. The following circumstances can lead to **termination by impossibility**:

- The loss or destruction of the subject matter of the agency

Example A principal employs an agent to sell his horse, but the horse dies before it is sold. The agency relationship terminates at the moment the horse dies.

- The loss of a required qualification

Example A principal employs a licensed real estate agent to sell her house, and the real estate agent's license is revoked. The agency terminates at the moment the license is revoked.

- A change in the law

Example A principal employs an agent to trap alligators. If a law is passed that makes trapping alligators illegal, the agency contract terminates when the law becomes effective.

TEST REVIEW TERMS AND CONCEPTS

Agency
Agency by ratification
Agency coupled with an interest
Agency law
Agent
Apparent agency (agency by estoppel)
Attorney-in-fact
Contingency-fee basis
Contractual capacity
Durable power of attorney
Duty of notification of termination of an agency
Duty to account (duty of accountability)
Duty to compensate
Duty to cooperate
Duty to indemnify
Duty to notify
Duty to perform
Duty to reimburse
Employer–employee relationship
Estopped
Exclusive agency contract
Express agency
Fiduciary relationship
General power of attorney
Implied agency
Imputed knowledge
Incidental authority
Independent contractor
Irrevocable agency
Power of attorney
Principal
Principal–agent relationship
Professional agent
Renunciation of authority
Restatement (Second) of Agency
Revocation of authority
Special power of attorney
Termination by acts of the parties
Termination by impossibility
Termination by operation of law
Wrongful termination

CASE PROBLEMS

1 Creation of an Agency Renaldo, Inc., doing business as Baker Street, owned and operated a nightclub in Georgia. On the evening in question, plaintiff Ginn became "silly drunk" at the nightclub and was asked by several patrons and the manager to leave the premises. The police were called, and Ginn left the premises. When Ginn realized that his jacket was still in the nightclub, he attempted to reenter the premises. He was met at the door by the manager, who refused him admittance. When Ginn persisted, an unidentified patron, without the approval of the manager, pushed Ginn, who lost his balance and fell backward. To break his fall, Ginn put his hand against the door jamb. The unidentified patron slammed the door on Ginn's hand and held it shut for several minutes. Ginn, who suffered severe injuries to his right hand, sued the nightclub for damages. Is the unidentified patron an agent of the nightclub? *Ginn v. Renaldo, Inc.*, 183 Ga.App. 618, 359 S.E.2d 390, **Web** 1987 Ga.App. Lexis 2023 (Court of Appeals of Georgia)

2 Independent Contractor Mercedes Connolly and her husband purchased airline tickets and a tour package for a tour to South Africa from Judy Samuelson, a travel agent doing business as International Tours of Manhattan. Samuelson sold tickets for a variety of airline companies and tour operators, including African Adventurers, which was the tour operator for the Connollys' tour. Mercedes fell while trying to cross a 6-inch-deep stream while the tour group was on a walking tour to see hippopotami in a river at a game reserve. In the process, she injured her left ankle and foot. She sued Samuelson for damages. Is Samuelson liable? *Connolly v. Samuelson*, 671 F.Supp. 1312, **Web** 1987 U.S. Dist. Lexis 8308 (United States District Court for the District of Kansas)

3 Contract Liability Leroy Behlman and 18 other football fans from Connecticut and New York decided to attend the Super Bowl football game in New Orleans. They entered into contracts with Octagon Travel Center, Inc. (Octagon), a tour operator, and paid $399 each for transportation, lodging, and a ticket to the Super Bowl football game. They purchased the tour package through Universal Travel Agency, Inc. (Universal), a travel agency that acts as a broker for a number of airline companies and tour operators. The individual contracts, however, were between the football fans and Octagon. When they arrived in New Orleans, no tickets to the Super Bowl were forthcoming. Upon returning, they sued Universal for breach of contract. Is Universal liable? *Behlman v. Universal Travel Agency, Inc.*, 4 Conn.App. 688, 496 A.2d 962, **Web** 1985 Conn. App. Lexis 1092 (Appellate Court of Connecticut)

4 Power of Attorney As a result of marital problems, Howard R. Bankerd "left for the west," and Virginia Bankerd, his wife, continued to reside in their jointly owned home. Before his departure, Howard executed a power of attorney to Arthur V. King, which authorized King to "convey, grant, bargain, and/or sell" Howard's interest in the property. For the ensuing decade, Howard lived in various locations in Nevada, Colorado, and Washington but rarely contacted King. Howard made no payments on the mortgage, for taxes, or for maintenance or upkeep of the home.

Nine years later, Virginia, who was nearing retirement, requested King to exercise his power of attorney and transfer Howard's interest in the home to her. King's attempts to locate Howard were unsuccessful. He believed that Howard, who would then be 69 years of age, might be dead. King gifted Howard's interest in the property to Virginia, who sold the property for $62,500. Four years later, Howard returned and filed suit against King, alleging breach of trust and fiduciary duty. Is King liable? *King v. Bankerd*, 303 Md. 98, 492 A.2d 608, **Web** 1985 Md. Lexis 589 (Court of Appeals of Maryland)

5 Apparent Agency Robert Bolus was engaged in various businesses in which he sold and repaired trucks. He decided to build a truck repair facility in Bartonsville, Pennsylvania. Bolus contacted United Penn Bank (Bank) to obtain financing for the project and was referred to Emmanuel Ziobro, an assistant vice president. Ziobro orally agreed that Bank would provide funding for the project. He did not tell Bolus that he only had express authority to make loans of up to $10,000. After extending $210,000 in loans to Bolus, Bank refused to provide further financing. When Bolus defaulted on the loans, Bank pressed judgment against Bolus. Bank sought to recover Bolus's assets in payment for the loan. Bolus sued Bank for damages for breach of contract. Who wins? *Bolus v. United Penn Bank*, 363 Pa. Super. 247, 525 A.2d 1215, **Web** 1987 Pa. Super. Lexis 7258 (Superior Court of Pennsylvania)

6 Imputed Knowledge Iota Management Corporation entered into a contract to purchase the Bel Air West Motor Hotel in the city of St. Louis from Boulevard Investment Company. The agreement contained the following warranty: "Seller has no actual notice of any substantial defect in the structure of the Hotel or in any of its plumbing, heating, air-conditioning, electrical, or utility systems."

When the buyer inspected the premises, no leaks in the pipes were visible. Iota purchased the hotel for $2 million. When Iota removed some of the walls and ceilings during remodeling, it found evidence of prior repairs to leaking pipes and ducts, as well as devices for catching water (e.g., milk, cartons, cookie sheets, buckets). The estimate to repair these leaks was $500,000. Evidence at trial showed that Cecil Lillibridge, who was Boulevard's maintenance supervisor for the four years prior to the motor hotel's sale, had actual knowledge of these problems and had repaired some of the pipes. Iota sued Boulevard to rescind the contract. Is Boulevard liable? *Iota Management Corporation v. Boulevard Investment Company*, 731 S.W.2d 399, **Web** 1987 Mo.App. Lexis 4027 (Court of Appeals of Missouri)

BUSINESS ETHICS CASES

7 Business Ethics The Hagues, husband and wife, owned a 160-acre tract that they decided to sell. They entered into a listing agreement with Harvey C. Hilgendorf, a licensed real estate broker, which gave Hilgendorf the exclusive right to sell the property for a period of 12 months. The Hagues agreed to pay Hilgendorf a commission of 6 percent of the accepted sale price if a bona fide buyer was found during the listing period.

By letter 5 months later, the Hagues terminated the listing agreement with Hilgendorf. Hilgendorf did not acquiesce to the Hagues' termination, however. One month later, Hilgendorf presented an offer to the Hagues from a buyer willing to purchase the property at the full listing price. The Hagues ignored the offer and sold the property to another buyer. Hilgendorf sued the Hagues for breach of the agency agreement. Did the Hagues act ethically in this case? Who wins the lawsuit? *Hilgendorf v. Hague*, 293 N.W.2d 272, **Web** 1980 Iowa Sup. Lexis 882 (Supreme Court of Iowa)

8 Business Ethics Elizabeth Krempasky, who was 82 years old, owned a house and four certificates of deposit (CDs) at a bank. In her will, Krempasky devised her estate to her niece, Lydia Vrablova Wanamaker. Krempasky died while a patient at a hospital. Wanamaker, who was appointed executrix of the decedent's estate, could not find the CDs. Upon further inquiry, she discovered that the name of Anna A. Parana, an acquaintance of Krempasky's, had been added to the CDs on the day of the decedent's death. Evidence showed that (1) Parana prepared the forms necessary to authorize the bank to add her name to the CDs, (2) the decedent signed the forms on the day of her death sometime before dying at 2:45 P.M., and (3) Parana presented the authorization forms to the bank sometime between 3:00 P.M. and 4:00 P.M. on the same day. A transfer of CDs to joint tenancy is not effective until the bank officially makes the transfer on its records, which it did because it did not have notice of Krempasky's death. Wanamaker, as executrix of the decedent's estate, filed a petition requesting that the CDs be ordered returned to the decedent's estate. Is Anna Parana an agent of Elizabeth Krempasky? Did Parana act ethically in this case? *Estate of Krempasky*, 348 Pa. Super. 128, 501 A.2d 681, **Web** 1985 Pa. Super. Lexis 10545 (Superior Court of Pennsylvania)

LIABILITY OF PRINCIPALS, AGENTS, AND INDEPENDENT CONTRACTORS

LIABILITY OF PRINCIPALS, AGENTS, AND INDEPENDENT CONTRACTORS

▲ **New York City** *These are taxis in New York City. If a taxi driver owns his or her vehicle, the taxi owner is liable for injuries he or she causes while driving the taxi. Many taxis, however, are owned by one party, and another party—the taxi driver—is hired to drive the taxi. In this case, the owner of the taxi is the principal, and the driver is the agent. The owner of the taxi is liable for the negligent conduct of the driver while the driver is acting within the scope of employment.*

CHAPTER OBJECTIVES

After studying this chapter, you should be able to:

1. Describe the duty of loyalty owed by an agent to a principal.
2. Identify and describe the principal's liability for the tortious conduct of an agent.
3. Describe the principal's and agent's liability on third-party contracts.
4. Describe how independent contractor status is created.
5. Describe the principal's liability for torts of an independent contractor.

CHAPTER CONTENTS

"The law, wherein, as in a magic mirror, we see reflected not only our lives, but the lives of all men that have been! When I think on this majestic theme, my eyes dazzle."

—Oliver Wendell Holmes, Jr.
To the Suffolk Bar Association (1885)

INTRODUCTION TO LIABILITY OF PRINCIPALS, AGENTS, AND INDEPENDENT CONTRACTORS

Principals and agents owe certain duties to each other and are liable to each other for breaching these duties. When acting for the principal, an agent often enters into contracts and otherwise deals with third parties. Agency law has established certain rules that make principals, agents, and independent contractors liable to third persons for contracts and tortious conduct.

This chapter discusses the liability of principals, agents, and independent contractors to each other and to third parties.

AGENT'S DUTY OF LOYALTY TO THE PRINCIPAL

Because an agency relationship is based on trust and confidence, an agent owes the principal a **duty of loyalty** in all agency-related matters. Thus, an agent owes a fiduciary duty not to act adversely to the interests of the principal. If this duty is breached, the agent is liable to the principal. The most common types of breaches of loyalty by an agent are discussed in the following paragraphs.

agent's duty of loyalty
A fiduciary duty owed by an agent not to act adversely to the interests of the principal.

Self-Dealing

Agents are generally prohibited from undisclosed **self-dealing** with the principal.

Example A real estate agent who is employed to purchase real estate for a principal cannot secretly sell his own property to the principal. However, the deal is lawful if the principal agrees to buy the property after the agent discloses his ownership of the property.

Usurping an Opportunity

An agent cannot **usurp an opportunity** that belongs to the principal. A third-party offer to an agent must be conveyed to the principal. The agent cannot appropriate the opportunity for himself or herself unless the principal rejects it after due consideration. Opportunities to purchase real estate, businesses, products, ideas, and other property are subject to this rule.

Competing with the Principal

Agents are prohibited from **competing with the principal** during the course of an agency unless the principal agrees to the competition. The reason for this rule is that an agent cannot meet his or her duty of loyalty when his or her personal interests conflict with the principal's interests. If the parties have not entered into an enforceable covenant not to compete, the agent is free to compete with the principal when the agency has ended.

Misuse of Confidential Information

In the course of an agency, the agent often acquires confidential information about the principal's affairs (e.g., business plans, technological innovations, customer lists, trade

If we are industrious, we shall never starve; for, at the workingman's house hunger looks in, but dares not enter. Nor will the bailiff or the constable enter, for industry pays debts, while despair increaseth them.

Benjamin Franklin

secrets). The agent is under a legal duty not to disclose or **misuse confidential information** either during or after the course of the agency. There is no prohibition against using general information, knowledge, or experience acquired during the course of the agency.

Dual Agency

An agent cannot meet a duty of loyalty to two parties that have conflicting interests. **Dual agency** occurs when an agent acts for two or more different principals in the same transaction. This practice is generally prohibited unless all the parties involved in the transaction agree to it. If an agent acts as an undisclosed dual agent, he or she must forfeit all compensation received in the transaction. Some agents, such as middlemen and finders, are not considered dual agents. This is because they only bring interested parties together; they do not take part in any negotiations.

▶ TORT LIABILITY TO THIRD PARTIES

No nation was ever ruined by trade.

Benjamin Franklin

A principal and an agent are each personally liable for their own tortious conduct. The principal is liable for the tortious conduct of an agent who is acting within the scope of his or her authority. The agent, however, is liable for the tortious conduct of the principal only if he or she directly or indirectly participates in or aids and abets the principal's conduct.

The courts have applied a broad and flexible standard in interpreting scope of authority in the context of employment. Although other factors may also be considered, the courts answer the following questions to determine whether an agent's conduct occurred within the scope of his or her employment:

- Was the act specifically requested or authorized by the principal?
- Was it the kind of act that the agent was employed to perform?
- Did the act occur substantially within the time period of employment authorized by the principal?
- Did the act occur substantially within the location of employment authorized by the employer?
- Was the agent advancing the principal's purpose when the act occurred?

Where liability is found, tort remedies are available to the injured party. These remedies include recovery for medical expenses, lost wages, pain and suffering, emotional distress, and, in some cases, punitive damages. As discussed in the following paragraphs, the three main sources of **tort liability** for principals and agents are negligence, intentional torts, and misrepresentation.

Negligence

respondeat superior
A rule that says an employer is liable for the tortious conduct of its employees or agents while they are acting within the scope of its authority.

Principals are liable for the negligent conduct of agents acting within the scope of their employment. This liability is based on the common law doctrine of ***respondeat superior*** ("let the master answer"), which, in turn, is based on the legal theory of **vicarious liability** (liability without fault). In other words, the principal is liable because of his or her employment contract with the negligent agent, not because the principal was personally at fault.

The doctrine of **negligence** rests on the principle that if the principal expects to derive certain benefits from acting through others (i.e., an agent), that person should also bear the liability for injuries caused to third persons by the negligent conduct of an agent who is acting within the scope of his or her employment.

frolic and detour
A situation in which an agent does something during the course of his or her employment to further his or her own interests rather than the principal's.

Frolic and Detour Agents sometimes do things during the course of their employment to further their own interests rather than the principal's. For example, an agent might take a detour to run a personal errand while on assignment for the principal. This is commonly referred to as **frolic and detour**. Negligence actions stemming from frolic and detour are examined on a case-by-case basis. Agents are always personally liable for their tortious conduct in such situations. Principals are generally relieved of liability if the agent's frolic and detour is substantial. However, if the deviation is minor, the principal is liable for the injuries caused by the agent's tortious conduct.

The following case involves frolic and detour.

CASE 1 Frolic and Detour

Siegenthaler v. Johnson Welded Products, Inc.

2006 Ohio 5588, Web 2006 OhioApp. Lexis 5616 (2006)
Court of Appeals of Ohio

"No reasonable finder of fact could find from this evidence that Spires was subject to the direction and control of Johnson Welded Products as to the operation of his truck at the time of the collision, while he was on his way to a friend's house for lunch."

—Judge Fain

Facts

Jesse Spires was employed as a welder by Johnson Welded Products, Inc. Johnson Welded Products provides a lunchroom equipped with a microwave, refrigerator, and vending machine for sandwiches, snacks, and drinks. Spires worked a shift that ran from 3:15 P.M. until 12:15 A.M. One day at work, Spires was on his way to a friend's house for lunch during his lunch break, driving his own pickup truck, when he collided with Donald Siegenthaler, who was riding a motorcycle. The collision, which was the result of Spires's negligence, caused injury to Siegenthaler.

Siegenthaler sued Johnson Welded Products, alleging that Spires was an agent of Johnson Welded Products at the time of the accident and that Johnson Welded Products was vicariously liable under the doctrine of *respondeat superior*. Johnson Welded Products argued that Spires was on personal business when he caused the accident. The trial court granted Johnson Welded Products's motion for summary judgment. Siegenthaler appealed.

Issue

Was Spires an agent of Johnson Welded Products, acting within the scope of his employment, at the time of the accident that injured Siegenthaler?

Language of the Court

Under the doctrine of respondeat superior, *an employer will be held liable for the negligent act of its employee if the employee was acting within the course and scope of his employment. No reasonable finder of fact could find from this evidence that Spires was subject to the direction and control of Johnson Welded Products as to the operation of his truck at the time of the collision, while he was on his way to a friend's house for lunch.*

There is nothing in this record to suggest that Spires's contract of employment with Johnson Welded Products purported to give Johnson Welded Products the right to control the manner in which Spires would drive his own vehicle to or from work, and the only reasonable inference is that Johnson Welded Products had no right to control Spires's conduct in that matter. We can see no reason why Johnson Welded Products would have any desire to control the manner in which its employees drive to or from work.

Decision

The court of appeals held that Spires was not acting within his scope of employment when he collided with and injured Siegenthaler. The court of appeals affirmed the trial court's grant of summary judgment to Johnson Welded Products.

Case Questions

Critical Legal Thinking Describe the doctrine of *respondeat superior*. What does the doctrine of frolic and detour provide?

Business Ethics Could Siegenthaler recover from Spires? If so, under what legal theory? Did Siegenthaler act ethically in bringing this case against Johnson Welded Products?

Contemporary Business How important is the element of control in determining whether an employee is acting within the scope of his or her employment?

Coming and Going Rule Under the common law, a principal is generally not liable for injuries caused by its agents and employees while they are on their way to or from work. This rule, called the **coming and going rule**, applies even if the principal supplies the agent's automobile or other transportation or pays for gasoline, repairs, and other automobile operating expenses. This rule is quite logical. Because principals do not control where their agents and employees live, they should not be held liable for tortious conduct of agents on their way to and from work.

In the following case, the court applied the coming and going rule.

coming and going rule
A rule that says a principal is generally not liable for injuries caused by its agents and employees while they are on their way to or from work.

CASE 2 Coming and Going Rule

American National Property and Casualty Company v. Farah

2006 Ohio 5519, Web 2006 Ohio App. Lexis 5496 (2006)
Court of Appeals of Ohio

"Therefore, the trial court applied the coming and going rule and determined that Morgenstern was not in the course of his company's business at the time of the accident."

—Judge Klatt

Facts

Daniel J. Morgenstern was a licensed chiropractor and owned and was the sole shareholder of Daniel J. Morgenstern, D.C., Inc., d.b.a. Morning Star Chiropractic. He treated patients in an office located in Gahanna, Ohio. One day, when he did not have any scheduled appointments, he planned on meeting his wife at her sister's house. Around 11:00 A.M., Morgenstern drove to a restaurant for lunch. After having lunch, he headed toward his sister-in-law's house. On the way, he stopped at a grocery store in Columbus, Ohio. After leaving the store, his lunch began to "weigh a little heavy" on his stomach, so he decided to go to his office to take some nutrients for his stomach. On the way, Morgenstern collided with Ayan Farah's automobile. Farah was seriously injured as a result of the collision. Farah sued Morgenstern personally as well as his company, alleging that Morgenstern's negligence caused her injuries and that the company was vicariously liable.

American National Property and Casualty Company (ANPAC) insured Morgenstern personally for $250,000 for liability and insured the company for $1 million for liability. ANPAC filed a declaratory judgment action to resolve its insurance liability. ANPAC conceded that Morgenstern's $250,000 personal liability automobile insurance policy provided Farah with coverage. ANPAC argued, however, that its $1 million commercial automobile policy on the company did not cover Farah because Morgenstern was not acting in the scope of his employment when the accident happened. ANPAC argued that the coming and going rule protected it from liability. The trial court agreed with ANPAC and entered judgment in favor of ANPAC. Farah appealed.

Issue

Did the coming and going rule protect the company, and therefore ANPAC, from liability to Farah?

Language of the Court

In determining whether an employee has a fixed place of employment, and therefore is subject to the coming and going rule, courts have focused on when and where the employee commences his substantial employment duties. If an employee commences substantial employment duties only after arriving at a specific and identifiable work place designated by the employer, the employee has a fixed place of employment and the coming and going rule applies. In the case at bar, the trial court found that Morgenstern has a fixed place of employment. Therefore, the trial court applied the coming and going rule and determined that Morgenstern was not in the course of his company's business at the time of the accident. Consequently, there was no coverage under the company's commercial policy. We agree.

In the normal context, an employee's commute to a fixed work site bears no meaningful relation to his employment contract and serves no purpose of the employer's business. Morgenstern was driving to his office primarily because he did not feel well. Simply because he was listening to an audiotape of his lecture notes at the time of the accident does not change the fundamental character of the drive to his office. In conclusion, Morgenstern was driving to his Gahanna office at the time of the accident. That office was a fixed place of employment for Morgenstern. Thus, under the coming and going rule, he was not in the course of his company's business when he collided with appellant. Accordingly, ANPAC's commercial policy does not provide Morgenstern with coverage.

Decision

The court of appeals held that Morgenstern was not acting within the course of the company's business when he collided with Farah and that the coming and going rule applied. The court of appeals affirmed the trial court's judgment, which held that ANPAC's $1 million commercial policy insuring the company was not available to Farah's claims.

Case Questions

Critical Legal Thinking What does the coming and going rule provide? Explain. What is the public policy that supports the coming and going rule?

Business Ethics Did Morgenstern want to be found to have been acting within the scope of his company's employment when the accident happened? Why or why not? Was it unethical for ANPAC to deny coverage on its commercial insurance policy?

Contemporary Business Why did the injured victim, Farah, want Morgenstern to be found to be acting in the scope of the company's employment when the accident happened?

Dual-Purpose Mission Sometimes, a principal requests that an agent run errands or conduct other acts on his or her behalf while the agent or employee is on personal business. In this case, the agent is on a **dual-purpose mission**. That is, he or she is acting partly for himself or herself and partly for the principal. Most jurisdictions hold both the principal and the agent liable if the agent injures someone while on such a mission.

dual-purpose mission
An errand or another act that a principal requests of an agent while the agent is on his or her own personal business.

Example Suppose a principal asks an employee to drop off a package at a client's office on the employee's way home. If the employee negligently injures a pedestrian while on this dual-purpose mission, the principal is liable to the pedestrian.

Intentional Tort

Intentional torts include such acts as assault, battery, false imprisonment, and other intentional conduct that causes injury to another person. A principal is not liable for the intentional torts of agents and employees that are committed outside the principal's scope of business.

Example If an employee attends a sporting event after working hours and gets into a fight with another spectator at the event, the employer is not liable.

However, a principal is liable under the doctrine of vicarious liability for intentional torts of agents and employees committed within the agent's scope of employment. The courts generally apply one of the following tests in determining whether an agent's intentional torts were committed within the agent's scope of employment:

- **Motivation test.** Under the **motivation test**, if the agent's motivation in committing an intentional tort is to promote the principal's business, the principal is liable for any injury caused by the tort. However, if an agent's motivation in committing the intentional tort is personal, the principal is not liable, even if the tort takes place during business hours or on business premises.

motivation test
A test that determines whether an agent's motivation in committing an intentional tort is to promote the principal's business; if so, the principal is liable for any injury caused by the tort.

Example Under the motivation test, an employer—the principal—is not liable if his employee, who is motivated by jealousy, injures on the job someone who dated her boyfriend. Here, the motivation of the employee was personal and not for the promotion of the principal's business.

- **Work-related test.** Some jurisdictions have rejected the motivation test as too narrow. These jurisdictions apply the **work-related test** instead. Under this test, if an agent commits an intentional tort within a work-related time or space—for example, during working hours or on the principal's premises—the principal is liable for any injuries caused by the agent's intentional torts. Under this test, the agent's motivation is immaterial.

work-related test
A test that determines whether an agent committed an intentional tort within a work-related time or space; if so, the principal is liable for any injury caused by the agent's intentional tort.

Example Under the work-related test, an employer—the principal—is liable if his employee, who was motivated by jealousy, injures on the work premises and during work hours someone who dated her boyfriend. Here, the motivation of the employee is not relevant. What is relevant is that the intentional tort was committed on work premises and during the employee's work hours.

ETHICS SPOTLIGHT
Intentional Tort

Kenya Massey and her fiancée, Raymond Rodriquez, entered a Starbucks coffee shop in Manhattan, New York City. The couple ordered two beverages from Starbucks employee Okang Wilson and paid for the drinks. When Massey and Rodriquez moved toward the seating area while waiting for their drinks to be prepared, Karen Morales, the shift supervisor at the store, told Massey and Rodriquez that they could not sit down because the store was closing. Massey asked Morales what time the store closed, and Morales told her that it closed at 10:00. Massey pointed at a large digital clock across the street that read 9:52. Morales responded that it was

10:00 according to her watch and that she was closing the store.

Massey, who had not yet received her drinks, informed Morales that when she received her drinks, she and Rodriquez intended to sit and enjoy them at Starbucks. Morales instructed Starbucks employee Louis Suriel to cancel Massey's beverage order and refund Massey's money. Massey asked to speak with a manager. Morales identified herself as the manager and told Massey to "get a life." Massey insisted she was not leaving until she could file a complaint about Morales's behavior.

At that point, Starbucks employee Melissa Polanco became involved in the argument. She told Massey, "I get off at ten o'clock, and we can go outside." Rodriquez suggested to Massey that they leave voluntarily, and Massey agreed. Suriel apologized to them as Morales, Polanco, and Wilson held the door open for Massey and Rodriquez as they exited. The couple walked away from the store while Massey and the employees yelled profanities at each other.

As Massey continued to walk away, Polanco ran after and caught her and punched Massey in the face. Morales then jumped on Massey's back. Massey and Morales fell into a snow bank on the sidewalk, and a physical altercation ensued. A pedestrian passerby finally separated Massey and Morales. Massey's face was bleeding when she got up.

Massey pressed criminal charges against Morales and Polanco the next morning. Morales and Polanco each pleaded guilty to assault. All three Starbucks employees who were involved in the altercation—Morales, Polanco, and Wilson—were terminated by Starbucks. Massey sued Starbucks for damages for the injuries she suffered. Starbucks moved for summary judgment, alleging that the employees were not acting within the scope of their employment when they assaulted Massey.

The U.S. District Court held against Massey and granted Starbucks's motion for summary judgment. The Court found that the Starbucks employees were acting outside the scope of their employment when they assaulted Massey on the street. The court stated:

> *Massey contends that because her assault was sparked by a dispute concerning whether the store should close, the employees were acting in an employment capacity even when they chased Massey down the street. Massey fails to consider that she suffered no damages as a result of the dispute, but only as a result of the assault. Thus, the question for this court is not whether employees were acting within the scope of their employment when they first began arguing with Massey. Rather, the question is whether they were acting within the scope of their employment when they assaulted her.*
>
> *While the dispute may have started when the employees were acting within the scope of employment; it ended in an assault that was clearly outside of that scope. In this case, the employees did not assault Massey as part of their job. They did not attack Massey on the sidewalk to remove her from the store at closing time, or for any other employment-related purpose. In fact, the employees deliberately waited until Massey had voluntarily left the store before they assaulted her.*

The U.S. District Court held that the Starbucks employees were not acting within the scope of their employment when they assaulted Massey. The U.S. District Court granted Starbucks's motion for summary judgment. *Massey v. Starbucks Corporation*, **Web** 2004 U.S. Dist. Lexis 12993 (United States District Court for the Southern District of New York, 2004)

Business Ethics Was it ethical for Starbucks Corporation to deny liability in this case? Why or why not?

Misrepresentation

intentional misrepresentation
A deceit in which an agent makes an untrue statement that he or she knows is not true.

Intentional misrepresentations are also known as **fraud** or **deceit**. They occur when an agent makes statements that he or she knows are not true. An **innocent misrepresentation** occurs when an agent negligently makes a misrepresentation to a third party. A principal is liable for the intentional and innocent misrepresentations made by an agent acting within the scope of employment. The third party can either (1) rescind the contract with the principal and recover any consideration paid or (2) affirm the contract and recover damages.

Example Assume that (1) a car salesman is employed as an agent to sell the principal's car and (2) the principal tells the agent that the car was repaired after it was involved in a major accident. If the agent intentionally tells the buyer that the car was never involved in an accident, the agent has made an intentional misrepresentation. Both the principal and the agent are liable for this misrepresentation.

CONCEPT SUMMARY

TORT LIABILITY OF PRINCIPALS AND AGENTS TO THIRD PARTIES

Agent's Conduct	Agent Liable	Principal Liable
Negligence	Yes	The principal is liable under the doctrine of *respondeat superior* if the agent's negligent act was committed within his or her scope of employment.

Agent's Conduct	Agent Liable	Principal Liable
Intentional tort	Yes	*Motivation test*: The principal is liable if the agent's motivation in committing the intentional tort was to promote the principal's business.
	Yes	*Work-related test*: The principal is liable if the agent committed the intentional tort within work-related time and space.
Misrepresentation	Yes	The principal is liable for the intentional and innocent misrepresentations made by an agent acting within the scope of his or her authority.

CONTRACT LIABILITY TO THIRD PARTIES

A principal who authorizes an agent to enter into a contract with a third party is liable on the contract. Thus, the third party can enforce the contract against the principal and recover damages from the principal if the principal fails to perform it. The agent can also be held liable on the contract in certain circumstances. Imposition of **contract liability to third parties** depends on whether the agency is classified as fully disclosed, partially disclosed, or undisclosed.

Fully Disclosed Agency

A **fully disclosed agency** results if a third party entering into a contract knows (1) that the agent is acting as an agent for a principal and (2) the actual identity of the principal.[1] The third party has the requisite knowledge if the principal's identity is disclosed to the third party by either the agent or some other source.

fully disclosed agency
An agency in which a contracting third party knows (1) that the agent is acting for a principal and (2) the identity of the principal.

In a fully disclosed agency, the contract is between the principal and the third party. Thus, the principal, who is called a **fully disclosed principal**, is liable on the contract. The agent, however, is not liable on the contract because the third party relied on the principal's credit and reputation when the contract was made. An agent is liable on the contract if he or she guarantees that the principal will perform the contract.

The agent's signature on a contract entered into on the principal's behalf is important. It can establish the agent's status and, therefore, his or her liability. For instance, in a fully disclosed agency, the agent's signature must clearly indicate that he or she is acting as an agent for a specifically identified principal.

Examples Examples of proper signatures for an agent include "Allison Adams, agent for Peter Perceival," "Peter Perceival, by Allison Adams, agent," and "Peter Perceival, by Allison Adams."

Example Poran Kawamara decides to sell her house and hires Mark Robbins, a real estate broker, to list and sell the house for a price of $1 million. They agree that Mark will disclose the existence of the agency and the identity of the principal to interested third parties. This is a fully disclosed agency. Mark shows the house to Heather, a prospective buyer, and discloses to Heather that he is acting as an agent for Poran. Heather makes an offer for the house at the $1 million asking price. Mark signs the contract with Heather on behalf of Poran by signing "Mark Robbins, agent for Poran Kawamara." Poran is liable on the contract with Heather, but Mark is not liable on the contract with Heather.

Partially Disclosed Agency

A **partially disclosed agency** occurs if the agent discloses his or her agency status but does not reveal the principal's identity and the third party does not know the principal's identity from another source. The nondisclosure may be because (1) the principal instructs the agent not to disclose his or her identity to the third party or (2) the agent forgets to tell the third party the principal's identity. In this kind of agency, the principal is called a **partially disclosed principal**.

partially disclosed agency
An agency in which a contracting third party knows that the agent is acting for a principal but does not know the identity of the principal.

In a partially disclosed agency, both the principal and the agent are liable on a third-party contract.[2] This is because the third party must rely on the agent's reputation, integrity, and credit because the principal is unidentified. If the agent is made to pay the contract, the agent can sue the principal for indemnification. The third party and the agent can agree to relieve the agent's liability. A partially disclosed agency can be created either expressly or by mistake.

Example A principal and an agent agree that the agent will represent the principal to purchase a business and that the agent will disclose the existence of the agency and the identity of the principal to third parties; this is a fully disclosed agency. Suppose the agent finds a suitable business for the principal and contracts to purchase the business on behalf of the principal, but the agent mistakenly signs the contract with the third party "Allison Adams, agent." This is a partially disclosed agency that occurs because of mistake. The principal is liable on the contract with the third party, and the agent is also liable.

Undisclosed Agency

undisclosed agency
An agency in which a contracting third party does not know of either the existence of the agency or the principal's identity.

An **undisclosed agency** occurs when a third party is unaware of either the existence of an agency or the principal's identity. The principal is called an **undisclosed principal**. Undisclosed agencies are lawful. They are often used when the principal feels that the terms of the contract would be changed if his or her identity were known. For example, a wealthy person may use an undisclosed agency to purchase property if he thinks that the seller would raise the price of the property if his identity were revealed.

In an undisclosed agency, both the principal and the agent are liable on the contract with the third party. This is because the agent, by not divulging that he or she is acting as an agent, becomes a principal to the contract. The third party relies on the reputation and credit of the agent in entering into the contract. If the principal fails to perform the contract, the third party can recover against the principal or the agent. If the agent is made to pay the contract, he or she can recover indemnification from the principal. An undisclosed agency can be created either expressly or by mistake.

Example The Walt Disney Company wants to open a new theme park in Chicago but needs to first acquire land for the park. Disney employs an agent to work on its behalf to acquire the needed property, with an express agreement that the agent will not disclose the existence of the agency to a third-party seller. If a seller agrees to sell the needed land and the agent signs her name "Allison Adams," without disclosing the existence of the agency, it is an undisclosed agency. Disney is liable on the contract with the third-party seller, and so is the agent.

Agent Exceeding the Scope of Authority

implied warranty of authority
A warranty of an agent who enters into a contract on behalf of another party that he or she has the authority to do so.

ratification
A situation in which a principal accepts an agent's unauthorized contract.

An agent who enters into a contract on behalf of another party impliedly warrants that he or she has the authority to do so. This is called the agent's **implied warranty of authority**. If the agent exceeds the scope of his or her authority, the principal is not liable on the contract unless the principal **ratifies** it. The agent, however, is liable to the third party for breaching the implied warranty of authority. To recover, the third party must show (1) reliance on the agent's representation and (2) ignorance of the agent's lack of status.

CONCEPT SUMMARY

CONTRACT LIABILITY OF PRINCIPALS AND AGENTS TO THIRD PARTIES

Type of Agency	Principal Liable	Agent Liable
Fully disclosed	Yes	No, unless the agent (1) acts as a principal or (2) guarantees the performance of the contract
Partially disclosed	Yes	Yes, unless the third party relieves the agent's liability
Undisclosed	Yes	Yes
Nonexistent	No, unless the principal ratifies the contract	Yes, the agent is liable for breaching the implied warranty of authority.

INDEPENDENT CONTRACTOR

Principals often employ outsiders—that is, persons and businesses that are not employees—to perform certain tasks on their behalf. These persons and businesses are called **independent contractors**. The party that employs an independent contractor is called a *principal.*

independent contractor
"A person who contracts with another to do something for him who is not controlled by the other nor subject to the other's right to control with respect to his physical conduct in the performance of the undertaking" [*Restatement (Second) of Agency*].

Example Lawyers, doctors, dentists, consultants, stockbrokers, architects, certified public accountants, real estate brokers, and plumbers are examples of people who commonly act as independent contractors.

Example Jamie is a lawyer who has her own law firm and specializes in real estate law. Raymond, a real estate developer, hires Jamie to represent him in the purchase of land. Raymond is the principal, and Jamie is the independent contractor.

A principal–independent contractor relationship is depicted in Exhibit 1.

Exhibit 1
PRINCIPAL–INDEPENDENT CONTRACTOR RELATIONSHIP

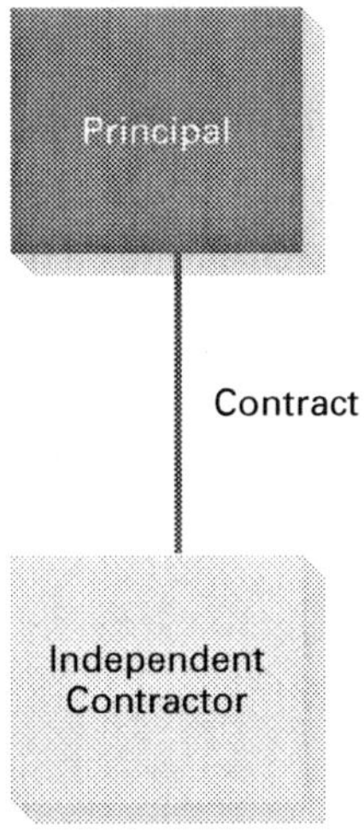

Factors for Determining Independent Contractor Status

Section 2 of the *Restatement (Second) of Agency* defines *independent contractor* as "a person who contracts with another to do something for him who is not controlled by the other nor subject to the other's right to control with respect to his physical conduct in the performance of the undertaking." Independent contractors usually work for a number of clients, have their own offices, hire employees, and control the performance of their work.

The crucial factor in determining whether someone is an independent contractor or an employee is the **degree of control** that the principal has over the agent. Critical factors in determining independent contractor status include:

- Whether the worker is engaged in a distinct occupation or an independently established business
- The length of time the agent has been employed by the principal
- The amount of time that the agent works for the principal
- Whether the principal supplies the tools and equipment used in the work
- The method of payment, whether by time or by the job
- The degree of skill necessary to complete the task
- Whether the worker hires employees to assist him or her
- Whether the employer has the right to control the manner and means of accomplishing the desired result

If an examination of these factors shows that the principal asserts little control, the person is an independent contractor. Substantial control indicates an employer–employee relationship. Labeling someone an independent contractor is only one factor in determining whether independent contractor status exists.

Liability for an Independent Contractor's Contracts

A principal can authorize an independent contractor to enter into contracts. Principals are bound by the authorized contracts of their independent contractors.

Nature seems to have taken a particular care to disseminate her blessings among the different regions of the world, with an eye to their mutual intercourse and traffic among mankind, that the nations of the several parts of the globe might have a kind of dependence upon one another and be united together by their common interest.

Joseph Addison

Example A client hires a lawyer as an independent contractor to represent her in a civil lawsuit against a defendant to recover monetary damages. If the client authorizes the lawyer to settle a case within a certain dollar amount and the lawyer does so, the settlement agreement is binding.

If an independent contractor enters into a contract with a third party on behalf of the principal, without express or implied authority from the principal to do so, the principal is not liable on the contract.

Liability for an Independent Contractor's Torts

Generally, a principal is not liable for the torts of its independent contractors. Independent contractors are personally liable for their own torts. The rationale behind this rule is that principals do not control the means by which the results are accomplished.

Example Qixia hires Harold, a lawyer and an independent contractor, to represent her in a court case. While driving to the courthouse to represent Qixia at trial, Harold negligently causes an automobile accident in which Mildred is severely injured. Harold is liable to Mildred because he caused the accident. Qixia is not liable to Mildred because Harold was an independent contractor when he caused the accident.

Exceptions in Which a Principal Is Liable for the Torts of an Independent Contractor

There are two exceptions in which the law imposes liability on a principal for the tortious conduct of an independent contractor he or she has hired:

1. **Inherently dangerous activities.** Principals cannot avoid strict liability for **inherently dangerous activities** assigned to independent contractors. For example, the use of explosives, clearing of land by fire, crop dusting, and such involve special risks that are shared by the principal.
2. **Negligence in the selection of an independent contractor.** A principal who hires an unqualified or known dangerous person as an independent contractor is liable if that person injures someone while on the job.

ETHICS SPOTLIGHT

Principal Liable for Repo Man's Tort

"The issue in this case is whether a secured creditor may avoid liability for breaches of the peace by using an independent contractor."

—Judge Mauzy

Yvonne Sanchez borrowed money from MBank El Paso (MBank) to purchase an automobile. She gave MBank a security interest in the vehicle to secure the loan. When Sanchez defaulted on the loan, MBank hired El Paso Recovery Service, an independent contractor, to repossess the automobile. The two men who were dispatched to Sanchez's house found the car parked in the driveway and hooked it to a tow truck. Sanchez demanded that they cease their efforts and leave the premises, but the men nonetheless continued with the repossession. Before the men could tow the automobile into the street, Sanchez jumped into the car, locked the doors, and refused to leave. The men towed the car at a high rate of speed to the repossession yard. They parked the car in the fenced repossession yard, with Sanchez inside, and padlocked the gate. Sanchez was left in the repossession lot with a Doberman Pinscher guard dog loose in the yard. Later, she was rescued by the police. The law prohibits the repossession of a vehicle if a breach of peace would occur. Sanchez filed suit against MBank, alleging that it was liable for the tortious conduct of El Paso Recovery Service. The trial court granted summary judgment to MBank, but the court of appeals reversed. MBank appealed.

The supreme court of Texas held that MBank, the principal, was liable for the tortious conduct of El Paso Recovery Service, an independent contractor. The court held that the act of repossessing an automobile from a defaulting debtor is an inherently dangerous activity and a nondelegable duty. The court concluded that El Paso Recovery Service had breached the peace in repossessing the car from Sanchez and caused her physical and emotional harm. The court held that MBank, the principal, could not escape liability by hiring an independent contractor to do this task. The court found MBank liable to Sanchez. *MBank El Paso, N.A. v. Sanchez*, 836 S.W.2d 151, **Web** 1992 Tex. Lexis 97 (Supreme Court of Texas)

Business Ethics Did the independent contractor act responsibly in this case? Should the principal bank have been held liable in this case? Why or why not?

TEST REVIEW TERMS AND CONCEPTS

Agent's duty of loyalty
Coming and going rule
Competing with the principal
Contract liability to third parties
Degree of control
Dual agency
Dual-purpose mission
Frolic and detour
Fully disclosed agency
Fully disclosed principal
Implied warranty of authority
Independent contractor
Inherently dangerous activity
Innocent misrepresentation
Intentional misrepresentation (fraud or deceit)
Intentional tort
Misuse of confidential information
Motivation test
Negligence
Partially disclosed agency
Partially disclosed principal
Ratification
Respondeat superior
Self-dealing
Tort liability
Undisclosed agency
Undisclosed principal
Usurping an opportunity
Vicarious liability
Work-related test

CASE PROBLEMS

1 Fiduciary Duty After Francis Pusateri retired, he met with Gilbert J. Johnson, a stockbroker with E. F. Hutton & Co., Inc., and informed Johnson that he wished to invest in tax-free bonds and money market accounts. Pusateri opened an investment account with E. F. Hutton and checked a box stating that his objective was "tax-free income and moderate growth." During the course of a year, Johnson churned Pusateri's account to make commissions and invested Pusateri's funds in volatile securities and options. Johnson kept telling Pusateri that his account was making money, and the monthly statement from E. F. Hutton did not indicate otherwise. The manager at E. F. Hutton was aware of Johnson's activities but did nothing to prevent them. When Johnson left E. F. Hutton, Pusateri's account—which had been called the "laughingstock" of the office—had shrunk from $196,000 to $96,880. Pusateri sued E. F. Hutton for damages. Is E. F. Hutton liable? *Pusateri v. E. F. Hutton & Co., Inc.*, 180 Cal.App.3d 247, 225 Cal.Rptr. 526, **Web** 1986 Cal.App. Lexis 1502 (Court of Appeal of California)

2 Fiduciary Duty Boettcher DTC Building Joint Venture (Boettcher) owned an office building in which it leased space to tenants. Harmon Wilfred, an independent leasing agent, contacted Boettcher on behalf of Landmark Associates (Landmark), which was interested in leasing office space in the Boettcher building. Wilfred represented Boettcher as a special agent in the transaction. Landmark executed a 68-month lease with Boettcher. Boettcher paid Wilfred a commission. Shortly thereafter, Landmark began negotiating with Boettcher for additional lease space. Landmark also contacted Wilfred to inquire about the availability of lease space in other buildings. When Wilfred found lease space for Landmark in another office building, Landmark vacated its premises at the Boettcher building and defaulted on its lease agreement. Boettcher sued Wilfred for damages, alleging that Wilfred had violated his fiduciary duty to Boettcher. Who wins? *Boettcher DTC Building Joint Venture v. Wilfred*, 762 P.2d 788, **Web** 1988 Colo.App. Lexis. 323 (Court of Appeals of Colorado)

3 Duty of Loyalty Peter Shields was the president and a member of the board of directors of Production Finishing Corporation for seven years. The company provided steel polishing services. It did most, if not all, of the polishing work in the Detroit area, except for that of the Ford Motor Company. (Ford did its own polishing.) On a number of occasions, Shields discussed with Ford, on behalf of Production Finishing, the possibility of providing Ford's steel polishing services. When Shields learned that Ford was discontinuing its polishing operation, he incorporated Flat Rock Metal and submitted a confidential proposal to Ford which provided that he would buy Ford's equipment and provide polishing services to Ford. It was not until he resigned from Production Finishing that he informed the board of directors that he was pursuing the Ford business himself. Production Finishing sued Shields. Did

Shields breach his fiduciary duty of loyalty to Production Finishing? Who wins? *Production Finishing Corporation v. Shields*, 158 Mich.App. 479, 405 N.W.2d 171, **Web** 1987 Mich.App. Lexis 2379 (Court of Appeals of Michigan)

4 Independent Contractor The Butler Telephone Company, Inc. (Butler), contracted with the Sandidge Construction Company to lay 18 miles of telephone cable in a rural area. In the contract, Butler reserved the right to inspect the work for compliance with the terms of the contract. Butler did not control how Sandidge performed the work. Johnnie Carl Pugh, an employee of Sandidge, was killed on the job when the sides to an excavation in which he was working caved in on top of him. Evidence disclosed that the excavation was not properly shored or sloped and that it violated general safety standards. Pugh's parents and estate brought a wrongful death action against Butler. Is Butler liable? *Pugh v. Butler Telephone Company, Inc.*, 512 So.2d 1317, **Web** 1987 Ala. Lexis 4468 (Supreme Court of Alabama)

5 Personal Guaranty Sebastian International, Inc. entered into a five-year lease to lease a building in Chadsworth, California. Just over two years later, with the consent of the master lessors, Sebastian sublet the building to West Valley Grinding, Inc. In conjunction with the execution of the sublease, the corporate officers of West Valley, including Kenneth E. Peck, each signed a guaranty of lease, personally ensuring the payment of West Valley's rental obligations. The guaranty contract referred to Peck in his individual capacity; however, on the signature line, he was identified as "Kenneth Peck, Vice President." Eight months later, West Valley went out of business, leaving 24 months remaining on the sublease. After unsuccessful attempts to secure another sublessee, Sebastian surrendered the leasehold back to the master lessors and brought suit against Peck to recover the unpaid rent. Peck argued that he was not personally liable because his signature was that of an agent for a disclosed principal and not that of a principal himself. Who wins? *Sebastian International, Inc. v. Peck*, 195 Cal.App.3d 803, 240 Cal.Rptr. 911, **Web** 1987 Cal. App. Lexis 2237 (Court of Appeal of California)

6 Contract Liability G. Elvin Grinder of Marbury, Maryland, was a building contractor who, for years, did business as an individual and traded as "Grinder Construction." Grinder maintained an open account on his individual credit, with Bryans Road Building & Supply Co., Inc. Grinder would purchase materials and supplies from Bryans on credit and later pay the invoices. G. Elvin Grinder Construction, Inc., a Maryland corporation, was formed, with Grinder personally owning 52 percent of the stock of the corporation. Grinder did not inform Bryans that he had incorporated, and he continued to purchase supplies on credit from Bryans under the name "Grinder Construction." Five years later, after certain invoices were not paid by Grinder, Bryans sued Grinder personally to recover. Grinder asserted that the debts were owed by the corporation. Bryans amended its complaint to include the corporation as a defendant. Who is liable to Bryans? *Grinder v. Bryans Road Building & Supply Co., Inc.*, 290 Md. 687, 432 A.2d 453, **Web** 1981 Md. Lexis 246 (Court of Appeals of Maryland)

7 Dual Agency Chemical Bank was the primary bank for Washington Steel Corporation. As an agent for Washington Steel, Chemical Bank expressly and impliedly promised that it would advance the best interests and welfare of Washington Steel. During the course of the agency, Washington Steel provided the bank with comprehensive and confidential financial information, other data, and future business plans.

At some point during the agency, TW Corporation and others approached Chemical Bank to request a loan of $7 million to make a hostile tender offer for the stock of Washington Steel. Chemical Bank agreed and became an agent for TW. Management at Chemical Bank did not disclose to Washington Steel its adverse relationship with TW, did not request Washington Steel's permission to act as an agent for TW, and directed employees of the bank to conceal from Washington Steel the bank's involvement with TW. After TW commenced its public tender offer, Washington Steel filed suit, seeking to obtain an injunction against Chemical Bank and TW. Who wins? *Washington Steel Corporation v. TW Corporation*, 465 F.Supp. 1100, **Web** 1979 U.S. Dist. Lexis 14391 (United States District Court for the Western District of Pennsylvania)

8 Tort Liability Ray Johnson and his eight-year-old son, David, were waiting for a "walk" sign before crossing a street in downtown Salt Lake City. A truck owned by Newspaper Agency Corporation (NAC) and operated by its employee, Donald Rogers, crossed the intersection and jumped the curb, killing David and injuring Ray. Before reporting for work on the evening of the accident, Rogers had consumed approximately seven mixed drinks containing vodka and had chugalugged a 27-ounce drink containing two minibottles of tequila. His blood alcohol content after the accident was .18 percent.

Evidence showed that the use of alcohol and marijuana was widespread at NAC and that the company made no effort to curtail such use. Evidence further showed that NAC vehicles were returned with beer cans in them and that on one occasion, an NAC supervisor who had observed drivers smoking marijuana had told the drivers to "do it on the road." Ray Johnson sued Rogers and NAC for the wrongful death of his child, David, and physical injury to Ray. Is NAC liable? *Johnson v. Rogers*, 763 P.2d 771, 90 Utah Adv.Rep.3, **Web** 1988 Utah Lexis 81 (Supreme Court of Utah)

9 Tort Liability Intrastate Radiotelephone, Inc., was a public utility that supplied radiotelephone utility service to the general public for radiotelephones, pocket pagers, and beepers. Robert Kranhold, an employee of Intrastate, was authorized to use his personal vehicle on company business. One morning, when Kranhold was driving his vehicle to Intrastate's main office, he negligently struck a motorcycle being driven by Michael S. Largey, causing severe and permanent injuries to

Largey. The accident occurred at the intersection where Intrastate's main office is located. Evidence showed that Kranhold acted as a consultant to Intrastate, worked both in and out of Intrastate's offices, had no set hours of work, often attended meetings at Intrastate's offices, and went to Intrastate's offices to pick things up or drop things off. Largey sued Intrastate for damages. Is Intrastate liable? *Largey v. Radiotelephone, Inc.*, 136 Cal.App.3d 660, 186 Cal.Rptr. 520, **Web** 1982 Cal.App. Lexis 2049 (Court of Appeal of California)

10 Tort Liability Donnie Joe Jackson hired Ted Green to do some remodeling work on his house. Jackson never paid Green for his work, and a dispute arose as to how much was owed to Green. Jackson worked at the Higgenbotham-Bartlett Lumber Company, a lumberyard where Green often purchased lumber and supplies. During the course of the following year, when Green went to the lumberyard to do business, Jackson verbally accosted him on at least three separate occasions. Each time, Green left the lumberyard. Green, accompanied by his son, made two trips to the facility. On the first trip, Jackson and Green had a verbal altercation. On the second trip, Jackson hit Green, knocking him unconscious and causing injuries. Green sued Jackson's employer for damages. Is the lumber company liable for the intentional tort of its agent? *Green v. Jackson*, 674 S.W.2d 395, **Web** 1984 Tex. App. Lexis 5592 (Court of Appeals of Texas)

BUSINESS ETHICS CASES

11 Business Ethics William Venezio, a real estate broker, conducted his business under the trade name King Realty and had properly filed the required name certificate in the Schenectady County clerk's office. King Realty entered into a contract to purchase property located in the town of Rotterdam, Schenectady County, from Ermino Bianchi. Venezio signed the end of the contract "King Realty for Customer." Four days later, King Realty entered into a contract to sell the property to Mario Attanasio. However, Bianchi refused to sell the property to King Realty, alleging that because the original contract had failed to adequately identify the purchaser, there was not a binding contract. Venezio, d.b.a. King Realty, brought an action for specific performance against Bianchi. Was it ethical for Bianchi to try to back out of the contract? Can King Realty, as an agent for a partially disclosed principal, enforce the contract against Bianchi? *Venezio v. Bianchi*, 124 A.D.2d 933, 508 N.Y.S.2d 349, **Web** 1986 N.Y.App. Div. Lexis 62252 (Supreme Court of New York)

12 Business Ethics National Biscuit Company (Nabisco) is a corporation that produces and distributes cookies and other food products to grocery stores and other outlets across the nation. Nabisco hired Ronnell Lynch as a cookie salesman-trainee and eventually assigned Lynch to his own sales territory. Lynch's duties involved making sales calls, taking orders, and making sure that shelves of stores in his territory were stocked with Nabisco products. During the first two months, Nabisco received numerous complaints from store owners in Lynch's territory that Lynch was overly aggressive and was taking for Nabisco products shelf space that was reserved for competing brands.

One day, after having been in his territory for two months, Lynch visited a grocery store that was managed by Jerome Lange. Lynch was there to place previously delivered merchandise on the store's shelves. An argument developed between Lynch and Lange. Lynch became very angry and started swearing. Lange told Lynch to stop swearing or leave the store because children were present. Lynch became uncontrollably angry and went behind the counter and dared Lange to fight. When Lange refused to fight, Lynch proceeded to viciously assault and batter Lange, causing severe injuries. When Lange sued Nabisco, Nabisco denied liability. Was it ethical for Nabisco to deny liability in this case? Do you think the prior complaints against Lynch had any effect on the decision reached in this case? Is Nabisco liable for the intentional tort (assault and battery) of its employee Ronnell Lynch? *Lange v. National Biscuit Company*, 297 Minn. 399, 211 N.W.2d 783, **Web** 1973 Minn. Lexis 1106 (Supreme Court of Minnesota)

ENDNOTES

1. *Restatement (Second) of Agency*, Section 4.
2. *Restatement (Second) of Agency*, Section 321.

PERSONAL PROPERTY AND BAILMENT

PERSONAL PROPERTY AND BAILMENT

▲ **Grand Hotel, Mackinac Island, Michigan** *Almost all states have enacted innkeepers' statutes that limit the liability of innkeepers for loss of guests' property if certain statutory requirements are met.*

CHAPTER OBJECTIVES

After studying this chapter, you should be able to:

1. Define *personal property*.
2. Describe the methods for acquiring and transferring ownership in personal property.
3. Describe and apply rules regarding ownership rights in mislaid, lost, and abandoned property.
4. List and describe the elements for creating a bailment.
5. Explain the liability of bailees for lost, damaged, or destroyed goods.

CHAPTER CONTENTS

"Property and law are born and must die together."

—Jeremy Bentham
Principles of the Civil Code, I Works 309

INTRODUCTION TO PERSONAL PROPERTY AND BAILMENT

Private ownership of property forms the foundation of our economic system. Therefore, a comprehensive body of law has been developed to protect property rights. The law protects the rights of property owners to use, sell, dispose of, control, and prevent others from trespassing on their rights.

This chapter discusses the kinds of personal property, methods of acquiring ownership in personal property, and property rights in mislaid, lost, and abandoned property. This chapter also discusses bailment, situations in which possession of (but not title to) personal property is delivered to another party for transfer, safekeeping, or some other purpose.

PERSONAL PROPERTY

There are two kinds of property: *real property* and *personal property*. Real property includes land and property that is permanently attached to it. For example, minerals, crops, timber, and buildings that are attached to land are generally considered real property. **Personal property** (sometimes referred to as *goods* or *chattels*) consists of everything that is not real property. Real property can become personal property if it is removed from the land. For example, a tree that is part of a forest is real property; a tree that is cut down is personal property.

personal property
Tangible property such as automobiles, furniture, and equipment, and intangible property such as securities, patents, and copyrights.

Personal property that is permanently affixed to land or buildings is called a **fixture**. Such property, which includes things like heating systems and storm windows, is categorized as real property. Unless otherwise agreed, fixtures remain with a building when it is sold. Personal property (e.g., furniture, pictures, other easily portable household items) may be removed by the seller prior to sale.

Personal property can be either tangible or intangible. **Tangible property** includes physically defined property, such as goods, animals, and minerals. **Intangible property** represents rights that cannot be reduced to physical form, such as stock certificates, certificates of deposit, bonds, and copyrights.

tangible property
All real property and physically defined personal property, such as buildings, goods, animals, and minerals.

intangible property
Rights that cannot be reduced to physical form, such as stock certificates, certificates of deposit, bonds, and copyrights.

Real and personal property may be owned by one person or by more than one person. If property is owned concurrently by two or more persons, there is *concurrent ownership*.

ACQUIRING OWNERSHIP OF PERSONAL PROPERTY

Personal property can be acquired or transferred with a minimum of formality. Commerce would be severely curtailed if the transfer of such items were difficult. The methods for acquiring ownership in personal property are possession or capture, purchase, production, gift, will, inheritance, accession, confusion, and divorce. These methods are discussed in the following paragraphs.

Possession or Capture

A person can acquire ownership in unowned personal property by **taking possession** of it, or **capturing** it. The most notable unowned objects are things in their natural state. This type of property acquisition was important when this country was being developed. In today's urbanized society, however, there are few unowned objects, and this method of acquiring ownership in personal property has become less important.

Example Someone who obtains the proper fishing license acquires ownership of all the fish he or she catches.

Purchase

The most common method of acquiring title to personal property is by *purchasing* the property from its owner.

Example Urban Concrete owns a large piece of equipment. City Builders purchases the equipment from Urban Concrete for $100,000. Urban Concrete transfers title to the equipment to City Builders. City Builders is now the owner of the equipment.

Production

Only a ghost can exist without material property.

Ayn Rand
Atlas Shrugged (1957)

Production is a common method of acquiring ownership in personal property. A manufacturer that purchases raw materials and produces a finished product owns that product.

Gift

gift
The voluntary transfer of title to property without payment of consideration by the donee. To be a valid gift, three elements must be shown: (1) donative intent, (2) delivery, and (3) acceptance.

donor
A person who gives a gift.

donee
A person who receives a gift.

gift *inter vivos*
A gift made during a person's lifetime that is an irrevocable present transfer of ownership.

gift *causa mortis*
A gift that is made in contemplation of death.

A **gift** is a voluntary transfer of property without consideration. The lack of consideration is what distinguishes a gift from a purchase. The person making a gift is called the **donor**. The person who receives a gift is called the **donee**. There are three elements of a valid gift:

1. **Donative intent.** For a gift to be effective, the donor must have intended to make a gift. **Donative intent** can be inferred from the circumstances or language used by the donor. The courts also consider such factors as the relationship of the parties, the size of the gift, and the mental capacity of the donor.
2. **Delivery.** **Delivery** must occur for there to be a valid gift. Although **physical delivery** is the usual method of transferring personal property, it is sometimes impracticable. In such circumstances, **constructive delivery** (or *symbolic delivery*) is sufficient. For example, if the property being gifted is kept in a safe-deposit box, physically giving the key to the donee is enough to signal the gift. Most intangible property is transferred by written conveyance (e.g., conveying a stock certificate represents a transfer of ownership in a corporation).
3. **Acceptance.** **Acceptance** is usually not a problem because most donees readily accept gifts. In fact, the courts presume acceptance unless there is proof that the gift was refused. Nevertheless, a person cannot be forced to accept an unwanted gift.

CONTEMPORARY ENVIRONMENT

Gift *Inter Vivos* and Gift *Causa Mortis*

A gift can be classified as either a gift *inter vivos* or a gift *causa mortis*. A gift made during a person's lifetime that is an irrevocable present transfer of ownership is a **gift *inter vivos***.

A **gift *causa mortis*** is a gift made in contemplation of death. A gift *causa mortis* is established when (1) the donor makes a gift in anticipation of approaching death from some existing sickness or peril and (2) the donor dies from such sickness or peril without having revoked the gift. A gift *causa mortis* can be revoked by the donor up until the time he or she dies. A gift *causa mortis* takes precedence over a prior conflicting will.

Example Sandy is a patient in a hospital. She is to have a major operation from which she may not recover. Prior to going into surgery, Sandy removes her diamond ring and gives it to her friend Pamela, stating, "In the event of my death, I want you to have this." This gift is a gift *causa mortis*. If Sandy dies from the operation, the gift is effective, and Pamela owns the ring. If Sandy lives, the requisite condition for the gift (her death) has not occurred; therefore, the gift is not effective, and Sandy can recover the ring from Pamela.

Uniform Gifts to Minors Act and Uniform Transfers to Minors Act

Many states have adopted in whole or part the **Uniform Gifts to Minors Act (UGMA)** or the **Uniform Transfers to Minors Act (UTMA)**. These acts were drafted by the National Conference of Commissioners on Uniform State Laws and do not become the law of a state until that state's legislature enacts the act as a statute. These laws establish procedures for adults to make irrevocable gifts of money and securities to minors. Gifts of money can be made by depositing the money in an account in a financial institution, with the donor or another trustee (e.g., another adult or bank) as custodian for the minor. Gifts of securities can be made by registering the securities in the name of a trustee as custodian for the minor.

Uniform Gifts to Minors Act and Uniform Transfers to Minors Act
Acts that establish procedures for adults to make gifts of money and securities to minors.

Will or Inheritance

Title to personal property is frequently acquired by **will** or **inheritance**. If the person who dies has a valid will, the property is distributed to the **beneficiaries**, pursuant to the provisions of that will. If a person dies without having executed a will, the property is distributed to the **heirs** as provided in the relevant state's inheritance statute.

Accession

Accession occurs when the value of personal property increases because it is added to or improved by natural or manufactured means. Accession that occurs naturally belongs to the owner.

accession
An increase in the value of personal property because it is added to or improved by natural or manufactured means.

Example Julie owns a mare named Echo. Echo gives birth to a colt. Pursuant to accession, Julie owns the newborn colt.

If an improvement is made wrongfully, the owner acquires title to the improved property and does not have to pay the improver for the value of the improvements.

Example Suppose a thief steals a car and puts a new engine in it. The owner is entitled to recover the car as improved and does not have to pay the thief for the improvements.

If an improvement is mistakenly made by an improver and the improvement can be easily separated from the original article, the improver must remove the improvement and pay any damages caused by such removal.

Example A builder who puts the wrong door on a house must replace that door with the correct door at his own cost.

If an improvement is mistakenly made by an improver, and the improvement cannot be removed from the original article, the owner owns title to the improved property and does not have to pay the improver for the improvement.

Example If a builder misreads blueprints and extends an addition to a building farther than the owner has contracted for, the owner of the building is entitled to keep the improvement at no extra cost.

Confusion

Confusion occurs if two or more persons commingle **fungible goods** (i.e., goods that are exactly alike, such as the same grade of oil, grain, or cattle). Title to goods can be acquired by confusion. The owners share ownership in the commingled goods in proportion to the amount of goods contributed by each owner. It does not matter whether the goods were

Personal property has no locality.

Chief Justice Lord Loughborough
Sill v. Worswick (1971)

commingled by agreement or by accident. If goods are wrongfully or intentionally commingled without permission, the innocent party acquires title to them.

Example If three farmers voluntarily agree to store the same amount of Grade B winter wheat in a silo, each of them owns one-third. When the grain is sold, the profits are divided into three parts; if the silo burns to the ground, each farmer suffers one-third of the loss.

Divorce

When a marriage is dissolved by a **divorce**, the parties obtain certain rights in the property that comprises the marital estate. Often, a settlement of property rights is reached. If not, the court must decide the property rights of the spouses.

▶ MISLAID, LOST, AND ABANDONED PERSONAL PROPERTY

Often, people find other people's personal property. Ownership rights to found property differ, depending on whether the property was mislaid, lost, or abandoned. The following paragraphs discuss these legal rules.

Mislaid Property

mislaid property
Property that an owner voluntarily places somewhere and then inadvertently forgets.

Property is **mislaid** when its owner voluntarily places the property somewhere and then inadvertently forgets it. It is likely that the owner will return for the property upon realizing that it was misplaced.

The owner of the premises where the property is mislaid is entitled to take possession of the property against all except the rightful owner. This right is superior to the rights of the person who finds it. Such possession does not involve a change of title. Instead, the owner of the premises becomes an involuntary bailee of the property and owes a duty to take reasonable care of the property until it is reclaimed by the owner. (Bailments are discussed later in this chapter.)

Example Felicity is on a business trip and stays in a hotel during her trip. Felicity accidentally leaves her diamond engagement ring in the hotel room she has stayed in and checks out of the hotel. The engagement ring is mislaid property, and the hotel has a duty to return it to Felicity, its rightful owner.

Lost Property

lost property
Property that the owner leaves somewhere due to negligence, carelessness, or inadvertence.

Property is considered **lost property** when its owner negligently, carelessly, or inadvertently leaves it somewhere. The finder obtains title to such property against the whole world except the true owner. The lost property must be returned to its rightful owner, whether the finder discovers the loser's identity or the loser finds the finder. A finder who refuses to return the property to the loser is liable for the tort of conversion and the crime of larceny. Many states require the finder to conduct a reasonable search (e.g., place advertisements in newspapers) to find the rightful owner.

Example If a commuter finds a laptop computer on the floor of a subway station in New York City, the computer is considered lost property. The finder can claim title to the computer against the whole world except the true owner. If the true owner discovers that the finder has her computer, she may recover it from the finder. If there is identification of the owner on the computer (e.g., name, address, and telephone number), the finder owes a duty to contact the rightful owner and give back the computer.

ETHICS SPOTLIGHT

Estray Statute

Most states have enacted **estray statutes** that permit a finder of mislaid or lost property to clear title to the property if:

- The finder reports the found property to the appropriate government agency and then turns over possession of the property to this agency.
- Either the finder or the government agency posts notices and publishes advertisements describing the lost property.
- A specified time (usually a year or a number of years) has passed without the rightful owner's reclaiming the property.

Many state estray statutes provide that the government receive a portion of the value of the property. Some statutes provide that title cannot be acquired in found property that is the result of illegal activity. For example, title has been denied to finders of property and money deemed to have been used for illegal drug purchases.

Business Ethics Do estray statutes encourage ethical behavior? Explain.

The following case involves the distinction between lost and mislaid property.

estray statute
A statute that permits a finder of mislaid or lost property to clear title to the property if certain prescribed legal formalities are met.

CASE 1 Estray Statute

Willsmore v. Township of Oceola, Michigan

106 Mich.App. 671, 308 N.W.2d 796, Web 1981 Mich.App. Lexis 2993
Court of Appeals of Michigan

"The Lost Goods Act provides certainty of title to property by eventually vesting clear title after a set period of time. It encourages honesty in finders."

—Judge Corsiglia

Facts

While hunting on unposted and unoccupied property in Oceola Township, Michigan, Duane Willsmore noticed an area with branches arranged in a crisscross pattern. When he kicked aside the branches and sod, he found a watertight suitcase in a freshly dug hole. Willsmore informed the Michigan State Police of his find. A state trooper and Willsmore together pried open the suitcase and discovered $383,840 in cash. The state police took custody of the money, which was deposited in an interest-bearing account. Michigan's Lost Goods Act provides that the finder and the township in which the property was found must share the value of the property if the finder publishes required notices and the true owner does not claim the property within one year.

Willsmore published the required notices and brought a declaratory judgment action, seeking a determination of the ownership of the money. Thomas Powell, the owner of the land on which the suitcase was found, claimed he was the owner of the suitcase. After Powell incorrectly named the amount of money in the suitcase, he asserted his Fifth Amendment right not to testify at his deposition and at trial. The trial court awarded the money equally to Willsmore and the Township of Oceola. Powell appealed.

Issue

Who is the owner of the lost briefcase and its contents?

Language of the Court

It is a universally accepted fundamental principle of property law that the true owner, assuming he presented himself within the one-year statute of limitations of the Lost Goods Act, would be entitled to the money before any other party in this case.

Voluntarily, and perhaps wisely, claimant Powell did not present himself at trial. At Powell's deposition, virtually the only answer he would give was the bald assertion that he was the true owner of the money. When asked the sum of money in the suitcase, his answer was incorrect. When faced with questions about how he obtained the money and hid it, claimant Powell had the right to assert his constitutional privilege to remain silent. However, the court not only had the right, but also the duty, to conclude from such silence that claimant Powell did not carry his burden of proof. Claimant Powell's claim as true owner fails as a matter of law. The

(case continues)

trial court was justified in granting a directed verdict against claimant Powell, claiming as the true owner.

The Lost Goods Act provides certainty of title to property by eventually vesting clear title after a set period of time. It encourages honesty in finders. The public obtains a portion of the benefit of a find through receipt of one-half of the value by the township. The finder receives an award for his honesty by receiving one-half of the value of the property plus costs.

Decision

The court of appeals held that Willsmore and the Township of Oceola were the owners of the briefcase and its contents. The court of appeals affirmed the judgment of the trial court and ordered that Willsmore and the township each receive one-half the proceeds of the find after Willsmore's costs were deducted.

Case Questions

Critical Legal Thinking What is an estray statute? What is the public policy underlying an estray statute?

Business Ethics If you had found the suitcase, would you have turned it in to the government? Or would you have opened it? If you had found the $383,840 in cash, would you have kept it or turned it in to the government?

Contemporary Business Should the government be entitled to half the find? Does this rule encourage finders to turn in their finds? Explain.

Abandoned Property

abandoned property
Property that an owner has discarded with the intent to relinquish his or her rights in it and mislaid or lost property that the owner has given up any further attempts to locate.

Property is classified as **abandoned property** if (1) an owner discards the property with the intent to relinquish his or her rights in it or (2) an owner of mislaid or lost property gives up any further attempts to locate it. Anyone who finds abandoned property acquires title to it. The title is good against the whole world, including the original owner.

Example Property left at a garbage dump is abandoned property. It belongs to the first person who claims it.

CONCEPT SUMMARY
MISLAID, LOST, AND ABANDONED PROPERTY

Type of Property	Ownership Rights
Mislaid property	The owner of the premises where property is mislaid is entitled to possession but does not acquire title. He or she holds the property as an involuntary bailee until the owner reclaims it.
Lost property	The finder acquires title to the property against the whole world except the true owner; the owner may reclaim his or her property from the finder.
Abandoned property	The finder acquires title to the property, even against its original owner.

▶ BAILMENT

bailment
A transaction in which an owner transfers his or her personal property to another to be held, stored, delivered, or for some other purpose. Title to the property does not transfer.

bailor
The owner of property in a bailment.

bailee
A holder of goods who is not a seller or a buyer (e.g., warehouse, common carrier).

A **bailment** occurs when the owner of personal property delivers his or her property to another person, either to be held, stored, or delivered or for some other purpose. In a bailment, the owner of the property is the **bailor**. The party to whom the property is delivered for safekeeping, storage, or delivery (e.g., warehouse, common carrier) is the **bailee** (see Exhibit 1). The law of bailment establishes the rights, duties, and liabilities of parties to a bailment.

A bailment is different from a sale or a gift because title to the goods does not transfer to the bailee. Instead, the bailee must follow the bailor's directions concerning the goods.

Example Hudson Corporation is relocating offices and hires American Van Lines to move its office furniture and equipment to the new location. American Van Lines (the bailee) must follow Hudson's (the bailor's) instructions regarding delivery.

Exhibit 1 BAILMENT

Elements Necessary to Create a Bailment

Three elements are necessary to create a bailment:

1. **Personal property.** Only *personal property* can be bailed. The property can be tangible (e.g., automobiles, jewelry, animals) or intangible (e.g., stocks, bonds, promissory notes).
2. **Delivery of possession.** **Delivery of possession** involves two elements: (1) The bailee must have exclusive control over the personal property, and (2) the bailee must knowingly accept the personal property.

   Examples No bailment is created if a patron goes into a restaurant and hangs her coat on an unattended coat rack because other patrons have access to the coat. However, a bailment is created if a patron checks her coat with a coatroom attendant because the restaurant has assumed exclusive control over the coat. If valuable property was left in the pocket of the coat, there would be no bailment of that property because the checkroom attendant did not knowingly accept it.

   Most bailments are created by *physical delivery*. For example, a bailment is created if Great Lakes Shipping, Inc., delivers a vessel to Marina Repairs, Inc., for repairs. *Constructive delivery* can create a bailment, too. For example, there has been constructive delivery of an automobile if the owner gives someone the keys and registration to his car.
3. **Bailment agreement.** The creation of a bailment does not require any formality. A bailment may be either express or implied. Most *express bailments* can be either written or oral. Under the Statute of Frauds, however, a **bailment agreement** must be in writing if it is for more than one year. An example of an *implied bailment* is the finding and safeguarding of lost property.

Laws are always useful to persons of property, and hurtful to those who have none.

Jean-Jacques Rousseau
Du Contrat Social (1761)

In the following case, the court had to decide whether a bailment had been created.

CASE 2 Bailment

Ziva Jewelry, Inc. v. Car Wash Headquarters, Inc.

897 So.2d 1011, Web 2004 Ala. Lexis 238 (2004)
Supreme Court of Alabama

"Thus, Ziva Jewelry cannot claim that CWH knew or that it should have reasonably foreseen or expected that it was taking responsibility for over $850,000 worth of jewelry when it accepted Smith's vehicle for the purpose of washing it."

—Judge Stuart

Facts

Ziva Jewelry, Inc., is a jewelry wholesaler. Stewart Smith was employed by Ziva Jewelry as a traveling sales representative. In connection with the employment, Smith drove his own vehicle to meet clients and attend trade shows. Smith testified that he knew that thieves are aware of jewelry trade shows and sometimes follow jewelry sales representatives, looking for an opportunity to steal the jewelry in the possession of the sales representatives and that they are most likely to strike when the car carrying the jewelry is unattended. Smith's practice was to keep the jewelry in the trunk of his vehicle while he was traveling on business. He kept the trunk padlocked and kept the only key to the padlock on the key ring with his ignition key.

One day, when Smith was traveling from a jewelry trade show, he stopped at Rain Tunnel Car Wash, owned by Car

(case continues)

Wash Headquarters, Inc. (CWH). At Rain Tunnel, the driver leaves his or her vehicle with employees of the car wash, and the vehicle is sent through a wash "tunnel." Upon completion of the car wash cycle, an employee drives the vehicle to another area of the car-wash premises to be hand dried. Once the vehicle is dried, the driver is signaled to retrieve the vehicle.

Smith left his car and the keys with a car-wash employee. Jewelry worth $850,000 was locked in the trunk of the vehicle. Smith watched the car as it went through the car wash tunnel. He watched as an employee dried the vehicle. As Smith was standing at the counter waiting to pay the cashier, he saw the employee wave a flag, indicating that the vehicle was ready for Smith. The employee then walked away from the vehicle. While Smith was standing at the cashier counter, someone jumped into Smith's vehicle and sped off. When the police recovered Smith's vehicle about 15 minutes later, the jewelry was gone.

Ziva Jewelry sued CWH to recover the value of the jewelry, alleging that a bailment had been created between Ziva and CWH and that CWH, as the bailee, was negligent in protecting the bailed goods. CWH defended, arguing that no bailment was created and therefore it was not liable for the loss of Ziva's stolen jewelry. The trial court held that no bailment had been created and entered summary judgment for CWH. Ziva Jewelry appealed.

Issue

Was a bailment created between Ziva Jewelry and CWH?

Language of the Court

A bailment is defined as the delivery of personal property by one person to another for a specific purpose, with a contract, express or implied, that the trust shall be faithfully executed, and the property returned or duly accounted for when the special purpose is accomplished, or kept until the bailor reclaims it. In order for a bailment to exist the bailee must have voluntarily assumed the custody and possession of the property for another.

In this case, Ziva Jewelry cannot establish that CWH expressly or impliedly agreed to take responsibility for the jewelry hidden inside Smith's trunk. Ziva Jewelry acknowledges that the jewelry was not plainly visible; that its presence was not made known to the car-wash employees; and that there was no reason that the employees should have expected expensive jewelry to be in the trunk of Smith's vehicle. Thus, Ziva Jewelry cannot claim that CWH knew or that it should have reasonably foreseen or expected that it was taking responsibility for over $850,000 worth of jewelry when it accepted Smith's vehicle for the purpose of washing it. Thus, there is no evidence indicating that CWH expressly or impliedly accepted responsibility for the jewelry in the trunk of Smith's vehicle. Without express or implied acceptance by the purported bailee, a bailment cannot arise.

Decision

The supreme court held that no bailment had been created between Ziva Jewelry and CWH. The supreme court affirmed the trial court's ruling that granted summary judgment to CWH.

Case Questions

Critical Legal Thinking What is a bailment? What is required for a bailment to be created? Why was a bailment not created in this case? Explain.

Business Ethics Did Ziva Jewelry have a good chance of winning this case? Why or why not? Do you think Smith was negligent in this case?

Contemporary Business Do you think that jewelry sales representatives are often subject to theft?

Types of Ordinary Bailments

There are three types of ordinary bailments: *bailment for the sole benefit of the bailor*, *bailment for the sole benefit of the bailee*, and *mutual benefit bailment*. Each of these types of bailments is discussed in the following paragraphs.

bailment for the sole benefit of the bailor
A gratuitous bailment that benefits only the bailor. The bailee owes only a *duty of slight care* to protect the bailed property.

Bailment for the Sole Benefit of the Bailor A **bailment for the sole benefit of the bailor** is a **gratuitous bailment** that benefits only the bailor. This ordinary bailment arises when the bailee is requested to care for the bailor's property as a favor. The bailee owes only a **duty of slight care** to protect the bailed property—that is, he or she owes a duty not to be grossly negligent in caring for the bailed goods.

Example The Watkins family is going on vacation and asks the neighbors, the Smiths, to feed its dog, which is allowed to run free. The Smiths diligently feed the dog, but the dog runs away and does not return. The Smiths are not liable for the loss of the dog.

Bailment for the Sole Benefit of the Bailee A **bailment for the sole benefit of the bailee** is a *gratuitous bailment* that solely benefits the bailee. This ordinary bailment arises when a bailee requests to use the bailor's property for personal reasons. In this situation, the bailee owes a **duty of great care** (or **duty of utmost care**) to protect the bailed property—that is, he or she owes a duty not to be slightly negligent in caring for the bailed goods.

bailment for the sole benefit of the bailee
A gratuitous bailment that benefits only the bailee. The bailee owes a *duty of utmost care* to protect the bailed property.

Example Mitch borrows Courtney's lawn mower (free of charge) to mow his own lawn. Mitch is the bailee, and Courtney is the bailor. This bailment is for the sole benefit of the bailee. Suppose Mitch, while mowing his lawn, leaves the lawn mower in his front yard while he goes into his house to answer the telephone. While he is gone, the lawn mower is stolen. Here, Mitch will be held liable to Courtney for the loss of the lawn mower because Mitch breached his duty of great care to protect the lawn mower.

Mutual Benefit Bailment A **mutual benefit bailment** is a bailment that *benefits both parties*. The bailee owes a **duty of reasonable care** (or **duty of ordinary care**) to protect the bailed goods. This means that the bailee is liable for any goods that are lost, damaged, or destroyed because of his or her negligence.

mutual benefit bailment
A bailment for the mutual benefit of the bailor and bailee. The bailee owes a *duty of ordinary care* to protect the bailed property.

Example ABC Garment Co. delivers goods to Lowell, Inc., a commercial warehouser, for storage. A fee is charged for this service. ABC Garment Co. receives the benefit of having its goods stored, and Lowell, Inc., receives the benefit of being paid compensation for storing the goods. In this example, Lowell, Inc. (the bailee), owes a duty of ordinary care to protect the goods.

CONCEPT SUMMARY

ORDINARY BAILMENT

Type of Bailment	Duty of Care Owed by Bailee	Bailee Liable to Bailor for
For the sole benefit of the bailor	Slight	Gross negligence
For the sole benefit of the bailee	Great	Slight negligence
For the mutual benefit of the bailor and bailee	Ordinary	Ordinary negligence

Duration and Termination of Bailments

A bailment generally expires at a specified time or when a certain purpose is accomplished. A **bailment for a fixed term** terminates at the end of the term or sooner, by mutual consent of the parties. A party who terminates a bailment in breach of the bailment agreement is liable to the innocent party for damages resulting from the breach. A bailment without a fixed term is called a **bailment at will**. A bailment at will can be terminated at any time by either party. Gratuitous bailees can generally terminate a fixed-term bailment prior to expiration of the term.

bailment for a fixed term
A bailment that terminates at the end of the term or sooner, by mutual consent of the parties.

bailment at will
A bailment without a fixed term; can be terminated at any time by either party.

Upon termination of a bailment, the bailee is legally obligated to do as the bailor directs with the property. Unless otherwise agreed, the bailee is obligated to return the identical goods bailed. Where commingled *fungible goods* are involved (e.g., grain), identically equivalent goods may be returned by the bailee.

▶ SPECIAL BAILMENTS

Several special forms of bailment require special procedures for formation and have their own special liability rules. There bailments involve *warehouse companies*, *common carriers*, and *innkeepers*. These special types of bailments are discussed in the following paragraphs.

Warehouse Company

A **warehouser**, or **warehouse company**, is a bailee engaged in the business of storing property for compensation. Warehousers are subject to the rights, duties, and liability of an ordinary bailee. As such, they owe a *duty of reasonable care* to protect the bailed property in their possession from harm or loss.[1] Warehousers are liable only for loss or damage to the bailed property caused by their own negligence. They are not liable for loss or damage caused to bailed goods by another person's negligence or conduct. Warehousers can limit the dollar amount of their liability if they offer the bailor the opportunity to increase the liability limit for the payment of an additional charge.

Warehouse Receipt A **warehouse receipt** is a document of title issued by a company that is engaged in the business of storing goods for hire, such as a warehouse company or a storage company.[2] A warehouse receipt that is issued to the bailor is often a preprinted form drafted by the warehouse company. A warehouse receipt includes the date of issue, a description of the goods or the packages containing the goods, the location of the warehouse where the goods are stored, and other terms related to the bailment. A warehouse company has a **lien** on the goods in its possession for necessary expenses incurred in storing and handling the goods. If the charges are not paid, the warehouse company may sell the goods at a public or private auction and apply the proceeds to pay the charges. Any excess proceeds must be held for the persons who had the right to demand delivery of the goods.

Common Carrier

Common carriers offer transportation services to the general public. For example, commercial airlines, railroads, public trucking companies, public pipeline companies, and such are common carriers. The delivery of goods to a common carrier creates a mutual benefit bailment. The person shipping the goods is the **consignor**, or **shipper** (the bailor). The transportation company is called the **common carrier** (the bailee). The person to whom the goods are to be delivered is called the **consignee**. (See Exhibit 2.)

consignor
A person shipping goods. The bailor.

consignee
A person to whom bailed goods are to be delivered.

Common carriers are held to a **duty of strict liability**:[3] If the goods are lost, damaged, destroyed, or stolen, the common carrier is liable even if it was not at fault for the loss. Common carriers are not liable for the loss, damage, or destruction of goods caused by (1) an act of God (e.g., a tornado), (2) an act of a public enemy (e.g., a terrorist activity), (3) an order of the government (e.g., statutes, court decisions, government regulations), (4) an act of the shipper (e.g., improper packaging), or (5) the inherent nature of the goods (e.g., perishability).

▶ Exhibit 2 COMMON CARRIER CONSIGNMENT

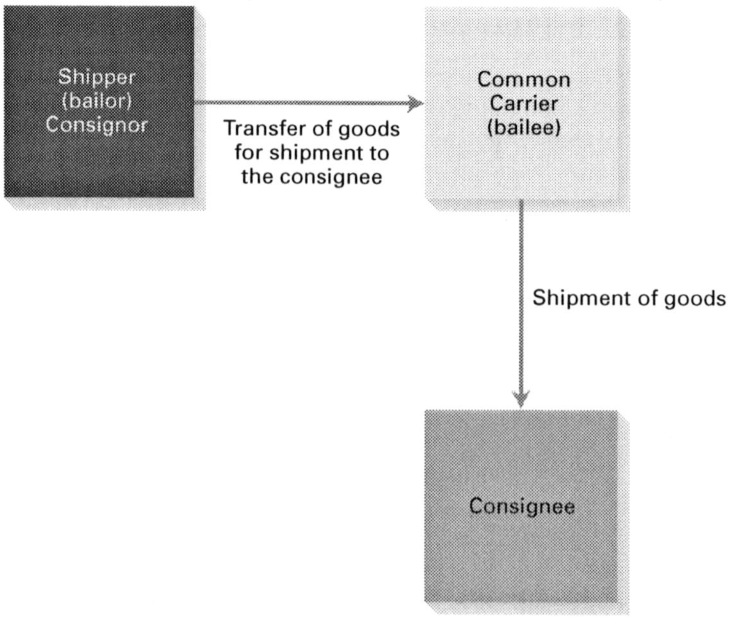

Common carriers can limit their liability to a stated dollar amount by expressly stating that in the bailment agreement. Federal law requires common carriers who take advantage of such limitation to offer shippers the opportunity to pay a premium and declare a higher value for the goods.[4]

Bill of Lading A **bill of lading** is a document of title that is issued by a carrier-bailee to the bailor when goods are received for transportation. A carrier has a lien on the goods in its possession covered by a bill of lading for necessary charges and expenses. If the charges are not paid, the carrier can sell the goods at public or private sale and apply the proceeds to pay the charges. Any excess proceeds must be held for the person who had the right to demand delivery of the goods.[5]

Mine is better than ours.

Benjamin Franklin

innkeepers' statutes
State statutes that limit an innkeeper's common law liability. An innkeeper can avoid liability for loss caused to a guest's property if (1) a safe is provided in which the guest's valuable property may be kept and (2) the guest is notified of this fact.

CONTEMPORARY ENVIRONMENT

Innkeeper's Statute

An **innkeeper** is the owner of a facility that provides lodging to the public for compensation (e.g., hotel, motel). Under the common law, innkeepers are held to a **strict liability standard** regarding loss caused to the personal property of transient guests. Permanent lodgers are not subject to this rule.

However, almost all states have enacted **innkeepers' statutes** that change the common law and limit the liability of innkeepers. These statutes allow innkeepers to avoid liability for loss caused to guests' property if a safe is provided in which the guests' valuable property may be kept and the guests are aware of the safe's availability. Most state laws also allow innkeepers to limit the dollar amount of their liability by notifying their guests of this limit (e.g., by posting a notice on each guest room door).

Example Hospitality Hotel, Inc., operates a hotel. The hotel is located in a state that has an innkeepers' statute that (1) eliminates a hotel's liability for guests' property not placed in the safe located at the hotel's registration desk and (2) limits a hotel's liability to $500 for any guest's property stored in the hotel's safe. The hotel has proper notices posted at the registration counter and in guests' rooms, notifying guests of these limitations on liability. Gion, a guest at the hotel, leaves expensive jewelry and cameras in his room when he temporarily leaves the hotel. When Gion returns, he finds that his jewelry and cameras have been stolen. Because of the innkeepers' statute, the hotel is not liable for Gion's loss. Suppose instead that Gion had taken items to the hotel's registration desk and had the hotel place the items in the hotel safe. If the items had been stolen from the hotel's safe, the innkeepers' statute would have limited the hotel's liability to $500.

CONCEPT SUMMARY

SPECIAL BAILMENTS

Type of Bailee	Liability	Limitation on Liability
Warehouse company	Ordinary negligence	May limit the dollar amount of liability by offering the bailor the right to declare a higher value for the bailed goods for an additional charge.
Common carrier	Strictly liable except for: 1. Act of God 2. Act of a public enemy 3. Order of the government 4. Act of the shipper 5. Inherent nature of the goods	May limit the dollar amount of liability by offering the bailor the right to declare a higher value for the bailed goods for an additional charge.
Innkeeper	Strictly liable	State innkeepers' statutes limit the liability of an innkeeper for others' negligence.

TEST REVIEW TERMS AND CONCEPTS

Abandoned property
Acceptance
Accession
Bailee
Bailment
Bailment agreement
Bailment at will
Bailment for a fixed term
Bailment for the sole benefit of the bailee
Bailment for the sole benefit of the bailor
Bailor
Beneficiary
Bill of lading
Common carrier
Confusion
Consignee
Consignor (shipper)
Constructive delivery
Delivery
Delivery of possession
Divorce
Donative intent
Donee
Donor
Duty of great care (duty of utmost care)
Duty of reasonable care (duty of ordinary care)
Duty of slight care
Duty of strict liability
Estray statute
Fixture
Fungible goods
Gift
Gift *causa mortis*
Gift *inter vivos*
Gratuitous bailment
Heir
Inheritance
Innkeeper
Innkeepers' statute
Intangible property
Lien
Lost property
Mislaid property
Mutual benefit bailment
Personal property
Physical delivery
Production
Strict liability standard
Taking possession (capturing)
Tangible property
Uniform Gifts to Minors Act
Uniform Transfer to Minors Act
Warehouser (warehouse company)
Warehouse receipt
Will

CASE PROBLEMS

1 Gift For 12 years, Theodore Alexander Buder's father made substantial gifts to his minor grandchildren. Theodore Buder and his wife divorced during this period. The cash gifts, typically in the form of checks made directly payable to the children, were given to Buder with the understanding that he would safeguard the money and invest it on behalf of the children. Buder invested various amounts of the children's money in "blue chip" stocks traded over the New York and American stock exchanges. Buder also invested substantial sums of the children's money in speculative penny stocks. The stocks were purchased in Buder's name as custodian for the children, as required by the Uniform Gifts to Minors Act (UGMA). At one point, almost half of the children's money was invested in penny stocks. All the penny stocks except one suffered substantial losses. Buder's ex-wife, Sartore, sued him, alleging that he had breached his fiduciary duty owed to the children under the UGMA. She sought to recover the funds lost by Buder's investment of the children's funds in penny stocks. Who wins? *Buder v. Sartore*, 774 P.2d 1383, **Web** 1989 Colo. Lexis 227 (Supreme Court of Colorado)

2 Lost Property Danny Lee Smith and his brother, Jeffrey Allen Smith, found a 16-foot fiberglass boat lying beside the roadway in Mobile County, Alabama. Seeing two sheriff's deputies, they stopped them to discuss the boat. Over the Smiths' objections, the deputies impounded the boat. The Smiths made it clear that if the true owner of the boat was not found, they wanted the boat. The true owner did not claim the boat. Mobile County claimed the boat and wanted to auction it off for sale to raise money for county recreational programs. The Smiths claimed the boat as finders. Alabama did not have an estray statute that applied to the situation. Who gets the boat? *Smith v. Sheriff Purvis*, 474 So.2d 1131, **Web** 1985 Ala. Civ. App. Lexis 1280 (Court of Civil Appeals of Alabama)

3 Abandoned Property Police officers of the city of Miami, Florida, responded to reports of a shooting at the apartment of Carlos Fuentes. Fuentes had been shot in the neck and shoulder, and shortly after the police arrived, he was removed to a hospital. In an ensuing search of the apartment, the police found assorted drug paraphernalia, a gun, and cash in the amount of $58,591. The property was seized, taken to the police station, and placed in custody. About nine days later, the police learned that Fuentes had been discharged from the hospital. All efforts by police to locate Fuentes and his girlfriend, a co-occupant of Fuentes's apartment, were unsuccessful. Neither Fuentes nor his girlfriend ever came forward to claim any of the items taken by the police from his apartment. About four years later, James W. Green and Walter J. Vogel, the owners of the apartment building in which Fuentes was a tenant, sued the city of Miami to recover the cash found in Fuentes's apartment. The state of Florida intervened in the case, also claiming an interest in the money. Who wins? *State of Florida v. Green*, 456 So.2d 1309, **Web** 1984 Fla.App. Lexis 15340 (Court of Appeal of Florida)

4 Bailment James D. Merritt leased a storage locker from Nationwide Warehouse Co., Ltd. (Nationwide), and agreed to pay a monthly fee to lease the locker. Merritt placed various items in the leased premises but never informed Nationwide as to the nature or quantity of articles stored therein. Merritt was free to store or remove whatever he wished without consultation with, permission from, or notice to Nationwide. Merritt locked the leased premises with his own lock and key. Nationwide was not furnished with a key. Subsequently, certain personal property belonging to Merritt disappeared from the storage space. Merritt sued Nationwide to recover damages of $5,275. Was a bailment created between Merritt and Nationwide? *Merritt v. Nationwide*

Warehouse Co., Ltd., 605 S.W.2d 250, **Web** 1980 Tenn.App. Lexis 338 (Court of Appeals of Tennessee)

5 Lost Goods Clarence Williams took his wife's fur coat to Debonair Cleaners for cleaning and storage. The clerk told him that the cleaner was experienced in such matters and that the charge would be 3 percent of the stated value of the coat. Williams stated that the coat was worth $13,000, and the clerk gave Williams a claim check and informed Williams that the total fee for storage would be $390, to be paid when the coat was retrieved. That evening, Williams related the substance of his conversation with the clerk to his wife, America, and gave her the claim check. Approximately eight months later, America Williams went to Debonair Cleaners to retrieve her coat. She presented the claim check to the clerk, who, after searching the premises for the coat, told her that it could not be located. Williams was informed that the coat had probably been stolen during a break-in and burglary. Williams sued Debonair Cleaners to recover the value of the coat. Who wins? *Mahallati v. Williams*, 479 A.2d 300, **Web** 1984 D.C.App. Lexis 419 (District of Columbia Court of Appeals)

6 Gratuitous Bailment Marsha Hamilton and Andrea Morris were guests at a dinner party attended by approximately 25 people. The party began about 7:00 P.M. and ended at approximately 1:00 A.M. Alcoholic beverages were served throughout the evening. At approximately 11:30, while working in the kitchen, Hamilton removed her watch and placed it on the counter. About midnight, Hamilton left the kitchen and went outside. After about 15 minutes, she became ill and fled to the bathroom. Shortly after Hamilton left the kitchen, Morris saw the watch on the counter and, fearing for its safety, picked it up and carried it in her hand as she looked for Hamilton. When Hamilton came out of the bathroom, she and her fiancé left the party. Morris was unable to find Hamilton and could not recall precisely what she did with the watch. She testified that she either gave it to Hamilton's fiancé or put it somewhere in the host's house for safekeeping. Hamilton's fiancé testified that Morris did not give him the watch. The next day, Hamilton discovered that she did not have her watch, but in a search of the host's home, the watch was not recovered. Hamilton sued Morris for damages. Who wins? *Morris v. Hamilton*, 225 Va. 372, 302 S.E.2d 51, **Web** 1983 Va. Lexis 231 (Supreme Court of Virginia)

7 Parking Lot's Liability Allright, Inc., was a parking lot operator in Houston, Texas. Kirkland Strauder drove his automobile to a Houston Allright parking lot and placed it in a row of cars to be parked by the attendant. When Strauder returned two hours later to reclaim his car, it could not be found. Strauder reported the car stolen. Allright could not explain the loss of the car, which was found weeks later, wrecked and stripped. Strauder sued Allright, Inc., for damages. Who wins? *Allright, Inc. v. Strauder*, 679 S.W.2d 81, **Web** 1984 Tex.App. Lexis 6006 (Court of Appeals of Texas)

8 Disclaimer of Liability Joseph Conboy, his wife, and a group of friends convened in Manhattan, New York, for a party at a club where patrons danced to recorded music. The Conboy party checked their coats, 14 in all, with the coatroom attendant. After paying a $0.75 charge per coat, they received seven check stubs. A small sign in the coatroom stated "Liability for lost property in this coat/check room is limited to $100 per loss of misplaced article." Conboy testified that he did not notice it when he checked his coat and that the coatroom attendant did not call his attention to the sign. At the end of the evening, Conboy and the other guests of the party attempted to reclaim their coats. Conboy's one-month-old $1,350 leather coat was missing. Conboy sued the club for damages. Is the disclaimer of liability enforceable? *Conboy v. Studio 54, Inc.*, 113 Misc.2d 403, 449 N.Y.S.2d 391, **Web** 1982 N.Y. Misc. Lexis 3309 (Civil Court of the City of New York)

BUSINESS ETHICS CASES

9 Business Ethics When Dr. Arthur M. Edwards died, leaving a will disposing of this property, he left the villa-type condominium in which he lived, its "contents," and $10,000 to his stepson, Ronald W. Souders. Edwards left the residual of his estate to other named legatees. In administering the estate, certain stock certificates, passbook savings accounts, and other bank statements were found in Edwards's condominium. Souders claimed that these items belonged to him because they were "contents" of the condominium. The other legatees opposed Souders' claim, alleging that the disputed property was intangible property and not part of the contents of the condominium. The value of the property was as follows: condominium, $138,000; furniture in condominium, $4,000; stocks, $377,000; and passbook and other bank accounts, $124,000. Who is entitled to the stocks and bank accounts? Do you think Souders acted ethically in this case? *Souders v. Johnson*, 501 So.2d 745, **Web** 1987 Fla.App. Lexis 6579 (Court of Appeal of Florida)

10 Business Ethics Darryl Kulwin was employed by Nova Stylings, Inc. (Nova), as a jewelry salesman. In that capacity, he traveled throughout the country, carrying with him jewelry owned and manufactured by Nova to show to prospective buyers. Kulwin was visiting Panoria Ruston, who was a guest registered with the Red Roof Inn in Overland Park, Kansas. Ruston and Kulwin met at the Red Roof Inn and later made plans to leave to go out for dinner. Kulwin asked Ruston to make arrangements with the desk clerk to leave his sample case in the office of the Red Roof Inn while they went out to dinner. Ruston asked the clerk if she could leave the bag in the manager's office of the Red Roof Inn, and the clerk agreed.

Ruston advised the clerk that the contents of the case were valuable but did not describe the contents of the bag.

Kansas Statute Section 36-402(b) provides:

No hotel or motel keeper in this state shall be liable for the loss of, or damage to, merchandise for sale or samples belonging to a guest, lodger, or boarder unless the guest, lodger, or boarder upon entering the hotel or motel, shall give notice of having merchandise for sale or samples in his possession, together with an itemized list of such property, to the hotel or motel keeper, or his authorized agent or clerk in the registration office of the hotel or motel office.

No hotel or motel keeper shall be liable for any loss of such property designated in this subsection (b), after notice an itemized statement having been given and delivered as aforesaid, in an amount in excess of two hundred fifty dollars ($250), unless such hotel or motel keeper, by specific agreement in writing, individually, or by an authorized agent or clerk in charge of the registration office of the hotel or motel, shall voluntarily assume liability for a larger amount with reference to such property. The hotel or motel keeper shall not be compelled to receive such guests, lodgers, or boarders with merchandise for sale or samples.

The inn posted the proper notice of the provisions of this act in all of the guests' rooms, including that of Ruston. An unidentified person obtained access to the manager's office and removed the case from the office. Nova sued Red Roof Inns for the alleged value of the jewelry, $650,000. Is Red Roof Inns liable? Did either party act unethically in this case? *Nova Stylings v. Red Roof Inns, Inc.*, 242 Kan. 318, 747 P.2d 107, **Web** 1987 Kan. Lexis 469 (Supreme Court of Kansas)

ENDNOTES

1. UCC 7-204(1), 7-403(1).
2. UCC 1-201(45).
3. UCC 7-301(1).
4. UCC 7-309(2).
5 UCC 7-308(1).

INTENTIONAL TORTS AND NEGLIGENCE

INTENTIONAL TORTS AND NEGLIGENCE

▲ **Children's Ride.** *In this children's "thrill" ride, the children are strapped in with their feet left dangling. The car goes up a 100-foot tower and then free-falls down, giving the riders a feeling of weightlessness. Operators of thrill rides carry liability insurance.*

CHAPTER OBJECTIVES

After studying this chapter, you should be able to:

1. List and describe intentional torts against persons.
2. List and explain the elements necessary to prove negligence.
3. Describe special negligence doctrines.
4. Describe assumption of the risk and other defenses to a charge of negligence.
5. Describe and apply the doctrine of strict liability.

CHAPTER CONTENTS

"Negligence is not actionable unless it involves the invasion of a legally protected interest, the violation of a right. Proof of negligence in the air, so to speak, will not do."

—Chief Judge Cardozo
Palsgraf v. Long Island Railroad Co., 248 N.Y. 339, 162 N.E. 99, 1928 N.Y. Lexis 1269 (1928)

▶ INTRODUCTION TO INTENTIONAL TORTS AND NEGLIGENCE

Tort is the French word for a "wrong." The law provides remedies to persons and businesses that are injured by the tortuous actions of others. Under tort law, an injured party can bring a *civil lawsuit* to seek compensation for a wrong done to the party or to the party's property. Many torts have their origin in common law. The courts and legislatures have extended tort law to reflect changes in modern society.

tort
A wrong. There are three categories of torts: (1) intentional torts, (2) unintentional torts (negligence), and (3) strict liability.

Tort damages are monetary damages that are sought from the offending party. They are intended to compensate the injured party for the injury suffered. Such injury may consist of past and future medical expenses, loss of wages, pain and suffering, mental distress, and other damages caused by the defendant's tortious conduct. If the victim of a tort dies, his or her beneficiaries can bring a *wrongful death action* to recover damages from the defendant. *Punitive damages*, which are awarded to punish the defendant, may be recovered in intentional tort and strict liability cases. Other remedies, such as injunctions, may be available, too.

This chapter discusses intentional torts, negligence, and defenses to tort actions.

▶ INTENTIONAL TORTS AGAINST PERSONS

The law protects a person from unauthorized touching, restraint, or other contact. In addition, the law protects a person's reputation and privacy. Violations of these rights are actionable as torts. **Intentional torts** against persons are discussed in the paragraphs that follow.

intentional tort
A category of torts that requires that the defendant possessed the intent to do the act that caused the plaintiff's injuries.

Assault

Assault is (1) the threat of immediate harm or offensive contact or (2) any action that arouses reasonable apprehension of imminent harm. Actual physical contact is unnecessary. Threats of future harm are not actionable.

assault
(1) The threat of immediate harm or offensive contact or (2) any action that arouses reasonable apprehension of imminent harm. Actual physical contact is unnecessary.

Examples Suppose a 6-foot-5-inch, 250-pound person makes a fist and threatens to punch a 5-foot, 100-pound person. If the threatened person is afraid that he or she will be physically harmed, that person can sue the threatening person to recover damages for the assault. If the threatened person is a black-belt karate champion and laughs at the threat, there is no assault because the threat does not cause any apprehension.

Battery

Battery is unauthorized and harmful or offensive physical contact with another person that causes injury. Basically, the interest protected here is each person's reasonable sense of dignity and safety. Direct physical contact, such as intentionally hitting someone with a fist, is battery.

battery
Unauthorized and harmful or offensive direct or indirect physical contact with another person that causes injury.

Indirect physical contact between the victim and the perpetrator is also battery, as long as injury results.

Examples Throwing a rock, shooting an arrow or a bullet, knocking off a hat, pulling a chair out from under someone, and poisoning a drink are all instances of actionable battery. The victim need not be aware of the harmful or offensive contact (e.g., it may take place while the victim is asleep).

Assault and battery often occur together, although they do not have to (e.g., the perpetrator hits the victim on the back of the head without any warning).

Transferred Intent Doctrine Sometimes a person acts with the intent to injure one person but actually injures another. The **transferred intent doctrine** applies to such situations. Under this doctrine, the law transfers the perpetrator's intent from the target to the actual victim of the act. The victim can then sue the defendant.

False Imprisonment

false imprisonment
The intentional confinement or restraint of another person without authority or justification and without that person's consent.

The intentional confinement or restraint of another person without authority or justification and without that person's consent constitutes **false imprisonment**. The victim may be restrained or confined by physical force, barriers, threats of physical harm, or the perpetrator's false assertion of legal authority (i.e., false arrest). A threat of future harm or moral pressure is not considered false imprisonment. The false imprisonment must be complete.

Examples Locking one's doors in a house or automobile and not letting the other person leave is false imprisonment. Merely locking one door to a building when other exits are not locked is not false imprisonment. However, a person is not obliged to risk danger or an affront to his or her dignity by attempting to escape.

Shoplifting and Merchant Protection Statutes

Shoplifting causes substantial losses to retail and other merchants each year. Oftentimes, suspected shoplifters are stopped by the store employees, and their suspected shoplifting is investigated. These stops sometimes lead to the merchant being sued for false imprisonment because the merchant detained the suspect.

merchant protection statutes
Statutes that allow merchants to stop, detain, and investigate suspected shoplifters without being held liable for false imprisonment if (1) there are reasonable grounds for the suspicion, (2) suspects are detained for only a reasonable time, and (3) investigations are conducted in a reasonable manner.

Almost all states have enacted **merchant protection statutes**, also known as the **shopkeeper's privilege**. These statutes allow merchants to stop, detain, and investigate suspected shoplifters without being held liable for false imprisonment if:

1. There are *reasonable grounds* for the suspicion.
2. Suspects are detained for only a *reasonable time.*
3. Investigations are conducted in a *reasonable manner.*

Proving these elements is sometimes difficult. The following case applies the merchant's protection statute.

CASE 1 False Imprisonment

Wal-Mart Stores, Inc. v. Cockrell

61 S.W.3d 774, Web 2001 Tex. App. Lexis 7992 (2001)
Court of Appeals of Texas

"He made me feel like I was scum. That I had no say-so in the matter, that just made me feel like a little kid on the block, like the bully beating the kid up. . . ."
—Karl Cockrell

Facts

Karl Cockrell and his parents went to the layaway department at a Wal-Mart store. Cockrell stayed for about five minutes and decided to leave. As he was going out the front door, Raymond Navarro, a Wal-Mart loss-prevention officer, stopped him and requested that Cockrell follow him to the manager's office. Once in the office, Navarro told him to pull his pants down. Cockrell put his hands between his shorts and underwear, pulled them out, and shook them. Nothing fell out. Next Navarro told him to take off his shirt. Cockrell raised his shirt, revealing a large bandage which covered a surgical wound on the right side of his abdomen. Cockrell had recently had a liver transplant. Navarro asked him to take off the bandage, despite Cockrell's explanation that the bandage maintained a sterile environment around his surgical wound. On Navarro's insistence Cockrell took down the bandage, revealing the wound. Afterwards Navarro apologized and let Cockrell go. Cockrell sued Wal-Mart to recover damages for false imprisonment. Wal-Mart defended, alleging that the shopkeeper's privilege protected it from liability. The trial court found in favor of Cockrell and awarded Cockrell $300,000 for his mental anguish. Wal-Mart appealed.

Issue

Does the shopkeeper's privilege protect Wal-Mart from liability under the circumstances of the case?

Language of the Court

Neither Raymond Navarro nor any other store employee saw Cockrell steal merchandise. However Navarro claimed he had reasons to suspect Cockrell of shoplifting. He said that Cockrell was acting suspiciously, because he saw him in the women's department standing very close to a rack of clothes and looking around. Later he saw Cockrell looking around and walking slowly by the cigarette aisle and then "pass out of the store." We conclude that a rational jury could have found that Navarro did not "reasonably believe" a theft had occurred and therefore lacked authority to detain Cockrell.

The extent to which Wal-Mart searched Cockrell compels us to address the reasonable manner of the detention. Navarro's search was unreasonable in scope, because he had no probable cause to believe that Cockrell had hidden any merchandise under the bandage. Removal of the bandage compromised the sterile environment surrounding the wound.

Evidence of Cockrell's mental anguish comes largely from the following testimony: Counsel asked Cockrell to describe his demeanor when he took down his bandage in the manager's office. He stated that Navarro: "Made me feel like I was scum. That I had no say-so in the matter, that just made me feel like a little kid on the block, like the bully beating the kid up and saying, 'Well, I didn't catch you with nothing; but I'm going to humiliate him, twist a knife a little bit more into them.'"

Cockrell testified that after Navarro let him go he was shaking, crying, nervous, scared, and looking around to make sure no one else was trying to stop him. Cockrell's parents saw him in the Wal-Mart store immediately after he was let go. They said he was upset, nervous, had tears in his eyes, and looked scared, pale, and badly shaken up. When he arrived at home he was crying, nervous, and still "pretty well shook up." His mother said that he stayed upset for a "long time" and would not go out of the house.

Decision

The court of appeals upheld the trial court's finding that Wal-Mart had falsely imprisoned Cockrell and had not proved the shopkeeper's privilege. The court of appeals upheld the trial court's judgment that awarded Cockrell $300,000 for mental anguish.

Case Questions

Critical Legal Thinking What is the tort of false imprisonment? Explain.

Business Ethics Did Navarro, the Wal-Mart employee, act responsibly in this case? Did Wal-Mart act ethically in denying liability in this case?

Contemporary Business What does the shopkeeper's privilege provide? What are the elements necessary to prove the shopkeeper's privilege? Do you think Wal-Mart had a good chance of proving the shopkeeper's privilege in this case?

Misappropriation of the Right to Publicity

Each person has the exclusive legal right to control and profit from the commercial use of his or her name and identity during his or her lifetime. This is a valuable right, particularly to well-known persons such as sports figures and movie stars. Any attempt by another person to appropriate a living person's name or identity for commercial purposes is actionable. The wrongdoer is liable for the **tort of misappropriation of the right to publicity** (also called the **tort of appropriation**).

tort of misappropriation of the right to publicity
An attempt by another person to appropriate a living person's name or identity for commercial purposes.

In such cases, the plaintiff can (1) recover the unauthorized profits made by the offending party and (2) obtain an injunction preventing further unauthorized use of his or her name or identity. Many states provide that the right to publicity survives a person's death and may be enforced by the deceased's heirs.

Example Brad Pitt is a famous movie star. If an advertising agency places Brad Pitt's likeness (e.g., photo) on a billboard advertising a product without Brad Pitt's permission, it has engaged in the tort of misappropriation of the right to publicity. Brad Pitt could sue and recover the profits made by the offending party as well as obtain an injunction to prevent unauthorized use of his likeness by the offending party.

Invasion of the Right to Privacy

The law recognizes each person's right to live his or her life without being subjected to unwarranted and undesired publicity. A violation of this right constitutes the tort of **invasion of the right to privacy**. If a fact is public information, there is no claim to privacy.

However, a fact that was once public (e.g., commission of a crime) may become private after the passage of time.

Examples Secretly taking photos of another person with a cell phone camera in a men's or women's locker room would constitute invasion of the right to privacy. Reading someone else's mail, wiretapping someone's telephone, and reading someone else's e-mail without authorization to do so are also examples of invasion of the right to privacy.

Placing someone in a "false light" constitutes an invasion of privacy.

Example Sending an objectionable telegram to a third party and signing another's name would place the purported sender in a false light in the eyes of the receiver.

Defamation of Character

A person's reputation is a valuable asset. Therefore, every person is protected from false statements made by others during his or her lifetime. This protection ends upon a person's death. The tort of **defamation of character** requires a plaintiff to prove that:

defamation of character
False statement(s) made by one person about another. In court, the plaintiff must prove that (1) the defendant made an untrue statement of fact about the plaintiff and (2) the statement was intentionally or accidentally published to a third party.

1. The defendant made an *untrue statement of fact* about the plaintiff.
2. The statement was intentionally or accidentally *published* to a third party. In this context, *publication* simply means that a third person heard or saw the untrue statement. It does not require appearance in newspapers, magazines, or books.

A false statement that appears in writing or other fixed medium is **libel**. The name for an oral defamatory statement is **slander**.

libel
A false statement that appears in a letter, newspaper, magazine, book, photograph, movie, video, and so on.

slander
Oral defamation of character.

Hard cases make bad law.

Legal Maxim

Examples False statements that appear in a letter, newspaper, magazine, book, photograph, movie, video, and the like would be libel. Most courts hold that defamatory statements in radio and television broadcasts are considered libel because of the permanency of the media.

The publication of an untrue statement of fact is not the same as the publication of an *opinion*. The publication of opinions is usually not actionable. Because defamation is defined as an untrue statement of fact, truth is an absolute defense to a charge of defamation.

Examples The statement "My lawyer is lousy" is an opinion and is not defamation. The statement "My lawyer has been disbarred from the practice of law," when she has not been disbarred, is an untrue statement of fact and is actionable as defamation.

Public Figures as Plaintiffs In ***New York Times Co. v. Sullivan***,[1] the U.S. Supreme Court held that *public officials* cannot recover for defamation unless they can prove that the defendant acted with "actual malice." Actual malice means that the defendant made the false statement knowingly or with reckless disregard of its falsity. This requirement has since been extended to *public figure* plaintiffs such as movie stars, sports personalities, and other celebrities.

CONTEMPORARY ENVIRONMENT

Eminem's Rap Song Is Not Slander

"It is therefore this court's ultimate position that Eminem is entitled to summary disposition."

—Judge Servitto

Eminem is a famous hip-hop artist and rapper who won a Grammy award for his music in the movie *8-Mile* in which he starred. Eminem's lyrics often contain references to his personal experiences. In "Brain Damage," a song from his 1999 CD *The Slim Shady LP*, Eminem sang lyrics he had written about his childhood experiences with DeAngelo Bailey. The lyrics read in part:

Way before my baby daughter Hailey
I was harassed daily by this fat kid named D'Angelo Bailey . . .
He banged my head against the urinal til he broke my nose . . .
Soaked my clothes in blood, grabbed me and choked my throat

DeAngelo Bailey sued Eminem for $1 million, alleging that the lyrics were untrue and slanderous. Eminem's mother publicly defended her son's account of the bullying by Bailey. Under questioning, Bailey admitted that when he was in the fourth grade, he was part of a group at school that did "bully type things" such as pushing Eminem down. Bailey described what was done to Eminem as "jokes, play games, you know, like we probably like—I mean this is kid stuff, so I'm saying." Bailey also testified that he was present when his friends pushed Eminem and that he would personally bump into Eminem by throwing a "little shove." Bailey offered no evidence to refute Eminem's claims in his deposition that Bailey was bigger than him, shoved him into walls, called him names, took his orange juice, and knocked over his books.

After hearing all the evidence, trial judge Deborah Servitto granted summary disposition in favor of Eminem. She wrote in her opinion:

Mr. Bailey complains that his rap is trash
So he's seeking compensation in the form of cash.
Bailey thinks he's entitled to some money gain
Because Eminem used his name in vain.
The lyrics are stories no one would take as fact
They're an exaggeration of a childish act.
It is therefore this court's ultimate position
That Eminem is entitled to summary disposition.

On appeal, the court of appeals of Michigan upheld the trial court's decision. *DeAngelo Bailey v. Marshall Bruce Mathers, III a/k/a/ Eminem*, 2005 Mich.App. Lexis 930 (Court of Appeals of Michigan, 2005)

Disparagement or Trade Libel

All slander must still be strangled in its birth, or time will soon conspire to make it strong enough to overcome the truth.

Sir William D'Avenant

Business firms rely on their reputation and the quality of their products and services to attract and keep customers. That is why state unfair-competition laws protect businesses from disparaging statements made by competitors or others. A disparaging statement is an untrue statement made by one person or business about the products, services, property, or reputation of another business.

To prove **disparagement**, which is also called **trade libel**, **product disparagement**, and **slander of title**, the plaintiff must show that the defendant (1) made an untrue statement about the plaintiff's products, services, property, or business reputation; (2) published that untrue statement to a third party; (3) knew the statement was not true; and (4) made the statement maliciously (i.e., with intent to injure the plaintiff).

product disparagement
False statements about a competitor's products, services, property, or business reputation. Also known as *trade libel*, *product disparagement*, and *slander of title*.

Intentional Misrepresentation (Fraud)

One of the most pervasive business torts is **intentional misrepresentation**. This tort is also known as **fraud** or **deceit**. It occurs when a wrongdoer deceives another person out of money, property, or something else of value. A person who has been injured by intentional misrepresentation can recover damages from the wrongdoer. Four elements are required to find fraud:

intentional misrepresentation
The intentional defrauding of a person out of money, property, or something else of value. Also known as *fraud* or *deceit*.

1. The wrongdoer made a false representation of material fact.
2. The wrongdoer had knowledge that the representation was false and intended to deceive the innocent party.
3. The innocent party justifiably relied on the misrepresentation.
4. The innocent party was injured.

He that's cheated twice by the same man, is an accomplice with the Cheater.

Thomas Fuller
Gnomologia (1732)

Item 2, which is called **scienter**, includes situations in which the wrongdoer recklessly disregards the truth in making a representation that is false. Intent or recklessness can be inferred from the circumstances.

Intentional Infliction of Emotional Distress

In some situations, a victim may suffer mental or emotional distress without first being physically harmed. The *Restatement (Second) of Torts* provides that a person whose *extreme and outrageous* conduct intentionally or recklessly causes severe emotional distress to another is liable for that emotional distress.[2] This is called the tort of **intentional infliction of emotional distress**, or the **tort of outrage**.

intentional infliction of emotional distress
A tort that says a person whose extreme and outrageous conduct intentionally or recklessly causes severe emotional distress to another person is liable for that emotional distress. Also known as the *tort of outrage*.

The plaintiff must prove that the defendant's conduct was "so outrageous in character and so extreme in degree as to go beyond all possible bounds of decency, and to be regarded as atrocious and utterly intolerable in a civilized society."[3] The tort does not require any publication to a third party or physical contact between the plaintiff and defendant.

An indignity, an annoyance, rough language, or an occasional inconsiderate or unkind act does not constitute outrageous behavior. However, repeated annoyances or harassment coupled with threats are considered outrageous.

The mental distress suffered by the plaintiff must be severe. Many states require that this mental distress be manifested by some form of physical injury, discomfort, or illness, such as nausea, ulcers, headaches, or miscarriage. This requirement is intended to prevent false claims. Some states have abandoned this requirement.

Examples Shame, humiliation, embarrassment, anger, fear, and worry constitute severe mental distress.

Malicious Prosecution

Businesses and individuals often believe they have a reason to sue someone to recover damages or other remedies. If the plaintiff has a legitimate reason to bring the lawsuit and does so, but the plaintiff does not win the lawsuit, he or she does not have to worry about being sued by the person whom he or she sued. But a losing plaintiff does have to worry about being sued by the defendant in a second lawsuit for **malicious prosecution** if certain elements are met. In a lawsuit for malicious prosecution, the original defendant sues the original plaintiff. In this second lawsuit, which is a *civil* action for damages, the original defendant is the plaintiff and the original plaintiff is the defendant. To succeed in a malicious prosecution lawsuit, the courts require the plaintiff to prove all of the following:

malicious prosecution
A lawsuit in which the original defendant sues the original plaintiff. In the second lawsuit, the defendant becomes the plaintiff and vice versa.

1. The plaintiff in the original lawsuit (now the defendant) instituted or was responsible for instituting the original lawsuit.
2. There was no *probable cause* for the first lawsuit (i.e., it was a frivolous lawsuit).
3. The plaintiff in the original action brought it with *malice*. (Caution: This is a very difficult element to prove.)
4. The original lawsuit was terminated in favor of the original defendant (now the plaintiff).
5. The current plaintiff suffered injury as a result of the original lawsuit.

The courts do not look favorably on malicious prosecution lawsuits because they feel such lawsuits inhibit the original plaintiff's incentive to sue.

Negligence is the omission to do something which a reasonable man would do, or doing something which a prudent and reasonable man would not do.

B. Alderson Blyth v. Birmingham Waterworks Co. *(1850)*

UNINTENTIONAL TORTS (NEGLIGENCE)

Under the doctrine of **unintentional tort**, commonly referred to as **negligence**, a person is liable for harm that is the *foreseeable consequence* of his or her actions. *Negligence* is defined as "the omission to do something which a reasonable man would do, or doing something which a prudent and reasonable man would not do."[4]

unintentional tort
A doctrine that says a person is liable for harm that is the foreseeable consequence of his or her actions. Also known as *negligence*.

To be successful in a negligence lawsuit, the plaintiff must prove that (1) the defendant owed a *duty of care* to the plaintiff, (2) the defendant *breached* this duty of care, (3) the plaintiff suffered *injury*, (4) the defendant's negligent act *caused* the plaintiff's injury and (5) the defendant's negligent act was the proximate cause of the plaintiff's injuries. Each of these elements is discussed in the paragraphs that follow.

CONCEPT SUMMARY

ELEMENTS OF NEGLIGENCE

1. The defendant owed a *duty of care* to the plaintiff.
2. The defendant *breached this duty*.
3. The plaintiff suffered *injury*.
4. The defendant's negligent act was the *actual cause* (or *causation in fact*) of the plaintiff's injuries.
5. The defendant's negligent act was the *proximate cause* (or *legal cause*) of the plaintiff's injuries. The defendant is liable only for the *foreseeable* consequences of his or her negligent act.

Duty of Care

To determine whether a defendant is liable for negligence, it must first be ascertained whether the defendant owed a **duty of care** to the plaintiff. *Duty of care* refers to the obligation people owe each other—that is, the duty not to cause any unreasonable harm or risk of harm.

duty of care
The obligation people owe each other not to cause any unreasonable harm or risk of harm.

Examples Each person owes a duty to drive his or her car carefully, not to push or shove on escalators, not to leave skateboards on the sidewalk, and the like. Businesses owe a duty to make safe products, not to cause accidents, and so on.

No court has ever given, nor do we think ever can give, a definition of what constitutes a reasonable or an average man.

Lord Goddard C.J.R. v. McCarthy *(1954)*

The courts decide whether a duty of care is owed in specific cases by applying a *reasonable person standard*. Under this test, the courts attempt to determine how an *objective, careful, and conscientious person would have acted in the same circumstances* and then measure the defendant's conduct against that standard. The defendant's subjective intent ("I did not mean to do it") is immaterial in assessing liability. Certain impairments do not affect the reasonable person standard.

Defendants with a particular expertise or competence are measured against a *reasonable professional standard*. This standard is applied in much the same way as the reasonable person standard.

Breach of Duty

Once a court finds that the defendant actually owed the plaintiff a duty of care, it must determine whether the defendant breached that duty. A **breach of the duty of care** is the failure to exercise care. In other words, it is the failure to act as a reasonable person would act. A breach of this duty may consist of an action.

breach of the duty of care
A failure to exercise care or to act as a reasonable person would act.

Example Throwing a lit match on the ground in the forest and causing a fire is a breach of a duty of care.

A breach of duty may also consist of a failure to act when there is a duty to act.

Example A firefighter who refuses to put out a fire when her safety is not at stake breaches her duty of care for failing to act when she has a duty to act.

Passersby are generally not expected to rescue others gratuitously to save them from harm. However, most states require certain relatives—parents to children, children to parents if the children are old enough—to try to save their relatives from harm.

CONTEMPORARY ENVIRONMENT

Ouch! McDonald's Coffee Is Too Hot!

McDonald's Corporation found itself embroiled in one of the most famous negligence cases of modern times. Many studies have shown that people care less about how good their coffee tastes than whether it is hot. So restaurants, coffee shops, and other sellers make their coffee hot. McDonald's, however, discovered that it was in hot water for making its coffee too hot.

Stella Liebeck, a 79-year-old resident of Albuquerque, New Mexico, visited a drive-through window of a McDonald's restaurant with her grandson Chris. Her grandson, the driver of the vehicle, placed the order for breakfast. When breakfast came at the drive-through window, Chris handed a hot cup of coffee to Stella. Because there were no cup holders in the vehicle, Chris pulled over so that Stella could put cream and sugar in her coffee. Stella took the lid off the coffee cup she held in her lap and the hot coffee spilled in her lap. The coffee spilled all over Stella, who suffered third-degree burns on her legs, thighs, groin, and buttocks. Stella was driven to the emergency room and was hospitalized for seven days. She required medical treatment and later returned to the hospital to have skin grafts. She suffered permanent scars from the incident.

Stella's medical costs were $11,000. Stella asked McDonald's to pay her $20,000 to settle the case, but McDonald's offered only $800. Stella refused this settlement and sued McDonald's in court for negligence for selling coffee that was too hot and for failing to warn her of the danger of the hot coffee it served. McDonald's went to trial.

At trial, McDonald's denied that it had been negligent and asserted that Stella's own negligence—opening a hot coffee cup on her lap—had caused her injuries. The jury heard evidence that McDonald's enforces a quality-control rule that requires its restaurants and franchises to serve coffee at 180 to 190 degrees Fahrenheit. Third-degree burns occur on skin in just two to five seconds when coffee is served at 185 degrees. Evidence at trial showed that McDonald's coffee temperature was 20 degrees hotter than coffee served by competing restaurant chains and approximately 40 to 50 degrees hotter than normal house-brewed coffee. Evidence also showed that McDonald's had received more than 700 prior complaints of people who had been scalded by McDonald's coffee, but McDonald's had failed to place a warning on its cups to alert patrons that the coffee it served would scald skin.

Based on this evidence, the jury turned its anger on McDonald's and concluded that McDonald's acted recklessly and awarded Stella $200,000 compensatory damages (reduced by $40,000 for her own negligence) and $2.7 million punitive damages. The trial court judge reduced the amount of punitive damages to $480,000, which was three times the amount of compensatory damages. McDonald's has not turned down the temperature of its coffee, but it does place warnings on its coffee cups. *Liebeck v. McDonald's Restaurants, P.T.S., Inc.* (New Mexico District Court, Bernalillo County, New Mexico, 1994)

In the following case, the court had to determine whether the defendant was liable for negligence.

CASE 2 Negligence

James v. Meow Media, Inc.

300 F.3d 683, Web 2002 U.S. App. Lexis 16185 (2002)
United States Court of Appeals for the Sixth Circuit

"Our inquiry is whether the deaths of James, Steger, and Hadley were the reasonably foreseeable result of the defendants' creation and distribution of their games, movie, and Internet sites."

—Judge Boggs

Facts

Michael Carneal was a 14-year-old freshman student at Heath High School in Paducah, Kentucky. Carneal regularly played the violent interactive video and computer games "Doom," "Quake," "Castle Wolfenstein," "Rampage," "Nightmare Creatures," "Mech Warrior," "Resident Evil," and "Final Fantasy." These games involved the player shooting virtual opponents with computer guns and other weapons. Carneal also watched videotaped movies, including one called *The Basketball Diaries*, in which a high-school-student protagonist dreams of killing his teacher and several of his fellow classmates. On December 1, 1997, Carneal took a .22-caliber pistol and five shotguns into the lobby of Heath High School and shot several of his fellow students, killing three and wounding many others. The three students killed were Jessica James, Kayce Steger, and Nicole Hadley.

The parents of the three dead children ("James") sued the producers and distributors of the violent video games and movies that Carneal had watched previous to the shooting. The parents sued to recover damages for wrongful death, alleging that the defendants were negligent in producing and distributing such games and movies to Carneal. The U.S. District Court applied Kentucky law and held that the defendants did not owe or breach a duty to the plaintiffs and therefore were not liable for negligence. The plaintiffs appealed.

Issue

Did the defendant video and movie producers and distributors owe a duty of care to the plaintiffs by selling and licensing violent video games and movies to Carneal, who killed the three children?

Language of the Court

Kentucky courts have held that the determination of whether a duty of care exists is whether the harm to the plaintiff resulting from the defendant's negligence was "foreseeable." Kentucky courts have struggled with the formless nature of this inquiry. Our inquiry is whether the deaths of James, Steger, and Hadley were the reasonably foreseeable result of the defendants' creation and distribution of their games, movie, and Internet sites.

It appears simply impossible to predict that these games, movie, and Internet sites would incite a young person to violence. We find that it is simply too far a leap from shooting characters on a video screen (an activity undertaken by millions) to shooting people in a classroom (an activity undertaken by a handful, at most) for Carneal's actions to have been reasonably foreseeable to the manufacturers of the media that Carneal played and viewed. Carneal's reaction was not a normal reaction. Indeed, Carneal is not a normal person. Individuals are generally entitled to assume that third parties will not commit intentional criminal acts.

Decision

The Court of Appeals held that the defendant video game and movie producers and distributors did not owe a duty of care to the plaintiffs by selling and licensing violent video games and movies to Carneal, who murdered the three children.

Case Questions

Critical Legal Thinking How do the courts define *foreseeability*? Did the Court of Appeals use a narrow, middle, or broad interpretation of foreseeability in deciding this case? Explain.

Business Ethics Do producers and distributors of video games and movies owe a duty of care to society not to produce and distribute violent games and movies?

Contemporary Business What would have been the consequences for the video game and movie industries if the court had held in favor of the plaintiffs? Are any free speech issues involved in this case? Explain.

Injury to Plaintiff

Even though a defendant's negligent act may have breached a duty of care owed to the plaintiff, this breach is not actionable unless the plaintiff suffers **injury** or injury to his or her property. That is, the plaintiff must have suffered some injury before he or she can recover any damages.

The damages recoverable depend on the effect of the injury on the plaintiff's life or profession.

injury
A plaintiff's personal injury or damage to his or her property that enables him or her to recover monetary damages for the defendant's negligence.

Examples Suppose that a man injures his hand when a train door malfunctions. The train company is found negligent. If the injured man is a star professional basketball player who makes $5 million per year, with an expected seven years of good playing time left, this plaintiff can recover multiple millions of dollars because he can no longer play professional basketball. If the injured man is a college professor with 15 years until retirement who is making only one-fortieth per year of what the basketball player makes, he can recover some money for his injuries. Because he makes a lot less per year than the professional basketball player and because he can continue working, albeit with more difficulty, the professor can recover much less for the same injury.

Actual Cause

actual cause
The actual cause of negligence. A person who commits a negligent act is not liable unless actual cause can be proven. Also called *causation in fact*.

A defendant's negligent act must be the **causation in fact**, or **actual cause**, of the plaintiff's injuries. The test is this: "But for" the defendant's conduct, would the accident have happened? If the defendant's act caused the plaintiff's injuries, there is causation in fact.

Examples Suppose a corporation negligently pollutes the plaintiff's drinking water. The plaintiff dies of a heart attack unrelated to the polluted water. Although the corporation has acted negligently, it is not liable for the plaintiff's death. There were a negligent act and an injury, but there was no cause-and-effect relationship between them. If, instead, the plaintiff had died from the polluted drinking water, there would have been causation in fact, and the polluting corporation would have been liable.

If two (or more) persons are liable for negligently causing the plaintiff's injuries, both (or all) can be held liable to the plaintiff if each of their acts is a substantial factor in causing the plaintiff's injuries.

Proximate Cause

Under the law, a negligent party is not necessarily liable for all damages set in motion by his or her negligent act. Based on public policy, the law establishes a point along the damage chain after which the negligent party is no longer responsible for the consequences of his or her actions. This limitation on liability is referred to as **proximate cause**, or **legal cause**. The general test of proximate cause is *foreseeability*. A negligent party who is found to be the actual cause—but not the proximate cause—of the plaintiff's injuries is not liable to the plaintiff. Situations are examined on a case-by-case basis.

proximate cause
A point along a chain of events caused by a negligent party after which this party is no longer legally responsible for the consequences of his or her actions. Also called *legal cause*.

LANDMARK LAW

Palsgraf v. The Long Island Railroad Company

"Negligence is not actionable unless it involves the invasion of a legally protected interest, the violation of a right. Proof of negligence in the air, so to speak, will not do."

—Justice Cardozo

The landmark case establishing the doctrine of proximate cause is ***Palsgraf v. The Long Island Railroad Company***, a New York case decided in 1928. Helen Palsgraf was standing on a platform, waiting for a passenger train. The Long Island Railroad Company owned and operated the trains and employed the station guards. As a man carrying a package wrapped in a newspaper tried to board the moving train, railroad guards tried to help him. In doing so, the package was dislodged from the man's arm, fell to the railroad tracks, and exploded. The package contained hidden fireworks. The explosion shook the railroad platform, causing a scale located on the platform to fall on Helen Palsgraf, injuring her.

Palsgraf sued the railroad for negligence. Justice Cardozo eloquently addressed the issue of proximate cause:

> *The conduct of the defendant's guard, if a wrong in its relation to the holder of the package, was not a wrong in its relation to the plaintiff, standing far away. Relatively to her it was not negligence at all. Nothing in the situation gave notice that the falling package had in it the potency of peril to persons thus removed. Negligence is not actionable unless it involves the invasion of a legally protected interest, the violation of a right. Proof of negligence in the air, so to speak, will not do. In every instance, before negligence can be predicated on a given act, in back of the act must be sought and found a duty to the individual complaining, the observance of which would have averted or avoided the injury.*
>
> *The argument for the plaintiff is built upon the shifting meanings of such words as "wrong" and "wrongful," and shares their instability. What the plaintiff must show is "a wrong" to herself, i.e., a violation of her own right, and not merely a wrong to some one else, nor conduct "wrongful" because unsocial. The risk reasonably to be perceived defines the duty to be obeyed, and risk imports relation; it is risk to another or to others within the range of apprehension. Here, by concession, there was nothing in the situation to suggest to the most cautious mind that the parcel wrapped in newspaper would spread wreckage through the station. If the guard had thrown it down knowingly and willfully, he would not have threatened the plaintiff's safety, so far as appearances could warn him.*

His conduct would not have involved, even then, an unreasonable probability of invasion of her bodily security. Liability can be no greater where the act is inadvertent.

Negligence, like risk, is thus a term of relation. Negligence in the abstract, apart from things related, is surely not a tort, if indeed it is understandable at all. One who seeks redress at law does not make out a cause of action by showing without more that there has been damage to his person. If the harm was not willful, he must show that the act as to him had possibilities of danger so many and apparent as to entitle him to be protected against the doing of it though the harm was unintended.

Justice Cardozo denied Palsgraf's recovery, finding that the railroad company was not the proximate cause of her injuries. *Palsgraf v. The Long Island Railroad Company*, 248 N.Y. 339, 162 N.E. 99, **Web** 1928 N.Y. Lexis 1269 (Court of Appeals of New York, 1928)

Automobiles, Las Vegas, Nevada *Most automobile and other vehicle drivers drive safely and are not often involved in accidents. However, vehicular accidents are a primary cause of injury and death. In the United States there are more than 40,000 fatalities of passenger car and SUV occupants, pedestrians, and cyclists each year. More than 4,000 motor cycle fatalities also occur each year.*

SPECIAL NEGLIGENCE DOCTRINES

The courts have developed many *special negligence doctrines*. The most important of these are discussed in the paragraphs that follow.

Professional Malpractice

Professionals, such as doctors, lawyers, architects, accountants, and others, owe a duty of ordinary care in providing their services. This duty is known as the *reasonable professional standard*. A professional who breaches this duty of care is liable for the injury his or her negligence causes. This liability is commonly referred to as **professional malpractice**.

professional malpractice The liability of a professional who breaches his or her duty of ordinary care.

Examples A doctor who amputates a wrong leg is liable for *medical malpractice*. A lawyer who fails to file a document with the court on time, causing the client's case to be dismissed, is liable for *legal malpractice*. An accountant who fails to use reasonable care, knowledge, skill, and judgment in providing auditing and other accounting services to a client is liable for *accounting malpractice*.

negligent infliction of emotional distress A tort that permits a person to recover for emotional distress caused by the defendant's negligent conduct.

Negligent Infliction of Emotional Distress

Some jurisdictions have extended the tort of emotional distress to include the **negligent infliction of emotional distress**.

Example The most common example of negligent infliction of emotional distress involve bystanders who witness the injury or death of a loved one that is caused by another's negligent conduct. Under this tort, the bystander, even though not personally physically injured, can sue the negligent party for his or her own mental suffering.

Generally, to be successful in this type of case, the plaintiff must prove that (1) a close relative was killed or injured by the defendant, (2) the plaintiff suffered severe emotional distress, and (3) the plaintiff's mental distress resulted from a sensory and contemporaneous observance of the accident. Some states require that the plaintiff's mental distress be manifested by some physical injury; other states have eliminated this requirement.

Negligence per Se

negligence per se
A tort in which the violation of a statute or an ordinance constitutes the breach of the duty of care.

Statutes often establish duties owed by one person to another. The violation of a statute that proximately causes an injury is **negligence per se**. The plaintiff in such an action must prove that (1) a statute existed, (2) the statute was enacted to prevent the type of injury suffered, and (3) the plaintiff was within a class of persons meant to be protected by the statute.

Example Most cities have an ordinance that places the responsibility for fixing public sidewalks in residential areas on the homeowners whose homes front the sidewalks. A homeowner is liable if he or she fails to repair a damaged sidewalk in front of his or her home and a pedestrian trips and is injured because of the damage. The injured party does not have to prove that the homeowner owed the duty because the statute establishes that.

Res Ipsa Loquitur

res ipsa loquitur
A tort in which the presumption of negligence arises because (1) the defendant was in exclusive control of the situation and (2) the plaintiff would not have suffered injury but for someone's negligence. The burden switches to the defendant to prove that he or she was not negligent.

If a defendant is in control of a situation in which a plaintiff has been injured and has superior knowledge of the circumstances surrounding the injury, the plaintiff might have difficulty proving the defendant's negligence. In such a situation, the law applies the doctrine of ***res ipsa loquitur*** (Latin for "the thing speaks for itself"). This doctrine raises a presumption of negligence and switches the burden to the defendant to prove that he or she was not negligent. *Res ipsa loquitur* applies in cases where the following elements are met:

1. The defendant had exclusive control of the instrumentality or situation that caused the plaintiff's injury.
2. The injury would not have ordinarily occurred but for someone's negligence.

Examples Haeran goes in for major surgery and is given anesthesia to put her to sleep during the operation. Sometime after the operation, it is discovered that a surgical instrument was left in Haeran during the operation. She suffers severe injury because of the left-in instrument. Haeran has no way to identify which doctor or nurse carelessly left the instrument in her body. In this case, the court can apply the doctrine of *res ipsa loquitur* and place the presumption of negligence on the defendants. Any defendant who can prove he or she did not leave the instrument in Haeran escapes liability; any defendant who does not disprove his or her negligence is liable. Other typical *res ipsa loquitur* cases involve commercial airplane crashes, falling elevators, and the like.

Good Samaritan Laws

Good Samaritan law
A statute that relieves medical professionals from liability for ordinary negligence when they stop and render aid to victims in emergency situations.

In the past, liability exposure made many doctors, nurses, and other medical professionals reluctant to stop and render aid to victims in emergency situations, such as highway accidents. Almost all states have enacted **Good Samaritan laws** that relieve medical professionals from liability for injury caused by their ordinary negligence in such circumstances. Good Samaritan laws protect medical professionals only from liability for their *ordinary negligence*, not for injuries caused by their gross negligence or reckless or intentional conduct. Most Good Samaritan laws protect licensed doctors, nurses, and laypersons who have been certified in CPR. Laypersons not trained in CPR are not generally protected by

Good Samaritan statutes—that is, they are liable for injuries caused by their ordinary negligence in rendering aid.

Examples Sam is injured in an automobile accident and is unconscious in his automobile alongside the road. Doctor Pamela Heathcoat, who is driving by the scene of the accident, stops, pulls Sam from the burning wreckage, and administers first aid. In doing so, Pamela negligently breaks Sam's shoulder. If Pamela's negligence is ordinary negligence, she is not liable to Sam because the Good Samaritan law protects her from liability; if Pamela was grossly negligent or reckless in administering aid to Sam, she is liable to him for the injuries she caused. It is a question of fact for the jury to decide whether a doctor's conduct was ordinary negligence or gross negligence or recklessness.

Every unjust decision is a reproach to the law or the judge who administers it. If the law should be in danger of doing injustice, then equity should be called in to remedy it. Equity was introduced to mitigate the rigour of the law.

Lord Denning
M.R. Re Vandervell's Trusts
(1974)

▶ DEFENSES AGAINST NEGLIGENCE

A defendant in a negligence lawsuit may raise several defenses to the imposition of liability. These defenses are discussed in the following paragraphs.

Superseding or Intervening Event

Under negligence, a person is liable only for foreseeable events. Therefore, an original negligent party can raise a **superseding event** or an **intervening event** as a defense to liability.

superseding or intervening event
An event for which a defendant is not responsible. The defendant is not liable for injuries caused by the superseding or intervening event.

Example Assume that an avid golfer negligently hits a spectator with a golf ball, knocking the spectator unconscious. While lying on the ground, waiting for an ambulance to come, the spectator is struck by a bolt of lightning and killed. The golfer is liable for the injuries caused by the golf ball. He is not liable for the death of the spectator, however, because the lightning bolt was an unforeseen intervening event.

Assumption of the Risk

If a plaintiff knows of and voluntarily enters into or participates in a risky activity that results in injury, the law recognizes that the plaintiff assumed, or took on, the risk involved. Thus, the defendant can raise the defense of **assumption of the risk** against the plaintiff. This defense assumes that the plaintiff (1) had knowledge of the specific risk and (2) voluntarily assumed that risk.

assumption of the risk
A defense a defendant can use against a plaintiff who knowingly and voluntarily enters into or participates in a risky activity that results in injury.

Example Under assumption of the risk, a race-car driver assumes the risk of being injured or killed in a crash.

In the following case, the court had to decide whether the plaintiff had assumed the risk.

CASE 3 Assumption of the Risk

Lilya v. The Greater Gulf State Fair, Inc.

855 So.2d 1049, Web 2003 Ala. Lexis 57 (2003)
Supreme Court of Alabama

"Here, the only evidence of danger stemming from the mechanical bull ride is the most open and obvious characteristic of the ride: the possibility of falling off the mechanical bull."

—Judge Houston

Facts

The Greater Gulf State Fair, Inc., operated the Gulf State Fair in Mobile County, Alabama. One of the events at the fair was a mechanical bull ride for which participants paid money to ride the mechanical bull. A mechanical bull is a ride where the rider sits on a motorized device shaped like a real bull, and the ride simulates a real bull ride as the mechanical bull turns, twists, and bucks. The challenge is to stay on the bull and not be thrown off the bull. A large banner above the ride read "Rolling Thunder."

John Lilya and a friend watched as a rider was thrown from the mechanical bull. Lilya also watched as his friend paid and rode the bull and also was thrown off. Lilya then paid the $5 admission charge and signed a release agreement that stated:

> *I acknowledge that riding a mechanical bull entails known and unanticipated risks which could result in physical or emotional injury, paralysis, death, or damage to myself, to property, or to third parties. I expressly agree and promise to accept and assume all of the risks existing in this activity. My participation in this activity is purely voluntary, and I elect to participate in spite of the risks.*

Lilya boarded the mechanical bull and was immediately thrown off onto a soft pad underneath the bull. Lilya reboarded the bull for a second ride. The bull ride began again and became progressively faster, spinning and bucking to the left and right until Lilya fell off the bull. On the fall, Lilya landed on his head and shoulders, and he suffered a fractured neck. Lilya sued Gulf State Fair to recover damages for his severe injuries. The trial court granted summary judgment to Gulf State Fair, finding that Lilya had voluntarily assumed an open and obvious danger. Lilya appealed.

Issue

Was riding a mechanical bull an open and obvious danger for which Lilya had voluntarily assumed the risk when he rode the mechanical bull?

Language of the Court

As the landowner, Gulf State Fair would owe Lilya, its invitee, the duty to use reasonable care. The owner of premises has no duty to warn an invitee of open and obvious defects in the premises which the invitee is aware of or should be aware of in the exercise of reasonable care. Here, the only evidence of danger stemming from the mechanical bull ride is the most open and obvious characteristic of the ride: the possibility of falling off the mechanical bull. Lilya was aware that the two riders who had ridden the mechanical bull immediately before he rode it had fallen off. He noticed the thick floor mat, and he knew that the mat was there to protect riders when they fell. Also, he signed a release that explicitly stated that riding the mechanical bull involved inherent risks and that the risks included falling off or being thrown from the bull which could result in head, neck, and back injuries. Additionally, the very name of the ride—"Rolling Thunder"—hanging on a banner above the ride, gives a somewhat graphic indication of what is the very nature of bull riding: an extremely turbulent, ride the challenge of which is to hang on and not fall off. The entertainment value—and, indeed, the concept—of bull riding becomes meaningless without the inherent possibility of falling off. "Volenti non fit injuria" (a person who knowingly and voluntarily risks danger cannot recover for any resulting injury).

Decision

The supreme court of Alabama held that riding a mechanical bull and being thrown and injured by the bull is an open and obvious danger and that Lilya had voluntarily assumed the risk when he rode the bull and was thrown and injured. The supreme court affirmed the trial court's grant of summary judgment in favor of Gulf State Fair.

Case Questions

Critical Legal Thinking What does the doctrine of assumption of the risk provide? Do you think the doctrine of assumption of the risk should be recognized by the law? Explain.

Business Ethics Did Gulf State Fair act ethically by making money from such a dangerous activity as mechanical bull riding? Did Lilya act ethically in suing for damages?

Contemporary Business What public purpose does the defense of assumption of the risk serve? What would be the consequences if this defense were not available? Explain.

Contributory Negligence

contributory negligence
A doctrine that says a plaintiff who is partially at fault for his or her own injury cannot recover against the negligent defendant.

Sometimes a plaintiff is partially liable for causing his or her own injuries. Under the common law doctrine of **contributory negligence**, a plaintiff who is partially at fault for his or her own injury cannot recover against the negligent defendant. Many states follow this rule.

Example Suppose a driver who is driving over the speed limit negligently hits and injures a pedestrian who is jaywalking. Suppose the jury finds that the driver is 80 percent responsible for the accident, and the jaywalker is 20 percent responsible. The pedestrian suffered

$100,000 in injuries. Under the doctrine of contributory negligence, the pedestrian cannot recover any damages from the driver.

Last Clear Chance Rule There is one major exception to the doctrine of contributory negligence: The defendant has a duty under the law to avoid the accident if at all possible. This rule is known as the *last clear chance rule*.

Example A driver who sees a pedestrian walking across the street against a "Don't Walk" sign must avoid hitting him or her if possible. When deciding cases involving this rule, the courts consider the attentiveness of the parties and the amount of time each had to respond to the situation.

Comparative Negligence

The application of the doctrine of contributory negligence could reach an unfair result where a party only slightly at fault for his or her injuries could not recover from an otherwise negligent defendant. Many states have replaced the doctrine of contributory negligence with the doctrine of **comparative negligence**, also called **comparative fault**. Under this doctrine, damages are apportioned according to fault.

comparative negligence
A doctrine under which damages are apportioned according to fault.

Example When the comparative negligence rule is applied to the previous example, the result is much fairer. The plaintiff-pedestrian, who was 20 percent at fault for causing his own injuries, can recover 80 percent of his damages (or $80,000) from the defendant-driver. This is an example of **pure comparative negligence**.

Several states have adopted **partial comparative negligence**, which provides that a plaintiff must be less than 50 percent responsible for causing his or her own injuries to recover under comparative negligence; otherwise, contributory negligence applies.

▶ STRICT LIABILITY

Strict liability, another category of torts, is *liability without fault*. That is, a participant in a covered activity will be held liable for any injuries caused by the activity, even if he or she was not negligent. This doctrine holds that (1) there are certain activities that can place the public at risk of injury even if reasonable care is taken and (2) the public should have some means of compensation if such injury occurs.

strict liability
Liability without fault.

Strict liability was first imposed for **abnormally dangerous activities**, such as crop dusting, blasting, fumigation, burning of fields, storage of explosives, and the keeping of wild animals as pets.

Peter Wilson © Dorling Kindersley

District of Shinjuku in Tokyo, Japan *Each country has developed its own civil law system. In Japan, for example, no class actions or contingency fee arrangements are allowed. Plaintiffs must pay their lawyers an upfront fee of up to eight percent of the damages sought, plus a nonrefundable filing fee to the court of one-half of one percent of the damages sought. No discovery is permitted. Even if the plaintiff wins the lawsuit, damage awards are low. Therefore, most legal disputes in Japan are decided by private arbitrators.*

TEST REVIEW TERMS AND CONCEPTS

Abnormally dangerous activities
Actual cause (causation in fact)
Assault
Assumption of the risk
Battery
Breach of the duty of care
Comparative negligence (comparative fault)
Contributory negligence
Defamation of character
Disparagement (trade libel, product disparagement, or slander of title)
Duty of care
False imprisonment
Good Samaritan law
Injury
Intentional infliction of emotional distress (tort of outrage)
Intentional misrepresentation (fraud or deceit)
Intentional tort
Intervening event
Invasion of the right to privacy
Libel
Malicious prosecution
Merchant protection statute (shopkeeper's privilege)
Misappropriation of the right to publicity (tort of appropriation)
Negligence (unintentional tort)
Negligence per se
Negligent infliction of emotional distress
New York Times Co. v. Sullivan
Palsgraf v. The Long Island Railroad Company
Partial comparative negligence
Professional malpractice
Proximate cause (legal cause)
Pure comparative negligence
Res ipsa loquitur
Scienter
Slander
Strict liability
Superseding event
Tort
Tort of appropriation
Transferred intent doctrine

CASE PROBLEMS

1 Intentional Tort The Baltimore Orioles, a professional baseball team, visited Boston's Fenway Park to play the Boston Red Sox, another professional baseball team. Ross Grimsley was a pitcher for the visiting Baltimore club. During one period of the game, Grimsley was warming up in the bullpen, throwing pitches to a catcher. During this warm-up, Boston spectators in the stands heckled Grimsley. After Grimsley had completed warming up, Grimsley wound up as if he were going to throw the ball in his hand at the plate but then turned and threw the ball at one of the hecklers in the stand. The ball traveled at about 80 miles an hour, passed through a wire fence protecting the spectators, missed the heckler that Grimsley was aiming at, and hit another spectator, David Manning, Jr., causing injury. Manning sued Grimsley and the Baltimore Orioles. Are the defendants liable? *Manning v. Grimsley*, 643 F.2d 20, **Web** 1981 U.S. App. Lexis 19782 (United States Court of Appeals for the First Circuit)

2 Merchant Protection Statute At about 7:30 P.M., Deborah A. Johnson entered a Kmart store located in Madison, Wisconsin, to purchase some diapers and several cans of motor oil. She took her small child along to enable her to purchase the correct size diapers, carrying the child in an infant seat that she had purchased at Kmart two or three weeks previously. A large Kmart price tag was still attached to the infant seat. Johnson purchased the diapers and oil and some children's clothes. She was in a hurry to leave because it was 8:00 P.M., her child's feeding time, and she hurried through the checkout lane. She paid for the diapers, the oil, and the clothing. Just after leaving the store, she heard someone ask her to stop. She turned around and saw a Kmart security officer. He showed her a badge and asked her to come back into the store, which she did. The man stated, "I have reason to believe that you have stolen this car seat." Johnson explained that she had purchased the seat previously. She demanded to see the manager, who was called to the scene. When Johnson pointed out that the seat had cat hairs, food crumbs, and milk stains on it, the man said, "I'm really sorry, there's been a terrible mistake. You can go." Johnson looked at the clock, which read 8:20 P.M., when she left. Johnson sued Kmart for false imprisonment. Is Kmart liable? *Johnson v. K-Mart Enterprises, Inc.*, 98 Wis.2d 533, 297 N.W.2d 74, **Web** 1980 Wisc.App. Lexis 3197 (Court of Appeals of Wisconsin)

3 Negligence George Yanase was a paying guest at the Royal Lodge-Downtown Motel in San Diego, California. Yanase was a member of the Automobile Club of Southern California. The Auto Club publishes a "Tourbook" in which it lists hotels and motels and rates the quality of their services, including the cleanliness of rooms, quality of the restaurant, level of personal service, and the like. Yanase had selected the Royal from the Tourbook. On the night of his stay at the Royal, Yanase was shot in the parking lot adjacent to the motel and died as a result of his injuries. Yanase's widow sued the Auto Club for negligence. Is the Auto Club liable? *Yanase v. Automobile Club of Southern California*, 212 Cal.App.3d 468, 260 Cal.Rptr. 513, **Web** 1989 Cal.App. Lexis 746 (Court of Appeal of California)

4 Causation W. L. Brown purchased a new large Chevrolet truck from Days Chevrolet. The truck had been manufactured by General Motors Corporation. One month later, an employee of Brown's was operating the truck when it ceased to function in rush-hour traffic on Interstate Highway 75 in the Atlanta suburbs. A defect within the alternator had caused a complete failure of the truck's electrical system. The defect was caused by General Motors's negligence in manufacturing the truck. When the alternator failed to operate, the truck came to rest in the right-hand lane of two north-bound lanes of freeway traffic. Because of the electrical failure, no blinking lights could be used to warn traffic of the danger. The driver, however, tried to motion traffic around the truck. Sometime later, when the freeway traffic had returned to normal, the large Chevrolet truck was still motionless on the freeway. At approximately 6:00 P.M., a panel truck approached the stalled truck in the right-hand lane of traffic at freeway speed. Immediately behind the panel truck, Mr. Davis, driving a Volkswagen fastback, was unable to see the stalled truck. At the last moment, the driver of the panel truck saw the stalled truck and swerved into another lane to avoid it. Mr. Davis drove his Volkswagen into the stalled truck at freeway speed, causing his death. Mr. Davis's wife brought a wrongful death action based on negligence against General Motors. Is there causation linking the negligence of the defendant to the fatal accident? *General Motors Corporation v. Davis*, 141 Ga.App. 495, 233 S.E.2d 825, **Web** 1977 Ga.App. Lexis 1961 (Court of Appeals of Georgia)

5 Negligence Per Se Julius Ebanks set out from his home in East Elmhurst, Queens, New York, en route to his employment in the downtown district of Manhattan. When Ebanks reached Bowling Green subway station, he boarded an escalator owned and operated by the New York City Transit Authority. While the escalator was ascending, Ebanks's left foot became caught in a two-inch gap between the escalator step on which he was standing and the side wall of the escalator. Ebanks was unable to free himself. When he reached the top of the escalator, he was thrown to the ground, fracturing his hip and causing other serious injuries. The two-inch gap exceeded the three-eighths-inch standard required by the city's building code. Ebanks sued the Transit Authority to recover damages for his injuries. Who wins? *Ebanks v. New York City Transit Authority*, 70 N.Y.2d 621, 518 N.Y.S.2d 776, **Web** 1987 N.Y. Lexis 17294 (Court of Appeals of New York)

6 Emotional Distress Gregory and Demetria James, brother and sister, were riding their bicycles north on 50th Street in Omaha, Nebraska. Spaulding Street intersects 50th Street. A garbage truck owned by Watts Trucking Service, Inc., and driven by its employee, John Milton Lieb, was backing up into the intersection of 50th and Spaulding streets. The truck backed into the intersection, through a stop sign, and hit and ran over Demetria, killing her. Gregory helplessly watched the entire accident but was not in danger himself. As a result of watching his sister's peril, Gregory suffered severe emotional distress. Gregory sued Watts and Lieb to recover damages for his emotional distress. Who wins? *James v. Watts Trucking Service, Inc.*, 221 Neb. 47, 375 N.W.2d 109, **Web** 1985 Neb. Lexis 1209 (Supreme Court of Nebraska)

7 Defense The New York Yankees professional baseball team played the Chicago White Sox at Shea Stadium, New York. Elliot Maddox played center field for the Yankees that night. It had rained the day before, and the previous night's game had been canceled because of bad weather. On the evening of the game, the playing field was still wet, and Maddox commented on this fact several times to the club's manager but continued to play. In the ninth inning, when Maddox was attempting to field a ball in center field, he slipped on a wet spot, fell, and injured his right knee. Maddox sued the City of New York, which owned Shea Stadium; the Metropolitan Baseball Club, Inc., as lessee; the architect; the consulting engineer; and the American Baseball League. Maddox alleged that the parties were negligent in causing the field to be wet and that the injury ended his professional career. Who wins? *Maddox v. City of New York*, 66 N.Y.2d 270, 487 N.E.2d 553, 496 N.Y.S.2d 726, **Web** 1985 N.Y. Lexis 17254 (Court of Appeals of New York)

BUSINESS ETHICS CASES

8 Business Ethics Radio station KHJ was a successful Los Angeles broadcaster of rock music that commanded a 48 percent market share of the teenage audience in the Los Angeles area. KHJ was owned and operated by RKO General, Inc. KHJ inaugurated a promotion titled "The Super Summer Spectacular." As part of this promotion, KHJ had a disc jockey known as "The Real Don Steele" ride around the Los Angeles area in a conspicuous red automobile. Periodically KHJ would announce to its radio audience Steele's location. The first listener to thereafter locate Steele and answer a question received a cash prize and participated in a brief interview on the air with Steele. One KHJ broadcast identified Steele's next destination as Canoga Park. Robert Sentner, 17 years old, heard the broadcast and immediately drove to Canoga Park. Marsha Baime, 19 years old, also heard the broadcast and drove to Canoga Park. By the time Sentner and Baime located Steele, someone else had already claimed the prize. Without the knowledge of the other, Sentner and Baime each decided to follow Steele to the next destination and to be first to "find" him.

Steele proceeded onto the freeway. For the next few miles Sentner and Baime tried to jockey for position closest to the Steele vehicle, reaching speeds of up to 80 miles per hour. There is no evidence that the Steele vehicle exceeded the speed limit. When Steele left the freeway at the Westlake off ramp, Sentner and Baime tried to follow. In their attempts to do so, they knocked another vehicle, driven by Mr. Weirum, into the center divider of the freeway, where it overturned. Mr. Weirum died in the accident. Baime stopped to report the accident. Sentner, after pausing momentarily to relate the tragedy to a passing police officer, got back into his car, pursued and successfully located Steele, and collected the cash prize. The wife and children of Mr. Weirum brought a wrongful death negligence action against Sentner, Baime, and

RKO General. Who wins? Did RKO General, Inc., act responsibly in this case? *Weirum v. RKO General, Inc.*, 15 Cal.3d 40, 539 P.2d 36, 123 Cal.Rptr. 468, **Web** 1975 Cal. Lexis 220 (Supreme Court of California)

9 Business Ethics Guy Portee, a seven-year-old, resided with his mother in an apartment building in Newark, New Jersey. Edith and Nathan Jaffee owned and operated the building. One day, Guy became trapped in the building's elevator, between its outer door and the wall of the elevator shaft. When someone activated the elevator, the boy was dragged up to the third floor. Another child who saw the accident ran to seek help. Soon afterward, Renee Portee, the boy's mother, and Newark Police Department officers arrived. The officers worked for hours, trying to release the boy, during which time the mother watched as her son moaned, cried out, and flailed his arms. The police contacted the Atlantic Elevator Company, which was responsible for the installation and maintenance of the elevator, and requested that the company send a mechanic to assist in the effort to free the boy. Apparently no one came. The boy suffered multiple bone fractures and massive internal hemorrhaging. He died while still trapped, his mother a helpless observer.

After her son's death, Renee became severely distressed and seriously self-destructive. Three years after the incident, she attempted to take her own life. She survived, and the wound was repaired by surgery, but thereafter she required considerable physical therapy. She had received extensive counseling and psychotherapy to help overcome the mental and emotional problems associated with her son's death. Renee sued the Jaffees and Atlantic to recover damages for her emotional distress. Who wins? Did either of the defendants act unethically in this case? *Portee v. Jaffee*, 84 N.J. 88, 417 A.2d 521, **Web** 1980 N.J. Lexis 1387 (Supreme Court of New Jersey)

ENDNOTES

1. 376 U.S. 254, 84 S.Ct. 710, 11 L.Ed.2d 686, Web 1964 U.S. Lexis 1655 (Supreme Court of the United States, 1964).
2. *Restatement (Second) of Torts*, Section 46.
3. *Restatement (Second) of Torts*, Section 46, Comment d.
4. Justice B. Anderson, *Blyth v. Birmingham Waterworks Co.*, 11 Exch. 781, 784 (1856).

STRICT LIABILITY AND PRODUCT LIABILITY

▲ **Hot Dog Stand** *The sellers of goods, including food, can be held liable under the doctrines of negligence and strict liability for injuries caused by the products they sell.*

CHAPTER OBJECTIVES

After studying this chapter you should be able to:

1. Describe and distinguish among the several legal theories of product liability.
2. Define the doctrine of *strict liability*.
3. Identify and describe defects in manufacture and design.
4. Identify and describe defects of failure to warn and in packaging.
5. Describe the damages recoverable in a product liability lawsuit.

CHAPTER CONTENTS

"A manufacturer is strictly liable in tort when an article he places on the market, knowing that it is to be used without inspection for defects, proves to have a defect that causes injury to a human being."

—Greenman v. Yuba Power Products, Inc.
59 Cal.2d 57, 27 Cal.Rptr. 697, 1963 Cal. Lexis 140 (1963)

INTRODUCTION TO STRICT LIABILITY AND PRODUCT LIABILITY

product liability
The liability of manufacturers, sellers, and others for the injuries caused by defective products.

If a product defect causes injury or death to purchasers, lessees, users, or bystanders, the injured party or the heirs of a deceased person may bring legal actions and recover damages under certain tort doctrines. These tort doctrines include negligence, misrepresentation, and the modern theory of strict liability. The liability of manufacturers, sellers, lessors, and others for injuries caused by defective products is commonly referred to as **product liability**. If a violation of strict liability has been found, the plaintiff may also recover punitive damages if the defendant's conduct has been reckless or intentional.

The various tort principles that permit injured parties to recover damages caused by defective products are discussed in this chapter.

NEGLIGENCE AND MISREPRESENTATION

Depending on the circumstances of the case, persons who are injured by defective products may be able to recover damages under the tort theories of *negligence* and *misrepresentation*. Both theories require the defendant to be *at fault* for causing the plaintiff's injuries. These theories are discussed in the paragraphs that follow.

Negligence

negligence
A tort related to defective products in which the defendant has breached a duty of due care and caused harm to the plaintiff.

An injustice anywhere is an injustice everywhere.

Samuel Johnson

A person injured by a defective product may bring an action for **negligence** against the negligent party. To be successful, the plaintiff must prove that the defendant breached a duty of due care to the plaintiff and thereby caused the plaintiff's injuries. In other words, the plaintiff must prove that the defendant was at fault for causing his injuries.

Failure to exercise due care includes failing to assemble a product carefully, negligent product design, negligent inspection or testing of a product, negligent packaging, failure to warn of the dangerous propensities of a product, and such. It is important to note that in a negligence lawsuit, only a party who was actually negligent is liable to the plaintiff.

Example Assume that the purchaser of a motorcycle is injured in an accident. The accident occurred because a screw was missing from the motorcycle. How does the buyer prove who was negligent? Was it the manufacturer, which left the screw out during the assembly of the motorcycle? Was it the retailer, who negligently failed to discover the missing screw while preparing the motorcycle for sale? Was it the mechanic, who failed to replace the screw after repairing the motorcycle? Negligence remains a viable, yet difficult, theory on which to base a product liability action.

Misrepresentation

intentional misrepresentation
A tort in which a seller or lessor fraudulently misrepresents the quality of a product and a buyer is injured thereby. Also known as *fraud*.

A buyer or lessee who is injured because a seller or lessor fraudulently misrepresented the quality of a product can sue the seller for the tort of **intentional misrepresentation**, or **fraud**. Recovery is limited to persons who were injured because they relied on the misrepresentation.

Intentional misrepresentation occurs when a seller or lessor either (1) affirmatively misrepresents the quality of a product or (2) conceals a defect in it. Because most reputable manufacturers, sellers, and lessors do not intentionally misrepresent the quality of their products, fraud is not often used as the basis for product liability actions.

STRICT LIABILITY

In the landmark case ***Greenman v. Yuba Power Products, Inc.***,[1] the California Supreme court adopted the **doctrine of strict liability in tort** as a basis for product liability actions. Most states have now adopted this doctrine as a basis for product liability actions. The doctrine of strict liability removes many of the difficulties for the plaintiff associated with other theories of product liability. This section examines the scope of the strict liability doctrine.

Liability Without Fault

Unlike negligence, strict liability does not require the injured person to prove that the defendant breached a duty of care. **Strict liability** is **liability without fault**. A seller can be found strictly liable even though he or she has exercised all possible care in the preparation and sale of his or her product. Strict liability may not be disclaimed.

strict liability
A tort doctrine that makes manufacturers, distributors, wholesalers, retailers, and others in the chain of distribution of a defective product liable for the damages caused by the defect, *irrespective of fault*.

The doctrine of strict liability applies to sellers and lessors of products who are engaged in the business of selling and leasing products. Casual sales and transactions by nonmerchants are not covered. Thus, a person who sells a defective product to a neighbor in a casual sale is not strictly liable if the product causes injury.

Strict liability applies only to products, not services. In hybrid transactions that involve both services and products, the dominant element of the transaction dictates whether strict liability applies. For example, in a medical operation that requires a blood transfusion, the operation would be the dominant element, and strict liability would not apply. Strict liability may not be disclaimed.

All in the Chain of Distribution Are Liable

All parties in the **chain of distribution** of a defective product are strictly liable for the injuries caused by that product. Thus, all manufacturers, distributors, wholesalers, retailers, lessors, and subcomponent manufacturers may be sued under the doctrine of strict liability in tort. This view is based on public policy. Lawmakers presume that sellers and lessors will insure against the risk of a strict liability lawsuit and spread the cost to their consumers by raising the price of products.

chain of distribution
All manufacturers, distributors, wholesalers, retailers, lessors, and subcomponent manufacturers involved in a transaction.

Example Suppose a subcomponent manufacturer produces a defective tire and sells it to a truck manufacturer. The truck manufacturer places the defective tire on one of its new-model trucks. The truck is distributed by a distributor to a retail dealer. Ultimately, the retail dealer sells the truck to a buyer. The defective tire causes an accident in which the buyer is injured. All the parties in the tire's chain of distribution can be sued by the injured party; in this case, the liable parties are the subcomponent manufacturer, the truck manufacturer, the distributor, and the retailer.

Exhibit 1 compares the doctrines of negligence and strict liability.

A defendant who has not been negligent but who is made to pay a strict liability judgment can bring a separate action against the negligent party in the chain of distribution to recover its losses.

Exhibit 1 NEGLIGENCE AND STRICT LIABILITY COMPARED

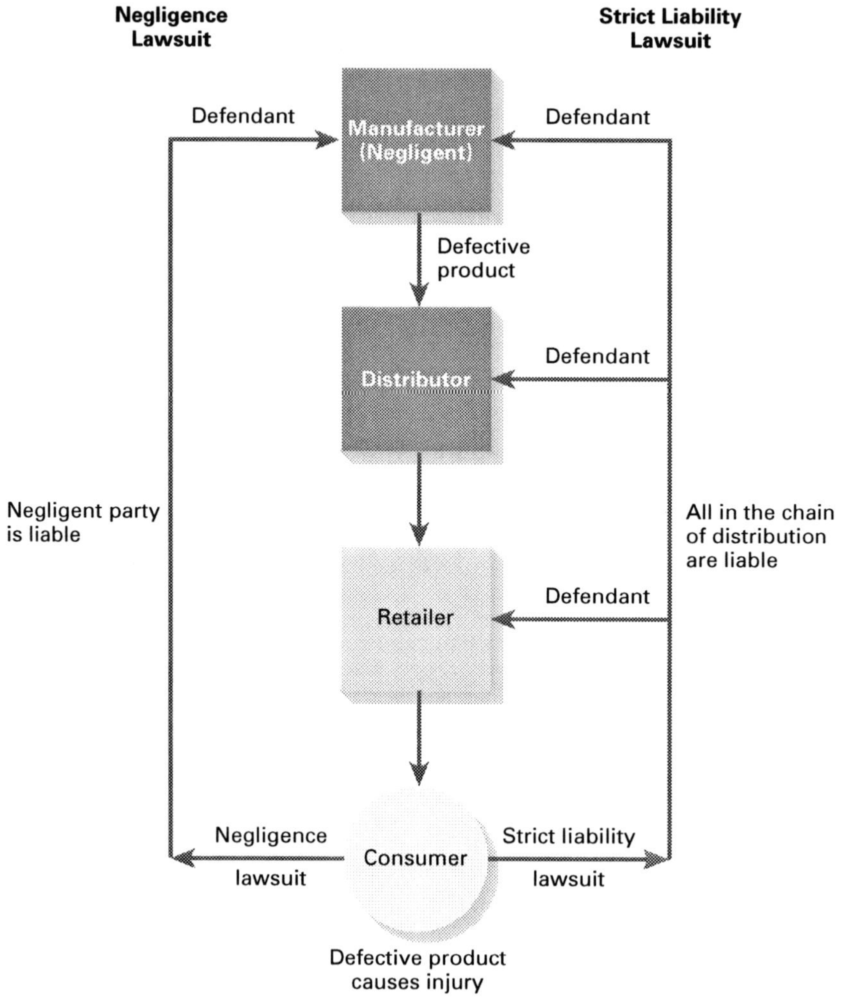

LANDMARK LAW

Restatement of Torts Definition of Strict Liability

Restatement (Second) of Torts

The most widely recognized articulation of the doctrine of strict liability in tort is found in *Section 402A* of the *Restatement (Second) of Torts*, which provides:

1. One who sells any product in a defective condition unreasonably dangerous to the user or consumer or to his property is subject to liability for physical harm thereby caused to the ultimate user or consumer, or to his property, if
   a. the seller is engaged in the business of selling such a product, and
   b. it is expected to and does reach the user or consumer without substantial change in the condition in which it is sold.
2. The rule stated in Subsection (1) applies although
   a. the seller has exercised all possible care in the preparation and sale of his product, and
   b. the user or consumer has not bought the product from or entered into any contractual relation with the seller.

Restatement (Third) of Torts

In 1997, the American Law Institute (ALI) adopted the *Restatement (Third) of Torts: Product Liability*. This new *Restatement* includes the following definition of *defect*:

A product is defective when, at the time of sale or distribution, it contains manufacturing defect, is defective in design, or is defective because of inadequate instructions or warnings.

A product:

a. contains a manufacturing defect when the product departs from its intended design even though all possible care was exercised in the preparation and marketing of the product;
b. is defective in design when the foreseeable risks of harm posed by the product could have been reduced or avoided by the adoption of a reasonable alternative design by the seller or other distributor, or a predecessor in the commercial chain of distribution, and the omission of the alternative design renders the product not reasonably safe;

c. is defective because of inadequate instructions or warnings when the foreseeable risks of harm posed by the product could have been reduced or avoided by the provision of reasonable instructions or warnings by the seller or other distributor, or a predecessor in the commercial chain of distribution, and the omission of the instructions or warnings renders the product not reasonably safe.

Parties Who Can Recover for Strict Liability

Because strict liability is a tort doctrine, *privity of contract* between the plaintiff and the defendant is not required. In other words, the doctrine applies even if the injured party had no contractual relations with the defendant. Thus, manufacturers, distributors, sellers, and lessors of a defective product are liable to the consumer who purchased the product and any user of the product. Users include the purchaser or lessee, family members, guests, employees, customers, and persons who passively enjoy the benefits of the product (e.g., passengers in automobiles).

Nobody has a more sacred obligation to obey the law than those who make the law.

Sophocles

The manufacturer, distributor, seller, and lessor of a defective product are also liable to third-party bystanders injured by the defective product. The courts have stated that bystanders who are injured by a defective product should be entitled to the same protection as a consumer or user. Bystanders and non-users do not even have the opportunity to inspect products for defects and to limit their purchases to articles manufactured by reputable manufacturers and sold by reputable retailers.

Damages Recoverable for Strict Liability

The damages recoverable in a strict liability action vary by jurisdiction. Damages for personal injuries are recoverable in all jurisdictions that have adopted the doctrine of strict liability, although some jurisdictions limit the dollar amount of the award. Property damage is recoverable in most jurisdictions, but economic loss (e.g., lost income) is recoverable in only a few jurisdictions.

Punitive damages, which are monetary damages awarded to punish the defendant, are generally allowed if the plaintiff can prove that the defendant either intentionally injured her or acted with reckless disregard for her safety.

DEFECTIVE PRODUCT

To recover for strict liability, the injured party must first show that the product that caused the injury was somehow *defective*. (Remember that the injured party does not have to prove who caused the product to become defective.) Plaintiffs can allege multiple **product defects** in one lawsuit. A product can be found to be defective in many ways. The most common types of defects are:

product defect
Something wrong, inadequate, or improper in the manufacture, design, packaging, warning, or instructions about a product.

- Defect in manufacture
- Defect in design
- Failure to warn
- Defect in packaging
- Failure to provide adequate instructions

These defects are discussed in the following paragraphs.

DEFECT IN MANUFACTURE

A **defect in manufacture** occurs when the manufacturer fails to (1) properly assemble a product, (2) properly test a product, or (3) adequately check the quality of a product.

defect in manufacture
A defect that occurs when a manufacturer fails to (1) properly assemble a product, (2) properly test a product, or (3) adequately check the quality of the product.

Example American Ladder Company designs, manufactures, and sells ladders. American Ladder Company manufactures a ladder, but a worker at the company fails to insert one of the screws that would support one of the steps of the ladder. The ladder is sold to Weingard Distributor, a wholesaler, which sells it to Reynolds Hardware Store, which sells the ladder to Heather, a consumer. When Heather is on the ladder painting her house, the step of the ladder breaks because of the missing screw, and Heather falls and is injured. The missing screw is an example of a defect in manufacture. Under the doctrine of strict liability, American Ladder Company, Weingard Distributor, and Reynolds Hardware Store are liable to Heather.

The following case is a classic example involving a defect in manufacture.

CASE 1 Defect in Manufacture

Shoshone Coca-Cola Bottling Company v. Dolinski

82 Nev. 439, 420 P.2d 855, Web 1966 Nev. Lexis 260 (1966) Supreme Court of Nevada

"In the case at hand, Shoshone contends that insufficient proof was offered to establish that the mouse was in the bottle of 'Squirt' when it left Shoshone's possession."

—Judge Thompson

Facts

Leo Dolinski purchased a bottle of Squirt, a soft drink, from a vending machine at a Sea and Ski plant, his place of employment. Dolinski opened the bottle and consumed part of its contents. He immediately became ill. Upon examination, it was found that the bottle contained the decomposed body of a mouse, mouse hair, and mouse feces. Dolinski visited a doctor and was given medicine to counteract nausea. Dolinski suffered physical and mental distress from consuming the decomposed mouse and thereafter possessed an aversion to soft drinks. The Shoshone Coca-Cola Bottling Company (Shoshone) had manufactured and distributed the Squirt bottle. Dolinski sued Shoshone, basing his lawsuit on the doctrine of strict liability. The state of Nevada had not previously recognized the doctrine of strict liability. However, the trial court adopted the doctrine of strict liability, and the jury returned a verdict in favor of the plaintiff. Shoshone appealed.

Issue

Should the state of Nevada judicially adopt the doctrine of strict liability? If so, was there a defect in the manufacture of the Squirt bottle that caused the plaintiff's injuries?

Language of the Court

In our view, public policy demands that one who places upon the market a bottled beverage in a condition dangerous for use must be held strictly liable to the ultimate user for injuries resulting from such use, although the seller has exercised all reasonable care.

Our acceptance of strict tort liability against the manufacturer and distributor of a bottled beverage does not mean that the plaintiff is relieved of the burden of proving a case. He must still establish that his injury was caused by a defect in the product and that such defect existed when the product left the hands of the defendant.

In the case at hand, Shoshone contends that insufficient proof was offered to establish that the mouse was in the bottle of "Squirt" when it left Shoshone's possession. The plaintiff offered the expert testimony of a toxicologist who examined the bottle and contents on the day the plaintiff drank from it. It was his opinion that the mouse "had been dead for a long time" and that the dark stains (mouse feces) that he found on the bottom of the bottle must have been there before the liquid was added. The jury apparently preferred the latter evidence that traced cause to the defendant.

Decision

The supreme court of Nevada adopted the doctrine of strict liability and held that the evidence supported the trial court's finding that there was a defect in manufacture. The supreme court affirmed the trial court's decision in favor of plaintiff Dolinski.

Case Questions

Critical Legal Thinking Describe the doctrine of strict liability. How does it differ from negligence? Explain.

Business Ethics Was it ethical for Shoshone to argue that it was not liable to Dolinski? Could this case have been "faked"?

Contemporary Business Should all parties in the chain of distribution of a defective product—even parties that are not responsible for the defect—be held liable under the doctrine of strict liability? Or should liability be based only on fault?

DEFECT IN DESIGN

A **defect in design** can support a strict liability action. Design defects that have supported strict liability awards include toys that are designed with removable parts that could be swallowed by children, machines and appliances designed without proper safeguards, and trucks and other vehicles designed without warning devices to let people know that the vehicle is backing up. A defect in design occurs when a product is designed incorrectly. In this case, not just one item but all of the defectively designed products can cause injury.

defect in design
A defect that occurs when a product is improperly designed.

In evaluating the adequacy of a product's design, the courts apply a risk–utility analysis. This requires the court to consider the gravity of the danger posed by the design, the likelihood that injury will occur, the availability and cost of producing a safer alternative design, the social utility of the product, and other factors.

In the following case, the courts had to decide whether there was a design defect.

CASE 2 Design Defect

Higgins v. Intex Recreation Corporation

123 Wn.App. 821, 99 P.3d 421, Web 2004 Wash.App. Lexis 2424 (2004)
Court of Appeals of Washington

"Now, the ride down a snow-covered hill backward at 30 miles per hour may be a thrill. But it has very little social value when compared to the risk of severe injury."

—Judge Sweeney

Facts

Intex Recreation Corporation designed and sold the Extreme Sno-Tube II. This snow tube is ridden by a user down snow-covered hills and can reach speeds of 30 miles per hour. The snow tube has no steering device, and therefore a rider may end up spinning and going down a hill backward.

Dan Falkner bought an Extreme Sno-Tube II and used it sledding the same day. During Falkner's second run, the tube rotated him backward about one-quarter to one-third of the way down the hill. A group of parents, including Tom Higgins, stood near the bottom of the hill. Higgins saw seven-year-old Kyle Potter walking in the path of Falkner's speeding Sno-Tube. Higgins ran and grabbed Potter to save him from harm, but while he was doing so, the Sno-Tube hit Higgins and threw him into the air. Higgins landed on his forehead, which snapped his head back. The impact severed Higgins's spinal cord and left him quadriplegic.

Higgins sued Intex for damages based on strict liability. Evidence was introduced at trial that showed that the Sno-Tube could rotate while going downhill and that it had no guiding mechanism and no steering device. Evidence also showed that Intex made a Sno-Boggan that went just as fast but did not rotate because of ridges on the bottom of the device. The jury found a design defect in the Sno-Tube and held Intex liable for 35 percent of Higgins's damages.

Issue

Was the Extreme Sno-Tube II defectively designed, thus supporting the judgment against Intex?

Language of the Court

There are two tests for determining whether a product is defective. The risk–utility test requires a showing that the likelihood and seriousness of harm outweigh the burden on the manufacturer to design a product that would have prevented that harm and would not have impaired the product's usefulness. The consumer-expectation test requires a showing that the product is more dangerous than the ordinary consumer would expect. This test focuses on the reasonable expectation of the consumer.

A plaintiff can satisfy its burden of proving an alternative design by showing that another product more safely serves the same function as the challenged product. There is evidence in this record from which a jury could conclude that the placement of ribs or ridges on the bottom of the Sno-Tube, like those used on Intex's Sno-Boggan, would keep the rider from facing downhill. The rider could then see obstacles and direct the tube. All this could be done without sacrificing speed. This is enough to prove an alternative safer design. Now, the ride down a snow-covered hill backward at 30 miles per hour may be a thrill. But it has very little social value when compared to the risk of severe injury. We do not think the Sno-Tube is a product that is necessary regardless of the risks involved to the user. We find ample evidence to support this verdict, applying the risk–utility test.

We next take up Intex's assertion that the tube was not unsafe to an extent beyond that which would be

(case continues)

contemplated by the ordinary consumer. Again, we find ample evidence in this record to support the Higgins's assertion to the contrary. And a reasonable jury could easily infer that the average consumer may expect the Sno-Tube to rotate. But he or she might not expect that it would continue in a backward position. Here, the Sno-Tube is inexpensive. But so is Intex's Sno-Boggan. And the Sno-Boggan provides a fast ride but not a blind high-speed ride. A jury could then find that a reasonable consumer would expect that a snow sliding product would not put him or her in a backward, high-speed slide. We find ample evidence in favor of the plaintiffs applying the consumer-expectation test.

Decision

The court of appeals held that the Sno-Tube was defectively designed and affirmed the judgment in favor of Higgins against Intex.

Case Questions

Critical Legal Thinking What is a design defect? Explain.

Business Ethics Should Intex have placed a ridge on the bottom of the Sno-Tube or equipped it with a steering device to make it safer? Would you have found for or against Intex in this case? Why or why not?

Contemporary Business What does the risk–utility test require? What does the consumer-expectation test require? How do these two tests differ?

Crashworthiness Doctrine

Often, when an automobile is involved in an accident, the driver or passengers are not injured by the blow itself. Instead, they are injured when their bodies strike something inside their own automobile (e.g., the dashboard, the steering wheel). This is commonly referred to as the "second collision." The courts have held that automobile manufacturers are under a duty to design automobiles to take into account the possibility of this second collision. This is called the **crashworthiness doctrine**. Failure to design an automobile to protect occupants from foreseeable dangers caused by a second collision subjects the manufacturer and dealer to strict liability.

crashworthiness doctrine
A doctrine that says automobile manufacturers are under a duty to design automobiles so they take into account the possibility of harm from a person's body striking something inside the automobile in the case of a car accident.

▶ FAILURE TO WARN

Certain products are inherently dangerous and cannot be made any safer and still accomplish the task for which they are designed. Many such products have risks and side effects caused by their use. Manufacturers and sellers owe a duty to warn consumers and users about the dangers of using these products. A proper and conspicuous warning placed on the product insulates the manufacturer and others in the chain of distribution from strict liability. **Failure to warn** of these dangerous propensities is a defect that will support a strict liability action.

failure to warn
A defect that occurs when a manufacturer does not place a warning on the packaging of products that could cause injury if the danger is unknown.

Example The Universal Drug Corporation develops a new prescription drug that has tremendous success in preventing and treating a certain type of cancer. The drug, however, has a three percent probability of causing an increased risk of heart disease in patients who take the drug. The drug cannot be made any safer and still possess its cancer treatment effects. The Universal Drug Corporation owes a duty to warn potential users of its drug of these heart-related risks. If it failed to do so and a user suffered a heart attack because of using the drug, the Universal Drug Corporation would be held strictly liable for failure to warn.

In the following case, the court had to decide whether there was a failure to warn.

CASE 3 Failure to Warn

Bunch v. Hoffinger Industries, Inc.

123 Cal.App.4th 1278, 20 Cal.Rptr.3d 780, Web 2004 Cal.App. Lexis 1869 (2004)
Court of Appeal of California

"We find that the danger of diving into a shallow aboveground pool is not open and obvious to an 11 year old as a matter of law."

—Judge Raye

Facts

Joe and Loretta Frank, husband and wife, received a used frame for an aboveground swimming pool as a gift. The pool frame measured 33 feet long, 18 feet wide, and 4 feet deep. The Franks purchased a pool liner from McMasker Enterprises, Inc. (McMasker), a swimming pool supplier. Hoffinger Industries, Inc. (Hoffinger) manufactured the pool liner.

The Franks placed the pool in the yard of their house. Mr. Frank built a deck around the pool at the level of the pool frame and built a wooden bench on the deck next to the pool. Hoffinger did not place warning labels on their pool liners about the dangers of diving into the shallow pool. Instead, Hoffinger provided consumers with labels and instructions on how to place the labels on the pool liner. The warning label stated: "Caution—no diving—shallow water." The warning label was 0.75 inch wide and 5.25 inches long. The Franks testified that they affixed a warning label to the pool liner.

Leesa Bunch, 11 years old, and her brother Eric, 9 years old, were using the Franks' pool. Mrs. Frank told the children "not to dive" into the pool and went into the house. Leesa had watched the summer Olympics and tried to imitate the shallow racing dives of the Olympic swimmers. Leesa dove from the bench into the pool. Eric then saw Leesa curled up and floating in the pool, and he jumped in and dragged her to the edge of the pool. Leesa was rendered a quadriplegic by the dive.

Leesa Bunch sued McMasker and Hoffinger for strict liability for failure to adequately warn her of the danger of diving into the pool. Evidence at trial proved that during the past 17 years, there had been 47 prior incidents of persons becoming quadriplegic from diving into Hoffinger pools. McMasker settled with Leesa for $1 million. At trial, the jury found that Hoffinger had provided inadequate warnings of the dangers of diving into the pool and awarded Leesa $12,526,890 in damages plus costs. Hoffinger appealed.

Issue

Did Hoffinger adequately warn Leesa, an 11-year old girl, about the dangers of diving into a 4-foot-deep pool?

Language of the Court

We find that the danger of diving into a shallow aboveground pool is not open and obvious to an 11 year old as a matter of law. In the context of products liability actions, the plaintiff must prove that the defective products supplied by the defendant were a substantial factor in bringing about his or her injury. The court instructed that the jury must find "that the design of the warning system for the pool liner was a substantial factor in causing harm to the plaintiff." The court also instructed that the jury must find a "lack of sufficient warnings was a substantial factor in causing plaintiff's harm."

Bunch presented testimony by Ross Buck, Ph.D., a professor of communication sciences and psychology at the University of Connecticut. According to Buck, effective warnings "act as brakes to stop dangerous behaviors." Buck outlined the components of an effective persuasive warning: it must command attention, galvanize memory, evoke emotion, contain an explicit instruction, and show a consequence. This kind of warning is especially important for children under the age of 12. Dr. Buck testified that a young diver standing at the edge of an aboveground pool cannot necessarily judge the depth of the pool. Warnings act as "brakes to stop dangerous behaviors." Warnings to children between the ages of seven and 12 must be concrete and spell out the dangers and consequences of actions in order to be effective. Buck found the labels supplied with the Hoffinger pool liner neither adequate nor effective. The labels failed to spell out any consequences of diving into shallow water.

Dr. Johnson, another of Bunch's experts, testified that based on his experience and research, the risk of spinal paraplegia was not readily apparent to an 11 year old. Many people who dive into pools are unable to gauge the depth of the water. After reviewing the facts, Johnson opined that Bunch was attempting a shallow racing dive and was unaware of the possible consequences of that dive.

Given the testimony of Bunch and her two expert witnesses, we find sufficient evidence to support the conclusion

(case continues)

that the lack of an adequate warning label was neither a negligible nor theoretical contribution to Bunch's injury. The evidence presented at trial revealed that the lack of a persuasive label outlining the consequences of diving into the pool was a substantial factor in causing the injury.

Decision

The court of appeal of California affirmed the trial court's finding that Hoffinger failed to adequately warn Leesa of the dangers of diving into the four-foot-deep pool. The court of appeal upheld the monetary judgment in favor of Leesa against Hoffinger.

Case Questions

Critical Legal Thinking Describe the doctrine of defect by failure to warn.

Business Ethics Based upon the previous 47 cases in which users of Hoffinger pools were rendered quadriplegic, should the warning on the pool liner in this case have been stronger?

Contemporary Business After the judgment of the trial court was issued, Hoffinger filed for bankruptcy. What are the consequences to Leesa of Hoffinger's filing for bankruptcy?

▶ DEFECT IN PACKAGING

Manufacturers owe a duty to design and provide safe packages for their products. This duty requires manufacturers to provide packages and containers that are tamperproof or that clearly indicate whether they have been tampered with. Certain manufacturers, such as drug manufacturers, owe a duty to place their products in containers that cannot be opened by children. A manufacturer's failure to meet this duty—a **defect in packaging**—subjects the manufacturer and others in the chain of distribution of the product to strict liability.

defect in packaging
A defect that occurs when a product has been placed in packaging that is insufficiently tamperproof.

Food Counter *Should sellers of foods that are not packaged but are easily tampered with be held liable if a consumer is injured by eating such tainted food?*

▶ OTHER DEFECTS

Sellers are responsible to provide adequate instructions for the safe assembly and use of the products they sell. **Failure to provide adequate instructions** for the safe assembly and use

failure to provide adequate instructions
A defect that occurs when a manufacturer does not provide detailed directions for safe assembly and use of a product.

of a product is a defect that subjects the manufacturer and others in the chain of distribution to strict liability.

Example Mother buys her four-year-old daughter Lia a tricycle manufactured by Bicycle Corporation. The tricycle comes in a box with many parts that need to be assembled. The instructions for assembly are vague and hard to follow. Mother puts together the tricycle, using these instructions. The first time that Lia uses the tricycle, the handlebar becomes loose, and Lia's tricycle goes into the street, where she is hit and injured by an automobile. In this case, Mother could sue Bicycle Corporation on behalf of Lia for strict liability to recover damages for failing to provide adequate instructions.

Other defects that support a finding of product liability based on strict liability include inadequate testing of products, inadequate selection of component parts or materials, and improper certification of the safety of a product. The concept of "defect" is an expanding area of the law.

PUNITIVE DAMAGES

In product liability cases, a court can award **punitive damages** if it finds that the defendant's conduct was committed with intent or with reckless disregard for human life. Punitive damages are meant to punish the defendant and to send a message to the defendant (and other companies) that such behavior will not be tolerated.

punitive damages
Monetary damages that are awarded to punish a defendant who either intentionally or recklessly injured the plaintiff.

DEFENSES TO PRODUCT LIABILITY

Defendants in strict liability or negligence actions may raise several defenses to the imposition of liability. These defenses are discussed in the paragraphs that follow.

Generally Known Dangers

Certain products are inherently dangerous and are known to the general population to be so. Sellers are not strictly liable for failing to warn of **generally known dangers**.

Example It is a known fact that guns shoot bullets. Manufacturers of guns do not have to place a warning on the barrel of a gun warning of this generally known danger.

generally known dangers
A defense that acknowledges that certain products are inherently dangerous and are known to the general population to be so.

Government Contractor Defense

Many defense and other contractors manufacture products (e.g., rockets, airplanes) to government specification. Most jurisdictions recognize a **government contractor defense** to product liability actions. To establish this defense, a government contractor must prove that (1) the precise specifications for the product were provided by the government, (2) the product conformed to those specifications, and (3) the contractor warned the government of any known defects or dangers of the product.

government contractor defense
A defense that says a contractor who was provided specifications by the government is not liable for any defect in the product that occurs as a result of those specifications.

Assumption of the Risk

Theoretically, the traditional doctrine of **assumption of the risk** is a defense to a product liability action. For this defense to apply, the defendant must prove that (1) the plaintiff knew and appreciated the risk and (2) the plaintiff voluntarily assumed the risk. In practice, the defense assumption of the risk is narrowly applied by the courts.

Misuse of the Product

Sometimes users are injured when they misuse a product. If a user brings a product liability action, the defendant-seller may be able to assert **misuse** as a defense. Whether the

misuse
A defense that relieves a seller of product liability if the user *abnormally* misused the product. Products must be designed to protect against *foreseeable* misuse.

defense is effective depends on whether the misuse was foreseeable. The seller is relieved of product liability if the plaintiff has **abnormally misused** the product—that is, if there has been an **unforeseeable misuse** of the product. However, the seller is liable if there has been a **foreseeable misuse** of the product. This reasoning is intended to provide an incentive for manufacturers to design and manufacture safer products.

Correction of a Product Defect

A manufacturer that produces a defective product and later discovers said defect must (1) notify purchasers and users of the defect and (2) **correct the defect**. Most manufacturers faced with this situation recall the defective product and either repair the defect or replace the product.

The seller must make reasonable efforts to notify purchasers and users of the defect and the procedure to correct it. Reasonable efforts normally consist of sending letters to known purchasers and users and placing notices in newspapers and magazines of general circulation. If a user ignores such notice and fails to have the defect corrected, the seller may raise this as a defense against further liability with respect to the defect. Many courts have held that reasonable notice is effective even against users who did not see the notice.

Supervening Event

supervening event or intervening event
An alteration or a modification of a product by a party in the chain of distribution that absolves all prior sellers from strict liability.

For a seller to be held strictly liable, the product it sells must reach the consumer or user "without substantial change" in its condition. Under the doctrine of **supervening event** or **intervening event**, the original seller is not liable if the product is materially altered or modified after it leaves the seller's possession and the alteration or modification causes an injury. A supervening or intervening event absolves all prior sellers in the chain of distribution from strict liability.

Example A manufacturer produces a safe piece of equipment. It sells the equipment to a distributor, which removes a safety guard from the equipment. The distributor sells it to a retailer, who sells it to a buyer. The buyer is injured because of the removal of the safety guard. The manufacturer can raise the defense of supervening event against the imposition of liability. However, the distributor and retailer are strictly liable for the buyer's injuries.

Statute of Limitation

statute of limitations
A statute that requires an injured person to bring an action within a certain number of years from the time that he or she was injured by a defective product.

Most states have **statutes of limitations** that require an injured person to bring an action within a certain number of years from the time that he or she was injured by a defective product. This limitation period varies from state to state. Failure to bring an action within the appropriate time relieves the defendant of liability.

In most jurisdictions, the statute of limitations does not begin to run until the plaintiff suffers an injury. This subjects sellers and lessors to exposure for an unspecified period of time because a defective product may not cause an injury for years, or even decades, after it was sold.

Statute of Repose

statute of repose
A statute that limits the seller's liability to a certain number of years from the date when the product was first sold.

Some states have enacted **statutes of repose**, which limit the seller's liability to a certain number of years from the date when the product was first sold. The period of repose varies from state to state.

CONCEPT SUMMARY

STATUTE OF LIMITATION AND STATUTE OF REPOSE

Statute	Begins to Run
Statute of limitations	When the plaintiff suffers injury
Statute of repose	When the product is first sold

Contributory Negligence and Comparative Fault

Sometimes a person who is injured by a defective product is negligent and contributes to his or her own injuries. The defense of **contributory negligence** bars an injured plaintiff from recovering from the defendant in a negligence action. However, this doctrine generally does not bar recovery in strict liability actions.

Many states have held that the doctrine of **comparative fault** applies to strict liability actions. Under this doctrine, a plaintiff who is contributorily negligent for his or her injuries is responsible for a *proportional share* of the damages. In other words, the damages are apportioned between the plaintiff and the defendant.

contributory negligence
A defense that says a person who is injured by a defective product but has been negligent and has contributed to his or her own injuries cannot recover from the defendant.

comparative fault
A doctrine that applies to strict liability actions that says a plaintiff who is contributorily negligent for his or her injuries is responsible for a proportional share of the damages.

Examples An automobile manufacturer produces a car with a hidden defect, and a consumer purchases the car from an automobile dealer. The consumer is injured in an automobile accident in which the defect is found to be 75 percent responsible for the accident, and the consumer's reckless driving is found to be 25 percent responsible. The plaintiff suffers $1 million worth of injuries. Under the doctrine of *contributory negligence*, the plaintiff would recover nothing from the defendants. Under the doctrine of *comparative negligence*, the plaintiff would recover $750,000 from the defendants (75 percent of $1 million).

CONCEPT SUMMARY
CONTRIBUTORY NEGLIGENCE AND COMPARATIVE FAULT

Doctrine	Description
Contributory negligence	A person who is partially responsible for causing his or her own injuries may not recover anything from the manufacturer or seller of a defective product.
Comparative fault	A person who is partially responsible for causing his or her own injuries is responsible for a proportional share of the damages. The manufacturer or seller of the defective product is responsible for the remainder of the plaintiff's damages.

Matthew Ward © Dorling Kindersley

South Korean Currency
Many countries have developed laws that permit lawsuits based on product defects. The Republic of Korea has enacted the Product Liability Act (PLA), which imposes strict liability on all parties along the chain of manufacture of a defective product, which would include the manufacturer of the product, an assembling manufacturer, and a manufacturer of defective component parts. Distributors, wholesalers, and the retailers that distribute defective products can be held liable if the manufacturer of the defective product cannot be found. Strict liability is imposed on importers of defective products.

TEST REVIEW TERMS AND CONCEPTS

Abnormal misuse (unforeseeable misuse)
Assumption of the risk
Chain of distribution
Comparative fault
Contributory negligence
Correction of a product defect
Crashworthiness doctrine
Defect in design
Defect in manufacture
Defect in packaging
Doctrine of strict liability in tort
Failure to provide adequate instructions
Failure to warn
Foreseeable misuse
Generally known dangers
Greenman v. Yuba Power Products, Inc.
Government contractor defense
Intentional misrepresentation (fraud)
Intervening event
Misuse of the product
Negligence
Product defect
Product liability
Punitive damages
Statute of limitations
Statute of repose
Strict liability (liability without fault)
Supervening event

CASE PROBLEMS

1 Strict Liability Jeppesen and Company produces charts that graphically display approach procedures for airplanes landing at airports. These charts are drafted from tabular data supplied by the Federal Aviation Administration (FAA), a federal agency of the U.S. government. By law, Jeppesen cannot construct charts that include information different from that supplied by the FAA. One day, the pilot of an airplane owned by World Airways was on descent to land at the Cold Bay, Alaska, airport. The pilot was using an instrument approach procedure chart published by Jeppesen. The airplane crashed into a mountain near Cold Bay, killing all six crew members and destroying the aircraft. Evidence showed that the FAA data did not include the mountain. The heirs of the deceased crew members and World Airways brought a strict liability action against Jeppesen. Does the doctrine of strict liability apply to this case? Is Jeppesen liable? *Brocklesby v. Jeppesen and Company*, 767 F.2d 1288, **Web** 1985 U.S. App. Lexis 21290 (United States Court of Appeals for the Ninth Circuit)

2 Failure to Warn The Emerson Electric Co. manufactures and sells a product called the Weed Eater XR-90. The Weed Eater is a multipurpose weed-trimming and brush-cutting device. It consists of a handheld gasoline-powered engine connected to a long drive shaft, at the end of which can be attached various tools for cutting weeds and brush. One such attachment is a 10-inch circular saw blade capable of cutting through growth up to 2 inches in diameter. When this saw blade is attached to the Weed Eater, approximately 270 degrees of blade edge are exposed when in use. The owner's manual contained the following warning: "Keep children away. All people and pets should be kept at a safe distance from the work area, at least 30 feet, especially when using the blade." Donald Pearce, a 13-year-old boy, was helping his uncle clear an overgrown yard. The uncle was operating a Weed Eater XR-90 with the circular saw blade attachment. When Pearce stooped to pick up something off the ground about 6 to 10 feet behind and slightly to the left of where his uncle was operating the Weed Eater, the saw blade on the Weed Eater struck something near the ground. The Weed Eater kicked back to the left and cut off Pearce's right arm to the elbow. Pearce, through his mother, Charlotte Karns, sued Emerson to recover damages under strict liability. Is Emerson liable? *Karns v. Emerson Electric Co.*, 817 F.2d 1452, **Web** 1987 U.S. App. Lexis 5608 (United States Court of Appeals for the Tenth Circuit)

3 Crashworthiness Doctrine One night Verne Prior, while driving on U.S. 101 under the influence of alcohol and drugs at speeds of 65 to 85 miles per hour, crashed his automobile into the left rear of a Chevrolet station wagon stopped on the shoulder of the freeway because of a flat tire. Christine Smith was sitting in the passenger seat of the parked car when the accident occurred. In the crash, the Chevrolet station wagon was knocked into a gully, where its fuel tank ruptured. The vehicle caught fire, and Smith suffered severe burn injuries. The Chevrolet station wagon was manufactured by General Motors Corporation. Evidence showed that the fuel tank was located in a vulnerable position in the back of the station wagon, outside the crossbars of the frame. Evidence further showed that if the fuel tank had been located underneath the body of the station wagon, between the crossbars of the frame, it would have been well protected in the collision. Smith sued General Motors for strict liability. Is the Chevrolet station wagon a defective product? *Smith v. General Motors Corporation*, 42 Cal.App.3d 1, 116 Cal.Rptr. 575, **Web** 1974 Cal.App. Lexis 1199 (Court of Appeal of California)

4 Failure to Warn Virginia Burke purchased a bottle of "Le Domaine" champagne that was manufactured by Almaden Vineyards, Inc. At home, she removed the wine seal from the top of the bottle but did not remove the plastic cork. She set the bottle on the counter, intending to serve it in a few minutes. Shortly thereafter, the plastic cork spontaneously ejected from the bottle, ricocheted off the wall, and struck Burke in the left lens of her eyeglasses, shattering the lens and driving pieces of glass into her eye. The champagne bottle did not contain any warning of this danger. Evidence showed that Almaden had previously been notified of the spontaneous ejection of the cork from its champagne bottles. Burke sued Almaden to recover damages for strict liability. Is Almaden liable? *Burke v. Almaden Vineyards, Inc.*, 86 Cal.App.3d 768,

150 Cal.Rptr. 419, **Web** 1978 Cal.App. Lexis 2123 (Court of Appeal of California)

5 Assumption of Risk Lillian Horn was driving her Chevrolet station wagon, which was designed and manufactured by General Motors Corporation, down Laurel Canyon Boulevard in Los Angeles, California. Horn swerved to avoid a collision when a car coming toward her crossed the center line and was coming at her. In doing so, her hand knocked the horn cap off the steering wheel, which exposed the area underneath the horn cap, including three sharp prongs that had held the horn cap to the steering wheel. A few seconds later, when her car hit an embankment, Horn's face was impaled on the three sharp exposed prongs, causing her severe facial injuries. Horn sued General Motors for strict liability. General Motors asserted the defense of assumption of the risk against Horn. Who wins? *Horn v. General Motors Corporation*, 17 Cal.3d 359, 551 P.2d 398, 131 Cal.Rptr. 78, **Web** 1976 Cal. Lexis 283 (Supreme Court of California)

6 Misuse The Wilcox-Crittendon Company manufactured harnesses, saddles, bridles, leads, and other items commonly used for horses, cattle, and other ranch and farm animals. One such item was a stallion or cattle tie, a five-inch-long iron hook with a one-inch ring at one end. The tongue on the ring opened outward to allow the hook to be attached to a rope or another object. A purchasing agent for United Airlines, who was familiar with this type of hook because of his previous experience on a farm, purchased one of these hooks from Keystone Brothers, a harness and saddlery wares outlet located in San Francisco, California. Four years later Edward Dosier, an employee of United Airlines, was working to install a new grinding machine at a United Airlines maintenance plant. As part of the installation process, Dosier attached the hook to a 1,700-pound counterweight and raised the counterweight into the air. While the counterweight was suspended in the air, Dosier reached under the counterweight to retrieve a missing bolt. The hook broke, and the counterweight fell and crushed Dosier's arm. Dosier sued Wilcox-Crittendon for strict liability. Who wins? *Dosier v. Wilcox-Crittendon Company*, 45 Cal.App.3d. 74, 119 Cal.Rptr. 135, **Web** 1975 Cal.App. Lexis 1665 (Court of Appeal of California).

BUSINESS ETHICS CASE

7 Business Ethics Celestino Luque lived with his cousins Harry and Laura Dunn in Millbrae, California. The Dunns purchased a rotary lawn mower from Rhoads Hardware. The lawn mower was manufactured by Air Capital Manufacturing Company and was distributed by Garehime Corporation. Neighbors asked Luque to mow their lawn. While Luque was cutting the lawn, he noticed a small carton in the path of the lawn mower. Luque left the lawn mower in a stationary position with its motor running and walked around the side of the lawn mower to remove the carton. As he did so, he slipped on the wet grass and fell backward. Luque's left hand entered the unguarded hole of the lawn mower and was caught in its revolving blade, which turns at 175 miles per hour and 100 revolutions per second. Luque's hand was severely mangled and lacerated. The word *Caution* was printed above the unguarded hole on the lawn mower. Luque sued Rhoads Hardware, Air Capital, and Garehime Corporation for strict liability. The defendants argued that strict liability does not apply to *patent* (obvious) defects. Was it ethical for the defendants to argue that they were not liable for patent defects? Would patent defects ever be corrected if the defendants' contention was accepted by the court? Who wins? *Luque v. McLean, Trustee*, 8 Cal.3d 136, 501 P.2d 1163, 104 Cal.Rptr. 443, **Web** 1972 Cal. Lexis 245 (Supreme Court of California)

ENDNOTE

1. 59 Cal.2d 57, 377 P.2d 897, 27 Cal.Rptr. 697, Web 1963 Cal. Lexis 140 (Supreme Court of California). For the complete opinion of this case, go to www.prenhall.com/cheeseman/.

Index

Page references followed by "f" indicate illustrated figures or photographs; followed by "t" indicates a table.